The Safety-Net Health Care System

D1219287

Gunnar Almgren, PhD, MSW, is Associate Professor of Social Work and Social Welfare at the University of Washington School of Social Work in Seattle. Dr. Almgren joined the academy after a 15-year career as a social work practitioner and administrator in not-for-profit and public health care systems. In addition to the numerous research articles he has published in peer review journals on the determinants of premature mortality in racially segregated neighborhoods, his previous book on health care policy (*Health Care Politics, Policy and Services: A Social Justice Analysis.* Springer Publishing, 2007) was selected for a Book of the Year Award by the *American Journal of Nursing*.

Taryn Lindhorst, PhD, MSW, LCSW, is an Associate Professor of Social Work at the University of Washington. Prior to receiving her doctorate in 2001, Dr. Lindhorst spent 15 years providing social work services in public health settings in New Orleans, Louisiana. Her research focuses on institutional policies and practices as sites for the creation of social inequalities, particularly as this relates to issues of violence against women and health. Her research has been funded by the U.S. National Institutes of Health, National Institute of Justice and the William T. Grant Foundation and has been honored with three national awards. She is currently engaged in policy and practice studies related to domestic violence, mental health, and end of life care. Dr. Lindhorst has co-authored two books and over 40 articles and chapters in journals such as *Social Service Review, Social Work, American Journal of Public Health,* and *Social Science and Medicine*.

The Safety-Net Health Care System
Health Care at the Margins

Gunnar Almgren, PhD, MSW

Taryn Lindhorst, PhD, MSW, LCSW

Property of
Baker College
of Allen Park

SPRINGER PUBLISHING COMPANY
NEW YORK

Copyright © 2012 Springer Publishing Company, LLC

All rights reserved.

No part of this publication may be reproduced, stored in a retrieval system, or transmitted in any form or by any means, electronic, mechanical, photocopying, recording, or otherwise, without the prior permission of Springer Publishing Company, LLC, or authorization through payment of the appropriate fees to the Copyright Clearance Center, Inc., 222 Rosewood Drive, Danvers, MA 01923, 978-750-8400, fax 978-646-8600, info@copyright.com or on the Web at www.copyright.com.

Springer Publishing Company, LLC
11 West 42nd Street
New York, NY 10036
www.springerpub.com

Acquisitions Editor: Jennifer Perillo
Composition: S4Carlisle Publishing Services

ISBN: 978-0-8261-0571-4
E-book ISBN: 978-0-8261-0572-1

11 12 13/ 5 4 3 2 1

The author and the publisher of this Work have made every effort to use sources believed to be reliable to provide information that is accurate and compatible with the standards generally accepted at the time of publication. The author and publisher shall not be liable for any special, consequential, or exemplary damages resulting, in whole or in part, from the readers' use of, or reliance on, the information contained in this book. The publisher has no responsibility for the persistence or accuracy of URLs for external or third-party Internet Web sites referred to in this publication and does not guarantee that any content on such Web sites is, or will remain, accurate or appropriate.

Library of Congress Cataloging-in-Publication Data

Almgren, Gunnar Robert, 1951-
  The safety-net health care system : health care at the margins / Gunnar Almgren, Taryn Lindhorst.
    p. ; cm.
  Includes bibliographical references and index.
  ISBN-13: 978-0-8261-0571-4
  ISBN-10: 0-8261-0571-8
  ISBN-13: 978-0-8261-0572-1 (e-book)
  I. Lindhorst, Taryn. II. Title.
    [DNLM: 1. Medically Uninsured--United States. 2. Delivery of Health Care--United States. 3. Health Services Needs and Demand--United States. 4. Insurance, Health--United States. 5. Professional-Patient Relations--United States. 6. Socioeconomic Factors--United States. W 250 AA1]
  LC classification not assigned
  368.38'200973--dc23

2011032268

Special discounts on bulk quantities of our books are available to corporations, professional associations, pharmaceutical companies, health care organizations, and other qualifying groups.

If you are interested in a custom book, including chapters from more than one of our titles, we can provide that service as well.

For details, please contact:
Special Sales Department, Springer Publishing Company, LLC
11 West 42nd Street, 15th Floor, New York, NY 10036-8002s
Phone: 877-687-7476 or 212-431-4370; Fax: 212-941-7842
Email: sales@springerpub.com

Printed in the United States of America by Hamilton Printing

To the patients, families, and staff of the University of Washington and Harborview Medical Centers of Seattle, and Charity Hospital and Hotel Dieu Community Hospital of New Orleans, as well as to the Sisters of St. Joseph of Peace, all of whom taught us everything we know about what it means to be caring professionals in the health care safety-net system.

And to Linda Viola Almgren and Cynthia Lynn Riche, without whose constant support this book would not have made it into your hands.

Contents

Foreword

The writing of this book comes at a time when, despite almost two decades of attention, health disparities by race/ethnicity and socioeconomic status are continuing to grow. These disparities occur in screening, incidence, treatment, and mortality across a wide variety of diseases and conditions, including cancer, cardiovascular disease, and diabetes. Those at the margins of society, by virtue of living in poverty or otherwise being cut off from the mainstream of society, bear a disproportionate burden of these disparities. We have come to realize their devastating consequences for the personal well-being, work, learning, and interpersonal relationships of individuals, and for the functioning of neighborhoods and communities in which they live.

Although we have become adept at quantifying health disparities, and in some cases have improved the health of individuals, we have made remarkably little progress in reducing disparities at the population level. This at least in part is due to our inattention to the safety-net health care system, the primary health care system for poor, incarcerated, and otherwise stigmatized and marginalized individuals and groups in the United States. Safety-net health care services are poorly understood by the majority of health care professionals and weakly integrated into the larger health care service delivery system. I continue to be surprised by the limited familiarity of my health care colleagues with the safety-net system. Yet, increasing numbers of persons in the United States live in poverty and operate outside the mainstream. Providing professional services to these persons requires a clear understanding of the safety-net health care system. Likewise, ensuring that the services provided are effective requires an understanding of challenges faced by marginalized persons living in all parts of the country, from very rural to very urban.

I am impressed with *The Safety-Net Health Care System: Health Care at the Margins,* because it eloquently addresses an important gap in professional medical training. Gunnar Almgren and Taryn Lindhorst are well versed in health care practice and policy and complement one another in terms of their experience in safety-net hospitals. They are well suited to guide the training of health care professionals, many of whom will at some point in their careers care for the growing population of marginalized persons living in the United States. The topic of safety-net health care is especially timely as the Patient Protection and Affordable Care Act (PPACA) is being implemented, and professions and training institutions are questioning how best to prepare students to provide services under the Act.

This book has the potential to provide much needed guidance for social workers, nurses, physicians, pharmacists, and other professionals who are involved in the provision of care to individuals, families, and communities who receive care through the safety-net health care system. It does so by providing information about the system itself, but also by effectively bringing their lives and the issues that shape those lives, such as poverty, social stratification and stigma, structural and social power, and homelessness, to the forefront in a way that will resonate with students and prepare them to be more effective practitioners.

Sarah Gehlert, PhD
E. Desmond Lee Professor of Racial and
Ethnic Diversity
The George Warren Brown School of
Social Work and Department of Surgery
School of Medicine, Washington University

Preface

This book is about professional practice in the safety-net health care system—defined as the clinics, hospitals, and individual health care providers that care for a disproportionate share of the poor, the uninsured, those afflicted by stigmatizing health conditions, and persons otherwise isolated from the mainstream health care system. The two authors who have collaborated on the research and writing of this book bring to bear not only their particular scholarly expertise in health care policy and practice, but more critically their many years of experience as social workers in safety-net hospitals. We intend this book for the nurses, physicians and social workers who anticipate internships and residencies in the hospitals and clinics that include a large proportion of persons who suffer from poverty and a range of other stigmatizing traits and health conditions that are associated with social isolation and exclusion from mainstream health care.

The genesis and orientation for this book originates from two experiences Many years ago, the first author had a conversation with a medical colleague, a gastroenterologist the author had complimented for his compassionate care of an impoverished woman dying from end-stage alcoholism. In response to the author's observation that other physicians too often treated patients with the twin stigmas of poverty and addiction with indifference and even contempt, the compassionate gastroenterologist shared his personal theory of why it was that so many of his colleagues harbored deep hostility toward patients that existed at the margins of society:

> In my view, one of the unintended consequences of the typical residency program is that doctors are taught to hate the poor, the addicted, and the mentally ill. I mean, here I was, a naïve 24-year-old with little more to offer than a newly minted medical degree, humanitarian instincts and the best of motivations;

plunked down in an urban hospital emergency department flooded with patients living lives I could not understand or in any way relate to….and suffering from problems and health conditions that neither I nor the system could seem to do much about. I hated feeling incompetent and helpless, and eventually I learned to hate the patients that made me feel this way—particularly the poor, [the] addicted, and the mentally ill. Eventually, if I could not find ways to avoid these kinds of patients, I at least learned to keep them at an emotional distance—dehumanize them, if you will. We need to do something different with our residency programs…we are teaching doctors to be indifferent and even to hate, not help.

The second experience was the recent death of the second author's sister after many years of chronic pain, addiction, and mental illness. Tracy was treated in many safety-net settings over the years. Despite her own strenuous efforts, those of her family and friends, and of the medical and mental health providers who worked with her, she died from her co-occuring conditions. Tracy felt cared for by some of the providers she met on her journey, but just as often, she would describe encounters where she felt discounted or shamed by a health professional.

People such as Tracy are some of the most challenging for health care professionals to help, and we will try to illuminate some of the reasons why in this book. At the same time, as we describe common situations of safety-net patients, we keep in mind that each of the patients the readers of this book may encounter is a Tracy—someone who was once an inquisitive, bright-eyed child full of wonder at the world; someone who often leaves behind family and friends who mourn the person she was and could have been.

This book is one attempt to do something different, not only with medical education but in the education of the other health care professions that are vital to safety-net health care as well. Instead of sidelining or containing discussions of poverty, homelessness, addictions, and chronic mental illness in either undergraduate courses or courses intended for specialists in such areas as addictions and mental health care, we seek to provide students and faculty with a resource book that delves into the nature of safety-net health care and the populations served by clinics and hospitals in the safety-net health care system. We hope that instructors of foundation practice courses in nursing, medicine, pharmacy, social work, and other health professions will use this text as a resource for classroom and seminar discussions that interrogate the nature of poverty, stigmatizing health conditions, and clinical practice in the context of safety-net health care, including the personal and professional challenges students are likely to confront.

Toward that end, we have organized this book in ten chapters that merge insights from an array of disciplines on the nature of safety-net health care, the populations served by safety-net health care systems, and the challenges clinical practitioners face in these settings. In addition to drawing upon evidence-based practice research in medicine, nursing, and social work, we include in this text decades of research on the communities and populations served by safety-net providers from the disciplines of sociology, anthropology, and social psychology.

The first section of the book focuses on larger social structural issues that affect care in the safety-net system. The first chapter provides historical background on the origins and functions of the safety-net health care system in the United States This is followed by a chapter that explains current statistics, theories, and controversies in the study of poverty. The next chapter interrogates the social processes that in many ways define the nature of safety-net health care—social stratification and stigma. The fourth chapter addresses the context of power and privilege that is at play between health care professionals and clients in safety-net systems. The fifth through seventh chapters provide an in-depth overview of the populations and communities that depend upon safety-net hospitals and clinics for health care, including the homeless, persons with addictions, and victims of violence and trauma. Chapter eight provides a larger look at processes involved in the creation of "difficulty" in clinical settings, paying special attention to the structural and social power issues at play. The ninth chapter interrogates and deconstructs the nature of a great source of practitioner frustration (and sometimes anger)—patients' failure to follow-through with treatment interventions that practitioners consider crucial to their health and well-being. The final chapter of the text considers the sources of motivation behind health care practice as a career choice, the emotional consequences of being a safety-net health care provider—and in the end why it is that so many of us are drawn to work that so challenges our personal resilience—and our capacities to rediscover, sustain, and elevate the humanity and dignity of those at the margins of society.

Acknowledgments

We are deeply grateful to Jennifer Perillo, former senior editor at Springer Publishing Company, for her patient encouragement and guidance throughout all stages of our contemplation, research, and writing of this book.

The Safety-Net Health Care System

PART I: SYSTEMIC FOUNDATIONS OF SAFETY-NET HEALTH CARE

1

Origins and Definitions of the Safety-Net Health Care System

INTRODUCTION

Poverty and sickness form a vicious partnership.
—Robert Hunter (1907, p. 144)

There must be strong incentives to get people to take a broader, societal view and work with those most in need. Otherwise, why should those with resources ever care about those without them?
—Wayne Lerner, President and CEO of Holy Cross Hospital,
Chicago, Illinois (Dialogue, 2009, p. 14)

*I*magine you are on a tightrope stretched between two poles. The person in front of you wasn't given a balancing pole to assist in the transit and fell part way across the rope. It is now your turn to walk out on the line. You received a pole, but now there are wind gusts. Will there be a net to catch you if you fall?

Metaphorically speaking, each person in the United States who is not independently wealthy is walking a tightrope when it comes to his or her health. Even people with insurance may lose their jobs and, therefore, their health insurance, or be unable to afford the uncovered costs of health care (e.g., insurance premiums, co-payments, and deductibles). Because of poverty, discrimination, and other factors that will be discussed in this book, some people have fallen from the tightrope into the patchwork system of health care that is known as the U.S. health care safety net. As we shall see in this chapter, no national consensus exists on specific definitions of the safety net. In this book, we take an expansive approach to understanding the health care safety net—it is the system of care that serves a disproportionate share of impoverished and otherwise vulnerable persons. Let's consider the situation of "John," a patient encountered by one of the authors who worked within a safety-net hospital whose story illustrates some of the dynamics that cause the fall from the tightrope, and what happens in the "net."

Case Study: Entry Into the Safety Net

John was 34 years old when he began to have severe pain in his stomach area. He had dropped out of school at 16 and worked as a part-time driver for a local trucking firm. The job did not offer any health insurance benefits, so when the pain he felt in his abdomen became too strong to ignore any longer, he went to a neighborhood health clinic, where he could see a doctor for a small charge. His 1- and 4-year-old sons had received their well-baby checkups at the clinic, so John was familiar with it. John arrived at 7:30 a.m. and was seen at 1 p.m. The nurse called the next day to say that John's laboratory results were abnormal and referred him for evaluation to the large public hospital located in the downtown core of the city. John knew the reputation of the hospital—it was crowded, run down, and unfriendly. So, it was with some trepidation that he brought his referral paperwork there. He spent 5 hours waiting before he was told that the next available appointment with a health care provider was 5 weeks away.

The day of his first appointment, John stood in line with 20 other people waiting to check in with the clerk. Plastic chairs were arranged in rows in front of the check-in desk, and the single window in the room had security bars across it. After 4 hours, John was escorted to a curtained alcove. The small space was separated by a thin drape from the next area, where another patient was being seen. John could hear bits of the conversations happening around him. A nurse practitioner arrived and told him she would be seeing him that day. John had lost over 20 Pounds because it hurt when he ate. He had also noticed what felt like a lump under his collarbone. John's provider told him he needed a CT scan and extensive laboratory tests of his blood. She asked if he had any insurance, because if he did, he could go to the hospital across the street, and receive the tests within a day. Without insurance, John discovered he would have to wait a week before he could receive the CT scan. The hospital had only one machine and there were higher priority clients. The nurse practitioner gave him a prescription for a mild pain reliever, but because John had not been able to work as much recently, he didn't have the money to obtain the medicine.

Once he received the CT scan, things began happening quickly. John was diagnosed with a rare and progressive form of cancer that was causing tumors to develop throughout his body, some the size of baseballs. He was immediately referred to the oncology clinic, whose next available appointment with a physician was 10 days away. John came to this appointment with his wife Keisha and their two young children. Keisha cared for their sons at home while John worked; the family couldn't afford child care. The family of four made the 20-mile trip to the hospital on three buses, a trip that took 2 hours.

The doctor recommended an aggressive treatment plan of chemotherapy and localized radiation to reduce the size of the tumors and make John more comfortable. The radiation treatments would require daily trips to the hospital for 2 weeks. John was told to expect that the treatments would make him too sick to work for the time being. Although he didn't have insurance, the hospital would provide his chemotherapy and radiation as "charity care," and not charge the family the thousands of dollars John's care would cost. The doctor suggested that the family speak with a social worker to see if they were eligible for other resources in the community. The social worker talked with John and Keisha about their understanding of what was happening, their concerns, and their needs. She referred John to both the local welfare office and the Social Security administration to apply for disability payments, food, and medical assistance. She also suggested resources in the community such as food banks and support groups for people with cancer and their loved ones.

Every morning that he arrived for radiation, John sat on an uncomfortable plastic chair in a room crowded with other people, and waited, sometimes several hours, to be called. There was no art on the walls; rather, the brown and white tiling was covered with photocopied papers telling patients to present their medical card, or to report experiences of unfair treatment to the nursing supervisor. The radiation clinic was near the street in a windowless room, and as he sat, he observed the uniformed security guards stationed at the entrance.

They carried guns and sometimes seemed to be arresting people who were yelling.

Despite the doctor's best efforts, the treatments didn't arrest the cancer and John became increasingly weaker. Within 5 months, he went from weighing 180 Pounds to 120 Pounds. His doctor suggested nutrition supplements, but John couldn't afford these because he and Keisha were relying on food stamps to feed the entire family. It was getting harder to travel to the clinic on multiple buses, his only consistent source of transportation.

Nine months after his diagnosis, he was referred to a local hospice program operated through a Catholic community hospital. John still had no insurance, so the program accepted him as a free-care patient because the hospital had a religious mission to serve the indigent. John's wife became his primary caregiver at home, providing his medication, helping him to get to the bathroom, arranging visits with various personnel, all while also mothering their two young sons. John was approved for Social Security disability income, but his rent was over half of what he received. His Social Security amount was a few dollars too high to allow him to be qualified for Medicaid, the indigent health insurance. The family received food stamps, and extra help from the Women, Infants, and Children nutrition program; their extended family members provided extra cash when they had it available.

The hospice nurse suggested that a hospital bed would make John more comfortable. John had no money to rent a bed, so the hospice social worker found an old hand-crank bed that could be donated to the family. John needed time-released morphine to ease the pain from the now numerous and ever-growing cancer tumors in his body. The amount of pain medicine he needed was substantial and cost more than $200 each month. Without insurance to cover the cost, the couple asked their extended family members for help. Sometimes they were only able to purchase a portion of the medicine John needed. John died at home, almost a year to the day after his initial diagnosis of cancer. His wife was unable to afford a funeral and burial, so John's remains were interred in the city's "potter's field," a cemetery for poor people.

John's story illustrates dynamics typical of those experienced by people without health insurance who must depend upon the health care safety net—he was one of the estimated 46.3 million Americans (U.S. Census, 2009) who did not have access to health insurance, in his case because of his part-time employment and his meager (but still too high) amount of Social Security. If John had lived for 30 months, he would have become eligible for Medicare health insurance from the

U.S. Social Security Administration as a person with a long-term disability, but he did not survive long enough. John was part of the working poor when he was healthy, but his illness forced his family into outright poverty. He turned to both the system of local health clinics and some of the hundreds of hospitals that provide specialty care to the indigent for his treatment. At the end of his life, a community hospital hospice provided his care without charge, because of its religious mission of service.

Professionals Need Specialized Knowledge to Work Effectively in Safety-Net Settings

Unlike every other major industrial democracy in the world, the United States lacks a coordinated national health program that covers all citizens. In 2006, 22,000 people died in the United States because they did not have access to health insurance (Redlener & Grant, 2009). Instead of viewing adequate health care as a right that is embedded in the social contract between a nation and its people, the United States' social, health, and economic policies treat health care as a privilege available only to those with certain forms of employment and levels of income. The safety-net system exists because there is no comprehensive commitment to the health of all in this country. As such, the existence of the health care safety-net system is both an indicator of underlying structural inequalities that beset the nation and an antidote for the worst of these inequities through the access to the health services it provides.

This book grows out of the professional work experiences both authors have had as service providers within the health care safety-net system and our personal commitment to preparing practitioners to be competent and caring resources within these settings. Working in these institutions poses serious challenges for health care professionals. Often, the physical structures of safety-net hospitals are antiquated, and limited funding is available for their upkeep. The clientele of these systems includes some of the most vulnerable and difficult-to-care-for patients within health practice. Their care is compromised by inadequate institutional funding and by the clients' own inability to pay for needed aspects of their care. Within this context, we have observed (and experienced ourselves) feelings of discouragement and despair in this work. For some practitioners, the difficulties attendant to working in the health care safety-net system can manifest in disdain for and frustration with clients. We believe that the antidote to these pessimistic feelings is a deeper understanding of the historical and structural issues of the health care safety-net system, and an understanding of the special needs and skills required to work effectively with our clientele.

Institutions within the health care safety net differ from typical middle-class medical settings because of their commitment to serving the poor. With that commitment come challenges that arise because of the poverty facing the clientele of these systems, and the funding instability that characterizes all services that focus primarily on the indigent in the United States. Practitioners who work within health care safety-net organizations need to understand their special history, setting, and context.

Our aim in this book is to encourage and strengthen the commitment of all health care professionals to the safety-net system and to the people within them most directly affected by poverty. This book is designed to give an overview of both the organizational characteristics of the safety-net system and some of the social problems such as homelessness, substance abuse, and violence that are disproportionately represented among the people seeking services in these institutions. In this chapter, we will explore some of the history that has led to the current configuration of the U.S. health care safety-net system, examine conflicting definitions of what constitutes the safety net, describe the chief components of this system and the problems it addresses, and end with a discussion of the challenges currently facing the safety net.

BRIEF HISTORY OF HEALTH CARE FOR THE MARGINALIZED IN THE UNITED STATES

Western health and medical care have a rich history that is centuries long (see, e.g., Thompson & Goldin, 1975), but for the purposes of understanding the contemporary safety net we will concentrate on four key time periods that have dramatically shaped the U.S. health care system: the period of industrialization that characterized the latter half of the 1800s and resultant shifts in care at the turn of the century, the governmental response to the Great Depression of the 1930s, the new health programs of the Great Society initiatives of the Johnson presidency, and the most recent decades that can be characterized by health care inflation, ever-increasing numbers of uninsured Americans, and repeated efforts at health care reform.

Institution Building in the Late 1800s

People in the latter half of the 19th century experienced massive dislocation as the United States transitioned from a primarily rural, farm-based economy to a system dominated by industrialization, the growth of factories, and wage earning. This shift was associated with rapid urbanization, high rates of internal migration and immigration, White retrenchment after the Civil War, the final defeat of indigenous nations for possession of land and natural resources, uprooting of families, and outbreaks of disease. These various forces strained the capacity of families and individual providers of health services to meet the growing demand for care of the injured, ill, disabled, and aged. As a result, compassionate institutional care that could address the needs of those without other resources became the primary focus of reformers. One well-known example of these efforts was the work of Dorothea Dix, a crusader for the humane care of the mentally ill and an advocate for the creation of state "insane asylums," as these institutions were called in this time period. Another example was the development of public hospitals whose major purpose was controlling infectious diseases such as tuberculosis, typhus, and syphilis. Public hospitals had a charitable mission of service to the poor, but were also strategic efforts on the part of the wealthy to protect themselves from diseases associated with poverty. By financing health care for the poor, the wealthy sought to contain illness outbreaks and to provide care during large-scale epidemics that threatened commercial interests (Waitzkin, 2005).

In the latter half of the 1800s, the wealthy who were ill or in need of care received that help in their own homes, but the poor who had no family resources were sent to institutions alternatively called poorhouses or almshouses. Poorhouses became the residence for the indigent, including orphaned children, unemployed men, the mentally ill, the frail elderly, and the disabled or ill. Poorhouses were financed by taxing local residents (much like the financing of contemporary "county" hospitals). In fact, one of the most famous public hospitals in the country, Cook County Hospital in Chicago, began as a poorhouse that provided medical services (History of Cook County Hospital, n.d.). The emphasis of these institutions was to provide essential, no-frills care so that people would view living in the poorhouse as an option of last resort. The idea that services for the poor should be spare with an eye toward discouraging "dependence" is a frequent theme in social welfare policy (Trattner, 1984).

Although much has been written about the poorhouse as a social phenomenon, few historians have delved into the day-to-day lives of the people who lived in these establishments. Wagner (2008) has provided an in-depth portrait of one of the largest poorhouses operating in the United States in the late 1800s. Located outside of Lowell, Massachusetts, Tewksbury opened in 1854 and came to house over 3,000 people a year. Anne Sullivan, Helen Keller's teacher, lived with her brother at Tewksbury from 1876 to 1880, after her mother died and her father was no longer able to care for the children. Sullivan told a biographer that the ward where she slept was "filled with old women, grotesque, misshapen, diseased and dying" (Wagner, 2008, p. 176). Being sent to the poorhouse filled people with dread. Jane Addams, noted 19th-century social reformer, sociologist, social worker, and Nobel Peace Prize winner, described a woman she met as she established Hull House, one of the first U.S. settlement houses (akin to today's neighborhood community centers) in Chicago. She remarked that, "the old woman . . . [looked] on with that gripping fear of the poorhouse in her eyes, she was a living embodiment of that dread which is so heart-breaking" (Addams, 1999, p. 106). Addams's experiences led her to include health services at Hull House, creating the prototypes for the community health clinics that would develop after the 1960s (Waitzkin, 2005).

No system of "long-term care" existed, so the poorhouse came to serve this function as families, increasingly mobile and pulled apart by the industrial revolution, were no longer able to care for their members. One-quarter of the residents of Tewksbury died within 3 years of arrival at the poorhouse (Wagner, 2008). As new institutions for orphans, the blind, and the deaf were created, people with these problems were moved from the poorhouses. As a result, a disproportionate percentage of poorhouse services came to be devoted to the care of the elderly, mostly elderly men without children (Katz, 1986). Additionally, most people with serious mental illness were cared for in poorhouses, particularly in rural areas, despite efforts by Dix and others to create separate institutions for the mentally ill (Katz, 1986). Poorhouses continued to exist in some locations until the 1960s, with many transitioning into long-term care facilities for the elderly and disabled during the 20th century.

By the turn of the 20th century, scientific breakthroughs in germ theory and surgical and medical treatments sparked a deepening interest in the provision of acute care, a medical model focused on diagnosis, intervention, and recovery or cure. In the 50 years from 1880 to

1930, the country's population doubled, but the number of acute care hospitals increased by over 2,500% (Risse, 1999). Acute care models contrasted sharply with the model of care delivered in the poorhouse, namely basic custodial services for people with chronic, incurable conditions. Acute care was driven by what would become one of the most important groups in the health policy debates of the coming century, the American Medical Association (AMA). By 1900, the AMA had solidified its standing as the main group representing medical doctors and the chief authority for the health of the nation.

The Great Depression and Missed Opportunities

The stock market crash of 1929 signaled the beginning of a decade-long period of severe economic deprivation in the United States and worldwide. One-quarter of the American population was unemployed (compared to about 10% unemployment during the recession of 2008–2010). A record number of homes and farms were foreclosed resulting in large numbers of homeless persons living in makeshift "towns" called Hoovervilles, in mocking deference to a president who many saw as ineffective and unconcerned with the needs of ordinary people.

Franklin Delano Roosevelt, a reformist governor from New York, was elected to the presidency in 1932. He promised a "New Deal" for the American people, one in which the federal government would adopt new roles and commitments in the provision of social and economic aid. Roosevelt's administration created a number of new employment programs including the Civilian Conservation Corps, the Works Progress Administration (WPA), and the Public Works Administration (PWA). These latter two programs were particularly important to the health infrastructure of the country, constructing buildings that are still in use today. In addition to public health projects such as sewer systems and water treatment plants, the WPA built 226 new hospitals and renovated an additional 2,324, and the PWA built 493 general hospitals and institutions, 205 insane asylums, and 146 specialty hospitals (Leighninger, 2007).

Although the WPA and PWA were dismantled during World War II, Roosevelt's most lasting contribution came with the passage of the Social Security Act. This legislation provided the first federal guarantee of a minimum standard of income for people who had worked and were retired or disabled. According to the Roosevelt Administration's Committee on Economic Security, poverty among the elderly prior to the passage of the Social Security Act exceeded 50% during the Great Depression.[1] This rate has steadily decreased over the decades so that now 9.7% of the elderly have incomes under the poverty level (U.S. Census Bureau, 2009). Social Security also provided financial assistance to survivors of deceased workers, the unemployed, and mothers and children in poverty through the Aid to Dependent Children program (which later became known as "welfare").

Conspicuously absent from the assistance provided through the Social Security Act is the inclusion of a comprehensive program to address health treatment. Throughout the drafting of the Social Security legislation, reformers made efforts to have national health insurance included. These efforts were frustrated in three primary ways. First, the AMA and state medical societies were deeply opposed to any efforts to create a national health insurance program, fearing a loss of their autonomy and the imposition of group practice models over the solo practices operated by physicians at the time (Starr, 1982). Second, President Roosevelt did not strongly favor national health care when compared to his adamant support for unemployment and old age assistance (Kooijman, 1999). Third, the Social Security Act was carefully constructed to maintain the racial status quo, particularly in Southern states (Lieberman, 1998). For example, domestic workers and agricultural laborers (disproportionately African American during this time period) were excluded from coverage under Social Security, a compromise with Southern legislators who feared increased economic independence of African Americans. If national health insurance was adopted, as was advocated by the National Association for the Advancement of Colored People and the National Medical Association (the leading African American physician organization created because of segregation and discrimination within the AMA), this would potentially tear apart the fragile coalition of Northern and Southern White representatives and senators needed to pass Social Security. As a result, policy planners within the Roosevelt Administration, and the president himself, came to believe that including any kind of national health plan would lead to the ultimate defeat of the entire Social Security effort.

[1] At the time that the Social Security Act of 1935 was passed, there were no precise estimates of poverty among persons aged 65 and older or even an official measure of poverty. Based on data from disparate sources such as state surveys and census counts of almshouse residents, the Roosevelt Administration's Committee on Economic Security estimated that at least one-half of the population of persons over age 65 lived in a state of economic dependence on others. For a critique of this 50% figure, see Gratton (1996) "The Poverty of Impoverishment Theory: The Economic Well-Being of the Elderly, 1890–1950." *Journal of Economic History* 56(1): 39–61.

Roosevelt assured disappointed supporters that national health insurance would be included in the next round of Social Security reforms, but, unfortunately, his optimism about the eventual creation of a national health care plan was ill-founded.

Although Social Security did not include a national health component, there were modest health efforts included in the legislation. The law funded state-based public health systems, vocational rehabilitation for people with disabilities, and maternal and child health efforts aimed at reducing infant and child mortality.

The People's Health: Johnson's Great Society, Medicare, and Medicaid

In the decades following World War II, other industrial democracies were enacting national health care or national insurance plans that provided a basic level of medical care to all citizens (Quadagno, 2005). Attempts to enact national health care in the United States had failed in the 1930s, and 30 years would pass before substantial reform was on the public policy agenda again. The 1960s opened with the lunch-counter sit-ins in Greensboro, North Carolina, protesting discrimination against African American citizens. Efforts to dismantle racial inequality sparked movements in diverse communities in response to other injustices. By the end of the decade, mass demonstrations against the Vietnam War, the creation of the feminist women's movement, occupation of land by Native Americans, and the emergence of the gay and lesbian liberation effort had all occurred. A common theme underlying all of these (and other) social justice struggles was the focus on wresting control of social problems from experts, politicians, or other institutional authorities and obtaining power for "the people"—typically referring to the segments of society with the least political voice and power through established political and economic institutions. As an example in the health system, several socially radical and progressive groups initiated their own health care programs, independent of the existing medical establishment. The Black Panther party opened clinics in Chicago, New York, Boston, and other cities; feminist clinics developed resources to place medical decision-making power in the hands of women rather than male doctors; and alternative health approaches flourished in the countercultural movement (Waitzkin, 2005). Many of these programs specifically focused their services on the poor, or provided care without charge as did the Haight Ashbury Free Clinic founded in 1967 (which continues to provide services today).

On the national policy front, efforts began in the Kennedy Administration and flourished under Lyndon Johnson to replace institutional care with accessible community-based services. In 1963, Kennedy signed the Community Mental Health Act, which facilitated the "deinstitutionalization" of persons with severe mental illness. One-hundred years earlier, Dorothea Dix had advocated the creation of insane asylums as a compassionate approach to the treatment and care of persons with serious mental disorders. From their progressive beginnings, these institutions deteriorated into places that were as dreaded as the poorhouses of the previous century. The advent of psychotropic medications and a national shift toward community-based care encouraged the return of persons who had been hospitalized (sometimes for decades) to family homes and neighborhoods. Unfortunately, Kennedy's vision of a network of community mental health centers to support care was never fully realized, as local governments displaced therapeutic and humanitarian goals with economic ones. Ongoing evaluations suggest that disproportionate numbers of the homeless are people with serious mental illnesses such as schizophrenia, bipolar disorder, or depression with psychotic features (Lamb & Bacharach, 2001).

Following these trends toward the provision of services at the community level, the Johnson Administration authorized a demonstration project to create neighborhood health centers to serve low-income communities. This project supported the empowerment of service recipients by requiring that 51% of the board of directors of any center be clients of the health program. Centers embraced other radical ideas about health care as demonstrated in this example of an early project in Mississippi:

> Malnutrition proved to be one of the most serious health problems . . . when the health center began stocking and prescribing food for the malnourished, some officials objected that its pharmacy was only supposed to carry drugs for the treatment of disease. To which the staff responded, "The last time we looked in the book, the specific therapy for malnutrition was food." The center also became involved in starting farm cooperatives, public transportation and other local projects. (Starr, 1982, p. 371)

By the mid-1970s, Congress authorized the full development of a national network of community health centers (CHC) that would provide primary care services to the indigent.

On the national health insurance front, discussions were underway during the Kennedy administration to introduce a program focused on the elderly. The costs of medical care had soared after World War II, but labor unions and others had negotiated private insurance plans that covered hospitalization for the majority of working Americans. However, the elderly did not have access to any affordable coverage of medical care, despite the fact that almost 20% of those over 65 were hospitalized in any given year (Starr, 1982). Kennedy proposed the creation of Medicare, a form of health insurance modeled on the popular "80/20" plans of the day. This type of insurance usually covered 80% of the allowable charges, and patients paid the remaining 20% of the bill. Policymakers also recognized that the "medically indigent" (including impoverished children and their mothers on welfare programs and younger disabled persons) could not obtain adequate health care. Medicaid, a health insurance program for those with incomes under the poverty line, was the policy solution for this group. Medicaid did not adopt the 80/20 model; rather, it paid the entire cost of allowed care, but its reimbursement rates for medical providers were set at a low level and certain procedures were not covered.

Again, the chief opponent of efforts to create national health insurance through Medicare and Medicaid was the AMA. The physician group fought expansion of public insurance, portraying it as a threat to the doctor–patient relationship, suggesting that the government would intervene to dictate the kinds of care a person would receive (Starr, 1982). To gain the cooperation of the AMA, Congress agreed to finance the costs of the new health insurance programs, but allowed financial intermediaries (chiefly Blue Cross) to administer the program.

Medicare and Medicaid reflect the deep split in the American policy psyche in regard to the creation of a social safety net for all citizens (see Table 1.1 for a summary of the differences between social insurance and "means-tested" programs). By the 1960s, Social Security had established itself as a profoundly popular program. Citizens felt entitled to its benefits as a result of their contributions through payroll deductions. Medicare was similarly viewed as a valued entitlement for those over 65 who had contributed to the nation through their work. Medicaid reflected a different orientation. As a means-tested program—indicating that a person had to have limited income or assets ("means") to qualify—Medicaid was seen as a form of welfare. Means-tested programs in the United States have typically suffered from a public perception that the people receiving them were undeserving of assistance, that they were living off "honest taxpayers," and getting something

TABLE 1.1
Social Insurance Versus Means-Tested Programs

SOCIAL INSURANCE	MEANS-TESTED "WELFARE" PROGRAMS
Programs	
• Social Security (retirement and disability programs) • Medicare	• Supplemental Security Income • Temporary Assistance to Needy Families ("welfare") • Medicaid
Characteristics	
• Universal—anyone who has worked for a certain amount of time is eligible regardless of level of income • Considered a social "right" • Generously funded	• Limited to those with a low enough income and no other resources • Considered a form of dependency • Highly stigmatized • Frequent reductions in funding

while doing nothing (Katz, 1986). Eligibility for Medicare was set by the federal government, but qualification for Medicaid was determined by each state, outside of federal mandates to cover children and mothers receiving welfare payments and other groups that were deemed "categorically" eligible (Coll, 1995). As a result, states differed dramatically in their income guidelines and the health care services covered. For example, some states cover dental services and mental health treatment whereas others do not (Kaiser Family Foundation, n.d.) In contrast to Medicare, no uniform national standards for coverage and services were set for Medicaid.

Medicare and Medicaid were clearly successful at providing the poor and aged with access to affordable health care. For example, by the mid-1970s, those on Medicaid visited physicians as often as the nonpoor and had as many surgical procedures as those with higher incomes, in contrast with utilization rates substantially lower than the nonpoor in the years before the programs existed (Starr, 1982). However, these improvements were not without certain costs, particularly for public health care systems. Medicare and Medicaid increasingly channeled public funds to private medical practitioners and nonprofit hospitals, siphoning off resources that were traditionally used to support public safety-net providers (Waitzkin, 2005). A further burden for the safety-net system was the fact that private providers would push patients back to the public system when their Medicaid benefits ended. Because poverty is not a constant event, people covered under Medicaid routinely lost their health insurance if they became employed, were disqualified from a program, or had temporary increases in income. At the same time, the low-income elderly, even with Medicare insurance, were unable to pay growing deductibles or co-payments for care and turned to the safety-net system. Although public hospitals have come to depend on these two public insurances to finance care, they faced declining revenues from traditional funders (the locales they served). With weakening of the rationale for their existence as the epidemics of the previous century were largely held at bay with improvements in public health and immunizations, public hospitals faced more precarious funding situations, as we will explore further later in this chapter.

From Reagan to Obama: Retrenchment, Failed Efforts, and (Limited) Success

Ronald Reagan was elected in 1980 and reelected in 1984 with more electoral votes than any candidate in American history. Riding a tide of increasing resentment against changes instituted under Johnson's presidency (both in terms of civil rights and War on Poverty programs), his policy was to shrink funding for social programs and "devolve" responsibility for these services to states, while also increasing funding to military and defense projects. Examples of these efforts were the Reagan Administration's decision to dramatically reduce funding of the community mental health system, while deinstitutionalization, ensured an increasing demand for outpatient services. If the 1960s were about designing systems to empower the poor, the 1980s were focused on preventing what conservative politicians believed were widespread efforts on the part of the poor to take fraudulent advantage of assistance programs. Reagan popularized these ideas in his first campaign for the presidency, frequently relating stories of the "welfare queen"—a pejorative term for poor women whom he believed were defrauding the system by having more children solely to collect more money from public assistance programs.

The largest health crisis of the Reagan presidency was the emergence of the HIV/AIDS epidemic. The first reports suggesting that a new disease was being seen among young gay men were issued by the Centers for Disease Control in 1981. Rare opportunistic infections such as *Pneumocystis carinii* pneumonia and Kaposi's sarcoma were occurring in men without any apparent reason for immune deficiency. In 1987, the World Health Organization estimated that between 5 and 10 million people were HIV infected worldwide (Chin & Mann, 1989).

Decades later, there are now an estimated 33.4 million people living with HIV, and in 2008 alone, 2 million people died of AIDS related conditions (World Health Organization, 2009).

Stigma associated with the initial emergence of the epidemic within the gay community in the United States, coupled with fear of contagion, led to examples of medical personnel refusing to treat people they suspected of being HIV positive (Shilts, 1987). As a result, many of the community-based services now available in the U.S. were begun and financed by members of the lesbian, gay, bisexual and transgender communities. Early in the epidemic, the average life expectancy of someone with AIDS was less than 6 months; people often died before they could be certified for Social Security and Medicaid benefits. Because of the stigma and financial issues, many people with AIDS (then and now) have received their care through the health care safety-net system. In 1990, Congress passed the Ryan White Comprehensive AIDS Resources Emergency Act to fund medical treatment for people with AIDS. The advent in the late 1990s of new antiretroviral medications that could check the progression of the disease put a further strain on public health care systems as the costs associated with drug treatment for a single month could be several hundred dollars and HIV positive persons needed these medications for the rest of their lives. These pharmaceuticals transformed AIDS from a terminal illness to a chronic one that could last for decades with substantial health care monitoring and treatment expenses. In response to the life-sustaining and expensive nature of these drugs, Congress created the AIDS Drug Assistance Program to provide resources for the purchase of drugs like AZT and, later, protease inhibitors. Even with federal assistance, some states are unable to provide AIDS treatment to everyone who needs it, which in several states has resulted in ongoing waiting lists for persons in need of these life-sustaining medications (Kaiser Family Foundation, 2011).

National efforts at major health care reform would not be undertaken again until the second year of Bill Clinton's presidency. Clinton made coverage of the uninsured a major policy initiative in his campaign. Soon after taking office, his wife Hillary Rodham Clinton, a respected attorney in her own right, chaired the Task Force on National Health Care Reform, which developed the proposal eventually presented to Congress for debate. The central feature of the Clinton plan to cover the uninsured was the mandate that employers had to provide health insurance coverage to employees. Initially, the AMA was supportive of a reform proposal, as were the professional associations of nurses, social workers, and pharmacists. Once the bill was introduced, the AMA qualified its endorsement stating that the mandate should only apply to "firms with over 100 employees and thereby excluding most private doctors, the majority of whom [did] not cover their own employees" (Starr, 1995, p. 21). As the debate progressed, the AMA became more opposed, citing its traditional concerns about national health care, namely that it would interfere with the doctor–patient relationship and undermine the quality of medical services (Pear, 1993). The Health Insurance Association of America (1997) (now known as America's Health Insurance Plans or AHIP) attacked the bill with a famous series of ads featuring "Harry and Louise" lamenting the proposed changes and urging people to oppose its passage. In 1994, the legislation was declared dead. However, the Clinton administration regrouped in 1997 to pass a smaller health insurance bill that covered low-income children not eligible for Medicaid, the State Children's Health Insurance Program (SCHIP).

Although Clinton pushed through piecemeal expansion of health coverage, he also signed legislation limiting or removing support to other indigent groups. For example, Clinton's efforts to "end welfare as we know it" resulted in the passage of the Personal Responsibility and Work Opportunity Act of 1996, which severely limited the availability of public financial assistance to poor women and children. The act imposed time limits on the receipt of assistance, so that eligible families could receive support for not more than 5 years, with some states limiting aid to even shorter periods. The act increased penalties for noncompliance with work requirements and other rules, allowing the complete removal of families from the program. A study of Medicaid usage after welfare reform in one state indicated that one-quarter of women who were sanctioned off the program needed Medicaid, but were unable to obtain it (Lindhorst & Mancoske, 2006). When welfare benefits end, a sizeable minority of recipients who remain income eligible for Medicaid may no longer receive it.

Similarly, Clinton also signed legislation prohibiting assistance through the Supplemental Security Income (SSI) program of Social Security for people who were disabled and unable to work as a result of drug addiction or alcoholism. SSI is the main income support program for people with disabilities or the elderly who cannot qualify for Social Security payments because they have not worked enough. SSI is another of the means-tested programs; a person cannot qualify for SSI payments if he or she has other income or resources. In 2009, 7.68 million Americans received SSI payments, 15.5% were children and 26.4% were over 65 years old (Social Security Administration, 2010). As part of their Contract with America, Republican Congress members pledged to stop financial support to people with addictions, although they represented less than 2% of people on SSI (Watkins & Podus, 2000). Evaluation of the effects of the policy suggested that SSI did not contribute to continued substance use (Watkins & Podus, 2000) and that a significant percentage of the people disqualified from services had been previously hospitalized for medical problems or serious mental disorders (Hanrahan, Luchins, Cloniger, & Swartz, 2004). The policy change resulted in over half of these former SSI recipients having no access to health insurance, despite their elevated health needs. The contraction in this program undoubtedly returned these persons to the rolls of safety-net providers.

The largest expansion to occur in any national health program since the passage of Medicare and Medicaid in the 1960s happened when the George W. Bush Administration shepherded a plan through Congress in 2003 creating a prescription drug benefit for recipients of Medicare. When enacted in 1965, Medicare covered hospitalization and physician services, but it did not cover any medications prescribed on an outpatient basis. Pharmaceuticals have played an increasing role in medical treatment, and their costs have risen significantly since the passage of Medicare. During the debate on the prescription drug bill, examples were given of seniors having to choose between paying for medications and food on their limited monthly incomes. The Medicare drug benefit passed by Congress provided coverage of medications (after payment of a premium, deductible, and co-payment) up to $2,400 annually. After a person exceeded this amount of outpatient medication, he or she became responsible for the full cost of the medicine until the beneficiary accumulated approximately $4,000 in out-of-pocket expenses, at which point Medicare again resumed coverage of prescriptions. This gap in coverage was commonly referred to as the "donut hole," and was created in response to political concerns about the cost of the drug benefit. Within 5 years, nearly three-quarters of Medicare recipients had signed up for the service (Goldstein, 2009).

In addition to Medicare prescription coverage, the Bush Administration also significantly expanded the CHC network. President Bush funded the establishment of 1,200 new health clinics in rural and medically underserved areas. The number of patients served more than doubled, with over 16 million people receiving treatment through the clinic system, the majority of whom are indigent (Sack, 2008).

The most recent chapter in efforts to ensure health care for all in the country has occurred with the passage of the Patient Protection and Affordable Care Act (PPACA) of 2010. The Obama Administration kept the idea of mandating insurance coverage from the Clinton reform efforts, but instead of requiring employers to cover work-ers, individuals will be required to purchase their own health insur-ance coverage or face an annual fine of several hundred dollars (up to 2.5% of an individual's income) for not doing so. In addition to requir-ing the purchase of health insurance, the Obama plan also prohibits insurance companies from refusing to cover preexisting conditions, or from dropping coverage of persons who have high-cost conditions. If all Americans purchase insurance as required under the plan, 94% of U.S. citizens and legal residents will have at least minimal health insurance coverage. People with incomes up to four times the federal poverty level who are unable to afford the cost of care will be eligible for governmental subsidies, so they will not have to pay more than 10% of annual income on health insurance. People with incomes up to 133% of the poverty line will be eligible for an expanded Medicaid program. However, the several mil-lion immigrants who are in the country without documentation will not be covered under the PPACA. It is unclear at this time whether this health reform will survive legal challenges from states—currently 18 states are contesting the law in court and over half of state legislatures are consider-ing bills that would nullify aspects of PPACA, including the mandate that individuals buy insurance.

Summary

This historical overview is brief, and other important moments in the history of health care for the marginalized are summarized in Table 1.2. Several key themes recur over the years. First, the system of financing and providing health care in the United States is a patchwork that allows substantial portions of people to fall through the cracks within the employer-based health insurance system because of "ac-cidents" of birth, geography, and employment (Meyer, 2004). This pieced-together system reflects structural inequalities (i.e., that poverty disproportionately affects certain groups of people such as children) and ameliorates some of the worst of these disparities by providing access to care within a safety-net context. Second, the country has been ambiva-lent about ensuring that all citizens have access to basic health resources. On the one hand, over time, certain groups have been made categori-cally eligible for health assistance (i.e., the elderly through Medicare), and entire systems of care such as the CHC network have been estab-lished. On the other hand, substantial portions of the U.S. population fall outside any coverage system, with thousands dying in any given year as a result of their inability to access care (Redlener & Grant, 2009).

TABLE 1.2
Chronology of Selected Dates in Safety-Net History

DATE	EVENT
1788	First veterans, hospital opened in Pittsburgh, PA
1833	Worcester State Insane Asylum Hospital opened, first hospital for the mentally ill
1841	Dorothea Dix publishes first report on treatment of "insane poor" of Massachusetts, resulting in the expansion of the hospital at Worcester
1849	Health care for American Indians provided under auspices of Bureau of Indian Affairs (BIA) transferred to newly created Department of the Interior
1890	State Care Act in NY—first law in which a state assumed the complete care and expense of the "insane poor"
1903	First study on the prevention and treatment of tuberculosis undertaken by the Charity Organization Society of New York
1911	First employer-sponsored group disability insurance policy issued
1921	Congress created health division within BIA
1921	Sheppard-Towner Act creates first maternal-child clinics to address infant mortality; repealed in 1927
1929	Baylor University Hospital offers hospitalization insurance, the origins of Blue Cross
1930	Establishment of Veterans Administration
1935	Passage of the Social Security Act
1937	Congress established the National Cancer Institute (the first illness-specific research center in what became known as the National Institutes of Health in 1944)
1946	Hospital Survey and Construction Act (Hill-Burton Act) provided funding for hospital construction with the requirement that hospitals provide a certain percentage of free care to indigent persons
1954	Indian Health Services (IHS) created within the U.S. Department of Health and Human Services, removed from the BIA
1962	Migrant Health Act creates first health clinics for seasonal and migrant farmworkers
1963	Community Mental Health Act leads to deinstitutionalization of persons with serious mental illness
1965	Passage of amendments to the Social Security Act creating Medicare and Medicaid
1972	End Stage Renal Disease program extends Medicare benefits to cover dialysis for persons with kidney failure
1972	Creation of National Health Service Corps to provide primary care in medically underserved areas

(continued)

TABLE 1.2
Chronology of Selected Dates in Safety-Net History *(Continued)*

DATE	EVENT
1973	Vocational Rehabilitation Act prevents any institution that receives federal funding from discriminating against persons on the basis of disability
1975	Permanent authorization of Neighborhood Health Centers, now known as Federally Qualified Health Centers
1977	Rural Health Clinic Services Act opens hundreds of new health centers mainly in the South and West
1982	Creation of Health Resources and Services Administration to improve care for medically underserved
1985	Disproportionate Share Hospital funding through Medicare and Medicaid mandated by Congress
1986	Emergency Medical Treatment and Labor Act requires all hospital emergency departments to provide medical screening to anyone who requests it regardless of ability to pay
1987	Stewart B. McKinney Homeless Assistance Act provides funding for health care for homeless children and adults
1990	Ryan White Care Act provided funding for primary care to HIV-infected persons; incorporated AIDS Drug Assistance Program funding started by Congress in 1987 to purchase AZT for HIV-infected persons
1990	Americans with Disabilities Act prevents discrimination on the basis of disability or perceived disabling condition
1997	State Children's Health Insurance Program (SCHIP) enacted
2003	Medicare Prescription Drug, Improvement and Modernization Act creates first outpatient drug benefit for Medicare beneficiaries
2010	Patient Protection and Affordable Care Act expands coverage of uninsured through Medicaid program and other public–private initiatives

Third, despite multiple policy interventions, a substantial number of people have not or cannot be "mainstreamed" into non-safety-net health systems. Programs such as Medicaid and even Medicare do not ensure that low-income persons can afford associated health care costs or remain enrolled in coverage over time, so a proportion of the population continues to require services provided by safety-net organizations. Fourth, the country's health resources have been devoted to an individual-oriented acute model of care that prioritizes medical intervention over preventive efforts (for instance, payment for expensive cardiac surgeries, but no reimbursement for weight loss interventions or investment in high-quality accessible food in all communities). In summary, these and other structural deficiencies are at the heart of the existence of the health care safety-net system.

FEATURES OF THE HEALTH CARE SAFETY-NET SYSTEM

Given the history of the health care safety-net system as a patchwork of programs, policies, and organizations, it should come as no surprise that there is a lack of consensus on how to determine who is a part of the system. In this section, we compare various definitions of who is a safety-net provider, followed by a listing of some of the major components of our system of care for the indigent. The final sections of this chapter touch on funding challenges of safety-net providers and debates about the quality of care in these systems.

Defining the Health Care Safety Net

No universally accepted definition for the safety net exists. The Institute of Medicine (IOM)—the national advisory body to the federal government on issues related to health and medical care—issued a report in 2000 entitled *America's Health Care Safety Net: Intact but Endangered*. The IOM definition is a good place to start in characterizing the U.S. safety-net system:

> The IOM committee defines safety net providers as those providers that organize and deliver a significant level of health care and other health-related services to uninsured, Medicaid, and other vulnerable patients. In most communities there is a subset of the safety net that the committee describes as "core safety net providers." These providers have two distinguishing characteristics: (1) by legal mandate or explicitly adopted mission, they maintain an "open door," offering patients access to services regardless of their ability to pay; and (2) a substantial portion of their patient mix is uninsured, Medicaid, and other vulnerable patients. (IOM, Lewin, & Altman, 2000, p. 21)

There are two important components to this definition. First, some people are more vulnerable than others based on their inability to pay for essential health care. As we shall see in the chapters on poverty and stigma, all people are not at equal risk for poverty or a lack of health insurance. Some people, because of their age, gender or race, are more likely to encounter these problems. Second, the safety-net system serves a disproportionately higher number of these people.

Table 1.3 further elaborates the idea of "vulnerability" as it is typically understood to apply to populations cared for in safety-net

TABLE 1.3
Vulnerable Populations Disproportionately Served Within Health Care Safety-Net Systems

Uninsured and Underinsured
- Working poor without employer health insurance
- Elders unable to afford co-pays and deductibles in private systems
- People covered by Medicaid who are not accepted for care by private health providers

Certain Health Conditions
- Chronically ill
- People with communicable diseases (HIV/AIDS, tuberculosis, and sexually transmitted infections)
- High-risk mothers and infants (those in need of neonatal intensive care)
- People with disabilities
- People with serious mental illness

Certain Social Problems
- Poverty
- Homelessness
- People addicted to drugs and/or alcohol
- Victims of violence and trauma
- Prisoners
- Victims of disasters

Certain Social Statuses
- Legal and undocumented immigrants
- Low-income people of color, especially American Indians (AI) and Alaska Natives (AN), African Americans, and Latinos
- People who speak limited or no English
- Migrant workers
- Refugees
- Veterans

NOTE: Adapted from Gage (1998).

systems. As this table shows, people are more likely to need assistance from the health care safety net if they have certain health conditions, experience certain social problems, or belong to certain social groups who are more likely to experience poverty. For example, safety-net hospitals are more likely to devote resources to culturally sensitive care such as the provision of medical interpreters. The safety-net hospital in Hennepin County, Minnesota, employs 42 full-time interpreters who respond to language requests in more than 60 languages (Meyer, 2004). The head of a Boston safety-net hospital noted, "We offer 18 languages onsite 24 hours a day. There's no other hospital in the state with that much cultural and linguistic competency" (Felland, Lauer, & Cunningham, 2009, pp. 7–8).

While satisfying as a general idea, the IOM definition is too vague to be of much use when we try to determine who and how many safety-net providers exist. How much is a "substantial portion" of a clientele? Who determines whether a legal mandate or mission exists? The IOM report itself excludes federally sponsored health care systems such as the Veterans Health Administration and the Indian Health Service (IHS) from its definition of the "core" health care safety net, despite the fact (as we will see later) that these systems serve disproportionate numbers of low-income people. Likewise, it does not take into account the growing amount of health care provided within state and federal prison systems (IOM et al., 2000).

As a result of this lack of clarity, others have suggested alternative approaches. These definitions generally focus on one of three methods for classifying a safety-net provider: the proportion of uncompensated care they provide, the number of Medicaid (i.e., low-income or indigent) patients they see, or the type of health care provider they are (i.e., teaching or public). As illustrated in Figure 1.1, a study of hospitals nationwide by McHugh, Kang, and Hasnian-Wynia (2009) determined that only 98 hospitals, or 2% of hospitals in the United States, qualified as safety-net providers under all three definitions; however, several hundred more met at least one of these three criteria.

Safety-net and non-safety-net hospitals clearly differ in the types of services they provide. Table 1.4 compares the two types of hospitals across a range of services including types of intensive care, mental

FIGURE 1.1   Alternative Measures to Define Safety-Net Hospitals

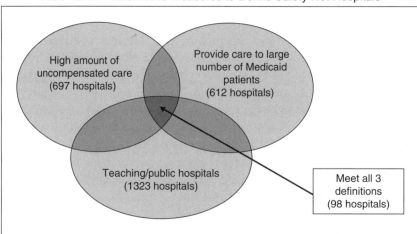

NOTE: Data in figure are from McHugh et al. (2009).

TABLE 1.4
Comparison of Services Provided by Safety-Net
and Non-safety-Net Hospitals

SERVICE	% OF SAFETY-NET HOSPITALS	% OF NON-SAFETY-NET HOSPITALS
Neonatal Intensive Care Unit	76.6	26.7
Trauma Center	74.5	22.9
Burn Unit	22.8	3.1
AIDS Services	83.5	49.0
Psychiatric Emergency Unit	77.9	42.4
Outpatient Substance Abuse Treatment	45.5	28.3

NOTE: Adapted from Bazzoll, Kang, Hasnain-Wynia, and Lindrooth (2005).

health services, and AIDS treatment. When these services are offered, they are far more likely to be provided by the safety-net hospital than for-profit or nonprofit community hospitals.

Health care researchers and policymakers have not agreed upon a set definition of what is a part of the health care safety-net system. As we have summarized, what is considered a safety-net provider varies widely among studies. In this text, our interest is in those people who are marginalized from care, meaning that they do not have the wealth or insurance coverage necessary to buy the care they need from "mainstream" medical systems. We define the safety-net health care system as comprising the clinics, hospitals, and individual health care providers that care for a disproportionate share of the poor, the uninsured, those afflicted by stigmatizing health conditions, and persons otherwise isolated from the mainstream health care system.

Components of the Health Care Safety Net

Within the health care safety net are institutions almost exclusively focused on care to the indigent, and others who have a mix of clientele but who serve a disproportionate number of those without insurance. These various institutions are funded primarily through federal or local taxes, including income taxes. As such, even for people who are not patients within these systems, the existence of these institutions is important to all U.S. citizens, as their funding rests on the (fragmented) "social contract" or agreement between citizens and their governing bodies for the kinds of services that will be provided collectively within a society. Table 1.5 provides a broad overview of programs or providers who are members of the health care safety-net system, along with estimates of the most recent annual amount of services provided,

TABLE 1.5
Selected Providers of Safety-Net Health Care Services

SERVICE PROVIDER	ESTIMATED AMOUNT OF SERVICE
Public hospitals[a]	1.8 million hospitalizations 36 million outpatient visits 6 million emergency department visits
Community hospitals[b]	5,010 hospitals 35.7 million hospitalizations 123 million emergency department visits 624 million outpatient visits
Teaching hospitals[c]	1,007 hospitals
Veteran's Administration[d]	171 medical centers 870 clinics 5.3 million patients served
IHS[e]	46 hospitals 633 ambulatory care centers 1.9 million AI/AN served
Prison health care[f]	1.6 million inmates in 1,821 federal or state facilities

Bureau of Primary Care (HRSA)[g]
    Community Health Centers
    Migrant Health Centers
    Healthcare for the Homeless
    Public Housing Primary Care
	17.1 million patients (1 in 18 nationally)
	1,080 grantees—half of which are located in rural areas
	7,500+ service sites

Public health departments	No information available
Long-term care facilities[h]	16,100 nursing homes 1,492,200 residents
Others (school-based health clinics, rural practitioners, rural pharmacists, and minority physicians serving inner-city populations)	No information available

[a] From 2008 data from 89 acute care public hospitals (Zaman, Cummings, & Spieler, 2009).

[b] From 2008 data; 5.8% of care is uncompensated (American Hospital Association, 2009).

[c] From 2007 data; 71% of care is uncompensated (Association of American Medical Colleges, 2009).

[d] From Oliver, 2007.

[e] From 2002 to 2009 (IHS, n.d.).

[f] As of 2005 (Stephan, 2008).

[g] Health Resources Services Administration (n.d.).

[h] From 2004 data (Centers for Disease Control, n.d.); nearly 46% of nursing home residents are covered by Medicaid (O'Brien, 2005).

where available. We briefly discuss five of these systems of care to illustrate their varying missions and programs.

Safety-Net Hospitals

When the words "health care safety net" are used, most people think of the network of "county," "public," or "charity care" hospitals primarily located in large metropolitan areas. However, small rural community hospitals that are the only source of health care for the poor and uninsured in sparsely populated areas are also a crucial and substantial component of the health care safety net.

In the United States, 10% of hospitals serve between 9% and 50% of the uninsured. The largest public hospital system in the country is the New York City Health and Hospital Corporation (IOM et al., 2000), but people are more likely to be familiar with Bellevue, the oldest public hospital in the New York City system, and in the country. Similar hospitals such as Cook County in Chicago or Charity Hospital in (pre-Hurricane Katrina) New Orleans serve indigent populations in other metropolitan areas. Approximately 1,300 public hospitals exist in the United States, although the majority are now quasi public–private partnerships funded through local tax revenues and insurance-based reimbursement for care (Gage, 1998). Safety-net hospitals care for special needs of the entire population such as traumas from mass casualties associated with gun violence or terrorist attacks and disaster preparedness, as well as the needs of special populations such as the poor (Lewin & Baxter, 2007).

In addition to the public hospitals in the country, not-for-profit, usually religiously affiliated hospitals also are considered safety-net hospitals under the IOM definition since they provide relatively larger levels of uncompensated care or have disproportionate numbers of Medicaid patients. Sectarian hospitals have historical foundations in providing services to members of their own faith communities, but have expanded their missions to serve people within certain geographical locations. For example, the Catholic Health Association (2010) states that there are over 600 Catholic hospitals in the United States and over 60 Catholic health care systems that provide community clinics, long-term care, and advocacy services to persons regardless of religious affiliation.

Finally, every hospital that operates an emergency department (ED), regardless of its typical requirements for payment for care, is a part of the health care safety net as the ED is the only part of the U.S. medical care system— indeed, the entire social welfare system— where "professional help is mandated by law, with guaranteed availability for all persons, all the time, regardless of the problem" (Gordon, 2001, p. 321). As a result, EDs become locations for both acute and nonemergency medical *and* social care. For example, many EDs provide sheltering space for homeless persons during emergency weather conditions. Although these departments are designed to assist people with acute needs (i.e., heart attack or trauma victims), many end up providing a variety of nonemergency services. Safety-net hospitals have experimented with approaches that triage and reroute nonacute medical patients to specialized psychiatric emergency care units, on-site primary care clinics, or to social workers for assessment and provision of resources (Gordon, 1999).

Indian Health Service

Federally recognized American Indian (AI) and Alaska Native (AN) nations have a unique state-to-state relationship with the U.S. government as sovereign and self-governing entities. The negotiations to end armed conflict against the indigenous peoples of the United States resulted in treaties in which the federal government became responsible for the provision of health care, formalizing this relationship through the Bureau of Indian Affairs (BIA) in 1849. In the 1950s, Congress created the Indian Health Services (IHS) and moved it from the BIA to the U.S. Department of Health and Human Services. IHS is "the only truly national health service for civilians in the United States" (Kunitz, 1996, p. 1466).

According to the IHS, AI/AN people make up approximately 1.2% of the U.S. population and belong to 564 federally recognized tribes in 35 states. However, the number of AI/AN people is believed by many to be much higher because of disputes over trial recognition and enrollment. One-quarter of AI/AN families live below the federal poverty level. As a result of poverty, discrimination, and other difficulties, AIs/ANs have high rates of health disparities (Call et al., 2006). For example, they are more likely to suffer from tuberculosis, diabetes mellitus, and alcoholism, and are also more likely to die as a result of homicide, suicide, motor vehicle accidents, and unintentional injuries (IHS, n.d.).

IHS services are generally provided in reservation-based hospitals or clinics that are accessible to about half of the AI/AN population (Zuckerman et al., 2004). However, most AIs/ANs live in cities (U.S. Census Bureau, 2001) as a result of federal policies of tribal termination and relocation in the mid-part of the 20th century, which resulted in the rapid urbanization of indigenous populations (Evans-Campbell,

Lindhorst, & Huang, 2006). Despite these high rates of urbanization, IHS allocates less than 2% of its funding to urban areas, leaving AIs/ANs in metropolitan areas with little or no access to the health care to which they are entitled by law (U.S. Commission on Civil Rights, 2003).

Recent changes in federal policy have allowed tribes to assume more direct control of health services provided by the IHS within their jurisdictions. This shift in control is accompanied with differing priorities including the need to focus health services on preventive as well as treatment-oriented services, using input from indigenous clients to develop health services, and training AI/AN community members to provide health-related care (Allison, Rivers, & Fottler, 2007).

Veterans Affairs

The federal government has established a national network of medical centers, community clinics, and long-term care (nursing homes) for veterans of the Army, Navy, Air Force, and Marines. Veterans who incur serious enough injuries as a result of their service in the armed forces are entitled to comprehensive health care (including hospitalization, rehabilitation, necessary tests, and medications) without charge at a local veterans affairs (VA) hospital or clinic (Hisnanick, 1995). Veterans may also receive care at VA facilities for nonservice-related conditions or for injuries incurred while a service member but that are not as serious. These veterans are charged co-payments for their care, depending on their income level.

VA clients are less likely to have insurance coverage than other veterans. For example, 21% of VA users were uninsured, compared to 9% of veterans overall, whereas almost one-third of VA clients under the age of 65 (i.e., not eligible for Medicare) were uninsured (Klein & Stockford, 2001). People using the VA tend to be "poorer, older, sicker, more likely to have social problems and mental illness" than people in the private sector (Oliver, 2007, p. 23).

Bureau of Primary Care

Another federal health program funded by U.S. taxpayers provides primary care services to a number of indigent and vulnerable people through four programs: CHC, Healthcare for the Homeless, Public Housing Primary Care, and Migrant (farmworker) Health Centers. Over 17 million people were seen through one of these programs; 70% of the clientele had incomes below the federal poverty line (Health

Property of
Baker College
of Allen Park

Resources Services Administration, n.d.). One in three people in poverty received health care through one of these programs.

With over 700 locations, CHCs are the largest component of this system. CHCs provide a broad spectrum of services to enable participation of low-income clients including case management, health education, nutrition counseling, transportation, translation, and child care. These centers focus on the one in six Americans who live in a medically underserved area—a location (rural or urban) where there are too few primary care providers, high infant mortality, high rates of poverty, or a large elderly population (Lefkowitz & Todd, 1999). The majority of clients of CHCs are poor, uninsured, or receiving Medicaid (Politzer et al., 2001). Millions of clients receive treatment for hyptertension, diabetes, alcoholism, drug, or mental health problems through CHCs.

CHCs have played a significant role in reducing poverty and race-related disparities in access to primary care and prevention services. Because of their physical locations in low-income neighborhoods, they are able to become a usual source of care that their patients perceive as user friendly and trustworthy. Unlike any other federally funded health program, CHCs are required to have a Board of Directors composed of at least 51% health center patients, ensuring a voice of the people receiving care in the decision making of the CHC.

Prisons

The United States has the highest prison population rate in the world, 756 per 100,000 persons, even exceeding the imprisonment rate of nations that have a long tradition of authoritarian regimes (Walmsley, 2009). People who are incarcerated are more likely to have health and mental health problems upon entrance to prison; and they are at high risk for acquiring serious communicable diseases because of prison overcrowding, drug use, and sexual behavior or sexual assault. When they are released and they return to their communities, they can transmit these illnesses to others. Researchers have noted that the prison population is growing older ("graying") as a result of changes in sentencing guidelines; is disproportionately composed of African American and Latino men ("browning") who are more likely to have been impoverished prior to incarceration; and has women, who are serving time largely for drug related crimes, as its fastest growing sub-population ("feminization"), (Delgado & Humm-Delgado, 2009).

Each of these groups has special health needs. For example, the graying of the prison population means that an increasing number of inmates are dying in prison from conditions such as cancer and heart disease. As a result, hospice programs are being developed in prisons across the country for the incarcerated who are dying but are ineligible for parole or compassionate release programs (Evans, Herzog, & Tillman, 2002). People living in poverty are less likely to have health insurance, and for many their first contact with any health provider comes in prison (Delgado & Humm-Delgado, 2009). Finally, because the number of women in prison has increased five fold since the late 1970s (Frost, Greene, & Pranis, 2006), local jails and large prison systems have needed to develop health services that are specific to the needs of women—including prenatal and maternal–child health services.

Summary

These five examples demonstrate the patchwork nature of the health care provided in the United States. Some services focus on certain populations, such as Medicare for disabled or older workers, or the VA's services to veterans of any age. Other systems focus on certain locations such as the county-based safety-net hospital system or CHCs targeted at geographic areas of need. The fragmented nature of this system means that some people live in the wrong place or don't have the right characteristic to allow them to access health care.

With the shift in the American economy from industrial to service sector employment, more Americans than ever are working part time or are contractual employees who don't receive benefits such as health insurance. Until the passage of the Obama health reforms, many people were unable to obtain health insurance if they had already been diagnosed with a medical problem (preexisting conditions exclusions). People can "fall" into the health care safety-net system for these reasons and more. Yet, safety-net providers are chronically underfunded and struggle to provide equitable levels of care for their clients; difficulties that are magnified in times of economic downturn and recession.

Challenges to Stable Funding in the Health Care Safety-Net System

Safety-net providers, particularly hospitals, tend to treat sicker patients with complications of poverty, which increases the costs of care (Meyer, 2004). As the economics of care have shifted, non-safety-net providers have scaled back or closed expensive services such as EDs or psychiatric care, concentrating the burden of these types of care within the health care safety-net system (Lewin & Baxter, 2007). Patients who are indigent are less likely to be able to afford medications that can treat their condition or to have access to high-quality, health-maintaining food and shelter. Patients within the health care safety net often require a variety of services that are not necessary for wealthier clients. Table 1.6 lists some of the services needed within the health care safety-net system, including financial and community resource counseling, social services, interpreters, and security officers. The poorest and most vulnerable in our society require some of the costliest care, but are served within institutions that are more likely to be underfunded and have the most unstable financing—they are in a "chronic [funding] crisis" (Waitzkin, 2005, p. 941).

Most safety-net providers rely on a variety of funding sources in order to see clients, regardless of their ability to pay. Table 1.7 summarizes the multitude of funding sources used by Denver Health, the largest safety-net provider in Colorado, to fund its operations. These sources of funding range from revenue generated by privately or publicly insured clients, to state and county disbursements and private fund-raising. The U.S. government spent a total of $22.8 billion on the health care safety net in 2004—in relative terms, less than 1% of the overall federal expenditures (Kaiser Commission on Medicaid and the Uninsured, 2005).

TABLE 1.6
Services More Likely to be Needed by Vulnerable Patients

- Financial counselors
- Social workers
- Additional security for urban providers
- Translators/interpreters
- Special services for HIV/AIDS patients
- Substance abuse diagnosis and treatment
- Nutrition assessment and counseling
- Transportation services
- Case management
- Mobile services for the homeless and homebound
- Communication services for patients without telephones
- Assistance obtaining housing
- Family violence prevention and intervention services
- Culturally sensitive providers
- Pharmaceutical company medication assistance programs

Adapted from Ginsberg, Gage, Martin, Gerstein, and Acuff (1994).

TABLE 1.7
Funding Sources for Denver Health

Federal

Medicaid (Title XIX)

Medicare (Title XVIII)

Medicaid Disproportionate Share Hospital (DSH) payments

Medicare DSH payments

FQHC payments

Health Resources and Services Administration Bureau of Primary Health Care Section 330 Grant

Title V (Maternal and Child Health Services Block Grant)

Medicaid, Early and Periodic Screening, Diagnosis and Treatment

Graduate Medical Education

Indirect Medical Education

Ryan White Comprehensive AIDS Resources Emergency Act

Medicaid Major Teaching Hospital

State

State Medicaid programs

SCHIP

State medically indigent care programs

State high-risk insurance program

State public health programs

Programs to subsidize care for special populations (i.e., infants and mothers)

Programs to subsidize care for special needs of all populations (e.g., poison center grant)

Health Department's transportation funds (federal block grant)

Special Supplemental Nutrition Program for Women, Infants and Children

Immunization Program

County

County indigent care programs

County contracts for services

Local public health programs

Other

National and state foundations

Local contributions

Self-pay

Managed care contracts

Other contracts for services

(continued)

TABLE 1.7
Funding Sources for Denver Health *(Continued)*

Indemnity insurance

No-fault insurance

Manufacturers' indigent drug assistance programs

Proceeds of sales and services

From Institute of Medicine, Lewin, M., & Altman, S. (Eds.). *America's health care safety net: Intact but endangered.* Reprinted with permission from the National Academies Press, Copyright 2000, National Academy of Sciences.

By far, the most important resources for most safety-net providers are revenues from Medicaid payments and from local governmental taxing authorities (Lewin & Baxter, 2007). Both of these sources tend to be highly volatile, rapidly diminishing during times of economic distress, and increasing at slow rates during more stable times. For example, because of economic troubles, the state of Oregon eliminated mental health and substance abuse coverage for adults receiving Medicaid (Meyer, 2004). Likewise, the state of Arizona in 2010 suspended payments for transplants under Medicaid as a result of a budget crisis, resulting in the deaths of patients no longer able to pay the thousands of dollars in transplantation expenses (Jones, 2010). Medicaid cutbacks in funding affect health care safety-net providers more dramatically than non-safety-net systems, which can continue to spend capital on facilities, equipment, and technology (Dialogue, 2009).

Systems that receive funding from local governments are faced with difficult decisions about who should be the beneficiaries of these limited resources. In Florida, Dade County has a one-half cent sales tax to generate revenue for Jackson Memorial Hospital, the county safety-net hospital, but other counties do not have earmarked funds, and their patients may be seen at Jackson if they require specialty care, meaning that the burden of paying for people outside the area is on people within the county. Urban safety-net providers become the "care of last resort" for suburban and rural providers. For example, Harborview Medical Center in Seattle, Washington, serves patients from across the state, although their taxing authority is limited to the metropolitan area. As one administrator there noted, "It wasn't uncommon to get patients from 100 miles away with a nice letter from their physician saying the person lost their insurance and they can't care for the patient anymore" (Felland et al., 2009, p. 9). Throughout the country, a debate rages over whether tax dollars should be spent on the provision of medical care to undocumented workers from other countries.

Hospitals outside of the safety-net have traditionally charged privately insured patients more than the cost of their hospital care to cover uncompensated care and costs associated with physician training (Fishman & Bentley, 1997). Financially strong hospitals are in systems that can leverage higher payments from insurers and can use costs from other patients to subsidize uncompensated care (Dialogue, 2009). As a result, a three-tiered system of health care providers exists. In the top tier are non-safety-net providers, next are economically viable health care safety-net providers, and, third, a larger group of smaller, less successful providers (Lewin & Baxter, 2007). As Waitzkin (2005) notes, private facilities often grow by drawing on public subsidies such as tax-exempt status and funding from public trust funds such as Medicare and Medicaid, whereas public institutions tend to deteriorate.

The Quality of Care Within the Health Care Safety-Net System

An implicit assumption exists that non-safety-net providers have higher-quality care. For example, safety-net hospitals (in this case, defined as those with a high proportion of Medicaid patients) scored lower on standardized quality indices (such as compliance with treatment of heart failure or pneumonia), were more likely to incur penalties, and were less likely to receive quality of care bonuses under "pay for performance" systems being created by the Centers for Medicare and Medicaid Services (Werner, Goldman, & Dudley, 2008). Quality appears to depend, however, on the definition used for a safety-net provider. When using McHugh and colleagues' (2009) definitions of safety-net providers as described in Figure 1.1, those institutions providing high levels of uncompensated care tended to have higher quality measures, whereas certain facility characteristics (such as being a teaching hospital) were associated with lower scores on quality measures. In a study of quality benchmarks at a large safety-net hospital in the West, no disparities in care were found; the quality of care met or exceeded available clinical benchmarks (Eisert, Mehler, & Gabow, 2008).

As noted previously, health care safety-net providers may be more able to create culturally sensitive care because they tend to have a higher number of ethnic minority providers, a history of commitment to the community that engenders trust, programs for language translation, open-door policies, sliding scale fee payments, and geographic location in underserved neighborhoods (Eisert et al., 2008). Within an ethnically diverse safety-net system patient population, implementation of a multidisciplinary program was associated with increased compliance with medication recommendations among patients; in fact, compliance exceeded the national average (Krantz et al., 2007). Findings such as these indicate that quality of care in some safety-net programs may actually improve outcomes for populations at highest risk for health disparities.

Receiving primary care can help prevent obesity and smoking as well as ensure early intervention for diseases such as cancer, diabetes, or hypertension that lead to high levels of disability and death if left untreated (Starfield, Shi, & Macinko, 2005). Yet, primary care is most likely to be unavailable to people who are uninsured, as we will discuss at length in the chapter on poverty. Many low-income people seek primary care through the network of federally funded CHCs operated by the federal Bureau of Primary Care. A national study of the quality of care provided in these centers concluded that, "the quality of care delivered in CHCs is comparable to that delivered in other settings that provide care for underserved populations and to some national benchmark data from other sources" (Hicks et al., 2006, p. 1718), although the authors did find room for significant improvement in meeting clinical benchmarks. The majority of patients in ambulatory safety-net care are ethnic minorities (Eisert et al., 2008). The care provided in these settings is likely to influence the rate of health care disparities, especially those experienced by people of color who are at the highest risk for lower-quality health overall. Closure or reduction of community-based health care safety-net systems will likely exacerbate these health care disparities.

CONCLUDING COMMENTS—PROTECTING THE HEALTH CARE SAFETY-NET SYSTEM

Enactment of universal health care insurance coverage legislation should increase access to primary care and help improve overall health by providing care to people who have previously been unable to access health services. However, increased insurance coverage alone will not reduce the gap between the "haves" and the "have nots" within the U.S. health care system. A primarily employment-based health insurance system will still exclude some groups from health insurance, such as undocumented immigrant workers and the seriously and persistently mentally ill. Safety-net health care providers will continue to exist in the American system of health care services and will face ongoing challenges to funding and care provision. As noted sociologist and physician Howard Waitzkin concluded, "Without a national health program, safety net organizations throughout the country will continue to struggle with the challenging, chronic problems of survival and responsiveness" (Waitzkin, 2005, p. 942).

Human societies are a web. Within the health care arena, this means that more generous provision of Medicaid or more employer-based coverage will result in less charity care (Meyer, 2004). As various economic, political, and social changes occur in the next decade, the safety-net health system will continue to provide services in an increasingly complex environment. Protecting the health care safety net will require creative thinking. For instance, more metropolitan areas may benefit from the creation of regional planning forums that consider taxing for services across county boundaries to provide fairer distribution of resources. Likewise, both for-profit and nonprofit health corporations could reinvent their connection to health care's original mission of quality care for all, while also being required to provide a certain amount of uncompensated care as a public good (Meyer, 2004). In the end, direct support will likely still need to be targeted to the safety-net providers themselves, but could be tied to systems changes that increase the likelihood of providing high-quality care (Hicks et al., 2006). Until a truly universal system of health care provision exists in the United States, safety-net providers will continue to be a key component within the patchwork system of U.S. health care.

REFERENCES

Addams, J. (1999). *Twenty years at Hull House with autobiographical notes and introduction by Victoria Bissell Brown.* Boston, MA: Bedford/St. Martin's Press.

Allison, M. T., Rivers, P. A., & Fottler, M. D. (2006). Future public health delivery models for Native American tribes. *Public Health, 121,* 296–307.

American Hospital Association. (2009). *Trendwatch chartbook 2009: Trends affecting hospitals and health systems.* Washington, DC: Author.

Association of American Medical Colleges. (2009). *Key facts about teaching hospitals.* Retrieved from http://www.aamc.org/newsroom/presskits/keyfactsaboutth.pdf

Bazzoll, G. J., Kang, R., Hasnain-Wynia, R., & Lindrooth, R. C. (2005). An update on safety-net hospitals: Coping with the late 1990s and early 2000s. *Health Affairs, 24,* 1047–1056.

Call, K. T., McAlpine, D. D., Johnson, P. J., Beebe, T. J., McRae, J. A., & Song, Y. (2006). Barriers to care among American Indians in public health care programs. *Medical Care, 44,* 595–600.

Catholic Health Association. (2010). Catholic health care in the United States. St. Louis, MO: Author.

Centers for Disease Control. (n.d.). *Nursing home care.* Retrieved from http:// www.cdc.gov/nchs/fastats/nursingh.htm

Chin, J., & Mann, J. (1989). Global surveillance and forecasting of AIDS. *Bulletin of the World Health Organization, 67,* 1–7.

Coll, B. D. (1995). *Safety net: Welfare and Social Security, 1929–1979.* New Brunswick, NJ: Rutgers University Press.

Delgado, M., & Humm-Delgado, D. (2009). *Health and health care in the nation's prisons: Issues, challenges, and policies.* Lanham, MD: Rowman & Littlefield.

Dialogue. (2009). Protecting the hospital safety net. *Inquiry, 46,* 7–16.

Eisert, S. L., Mehler, P. S., & Gabow, P. A. (2008). Can America's urban safety net systems be a solution to unequal treatment? *Journal of Urban Health, 85,* 766–778.

Evans, C., Herzog, R., & Tillman, T. (2002). The Louisiana State Penitentiary: Angola prison hospice. *Journal of Palliative Medicine, 5(4),* 553–558.

Evans-Campbell, T., Lindhorst, T., & Huang, B. (2006). Violent victimization among American Indian women. *American Journal of Public Health, 96(8),* 1416–1422.

Felland, L. E., Lauer, J. R., & Cunningham, P. J. (2009). Suburban poverty and the health care safety net. *Research Briefs of the Center for Studying Health System Change, 13,* 1–12.

Fishman, L. E., & Bentley, J. D. (1997). The evolution of support for safety-net hospitals. *Health Affairs, 16,* 30–47.

Frost, N. Greene, J., & Pranis, K. (2006). *The punitiveness report: Hard hit: The growth in the imprisonment of women, 1977–2004.* New York: Institute on Women & Criminal Justice, Women's Prison Association.

Gage, L. S. (1998). The future of safety-net hospitals. In S. H. Altman, U. E. Reinhardt, & A. E. Shields (Eds.), *The future U.S. health care system: Who will care for the poor and uninsured?* (pp. 123–150). Chicago, IL: Foundation of the American College of Healthcare Executives.

Ginsberg, C., Gage, L., Martin, V., Gerstein, S., & Acuff, K. (1994). *America's urban safety net hospitals: Meeting the needs of our most vulnerable populations.* Washington, DC: National Association of Public Hospitals.

Goldstein, A. (2009, December 28). The not-so-sweet side of closing the "doughnut hole." *Washington Post.* Retrieved from http://www.washingtonpost. com/wp-dyn/content/article/2009/12/27/AR2009122701206.html

Gordon, J. A. (1999). The hospital emergency department as a social welfare institution. *Annals of Emergency Medicine, 33,* 321–325.

Gordon, J. A. (2001). Cost-benefit analysis of social work services in the emergency department: A conceptual model. *Academic Emergency Medicine, 8,* 54–60.

Gratton, B. (1996). The poverty of impoverishment theory: The economic well-being of the elderly, 1890–1950. *Journal of Economic History, 56(1),* 39–61.

Hanrahan, P., Luchins, D. J., Cloniger, L., & Swartz, J. (2004). Medicaid eligibility of former Supplemental Security Income recipients with drug abuse or alcoholism disability. *American Journal of Public Health, 94,* 46–47.

Health Insurance Association of America. (1997). *Fundamentals of health insurance.* Washington, DC: Author.

Health Resources Services Administration. (n. d.). *Primary health care: The health center program.* Retrieved from http://bphc.hrsa.gov/

Hicks, L. S., O'Malley, A. J., Lieu, T. A., Keegan, T., Cook, N. L., McNeil, B. J., . . . Guadagnoli, E. (2006). The quality of chronic disease care in U.S. community health centers. *Health Affairs, 25,* 1712–1723.

Hisnanick, J. J. (1995). *How much of a safety net is VA?* Statistical Report No. SR-008-95-5. Washington, DC: National Center for Veteran Analysis and Statistics.

History of Cook County Hospital. (n.d.). Retrieved from http://johnstroger-hospital.org/dom/cchhistory.html

Hunter, R. (1907). *Poverty.* New York: MacMillan.

Indian Health Service. (n.d.) *Trends in Indian Health, 2002–2003.* Washington, DC: U.S. Department of Health and Human Services. Retrieved from http://www.ihs.gov/NonMedicalPrograms/IHS_Stats/files/Trends%20Cover%20Page%20&%20Front%20Text.pdf

Institute of Medicine, Lewin, M., & Altman, S. (Eds.) (2000). *America's health care safety net: Intact but endangered.* Washington, DC: National Academies Press.

Jones S. (2010, October 5). *Gov't-run health care death sentence in AZ: No more liver transplants for Hep-C patient.* CNS.NEWS.COM. Retrieved May 28, 2011, from http://www.cnsnews.com/news/article/arizonas-medicaid-program-will-no-longer

Kaiser Commission on Medicaid and the Uninsured. (2005). *Federal Spending on the Health Care Safety Net from 2001–2004: Has Spending Kept Pace with the Growth in the Uninsured?* Menlo Park, CA: Henry J. Kaiser Family Foundation.

Kaiser Family Foundation. (n.d.). *Medicaid benefits: Online database.* Retrieved from http://medicaidbenefits.kff.org/

Kaiser Family Foundation. (2011). *U.S. Federal Funding for HIV/AIDS: The President's FY 2012 Budget Request.* Retrieved from http://www.kff.org/hivaids/7029.cfm

Katz, M. B. (1986). *In the shadow of the poorhouse: A social history of welfare in America.* New York: Basic Books.

Klein, R. E., & Stockford, D. D. (2001). *Data on the socioeconomic status of veterans and on VA program usage.* Washington, DC: U.S. Department of Veterans Affairs. Retrieved from http://www1.va.gov/VETDATA/Specialreports/Special_Reports.asp

Kooijman, J. (1999). Soon or later on: Franklin D. Roosevelt and national health insurance, 1933–1945. *Presidential Quarterly, 29,* 336–350.

Krantz, M. J., Baker, W. A., Estacio, R. O., Haynes, D. K., Mehler, P. S., Fonarow, G. C., et al. (2007). Comprehensive coronary artery disease care in a safety-net hospital: Results of Get with the Guidelines quality improvement initiative. *Journal of Managed Care Pharmacy, 13,* 319–325.

Kunitz, S. J. (1996). The history and politics of U.S. health care policy for American Indians and Alaska Natives. *American Journal of Public Health, 86,* 1464–1473.

Lamb, H. R. & Bacharach, L. L. (2001). Some perspectives on deinstitutionalization. *Psychiatric Services, 52,* 1039–1045.

Lefkowitz, B., & Todd, J. (1999). An overview: Health centers at the crossroads. *Journal of Ambulatory Care Management, 22(4),* 1–11.

Leighninger, R. D. (2007). *Long-range public investment: The forgotten legacy of the New Deal.* Columbia, SC: University of South Carolina Press.

Lewin, M. E., & Baxter, R. J. (2007). America's health care safety net: Revisiting the 2000 IOM report. *Health Affairs, 26,* 1490–1494.

Lieberman, R. (1998). *Shifting the color line: Race and the American welfare state.* Cambridge, MA: Harvard University Press.

Lindhorst, T., & Mancoske, R. J. (2006). The social and economic impact of sanctions and time limits on recipients of Temporary Assistance to Needy Families. *Journal of Sociology and Social Welfare, 33(1),* 93–114.

McHugh, M., Kang, R., & Hasnian-Wynia, R. (2009). Understanding the safety net: Inpatient quality of care varies based on how one defines safety-net hospitals. *Medical Care Research and Review, 66,* 590–605.

Meyer, J. A. (2004). *Safety net hospitals: A vital resource for the U.S.* Washington, DC: Economic and Social Research Institute.

O'Brien, E. (2005). *Medicaid's coverage of nursing home costs: Asset shelter for the wealthy or essential safety net?* Washington, DC: Georgetown University Long-Term Care Financing Project.

Oliver, A. (2007). The Veterans Health Administration: An American success story? *Milbank Quarterly, 85,* 5–35.

Pear, R. (1993, September 30). Clinton's health plan: AMA rebels over plan in major challenge to the president. *New York Times.* Retrieved from http://www.nytimes.com/1993/09/30/us/clinton-s-health-plan-ama-rebels-over-health-plan-major-challenge-president.html

Politzer, R. M., Yoon, J., Shi, L., Hughes, R. G., Regan, J., & Gaston, M. H. (2001). Inequality in America: The contribution of health centers in reducing and eliminating disparities in access to care. *Medical Care Research Review, 58,* 234–248.

Quadagno, J. (2005). *One nation, uninsured: Why the U.S. has no national health insurance.* New York: Oxford University Press.

Redlener, I., & Grant, R. (2009). America's safety net and health care reform—What lies ahead? *New England Journal of Medicine, 361,* 2201–2204.

Risse, G. B. (1999). *Mending bodies, saving souls: A history of hospitals.* New York: Oxford University Press.

Sack, K. (2008, December 25). *Expansion of clinics shapes Bush legacy. New York Times,* A1. Retrieved from http://www.nytimes.com/2008/12/26/health/policy/26clinics.html.

Shilts, R. (1987). *And the band played on: Politics, people and the AIDS epidemic.* New York: St. Martin's Press.

Social Security Administration. (2010). *SSI recipients by state and county, 2009.* SSA Publication No. 13–11976. Washington, DC: Author.

Starfield, B., Shi, L., & Macinko, J. (2005), Contribution of primary care to health systems and health. *Milbank Quarterly, 83,* 457–502.

Starr, P. (1982). *The social transformation of American medicine: The rise of a sovereign profession and the making of a vast industry.* New York: Basic Books.

Starr, P. (1995). What happened to health care reform? *The American Prospect, 20,* 20–31.

Stephan, J. J. (2008). *Census of state and federal correctional facilities, 2005.* NCJ 222182. Washington, DC: Department of Justice, Bureau of Justice Statistics.

Thompson, J. D., & Goldin, G. (1975). *The hospital: A social and architectural history.* New Haven, CT: Yale University Press.

Trattner, W. I. (1984). *From poor law to welfare state: A history of social welfare in America.* New York: Free Press.

U.S. Census Bureau. (2001). *2000 Census Counts of American Indians, Eskimos, Aleuts, and American Indian and Alaska Native Areas.* Washington, DC: Racial Statistics Branch, Population Division.

U.S. Census Bureau. (2009). Income, poverty and health insurance coverage in the United States: 2008. Washington, DC: Department of Commerce.

U. S. Commission on Civil Rights. (2003). *A Quiet Crisis: Federal Funding and Unmet Needs in Indian Country.* Washington, DC: Author.

Wagner, D. (2008). *Ordinary people: In and out of poverty in the Gilded Age.* Boulder, CO: Paradigm Publishers.

Waitzkin, H. (2005). Commentary—The history and contradictions of the health care safety net. *Health Services Research, 40,* 941–952.

Walmsley, R. (2009). *World Prison Population List (8ᵗʰ ed.).* London: International Centre for Prison Studies, King's College.

Watkins, K., & Podus, D. (2000). Alcohol and drug abuse: The impact of terminating disability benefits for substance abusers on substance use and treatment participation. *Psychiatric Services, 51,* 1371–1381.

Werner, R. M., Goldman, L. E., & Dudley, R. A. (2008). Comparison of change in quality of care in safety-net and non-safety-net hospitals. *Journal of the American Medical Association, 299,* 2180–2187.

World Health Organization. (2009). *AIDS epidemic update.* Geneva, Switzerland: Author. Retrieved from http://data.unaids.org/pub/Report/2009/JC1700_Epi_Update_2009_en.pdf

Zaman, O. S., Cummings, L. C., & Spieler, S. S. (2009). *America's public hospitals and health systems, 2008: Results of the annual NAPH Hospital Characteristics Survey.* Washington, DC: National Association of Public Hospitals and Health Systems.

Zuckerman, S., Haley, J., Roubideaux, Y., & Lillie-Blanton, M. (2004). Health service access, use and insurance coverage among American Indians/Alaska Natives and Whites: What role does the Indian Health Service Play? *American Journal of Public Health, 94,* 53–59.

2

Poverty and Being Poor

POVERTY AS A SOCIAL PHENOMENON

The Nature of Poverty

Just as human societies are organized at multiple levels (individuals, groups, formal communities, societal institutions), poverty in its definition and effects entails inquiry at multiple levels. That is, poverty can be thought of as an individual status or personal experience, a family or community trait, or as a structural factor that shapes and is shaped by social institutions (like the education system). Before exploring the prevalence of poverty and how it manifests itself at different levels of society, we begin by interrogating alternative definitions of poverty.

Alternative Definitions of Poverty

In its most basic sense, poverty is about living in a state of deprivation from whatever it is that is deemed essential. All definitions of poverty share this conceptual common denominator. However, from there, definitions of poverty diverge in dramatic ways that have very different implications for the way we think about poverty and even the extent to which we believe there is a significant poverty problem in the United States (or, for that matter, most parts of the world). First, different definitions of poverty disagree on their meanings of "essential"; in some definitions of poverty, what is "essential" pertains only to what is required for day-to-day human survival. That is, a person is not truly poor unless he or she is deprived of what is essential for human survival—food to eat, clothes to wear, and a place to sleep in safety and in comfort. By other definitions of poverty (in particular the definition argued by Nobel Prize-winning economist Amartya Sen), poverty entails the deprivation of the things that are essential for the development of human capabilities—not only food and shelter, but education, health care, and certain other rights and freedoms that may be essential to the development of human capacities (Sen, 1999). Second, definitions of poverty differ on the meaning of "deprivation"; that is, whether an individual or group is deprived of things deemed essential in the *absolute* sense or in the *relative* sense. In fact, it is this distinction between *absolute* versus *relative* poverty that most distinguishes alternative conceptualizations of poverty and the meaning of being poor.

In the United States, the so-called poverty line is defined as an *absolute* measure of poverty. The Federal Poverty Line (FPL) essentially defines poverty on the basis of a minimum income threshold relative to family size, and assumes that a family that falls below this income threshold would be unable to afford even the very basics in food, clothing, and decent shelter. Developed by economist Mollie Orshansky of the Social Security Administration over four decades ago, the FPL based its minimum income threshold on what was assumed to be the grocery store cost of the U.S. Department of Agriculture's minimum-level food plan for essential nutrition. Whether or not a person "falls below the poverty line" depends on where their household falls within a 48-cell matrix of family types that factors in income level, family size, number of children, and, for small households (one and two persons), whether or not they are elderly. The FPL assumes that the cost of groceries is a good indicator of the cost of all other "essentials" a family needs to purchase for its members—food, housing, clothing, and so forth.

There are a number of problems with this assumption, including dramatic regional variations in the cost of housing relative to food, and of course the essential consumption needs of different kinds of families that are not captured in the crude FPL tables. Although Orshansky developed her FPL measure for a very limited purpose, it quickly became institutionalized as the "official" measure of poverty and is generally thought to underestimate absolute levels of material deprivation (O'Connor, 2001). There are several reasons for this, including the FPL's failure to adjust for the costs of day care, the actual costs of housing and transportation relative to grocery expenditures, the FPL's use of pre-tax dollars as its measure of income, and explosive health care costs for many low-income families who do not qualify for SCHIP or Medicaid.[1] Still, despite decades of criticism, we appear politically locked in to the FPL as the nation's primary measure of poverty.

By contrast to the *absolute* poverty approach taken by such measures as the FPL, *relative* measures of poverty are based on disparities in economic resources among persons, households, and different segments of the population. The primary measure of poverty employed by the Organization for Economic Co-operation and Development (OECD) defines poverty on the basis of relative income, with median income as the reference point. According to the OECD, relative poverty is defined as having an income that is no more than 50% of the median income. For example, a family household is counted as living in poverty if (adjusted for family size) their income is no more than one-half of the median income of all other family households (median income is the level of income achieved by 50% of all family households). In the United States during 2009, the median family household income for a family of four was $70,354 (Administration for Children and Families, 2009), which would therefore mean that a family of four would be considered to be in poverty if the annual income was no more than $35,177. In contrast, the FPL as the absolute measure would consider the same four-person family to be living in poverty only if their annual income was no more than $22,490[2]—a difference in the poverty threshold of $12,687! So which measure of poverty is correct, the relative measure or the absolute measure?

While we take the position in this text that the FPL is an overly conservative measure of poverty and in general underestimates the depth and extent of poverty in the United States, whether one approach to the measure of poverty is superior to the other has more to do with how one thinks about poverty. If poverty is thought about in very narrow terms, in essence being deprived of the essential necessities for

---

[1] There are good arguments that there are aspects of the FPL measure that overestimate poverty by failing to account for other kinds of subsidies that many low-income households receive, such as food stamps and federally subsidized housing. While these are valid considerations, on balance the FPL fails to account for more in essential expenditures and deductions from income than it does in subsidies.

[2] The FPL would have an even lower poverty threshold if the four-person household had no children, since that measure makes a small adjustment for the higher consumptive needs of children.

subsistence (food, shelter, clothing), then absolute measures of poverty that are based specifically on essential resource deprivation would be considered the more valid measure of poverty. On the other hand, relative measures of poverty do a better job of capturing significant disparities in the prevailing standards of living—in essence, the extent to which an individual or family has the resources to live pretty much "like everyone else." Proponents of relative poverty measures would argue that poverty is not only about the risk of not having the essential necessities of subsistence (food, shelter, clothing), but also the daily experience of *difference*—not being able to live at the same level of material comfort or having the same opportunities as most other persons in a given society. If we are concerned about persons or families being largely deprived of the resources and opportunities that are available to typical Americans, then relative poverty measures are the more valid means of assessing the prevalence of poverty.

The Scope and Distribution of Poverty in the United States

If the FPL is used as the estimator of the U.S. poverty rate, then the most recent general U.S. poverty rate estimate (as of 2008) is 13.2%, meaning about 40 million U.S. residents are living in poverty (DeNavas-Walt, Proctor, & Smith, 2009). The child poverty rate is much higher; at 19.0% of all children it means that about one out of every five children in the United States lives in poverty. We should keep in mind that the FPL is a very conservative measure of poverty, which suggests that the actual prevalence of poverty is likely much higher. In fact, if the OECD *relative* poverty measure is employed, the general U.S. poverty rate for the same period was closer to 17%, and the child poverty rate about 21%[3] (OECD, 2009b).

Although the United States ranks among the highest of all OECD countries in net per capita income, its relative poverty rate is also very high. In fact, among OECD countries the relative poverty rate in the United States is exceeded only by Turkey and Mexico (OECD, 2010b). This disturbing paradox is reflective of two primary factors. First, relative to other OECD member states the United States has a much higher level of overall income inequality. In the United States, the households that are at the highest fifth of the income scale have household incomes that are nearly eight times that of the lowest income fifth of households.

---

[3] The OECD estimates for child poverty are less current, based on 2005 estimates.

By contrast, in Sweden this household income equity ratio is closer to three (OECD, 2007). Second, relative to other OECD countries the United States ranks among the lowest in social spending—either in cash transfers to low income households or in social services to populations at risk for poverty (OECD, 2009b).[4] Taken together, these two factors reflect the dominance of a political philosophy in the United States that places emphasis on the free flow of capital as the essential anti-poverty strategy—as opposed to political philosophies in other modern democracies that place more emphasis on a balance between market-based solutions and universalistic public programs to reduce poverty.

While the general poverty rate is useful as a broad measure of the national poverty trend, by itself it tells us nothing about either the factors that are associated with poverty or the prevalence of poverty among the groups most at risk for poverty. Race, ethnicity, age, gender, and geographic location are all important correlates of poverty. We will begin with age, since poverty rates by age differ substantially and illuminate quite clearly the relationship between political power and social policy choices. The graph in Figure 2.1, taken from the U.S. Census Bureau's *Income, Poverty, and Health Insurance Coverage in the United States: 2008* report, shows FPL poverty trends by age group over the past 50 years, beginning with 1959.

As shown in Figure 2.1, over the last 50 years the group that has benefited the most from anti-poverty policies are persons aged 65 years and older. Older Americans went from the age group that had the highest prevalence of poverty (one in three older adults living in poverty) to the age group with the least prevalence of poverty (down to one in 10 older adults in poverty). Although the prevalence of poverty among children in America has generally declined over the past 50 years, at two different points (the early 1980s and the early 1990s), the achievements in child poverty rate reductions all but evaporated before trending downward again. However, even after 50 years, about one out of every five children in the United States is counted among the poor. As for the working age population (18 to 64 years), after an initial decline in the 1960s the prevalence of poverty has fluctuated only a few percentage points one way

---

[4] While the exception to this general trend is in health care expenditures, where the United States ranks first, health care dollars in the United States do not have the same level of purchasing power relative to other OECD countries. Moreover, most health care expenditures are not distributed with nearly the same level of equity in the United States relative to the typical OECD country.

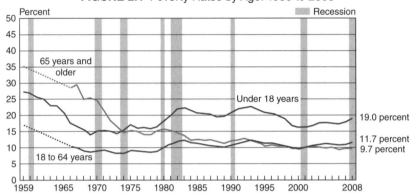

FIGURE 2.1 Poverty Rates by Age: 1959 to 2008

From DeNavas-Walt et al. (2009). Income, Poverty, and Health Insurance Coverage in the United States: 2008. Washington DC: U.S. Census Bureau.

or the other from a 10% poverty rate. So we are left to ponder, why has poverty declined so dramatically among older Americans over the past several decades, but so little among children?

Age Variations in Poverty

There are a range of answers to this question, some having to do with the changing demography of the American family and others having to do with the different social protections afforded to older adults relative to those afforded to families with children. Although we will explore these issues in more depth in the section that follows on the causes of poverty, we can at least cite two of the leading explanations for weak poverty protections for children relative to those afforded older adults.

First, unlike older adults, the income needs of children are tied more directly to the functioning of the labor market for their working-age parents, which in turn is tied directly to the race, gender, marital status, and educational level of the parents. That is, all of the factors that impede parents' capacities to earn a living wage (racial and gender disparities in earnings, low levels of education, and lack of marketable job skills) help to keep families with children in poverty. Marital/partnership status is another labor market relevant factor that has more of an effect on families with children than older adults, because in general the consumption needs of families with children are higher relative to the consumption needs of older adults. Thus, poverty rates are very high among single-parent (one-earner) families with children relative to two-parent (two-earner) families with children.[5]

Second, aside from greater dependence of children on the labor market, children are dependent on means-tested social safety-net programs to protect them from poverty, whereas older adults are, by definition, entitled to far more extensive and generous social entitlements. All but a very small fraction of older adults are eligible at age 65 for full Social Security income benefits as well as universal entitlement to Medicare health insurance benefits. Both Social Security income benefits[6] and Medicare health insurance are universal social insurance entitlements that are based on age rather than income status, whereas the safety-net programs targeted toward children (Temporary Assistance to Needy Families or TANF, and Medicaid) are means-tested programs—essentially requiring that families with children must be low income or even in severe poverty to be eligible.

In contrast to Social Security and Medicare, which are federal programs that remain in place once an older adult becomes eligible, both TANF and Medicaid require periodic redeterminations of eligibility, which can be quite onerous. In fact, states have very strong incentives to make it difficult for eligible poor families to access TANF benefits, and as a result, even the federal government estimates that only about 40% of TANF-eligible poor families actually receive income assistance from the TANF program (Schott, 2009). Finally, a particularly important distinction between the Social Security entitlements available to older adults and the means-tested programs targeted at poor children concerns the actual generosity of benefits and periodic adjustments for inflation. In contrast to the income assistance programs targeted to poor families with children, which have lost their inflation-adjusted real dollar value over time, Social Security benefits are by federal law adjusted annually to offset the effects of inflation. As a result, the Social Security income benefits have remained a strong protection against poverty while TANF benefits only keep poor children from being even poorer.[7]

---

[5] The U.S. Census Bureau estimates that the poverty rate among married-couple families with children is 6.4%, whereas for families with children headed by a single female the poverty rate is estimated at 36.5% (U.S. Census Bureau, 2010a).

[6] Officially referred to as the Old Age and Survivors Insurance (OSAI) benefit.

[7] The effects of the disparity between inflation-adjusted Social Security benefits and the decline in the real value of both welfare benefits (and also the federal minimum wage) can be seen in a comparison of the poverty rate trend lines for older adults versus children shown in Figure 2.1. In the inflation plagued 1970s, child poverty rates begin to rise again while older adult poverty rates continue to decline.

Racial and Ethnic Variations on Poverty

While the most recent general U.S. poverty rate estimates place the U.S. poverty rate at 13.2%, among African Americans and persons of Hispanic origin the poverty rates are, respectively, 24.7% and 23.2% (DeNavas-Walt et al., 2009). Even though it appears that the poverty rate among the U.S. Asian population at 11.8% is somewhat more favorable than the national average, the story differs remarkably depending on which sub-groups within the Asian population are considered. For example, poverty rates among Asians of Hmong or Laotian origin are quite comparable to the poverty rates of African Americans and Hispanics, while Asians of Filipino and Japanese origin have poverty rates below those of Whites (DeNavas-Walt et al., 2009; Le, 2010). The poverty rate among the American indigenous peoples (Native Americans and Alaska Natives) is 23.5%, and even higher for some reservation populations (U.S. Census Bureau, 2010b).

The disparities in poverty rates that correlate with racial and ethnic categories cannot legitimately be explained by either race or ethnicity, despite decades of attempts to do so by the proponents of racist and xenophobic ideologies. Rather, racial and ethnic disparities in poverty rates reflect both the legacies of different forms of racial/ethnic structural oppression and also differing contexts of migration. For example, the high poverty rates of both African Americans and Native Americans are consequential to violent dislocation, the near eradication of tribal cultures, and centuries of continuous racial oppression by European Whites. In contrast to other groups of voluntary immigrants (most notably immigrants from Northern Europe), the migration of African Americans to North America was involuntary—in the holds of slave ships. Even after emancipation from involuntary servitude, African Americans were systematically excluded from education, living-wage employment, decent housing, and health care over the entirety of the century that followed. In the case of Native Americans, few Americans can truly grasp the fact that mortality rates of indigenous Americans immediately following European contact were typically in the 90% range, and that by the beginning of the 20th century no more than 375,000 indigenous North Americans had survived European contact and the effects of European colonization from a pre-European contact population that may have been as high as 18 million (Thornton, 1997).[8]

For other racial/ethnic groups, racial and ethnic disparities in poverty rates are tied to such factors as the educational level of different groups of immigrants, the economic conditions at the time of migration, and the extent to which some racial/ethnic groups have been more subject to racial stereotyping and discriminatory practices in employment, housing access, and education (Portes, Fernández-Kelly, & Haller, 2009).

Gender and Poverty

Poverty rates for women are higher than for men, according to the most recent estimates: 14.5% and 11.4%, respectively. Although this difference would appear to be modest, the gender disparities in poverty rates are much higher during periods in the life course where there are gender disparities in earnings, dependent responsibilities, and survival into advanced old age. Women earn less than men, even where they have the same level of education and share the same occupation—in fact, the higher the status of the occupation the larger the gap in earnings (Massey, 2007). The vast majority of single parent families are also headed by women (some 77%), and, as highlighted previously, the poverty rates for single parent families headed by females is 36.5% (U.S. Census Bureau, 2010a). As Massey (2007) points out, in the decades since the sexual revolution men have had fewer incentives to marry and can more easily shirk their parental responsibilities than women.[9] Finally, women are more likely than men to survive into advanced old age, the point at which many of their needs for care and support exceed their dwindling income and assets. For this reason, as well as their disadvantaged economic status throughout the life course, the poverty rate among women aged 65+ is nearly twice (1.8 times) that of men (U.S. Census Bureau, 2009).

_____

[8] Contemporary estimates of the pre-Columbian North American indigenous population range from 2 million to 18 million, with no scientific consensus on the best estimate. However, there is clear scientific consensus on the fact of the near extinction of North American tribal peoples in the wake of disease, forced dislocations, destruction of indigenous cultures, and periodic massacres. The point is also made that not only mortality, but also declining birth rates in the face of brutal colonization, played a role in the decline of the Native American population (Thornton, 1997).

[9] In part, this is because men can find a variety of ways to evade child support enforcement laws. In addition, men who abandon their children both emotionally and financially, are more likely to be excused for their behavior than women who do so.

It should be pointed out that women of color encounter a kind of economic double jeopardy. They are more likely to be poor because they are economically disadvantaged relative to Whites, and they are also at higher risk for poverty relative to men of the same race. For example, African American women are 1.2 times more likely to be poor than African American men. If the effects of race and gender on poverty risk are considered together, African American women are 2.6 times more likely to be poor than White men. Women of Hispanic origin are similarly disadvantaged, with a poverty rate that is 1.2 times that of Hispanic men and 2.4 times that of non-Hispanic White men (U.S. Census Bureau, 2009).

The Geography of Poverty and the Phenomenon of Concentrated Poverty

Poverty varies along spatial dimensions just as it does along dimensions of race, ethnicity, and gender. There is a geography of poverty that reflects a myriad of complex social processes, including the distribution of natural resources, historic patterns of industrialization and urbanization, spatially expressed legacies of centuries of racial domination and oppression, and variations in local government antipoverty policies. Although there are local geographies of poverty that are readily visible in any typical city or town, we will begin by examining and deconstructing somewhat the geography of poverty that is apparent in the spatial distribution of child poverty by U.S. states and territories.

As shown in Figure 2.2, there are two obvious features in the geographic distribution of child poverty in the United States. First, there are dramatic variations in the prevalence of child poverty by state and by region of the country. Among U.S. states, the child poverty rate varies from a high of 29.7% (Mississippi) to a low of 9.3% (New Hampshire). In Puerto Rico, a U.S. territory, the child poverty rate is 56.9%. Second, the prevalence of child poverty increases dramatically south of the Mason-Dixon Line, the demarcation that in the pre-Civil War era separated northern free states from southern slave states. In part, the higher prevalence of child poverty in many southern states reflects an overlap between the racial distribution of poverty and the geographic distribution of poverty—meaning that the southern states shown with high rates of child poverty also have higher proportions of African American residents. Although some might argue that the high child poverty rates in these southern states reflect only the unfortunate legacies of slavery and long-abolished Jim Crow laws

FIGURE 2.2 Percentage of Children Under 18 Years Below Poverty Level in the Past 12 Months (For Whom Poverty Status Is Determined): 2008

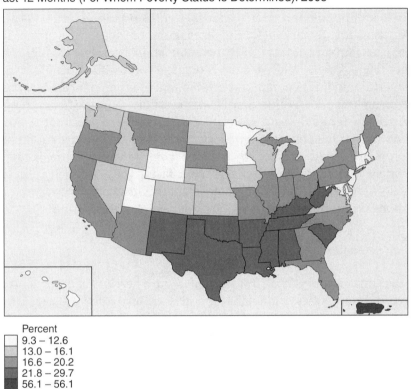

Percent
☐ 9.3 – 12.6
▢ 13.0 – 16.1
▢ 16.6 – 20.2
▢ 21.8 – 29.7
■ 56.1 – 56.1

From 2006–2008 American Community Survey 3-Year Estimates.

that disproportionately impoverished African Americans, states with higher proportions of African Americans also have been shown to have far more restrictive and punitive social welfare policies (Lieberman, 1998; Soss, Schram, & O'Brien, 2001). In essence, the high prevalence of child poverty among most of the former states of the Confederacy reflects not only the legacies of slavery and Jim Crow, but also contemporary policy choices that extend and deepen child poverty.

There is also a rural versus urban geographic dimension to poverty. Although most of the nation's poor are located in urban areas (in fact by a ratio of about 4 to 1), the poverty rate is somewhat higher among the nonurban population, 15.1% compared with an urban poverty rate of 12.9% (DeNavas-Walt et al., 2009). Over the 50 years that the United States has systematically tracked poverty, rural poverty has exceeded urban poverty—not only generally but also with each racial and ethnic group. The rural/urban poverty gap is particularly pronounced among Native Americans, with rural Native Americans almost twice as likely to live in poverty relative to the urban Native American population (U.S. Department of Agriculture, 2004).[10] There are also some remarkable differences in the impacts of poverty based on rural/urban location and the interaction between location and race. For example, while the psychological well-being of rural African American poor is generally better than that of urban African American poor, among poor Whites it appears the urban poor fare better in psychological terms (Amato & Zuo, 1992). In terms of health, it appears that at least in subjective terms the rural poor do better than the urban poor (Amato & Zuo, 1992). These considerations aside, it seems evident that every major poverty risk factor (race/ethnicity, limited education, and being in a female-headed household) is exacerbated among the rural population (U.S. Department of Agriculture, 2004).

Concentrated Poverty

Concentrated poverty is the phenomenon whereby the poor tend to live in communities and neighborhoods that have a disproportionately high representation of the poor. Although there is no scientific consensus on a precise definition of concentrated poverty, the conventional benchmark for designating a community or a neighborhood as an area of concentrated poverty is a poverty rate of at least 40% (Bishaw, 2005). Concentrated poverty occurs through a variety of mechanisms, almost always the product of deliberate social policies intended to isolate the poor from everyone else—sometimes because of poverty itself and other times because poverty is confounded with race. There are two prime examples of socially engineered concentrated poverty in America (among many), both of which are tied to race: the reservation system that was created in the wake of the European conquest of the indigenous tribes of North America, and the African American ghettos of America's largest cities.

In the first example of socially engineered concentrated poverty, indigenous peoples were coerced to migrate to lands designated by the federal government as tribal reservations—in order to permit wholesale expropriation of the North American continent by Whites

---

[10] A principal reason that poverty rates are higher among rural Native Americans than the urban Native American population is the very high prevalence of poverty among the Native American reservation population—an issue to be considered in the discussion that follows on *concentrated poverty.*

of European origin. Once their confinement to often desolate reservations was accomplished, Native Americans were isolated from both their traditional means of subsistence and the economic opportunities made available to Americans of European descent. The textbook case of this particular form of racially targeted concentrated poverty is the Pine Ridge Reservation of South Dakota, the coerced home of the Oglala Lakota Sioux Nation. Shannon County, South Dakota, one of three counties constituting the Pine Ridge Reservation and home to 11,855 tribal members, has a poverty rate of 52% and an infant mortality rate of 18.41 deaths per 1,000 live births—nearly 3 times that of the national infant mortality rate of 6.69 infant deaths per 1,000 live births (South Dakota Department of Health, 2008).[11]

In the second example of socially engineered concentrated poverty, African Americans were confined to certain neighborhoods within U.S. cities through a range of urban development, housing, and mortgage lending policies carried out throughout most of the 1900s—policies that worked in has many with racial violence and intimidation. Social policies that have promoted concentration of poverty include the creation of massive public housing projects in geographic isolation from middle-class neighborhoods and areas of job growth (which are often tied at least covertly to segregationist racial objectives), city planning policies that segregate low rent/high occupancy housing from proximity to owner-occupied housing, and local governance and taxation structures that locate amenities (like parks and good schools) within certain neighborhoods to the exclusion of others (Massey, 2007).

There have been countless public health studies in recent decades that document the relationships among racial segregation, concentrated poverty, and premature mortality in the African American ghettos of our largest cities. Perhaps the most famous of these is a case study of New York City's Harlem published two decades ago in the *New England Journal of Medicine*, which showed that African American men living in Harlem were less likely to reach age 65 than men in Bangladesh (McCord & Freeman, 1990). Later studies replicated these disturbing findings in the African American ghettos of other large cities (Guest, Almgren, & Hussey, 1998).

---

[11] While it is true that in recent decades the economic prospects of many tribal reservations have improved remarkably in the wake of federal legislation that promoted a tribal gaming industry, many tribes (like the Oglala Lakota Sioux of Pine Ridge) are not geographically positioned to support gaming enterprises—which in essence requires reservation proximity to large urban populations.

Although it is true that the wealthy have always preferred to separate themselves spatially from the working class and the poor, the spatial concentration of affluence in the United States has grown only modestly over the past several decades. However, the spatial concentration of poverty increased 80% between 1970 and 2000 (Massey, 2007), not so much because of the migration of poor into certain neighborhoods but because of three other factors: (a) the decline of living wage blue-collar jobs in U.S. cities in the wake of deindustrialization, (b) a general increase in urban poverty rates that disproportionately concentrated the burden of poverty in already poor neighborhoods (Massey & Denton, 1993), and (c) growing levels of income inequality in the United States between 1970 and 2000, which greatly increased concentrated affluence as well as concentrated poverty (Massey, 2007).

As the American metropolitan landscape has devolved further into a patchwork of affluent neighborhoods and poor ones, certain sequences have ensued that are highly relevant to the relationships between income, poverty, and health. Within poor neighborhoods, disorder in the form of crime, violence, family disruption, and school failure becomes endemic and entrenched (Massey, 2007; Massey & Denton, 1993; Wilson, 1996). In turn, affluent neighborhoods become increasingly more capable and motivated to use their relative wealth and disproportionate political influence to their exclusive advantage, both in favorable taxation policies and in the distribution of public goods—like well-funded schools, the best hospitals, well-maintained parks, and vigilant police protection.

The isolation of poor people living in high-poverty neighborhoods from health care is a particular concern of health care professionals, and on this front the evidence is disconcerting. For example, in the city of Chicago, between 1970 and 1990 some 39% of that city's hospitals closed, the majority of them small community hospitals serving the populations of high poverty, African American neighborhoods. Paradoxically, the higher the level of mortality in a given neighborhood the more likely it was that the neighborhood would lose its local hospital (Almgren & Ferguson, 1999). As a parallel trend, an ever-larger share of American hospitals has been shifting from public and not-for-profit ownership to corporate for-profit ownership, thus diminishing further the already limited health care access in high poverty neighborhoods and communities. In case there is doubt about whether the form of hospital ownership affects the health care available to the poor, readers are urged to consider the object lesson of Hurricane Katrina in New Orleans discussed in Chapter 3 (see Chapter 3, Stratification and Stigma).

Poverty Trends

Although we have argued that the Federal Poverty Line (FPL) underestimates the level of poverty in America, it is the only measure of poverty available that tracks poverty trends over time. As shown by Figure 2.1, after 1975 the FPL has fluctuated both for adults and children, in general correspondent to periods of recession. The poverty rate rises during periods of recession, and then falls substantially during longer periods of sustained economic growth. Figure 2.1 also makes it evident that there are more dramatic fluctuations in the poverty rate for children than for either working-age adults or older adults, and that as poverty rates rise generally the gap between the child poverty rate and the adult poverty rate grows. Finally, it should be evident from Figure 2.1 that at the point when the most recent poverty trends were made available (in September of 2009), consistent with history, poverty is once more on the rise in the wake of economic recession. As worrisome as this is, we should be even more concerned about evidence of the past three decades that shows that the more prolonged the recession, the more prolonged the lag between economic recovery and a discernable fall in the poverty rates for both children and adults.

Hidden beneath the widely utilized poverty line, and not considered in most discussions of poverty, are those living in more extreme or "deep poverty," conventionally measured at below 50% of the official FPL. Although the most recent official Census Bureau summary of poverty in the United States[12] does not report deep poverty data, other summaries of Census Bureau data show that the percentage of children living in deep poverty is at least 8% or nearly 1 in 10 of the nation's children (Moore, Redd, Burkhauser, Mbwana, & Collins, 2009). It is also suggested that, in contrast to the 1990s, children living in deep poverty in more recent years may be worse off because their families are less likely to access the public subsidies they are technically eligible to receive (Moore et al., 2009, p. 2). We believe that this disturbing decrease in the use of potentially accessible public subsidies by poor families reflects a deliberate social policy aimed at increasing the level of stigma attached to the receipt of means-tested public benefits (Soss et al., 2001).

---

[12] U.S. Census Bureau, *Income, Poverty, and Health Insurance Coverage in the United States, 2008*, released September, 2009.

Another poverty trend worth highlighting, less recent in origin but very much in play in both the national politics of poverty and in the real daily lives of poor women and children, is the enduring disadvantage of families that are headed by a single woman. In 1959, the first year that the Census Bureau reported the national poverty rate, about one-half of the families headed by single females fell below the poverty line, relative to an overall family poverty rate of about 1 in 5 families. Fifty years later, during which there were major state and federal investments in the antipoverty programs, the overall family poverty rate has fallen to about 1 in 10 families—a significant social achievement. However, the poverty rate for families headed by single women has remained very high; about 1 in 3 families headed by single women remains below the poverty line. For both African American and Hispanic families headed by women, the poverty rates still exceed 40% (DeNavas-Walt et al., 2009). Although the economic gap between family households headed by women and two-parent households are generally large in other countries that are politically and economically comparable to the United States, the gap is considerably larger in the United States than the average of other prosperous democracies (OECD, 2009c). The federal government has, since 1996, adopted an antipoverty strategy that promotes marriage as the antidote for the high poverty rate among single-parent families headed by women. However, there is no evidence that this has been successful as one considers either the persistently high rates of child poverty or the limited prospects of marriage for the low-income women targeted by federal pro-marriage/antipoverty strategies (McLanahan, 2004).

A final poverty trend of note is the worrisome growth in income inequality that the United States has experienced since the 1970s (Nielsen, Alderson, & Beckfield, 2005)—according to the most recent evidence, by some 24% over the past few decades (OECD, 2010a).[13] Income inequality can be measured in a variety of ways, but one of the more useful and intuitive measures is the income ratio between households that are at the highest fifth of all households in income relative to the lowest fifth. As we pointed out previously (in the discussion of relative poverty), the U.S. households that are at the highest fifth of the income scale have household incomes that are nearly eight times that of households at the lowest fifth of income (OECD,

---

[13] From the mid-1970s through the mid-1990s, the "gini-coefficient" of income inequality for the United States has increased from .37 to .46. In essence, this means that 46 cents out of every dollar would have to be redistributed to achieve equality of income among households.

2007). Although many European democracies also have high levels of income inequality, they tend to maintain tax and social support policies that transfer income and in-kind benefits (like subsidized child care) to lower-income households, thus reducing the impact of extreme levels of income inequality on the poorest segment of the population. As a result, the average level of "after-tax/in-kind transfer" or "de facto" income inequality in other modern democracies is about 20% lower than it is in the United States (OECD, 2010a). If income inequality continues to grow and is not offset by social investments that directly benefit low-income and poor families (like access to good schools and health care), the evidence is that poverty tends to become entrenched (Massey, 2007)—or as the adage goes, "the rich get richer and the poor get poorer."[14]

Causes of Poverty: The Interplay of Individual Risk Factors, Structural Conditions, and Proximate Causal Events

Although we often speak of the "causes of poverty," the term "cause" in the context of poverty is quite problematic. When it comes to poverty, there are not pure causes per se, but rather a variety of factors that make some persons more at risk for poverty than others. In fact, poverty is more typically a product of interactions among individual risk factors, structural conditions, and deleterious life events than any single cause. Some of the most important individual risk factors behind poverty include limited educational attainment, lack of job skills, having a chronic illness or disability, or possessing an ascribed characteristic that is economically and socially disadvantageous (think gender, ethnicity and race). Structural conditions that produce and replicate poverty include the existence of impoverished neighborhoods and communities, school funding policies that ensure that the poorest schools are in the poorest neighborhoods, minimum wage and taxation policies that work together to concentrate both wealth and poverty, and gross disparities in access to affordable health care by both race and social class. A short list of the typical proximate events

---

[14] It should be noted that the serious worries about increased levels of income inequality in the United States are not limited to social scientists—liberal, libertarian, or otherwise. Kevin Phillips, former campaign strategist for the Republican Party and Richard Nixon, has written a series of books connecting the decline of prosperous nations to rising levels of income inequality and concentrations of wealth, among them *Wealth and Democracy* (Broadway Books, NY; 2002) and *The Politics of Rich and Poor: Wealth and Electorate in the Reagan Aftermath* (Random House, NY; 1990).

that can either trigger episodes of poverty or become obstacles to escape from poverty include job loss, illness or injury, family disruption (divorce/separation/widowhood), and unplanned pregnancy.

A very illustrative and sadly prevalent example of how poverty is produced through the interplay of individual risk factors, structural conditions, and proximate events can be witnessed through the medical bankruptcy epidemic that has been accelerating in the wake of rising health care costs and the declining availability of affordable health care insurance. Based on evidence from a recent national sample of personal bankruptcies, it is conservatively estimated that 62% of bankruptcies are directly attributable to medical debt, an increase in such medical bankrupcies by some 49% between 2001 and 2007 (Himmelstein, Thorne, Warren, & Woolhandle, 2009). Medical bankruptcy is not a random kind of event that is just as likely to befall one person as another, but is more likely to affect people with some specific personal traits that are risk factors for this form of poverty—being an older worker, having less income, and having less education (Himmelstein et al., 2009). The structural conditions are self-evident, in particular an employer-based system of health insurance that provides an inadequate level of insurance access and protection in the face of rising health care costs. The proximate events that are typical to medical bankruptcy include either an illness that produces unaffordable health care expenditures, job loss/wage loss as a consequence of illness, or a combination of both (Himmelstein et al., 2009).

While all cases and examples of poverty can be dissected and understood through the interplay of individual risk factors, structural conditions, and seminal events in the life course (like job loss, illness, and family disruption), general theories of poverty attempt to explain how poverty is systematically produced through particular individual traits and/or specific structural conditions in ways that are relevant to social and economic policies aimed at the reduction of poverty.

Theories of Poverty

Theories of poverty, in their essence, try to respond to two fundamental questions:

1. Why are some persons poor and others not?
2. Why is poverty more prevalent in some groups than others?

Throughout human history, religious and ideological responses to these two questions have both preceded and dominated scientific efforts to grapple with these questions. Despite decades of supposedly ideologically neutral social science, the dominant theories of poverty (those that influence social policy) remain closely aligned with the two dominant political traditions in American politics—liberalism and conservatism. In fact, the policy think tanks that produce a large and influential share of the research on poverty (e.g., the Brookings Institute, the Heritage Foundation, the American Enterprise Institute, and the Urban Institute) are themselves positioned at different points on the continuum between the politics of left and right. There is one essential reason why this is so, and it entails the contrast and political implications between individualist explanations of poverty that emphasize the causal role of particular traits of the poor (intelligence, motivation, destructive morals and habits), and structural explanations of poverty that emphasize the causal role of structural conditions (e.g., laissez-faire economic policies and embedded hierarchies such as gender, class, and race). Conservative political thought tends to frame poverty as a problem of individual character traits and genetic endowments, while liberal theory tends to frame poverty as a problem of structural arrangements that disadvantage some groups more than others. To the extent that poverty is a problem that can be primarily attributed to the dysfunctional traits of the poor, or to government policies that reward bad choices, then conservative political and economic ideologies and policies that favor retention of the status quo gain credibility. On the other hand, to the extent that poverty is produced by the dysfunctional aspects of a market economy and entrenched hierarchies of political and economic power, policies that focus on structural reforms are called for that are more typically supported by liberals.[15]

Conservative Theories of Poverty

Within the conservative theoretical tradition, there are three dominant general theories of poverty that have deeply influenced the political discourse and social policies focused on poverty. The first general

---

[15] The conservative-liberal dichotomy in poverty theory and poverty policy, though dominant in the American poverty discourse, is an oversimplification that leaves out (in particular) more radical theoretical traditions that see poverty as a function of the interests of the dominant segments of society. Both radical feminist and neo-Marxist theories of poverty adopt this stance.

theory of poverty, "neo-culture of poverty theory," implicates the social programs intended to alleviate poverty to the de facto central problem of poverty.[16] Promulgated by conservative sociologist Murray in his *Losing Ground: American Social Policy, 1950–1980* (1984), this general theory of poverty is centered on three propositions:

- People are not motivated to engage in low-wage work where there are viable alternatives in the form of generous welfare transfers.
- Welfare transfers, rather than relieving poverty, perpetuate through such mechanisms as: welfare dependence, decreased investments in human capital, the promotion of sexual promiscuity, family dissolution, and intergenerational welfare dependence via both out-of-wedlock childbearing and dependence socialization of children.
- Welfare utilization rises in direct proportion to the generosity of benefits without decreasing real poverty levels.

While Murray's propositions were quickly refuted by evidence-based arguments to the contrary (McLanahan, 1985; Wilson, 1987), his theoretical propositions remain quite persuasive to a significant share of American voters and politicians, because at their core they reinforce common beliefs about the nature of welfare dependence and welfare recipients. Moreover, Murray's *Losing Ground* emerged at a time when national politics had taken a sharp turn to the right—toward the politics and policies of the Reagan Administration.

A second highly influential general theory of poverty promulgated by Charles Murray appeared in 1994 in a book he coauthored with the late Richard Herrnstein, *The Bell Curve: Intelligence and Class Structure in American Life*. Like Murray's earlier arguments in his *Losing Ground*, the arguments made by Murray and Herrnstein in *The Bell Curve* both resonated with conservative political ideology

---

[16] In its original form, culture of poverty theory was formulated 50 years ago by anthropologist Oscar Lewis as a *structural* explanation of poverty. Based on ethnographic studies of the poor in New York, Puerto Rico, and Mexico, "classic culture of poverty theory" holds that under extremely disadvantageous structural conditions, the poor would adapt to their circumstances by adopting attitudes, behaviors, and social arrangements that, while functional under their circumstances, would be dysfunctional to their prospects for escaping poverty. Murray and other conservative theorists that followed Lewis expropriated aspects of Lewis's "classic culture of poverty theory" into a "neo-culture of poverty theory" to argue that poverty *originates* in the attitudinal and behavioral traits of the poor—and is further promoted by public welfare programs that incentivize dysfunctional values and behaviors. Thus we have used the titles "neo-culture of poverty theory" and "classic culture of poverty theory" to make clear this critical distinction.

and appealed to the beliefs about the poor harbored by a significant share of the American electorate—that poor people are poor because they are defective in very fundamental ways. Unlike Murray's earlier works, the arguments in *The Bell Curve* are quite explicit in their linkage of race to poverty. In fact, the *The Bell Curve* strongly suggests that the gaps in income, educational attainment, and rates of poverty among races are accounted for in part by racial differences in the distribution of intelligence (Murray & Herrnstein, 1994). While the publication of *The Bell Curve* created a furor and its central arguments were quickly debunked by evidence-based critiques (Massey, 1995),[17] the racial arguments and deeply flawed evidence it presented found strong appeal among a small but significant share of the conservative electorate that has never embraced racial equity and has harbored beliefs that poverty and welfare dependence are in essence a racial trait. Despite the fact that most conservatives repudiate welfare dependence as specifically a racial trait, there is clear evidence that the more punitive aspects of the nation's primary means-tested public welfare program (Temporary Assistance to Needy Families or TANF) are targeted at African American families (Soss et al., 2001). It must be acknowledged that both the appeal of *The Bell Curve* as a legitimate basis of social policy and racially targeted welfare dependence sanctions are tied to a disturbing thread in American social thought and politics that continues to see poverty as a racial trait—as opposed to a legacy of centuries of racial oppression.

The third and final general theory of poverty that resonates with conservative political thought is a neopaternalistic theory of normative decline, advanced by political scientist and public policy scholar Lawrence Mead. While Charles Murray's *Losing Ground* played a strong role in defining *dependence* as the central concern of American social welfare policy as opposed to *poverty*, Lawrence Mead can be said to be the theoretical architect of the massive welfare reform legislation that was passed by the Republican-dominated Congress and signed into

---

[17] There are a number of evidence-based critiques of *The Bell Curve*, among the most lucid and direct of which is Massey's (1995) review of *The Bell Curve* in the *American Journal of Sociology*. Massey, former President of the American Sociological Association and the Population Association of America, takes Murray and Herrnstein to task on arguments based on selective and contradictory evidence and erroneous methodologies—in particular, poorly measured constructs and disregard for the conventions of theory-based statistical modeling. However, Massey's essay also takes to task the liberal social science establishment's tradition of self-censorship—in essence an embedded aversion to rigorously interrogate distasteful and repugnant propositions.

law in 1996 by President Bill Clinton. Many of the core provisions of the Personal Responsibility and Work Opportunity Reconciliation Act of 1996 derive directly from Mead's seminal book on poverty and social welfare policy *Beyond Entitlement: The Social Obligations of Citizenship*, first published in 1986. Central to the theory of poverty embedded in Mead's book is the idea that poverty is consequent to problematic behavioral traits of the poor, primary among them learned dependency and detachment from the obligations of citizenship—in particular, the obligation to work. According to Mead, both poverty and long-term welfare use are a result of a breakdown of public authority to enforce appropriate attitudes and behaviors toward work, education, and the human capital investments necessary for individuals to succeed in the labor market (Mead, 1986, 1992). Consistent with this view of poverty and the poor, government and agents of the human service system therefore have a distinctive responsibility to enforce social obligations and to teach the poor to act in responsible ways (Mead, 1986).

In contrast to other mainstream conservative poverty theorists, Mead does not consider reasonable levels of welfare assistance to be inherently destructive to the interests of the poor or contrary to the interests of society; rather, Mead sees sufficient welfare benefits as beneficial as long as they are tied to the enforcement of appropriate attitudes and behaviors. Mead's arguments about the nature of poverty and the paternalistic role of government are reflected clearly in the core purposes of the federal government's TANF Program, which pertain to ending the dependence of parents on government benefits through the promotion of work, marriage, and the reduction of out-of-wedlock childbearing.

Although the three conservative theories of poverty we briefly reviewed differ in some important ways, the common thread that binds these theories together is their common premises that (a) the causes of poverty originate in common traits of the poor that are different from the traits of people in mainstream society, and (b) poverty reduction strategies entail a focus on changing the attitudes, motivations, and behaviors of the poor.

Liberal Theories of Poverty

Although there are many theories of poverty that frame poverty as a problem of structural conditions as opposed to the deficits of people in poverty, we consider three that have originated in the theoretical tradition and inform liberal approaches to poverty policy. The first, "classic cultural of poverty theory," advanced 50 years ago by anthropologist Oscar Lewis, holds that under extremely disadvantageous structural conditions, the poor adapt to their circumstances by adopting attitudes, behaviors, and social arrangements that, while functional under the oppressive circumstances of sustained poverty, are often dysfunctional to their prospects for eventually escaping poverty (Lewis, 1959, 1975). There is a critically important distinction between the "classic culture of poverty theory" formulated by Oscar Lewis and the "neo-culture of poverty theory" advanced by conservative theorists. In its original form, Lewis's culture of poverty theory places strong emphasis on the self-defeating attitudes and behaviors of the poor as *functional adaptations to dysfunctional structural conditions*, not as the original or primary cause of poverty. In Lewis's original "classic culture of poverty theory," dismal and sustained poverty *precedes* adaptations of the poor that ultimately become self-defeating and maladaptive to mainstream society. In contrast to Lewis's original theory, conservative theorists discount the importance of structural causes of poverty (like decades of racial segregation and deindustrialization) and instead attribute the primary causes of poverty to maladaptive traits of the poor and the social programs that promote them. Liberal theorists argue that by ignoring the fundamental premise of Lewis's theory (structural conditions *precede* maladaptive attitudes and behaviors), conservative variations of culture of poverty theory engage in logical fallacy.

Despite the clear emphasis on the primary causal role of structural conditions in the original "classic culture of poverty theory" formulated by Oscar Lewis, many liberal scholars and activists disavow the liberal origins of culture of poverty theory and consider it to be only a tool of reactionary right-wing politicians and policies—akin to "blaming the victim."[18] However, the two most influential scholars of the liberal social science tradition, Douglas Massey and William Julius Wilson, both discuss in very frank terms the kinds of maladaptive values and behaviors that emerge under conditions of sustained

---

[18] As noted by Massey (1995), Oscar Lewis was roundly condemned by the liberal social science establishment for his original culture of poverty theory, despite his theory's emphasis on structural conditions as being the principal and original cause of poverty. Ironically, Lewis himself grew up in poverty and his groundbreaking ethnographies of the poor illuminated the connections between structural disadvantage and the adaptive responses of poor communities.

structural disadvantage and endemic poverty. In his analysis of the effects of deindustrialization on urban working-class neighborhoods (*When Work Disappears*, 1996), William Julius Wilson describes the normative breakdowns that ensue in the wake of sustained and endemic joblessness—including violent crime, family disintegration, and eventual detachment from work as a means of esteem and organizing one's life. Both in *American Apartheid* (Massey & Denton, 1993) and in *Categorically Unequal* (Massey, 2007), Douglas Massey describes in stark terms the behavioral effects of concentrated poverty on the inhabitants of poor neighborhoods:

> As poverty [becomes] more concentrated, so does everything associated with it: crime, violence, disorder, substance abuse, welfare dependency, poor health, and lagging educational achievement. (p. 195)

Notably, both Massey and Wilson identify the detrimental effects of high rates of incarceration as a significant structural antecedent to the kinds of normative dysfunctions that are typically used as evidence of a "culture of poverty" among the inhabitants of barrios and ghettos (Massey, 2007; Massey & Denton, 1993; Wilson, 1987, 1996). In fact, by 2001 the U.S. rate of incarceration (6.9 per 1,000 persons) exceeded that of both Russia (6.3/1,000) and South Africa (4.0/1,000)—among African Americans of working age, this rate is 79/1,000 (Massey, 2007, pp. 98–99).

Closely akin in some respects to "classic culture of poverty theory" is social disorganization theory. In particular, both theories of poverty have been used to explain the social pathologies (crime, family breakdown, endemic drug addiction, school dropout) that arise from sustained structural disadvantage and concentrated poverty. These theories have also been widely applied to the plight of African Americans residing in the nation's urban ghettos. A critical distinction between "classic culture of poverty theory" and social disorganization theory is that the former derives from the discipline of anthropology's focus on "culturally" ingrained values, attitudes, and norms of behavior, whereas social disorganization theory (as a sociological theory) focuses much more on the role of formal and informal social control mechanisms over social behaviors that are sustained by a neighborhood's or community's social institutions (e.g., schools, the family, churches, police, local businesses, and neighborhood civic clubs). Social disorganization, then, refers to a weakening of formal and informal controls over individual and collective behavior that results when there is a sustained decline in the viability and influence of local institutions (Almgren, 2005). Although social disorganization theory had its beginnings in American sociology's focus on the rapid cultural transformation of 19th century urban neighborhoods in the wake of the mass immigration of the late 1800s and early 1900s, in more recent decades social disorganization theory has been resurrected and modified to account for the decline in formerly stable urban neighborhoods in the wake of the post-1970s deindustrialization of America's largest manufacturing cities (e.g., Chicago, Milwaukee, Detroit, Newark).

A deeply problematic aspect of both "classic culture of poverty theory" and social disorganization theory is that they have been primarily applied to urban African American populations, and to some extent have been employed in disingenuous ways to both reinforce racial stereotypes and pathologize already disadvantaged African American neighborhoods.

The third and final theory of poverty that is strongly associated with the liberal tradition, human capital theory, has neither of those two drawbacks. Although human capital theory originated in the conservative Chicago School of Economics (most notably in the theories of Noble Prize Laureate Gary Becker), the antipoverty social investment strategies supported by human capital theory tend to be far more embraced by liberals than by conservatives. The key propositions of human capital theory are essentially as follows:[19]

1. Individuals, like capital in the free market, behave in a rational manner in response to a structure of incentives and constraints.

2. Individuals, like capital in the free market, will seek to delay gratification, invest in education or training, and in other ways will engage in socially desirable behavior to the extent they believe they can maximize returns by doing so.

3. To the extent that individuals are offered both the motivation and the opportunity to invest in education and training, production and economic growth will be enhanced (e.g., the post-World War GI Bill).

4. Gains by workers are not a matter of "institutional factors" such as labor unions, government policies, or corporate practices, but instead represent market returns on individual investments.

---

[19] Our synopsis of human capital theory is based primarily on Alice O'Connor's *Poverty Knowledge : Social Science, Social Policy, and the Poor in Twentieth-Century U.S. History* (Princeton University Press, 2001).

5. Poverty is explained by individual differences in skills and behavior that affect labor force participation and earnings.

6. The best poverty strategy is human capital investment.

The two propositions that resonate most strongly with liberal ideological traditions are propositions 2 and 3, because they speak directly to the importance of enhancing aspirations, motivation, and opportunities and proposition 6, because it supports the notion that social investments in education, health care, and basic material well-being are effective antipoverty strategies.

A Critique of Both Conservative and Liberal Theories of Poverty

Alice O'Connor, in her groundbreaking critique of both the conservative and liberal poverty research traditions, argues that both research traditions and the theories of poverty they promulgate are in reality an impediment to a more critical examination of the origins of poverty in the nation's embedded structures of social inequality. That is, both theoretical traditions focus on poverty and the poor as the focus of inquiry rather than entrenched hierarchies of social inequality. In essence, O'Connor argues that, rather than making poverty and the "poor" social problems to be addressed by public policy, poverty needs to be reframed as a phenomenon that is part and parcel of the larger problem of the growth of economic, political, and social inequality that cuts across all segments of society and all social institutions (O'Connor, 2001). The approach to poverty research advanced by O'Connor suggests that researchers that are committed to the reduction of poverty (as opposed to merely the study of it) must expand the scope of inquiry from the poor to an examination of the institutions, social and economic processes, work conditions, and especially the policy decisions that shape the economy and distribute economic opportunities. O'Connor further suggests that doing so entails a more critical examination of economic markets as social and political institutions that are shaped by the relationships of class, race, and gender as much as they are by the laws of supply and demand (O'Connor, 2001, pp. 292–293). We believe this critique is quite on target.[20]

---

[20] We also believe Douglas Massey's *Categorically Unequal: The American Stratification System* (2007, Russell Sage Foundation) meets the criteria for the kind of scholarship on poverty and inequality that O'Connor's critique suggests is essential. Readers might note that we cite this book extensively both in this chapter and the chapter that follows on stigma and social stratification.

*Public Beliefs About the Causes of Poverty and the Characteristics
of the Poor*

Two decades ago, public opinion researcher Tom Smith demonstrated that Americans tended to respond either pejoratively or
sympathetically to the poor depending on whether or not the term
"welfare" was used in the wording of survey questions (Smith,
1987). Smith found that where the term "welfare" was used, respondents on national surveys tended be more judgmental of the
poor and less inclined to suggest that government assistance was
warranted. Conversely, where the term "welfare" did not appear
in the question, responses tended to favor more government assistance to the poor. These findings get to a crucial paradox in
American ideology and politics, the distinctly different attitudes
Americans tend to have toward *poverty* on the one hand and *dependency* on the other. This paradox is itself reflective of the fundamental conflict between two American core values that arise from the
influence of the Protestant Ethic in American culture and politics:
charity and self-reliance (Weber, 1998). The former calls for a generous response for those in need, while the latter equates *dependence*
with personal failure and insinuations of flawed character. Many
Americans, both in their personal sentiments and voting preferences, seem to vacillate between these two contradictory core values—and as a result are easily swayed by disingenuous political
rhetoric and misleading media depictions of poverty and stereotypes of the poor.
    One particular strain of stereotypical media depictions of the
poor that has both fueled political rhetoric and shaped public policy
entails the racialization of poverty—in essence causing poverty
to be seen by many Americans as a racial characteristic. Based on
several decades of research on the relationship between race and
media depictions of poverty, political scientist Martin Gilens found
that although the true rate of African American poverty remained
fairly constant at between 25% and 30% over the 30-year period
following the passage of the Civil Rights Act of 1964, at various
points over these decades between 60% and 80% of media depictions of poverty showed only African American faces (Gilens, 1999).
In his analysis of these trends, Gilens also found a clear relationship between disproportionate media representations of African
Americans in poverty and unsympathetic public attitudes toward
the poor. The evidence cited by Gilens suggests that this occurs

for two reasons: (a) the frequency of media depictions of the poor (and African American poor in particular) tends to increase as the political rhetoric around poverty and welfare dependence heats up, and (b) the disproportionate numbers of African Americans as the "face" of poverty in America also tend to be unsympathetic portrayals that reinforce racial stereotypes. Aside from the disturbing level of covert racism in the media this represents, racially pejorative beliefs among voters then become linked to the goals and structure of poverty programs and policy. In this vein, it is worth noting that in the decade immediately preceding the passage of the 1996 TANF legislation, media depictions of poverty that disproportionately represented African Americans showed a dramatic upward trend (Gilens, 1999). We have noted previously that TANF is not structured to be an antipoverty program, but rather an antidependency program.

Aside from the issue of race, Americans' attitudes toward poverty and the poor are also shaped by two other crucial factors, each having to do with direct exposure to poverty. The first of these "exposure" factors pertains to broad economic trends. Intuitively enough, as the national economy falters and ordinarily nonpoor households sink into poverty, national survey trends show a significant drop in the proportion of Americans who assign the blame for poverty to the poor themselves (Gilens, 1999). In this regard, it worth noting that the nation's first antipoverty social insurance programs were passed by Congress in 1935, during the depths of the Great Depression. The second "exposure" factor has to do with the effect of personal income and wealth on beliefs about the nature of poverty. In essence, the higher the income level, the more likely it is that a person will see poverty as an individual problem that is not a priority for government attention and assistance. In fact, during both good times and bad, lower-income households are more willing to spend their tax dollars on assistance to the poor than either middle-income or upper-income households (Gilens, 1999). Aside from higher-income households simply not wanting to be taxed, under U.S. tax policies lower-income households actually pay a higher proportion of their earnings to programs targeting poverty than do the highest-income households. We (like Gilens) see this more generous response as one consequence of either knowing more people in poverty or having had more direct personal experiences of poverty.

Antipoverty Programs: Targeting Poverty or Targeting Dependency?

We made the point previously that there is a distinction between social programs that target *dependency* and those that target *poverty*. When President Bill Clinton spoke in his 1993 State of the Union Address about "ending welfare as we know it," he was not speaking of ending poverty; he was speaking of ending AFDC (Aid to Families with Dependent Children). AFDC, a federalized public assistance program that had originated in the 1935 Social Security Act as an antipoverty program, had over the decades become popularly viewed as a vehicle for the perpetuation of dependency. Clinton kept this particular political promise, and in bipartisan cooperation with the Republican-dominated Congress, the TANF (Temporary Assistance to Needy Families) program was signed into law in 1996. The central goal, the reduction of dependency on welfare, made the TANF program one of the few government programs that could in its first years be described as wildly successful. In the first few years of implementation, the proportion of the population receiving public assistance (a.k.a. welfare) had plummeted by over 40% (Health and Human Services, 2002). However, the larger question, at least in the minds of many, was whether or not TANF had also made inroads into the reduction of poverty. After all, a key premise of the TANF program, which imposed time limits on the duration of public assistance to poor families, was that public assistance dependency itself in various unintended ways perpetuated poverty. In fact, the evidence is that the passage of TANF, though not as disastrous to poor families and children as many predicted, certainly did not help poor families. As discussed earlier in this chapter, under the TANF program only about 40% of eligible poor families actually receive assistance (Schott, 2009) and there is no credible evidence that poverty has in any way been reduced as a result of TANF—either in good times or bad.

In contrast to TANF (as well as its precursor, AFDC) the Social Security OSAI and the Medicare insurance programs (originally Part A and Part B), were conceptualized and structured specifically as antipoverty measures. As a result, the poverty rates for Americans aged 65 and older have remained both stable and low at around 10% while the poverty rates for other groups of Americans, most notably children, have remained much higher and far more sensitive to national economic fluctuations (see again Figure 2.1). We made the point earlier (see the section "Age Variations in Poverty") that as an antipoverty program, the Social Security's Old Age Survivors Insurance provision of universal retirement income to millions of elderly Americans has been far more effective in reducing old age poverty for two reasons:

1. The income benefits from the very beginning were more closely calibrated to the consumption needs of the recipient households.
2. In contrast to public assistance to poor families with children (TANF and its AFDC precursor), as well as the federal minimum wage, Social Security benefit payments have been regularly adjusted to keep pace with inflation.

With respect to the Medicare Hospital Insurance program, it works very well as a major buffer against poverty because (a) older adults are universally entitled to a generous array of health care benefits, and (b) they carry an insurance card that gives them entrée into physicians and hospitals that are only too eager to provide Medicare beneficiaries with diagnostic and therapeutic services that are typically generously reimbursed by Medicare. In contrast is Medicaid, the primary healthcare entitlement program for poor and low-income families with children that has very restrictive eligibility standards requiring poverty as a condition of coverage and much lower levels of provider reimbursement than either Medicare or private health insurance. As a result of this, as well as the stigma associated with a Medicaid coupon, it is well documented that low-income and poor families have a much more difficult time accessing the health care that is often essential to getting out of poverty (Stuber, Meyer, & Link, 2008).

The contrasts between the values and the political rhetoric underlying the antipoverty programs benefiting older adults and the anti-dependency programs targeted at poor families with children obscure the reality that both kinds of programs concern the two segments of the nation's population that are unable to provide for their food, shelter, and health care through work—children and the aged. Both populations are, by definition, dependent, unless we are prepared to reintroduce the factories and sweatshops of the 19th century that always had a place for children—and which, through their harsh conditions, largely eliminated the problem of old age.

POVERTY, HEALTH, AND THE HEALTH CARE SYSTEM

The Causal Relationships Between Poverty and Health

A common and enduring feature of industrialized societies is the so-called *"SES health gradient,"* which refers to the consistently linear relationship between health status and socioeconomic status. Essentially, to the extent that individuals and groups are disadvantaged in the social and economic hierarchy, they are observed to be in poorer health. Conversely, to the extent that individuals and groups are advantaged in the social and economic hierarchy, they tend to be in better health (Marmot, 2002). This relationship holds both for men and for women, and it is consistent across all three dimensions of the SES gradient—income, occupation, and education. The *SES health gradient* is also apparent regardless of whether the measure of health is subjective (how people rate their own health) or objective (observed through specific health conditions). Among the scholars that have devoted their lives to the study of the *SES health gradient*, there is great disagreement on the extent to which material deprivation is the principal factor that explains why poorer people tend to be in poorer health, or whether the negative social status (or stigma) of poverty does more to explain why poor people tend to be in poorer health (Lynch et al., 2004). To complicate matters further, the causal relationship between poverty and health obviously runs in both directions; not only do the deprivations and stigma associated with poverty lead to poor health, but poor health itself places one at a higher risk of poverty due to such factors as disadvantaged employment prospects and unaffordable health care costs (Marmot, 2002).

Although it is clearly well beyond the purpose and scope of this text to disentangle the complex relationships between poverty and health (we also do not pretend that we could), we can highlight some illuminating theories and arguments on this critical relationship. The two theories and arguments we will discuss fall within the emerging discipline of *social epidemiology*. Unlike traditional epidemiology, which incorporates social context as a background to its investigations into the biological processes of disease and population health, *social epidemiology* explicitly investigates the *social* determinants of disease and population health (Krieger, 2002).

One of social epidemiology's earliest and most influential theories, fundamental social cause theory, was formulated in the 1990s by sociologists Bruce Link and Jo Phelan (Link & Phelan, 1995, 1996). Their theory addresses two enduring paradoxes of population health that are directly relevant to the causal connections between poverty and health:

1. The growth of disparities in mortality and longevity by such factors as race, gender, and social class that follow significant advancements in the knowledge base, methods, and technologies of health care.
2. The tendency of intergroup disparities in mortality to persist even though the specific disease mechanisms linked to disparities in mortality change significantly over time.

In its essence, fundamental social cause theory argues that the poor (and other disadvantaged groups) carry a disproportionate share of disease and early mortality due to structural disparities in the access to resources critical to the avoidance of disease risk and, where disease occurs, to the minimization of its detrimental consequences. These critical resources include specifically "money, knowledge, power, prestige and social connectedness" (Link & Phelan, 1995, p. 87).

Taking these critical resources one at a time, it can be seen that *money* buys better health and longevity through better health care throughout the life course, better and more nutritious food, better housing, and even better places to live—away from environmental toxins and closer to parks and other sources of recreation/renewal. *Knowledge* about health and management of illness comes from many sources that are less accessible to the poor, such as good schools and a good education. *Power* has many definitions, one of which is political power: in essence the capacity to advance one's interests in the political process. The poor clearly lack political power, manifested in ways that are clearly detrimental to health. Toxic landfills are located in their neighborhoods; they are disproportionately taxed for the basic necessities of life; they work in more dangerous occupations and conditions; and they are far less likely to have access to adequate health care—despite the fact that the United States spends as many *public* dollars on health care as the average *total* dollars of other countries that provide health care for all their citizens (OECD, 2009a). *Prestige* (social respect or being well thought of by others) is a well-established asset to human health, just as its opposite (stigma) has been shown to be detrimental to health (Marmot, 2002; Stuber et al., 2008). Finally, *social connectedness* (the relationships that people have with others) is the primary source of material and emotional support throughout every phase of life and is also the primary source of esteem, belongingness, and a sense of purpose. The opposite, social isolation, has been shown to be a principal source of detriment to both physical and mental health (Berkman, Glass, Brissette, & Seeman, 2000). Poverty and social isolation go hand in hand, though it is often difficult to determine which precedes the other; in essence because poverty isolates people and social isolation diminishes the relational buffers against poverty (Almgren, 2007).

A second theory that illuminates the relationships between poverty and health, the *ecosocial framework of human health and disease,* sees health and disease as manifestations of an ongoing adaptive and evolutionary process occurring between human beings and their environments—with each shaping the other at multiple levels of interaction (Krieger, 2001). Although a full explication of this theory and its insights on the complex relationships between poverty and health is too formidable an enterprise to undertake in this already lengthy book chapter, at the core of this theory is the idea of *embodiment*—the idea that we incorporate into our individual biological structures and processes the material and social world we interact with in an ongoing process from birth through death (Krieger, 2001). The poor thus embody, in their physiologies, a material world that is characterized by deprivation and injury and a social world that is often characterized by disrespect and despair. The poor among us are not, in fact, generally invisible but often readily discerned in their manner of dress, their appearance of health, and even physical attractiveness by the prevailing cultural conventions. The "embodiment" of poverty is manifested in suppressed immune systems, dental decay, uncontrolled diabetes, addiction to tobacco, and in scars and disabilities from occupational injuries.

Disparities in Health and Disparities in Health Care Among the Poor

Disparities in health concern differences between populations and population subgroups in the overall level of health as well as the distributions of disease and death, whereas *disparities in health care* encompass the health outcomes of care and specific dimensions of health care, in particular access, quality, and equity (Almgren, 2007, p. 221).

Disparities in Health Among the Poor: Counting the Human Costs of Poverty

Disparities in health are generally thought of as differences in the *burden of disease* carried by a disadvantaged subgroup, relative to either the population as a whole or some advantaged segment of the population. Burden of disease refers to the prevalence and distribution of diseases, disabilities, and mortality that is carried by the population. There are a range of burden-of-disease measures, from overall measures of mortality such as average years of life expectancy to disease-specific measures that implicate the specific linkages among various forms of disadvantage and their effects on human health. In the United States, where the health consequences of poverty are often confounded with disadvantages that are also caused by race and ethnicity, one way of isolating the income effects on the burden of disease is to observe the income effects on health within the same subgroup of the population. This is the approach undertaken by Banks, Marmot, Oldfield, and Smith (2006) in their study of the *SES health gradient* among comparable samples of middle-aged males in the United States and in the United Kingdom.[21] Because the Banks et al. study focused on a cluster of diseases that are highly influential in health differences by income level and affect the ability to function in the home and in the workplace (diabetes, hypertension, all heart diseases, heart attacks, strokes, diseases of the lung, and cancer), their findings provide a compelling illustration of the health consequences of poverty (Banks et al., 2006). However, data from their investigation also show remarkable disparities by income on self-reported health, which have been shown in multiple studies to correspond quite closely with the true levels of risk for premature mortality (Idler & Benyamini, 1997). Because self-reported poor health is such a powerful predictor of premature mortality, we will begin with their findings on this measure.

Figure 2.3 provides a straightforward and sobering comparison of self-reported poor health by income level, as the men in the Banks et al. study sample transition from their middle years to old age. The lowest income quartile, representing the men who are either living in poverty or are very close to it, have a prevalence of poor health in their early 50s that is three times higher than their middle-income

---

[21] The national survey data employed by the Banks et al. study (2006) excluded Hispanic, and African Americans. Although the data included other racial minorities, their counts in these national survey samples were very low.

counterparts and several times higher than the highest-income males. While the income gap in poor health begins to get smaller as the men in the sample transition toward old age, even by age 70 it is far from convergence—particularly if the contrast between the richest and poorest income levels are considered. In addition, the prevalence of poor health among the lowest-income males seems to peak at around 43% by age 62, while for the more economically advantaged there is a gradual trend toward modest incidence of poor health well into old age. Taken as a whole, the trends shown in Figure 2.3 illustrate perfectly the dramatic effects of poverty on premature aging and early mortality.

Disparities by income on disease-specific measures are also quite dramatic; for example, the Banks et al. study shows that in comparisons between low-, middle-, and high-income males, the incidences of diabetes is over two times higher in the lowest income group relative to the middle-income group and nearly three times higher relative to the highest-income group. Although disparities in hypertension by income level are less dramatic, they are still of large magnitude. That is, the prevalence of hypertension among the lowest-income group is 27% higher among low-income males relative to middle-income males (Banks et al., 2006).

FIGURE 2.3 Percentage of U.S. Males in Poor Health by Age and Level of Income, 1999–2000

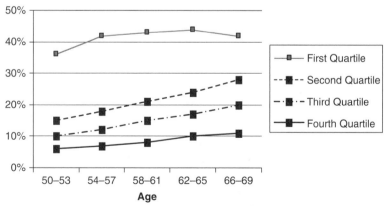

Constructed from data in Table 12A: Poor Health and Work by Income Quartile-United States in Banks et al., (2006). The SES Health Gradient on Both Sides of the Atlantic. NBER Working Paper Series (No. 12674). Estimates are derived from Banks et al.'s analysis of 1999–2000 National Health and Nutrition Examination Survey (NHANES) data. For purposes of comparability with the United Kingdom, Banks et al. excluded African American and Hispanic males from their analysis, which produces estimates that are more specific to the effects of income on health (as opposed to race and ethnicity).

A second example that shows, in statistical terms, the human costs of poverty is the incidence of premature mortality among the Oglala Lakota Sioux of the Pine Ridge Reservation in South Dakota— discussed earlier in this chapter as an exemplar of the deleterious effects of *concentrated poverty*. Although we have pointed out the clear relationship between concentrated poverty, harsh living conditions, and an infant mortality rate that was three times that of the national average (South Dakota Department of Health, 2008), we did not refer to disparities in death rates due to diabetes, heart disease, accidents, respiratory disease, or a host of other causes. These we show in Table 2.1, via a comparison between the age-adjusted mortality rates on the Native American population living on Pine Ridge Reservation relative to the age-adjusted mortality rates for the U.S. population as a whole.[22] Unlike the Banks et al. study cited in the preceding discussion, racial effects on mortality are confounded by income effects on mortality, in the sense that Pine Ridge Oglala Lakota Sioux suffer the combined effects of nearly two centuries of racial oppression and desperate poverty.

The 40,000-person population of the Pine Ridge Reservation has several demographic features that set it apart from the United States. In socioeconomic terms, it has a poverty rate of 52.3%, an unemployment rate of 80%, and is 95% Native American (Friends of Pine Ridge Reservation, 2010; South Dakota Department of Health, 2008). As shown in Table 2.1, Shannon County, South Dakota (located in the heart of Pine Ridge Reservation), has an overall age-adjusted mortality rate that is 2.2 times the national average. Causes of this dramatic disparity in population mortality include disparities in death rates due to heart failure (4.29 times the national average), chronic lower respiratory diseases (13.51 times the national average), accidents and motor vehicle accidents (respectively, 4.92 and 8.52 times the national average), influenza and pneumonia (3.09 times the national average), and diabetes (6.22 times the national average). In addition to these tragic statistics, the combination of endemic alcoholism and grinding poverty is clearly manifested in both the high rates of suicide and infant mortality.

Considered together, the Banks et al. study on the social class effects on the mortality of middle-aged White men and the high rates of premature mortality among the Oglala Lakota Sioux of the Pine

---

[22] Age-adjusted mortality estimates control for differences in population age distributions.

TABLE 2.1
Health Indicator Profile of the Pine Ridge Tribal Reservation
(Shannon County, South Dakota) Relative to the Entire United States

MORTALITY	UNITED STATES	SHANNON COUNTRY, SD	RATIO
ALL CAUSES	847.3	1883.9	2.22
Heart disease	241.3	379	1.57
Acute myocardial infarction	62.3	54.2	0.87
Heart failure	19.6	84.1	4.29
Atherosclerotic cardiovascular disease	23.6	LNE	
Malignant neoplasms (cancer)	193.2	291.9	1.51
Cererbrovascular disease	56.4	103.9	1.84
Accidents	37	182.2	4.92
Motor vehicle accidents	15.7	133.7	8.52
Chronic lower respiratory diseases	4.3	58.1	13.51
Influenzea and pneumonia	22.8	70.5	3.09
Diabetes mellitus	25.4	158	6.22
Alzheimer's disease	20.4	LNE	
Nephritis, nephrotic syndrome, and nephrosis	14.2	69.2	4.87
Intentional self-harm (suicide)	11	21.5	1.95
Infant mortality	7	13	1.86
Natality			
Percent of low birth weight infants	7.8%	7.1%	0.91
Percent of mothers receiving care in first trimester	83.7%	63.1%	0.75
Percent of mothers who use tobacco while pregnant	11.4%	19.3%	1.69
Percent of mothers who consumed alcohol while pregnant	0.8%	7.3%	9.13
Teenage pregnancy rate	53.5%	71.2%	1.33
Population under 100% of poverty	12.4%	52.3%	4.22
Percent Native American	0.9%	95.1%	105.67

From Table 7.1 Health Indicator Profile Pine Ridge Tribal Reservation (Shannon County, SD) Relative to Entire United States, in Almgren, G. (2007). Health Care Politics, Poverty and Services, Springer Publishing Company, NY. Used by permission.
Note: LNE refers to low number of events, resulting in an estimate that is omitted.

Ridge Reservation illustrate both the deleterious effects of poverty itself on health, and the even more deadly effects of poverty in combination with enduring racial oppression.

Disparities in Health Care Among the Poor

Since 2003, the Agency for Healthcare Research and Quality (AHRQ) has produced an annual *National Healthcare Disparities Report*, which functions as a kind of national report card on progress toward reducing differences in health care access and quality on the basis of such factors as age, gender, race, ethnicity, and income level. Although there are other organizations such as the Henry J. Kaiser Foundation, the Commonwealth Fund, and the Robert Wood Johnson Foundation that have a definitive commitment to the advancement of equitable access to quality health care for all Americans and provide a wealth of data on income-based health care disparities, we will draw on the *2009 National Health Care Disparities Report* (NHDR-2009) as our source for the illumination of health care disparities that are related specifically to poverty. We will begin with issues of access.

Access to health care is generally defined as the ability to engage in timely use of the health care services that achieve the optimal health outcomes (Institute of Medicine, 1993). The NHDR-2009 examines access to health care in terms of three crucial factors that can be either facilitators or barriers to health care: health insurance, having a usual source of care, and patient perceptions of need for care (AHRQ, 2009).

It is generally known that the United States stands alone among affluent democratic societies in its failure to provide universal health insurance coverage for its citizens. Although some politicians have claimed that Americans without insurance can still access health care through any hospital emergency department, the reality is that the essential requisite for adequate health care in America is the possession of some form of a health insurance card. Figure 2.4, taken from NHDR-2009, illuminates quite clearly the relationship between income and the likelihood of health insurance coverage.

There are three findings in Figure 2.4 that are particularly worth highlighting. The first is the obvious sustained gap between the poor and the near poor and the higher-income groups in health insurance coverage. The second finding worth highlighting is that health care insurance coverage is close to universal only for the Americans in the high-income bracket; even a large share of the middle class does not have insurance coverage. Finally, it is also quite clear that for the middle class, health care insurance coverage was on the decline in the years *preceding* the most recent recession. We also would argue that Figure 2.4 is, in some respects, deceptively optimistic in that a large share of the poor and near poor are insured only through the Medicaid program—a form of health care coverage that is often rejected by physicians, pharmacies, and other health care providers (Stuber et al., 2008). The NHDR-2009 report also points out that while health care expenditures for high-income Americans account for less than 10% of their income, health care expenditures for the poor consume about 33% of their income (AHRQ, 2009).

The second crucial access factor identified by the NHDR-2009 report, having a usual source of care, shows remarkable disparities by

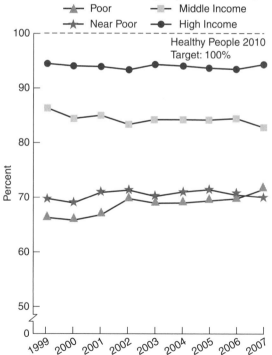

FIGURE 2.4 Health Insurance Coverage by Income Level, 1999–2007

From Figure 3.1. (graph 3) People under age 65 with health insurance, by race, ethnicity, income, and education, 1999–2007. AHRQ, 2009 National Health Care Disparities Report.

income, with only 70% of the poor having a usual primary care provider, compared with a figure of about 82% for high-income Americans. It is also the case that the poor are more likely to depend on hospital emergency departments for their usual-source primary care, which often means long waits, hurried examinations, no emphasis on preventive care, and greater expenditures for the health care system.

Finally, the poor are far more likely to either delay or forego altogether getting needed care for serious health problems. According to the NHDR-2009 estimates, two times as many poor and low-income Americans forego getting needed care because they believe they cannot afford it than do high-income Americans—and it should be obvious that for high-income Americans who defer health care for financial reasons, the issue is really about personal preferences as opposed to need.

The health consequences of barriers to health care access show up in a range of diseases and conditions, some more directly attributable to access than others. For example, poorly controlled hypertensive disease is often associated with lack of access to health care, but it can also reflect a large component of individual behavioral choices and genetic propensities. However, this is not so for health conditions such as a perforated appendix. The progression of appendicitis to perforation of the appendix entails excruciating abdominal pain, symptoms that if brought to the attention of a physician can quickly lead to a timely diagnosis of appendicitis. People suffering these kinds of excruciating symptoms who have health insurance (or other means to pay for care) tend to seek care in the early stages of abdominal pain, whereas people without health insurance are more likely to delay care and hope that the pain subsides and does not mean something serious—and as a result both poor people and even middle-class people without health insurance have a high incidence of hospital admissions for perforated appendix secondary to appendicitis.

For this reason, the NHDR-2009 used the incidence of hospital admissions for perforated appendix as one of the clinical indicators for the consequences of disparities in health care access by race/ethnicity, income, and health insurance status. Figure 2.5 shows NHDR-2009 data that are specific to differences in the incidence of hospital admissions for perforated appendix by community income quartile (with Quartile 1 representing the poorest communities). The figure shows that, while the incidence of hospital admissions for perforated appendix has generally been on the decline in recent years

FIGURE 2.5 Perforated Appendixes per 1,000 Admissions with Appendicitis, by Area Income Quartile, 2001–2006

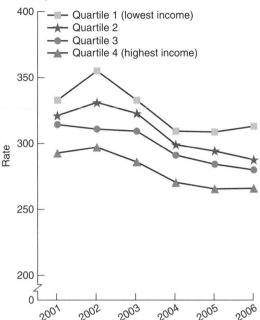

From Figure 3.14: Perforated appendixes per 1,000 admissions with appendicitis, by race/ethnicity, area income (median income of ZIP Code of residence), and insurance status, 2001–2006. AHRQ, 2009 National Health Care Disparities Report.

for communities at all income levels, the significant disparities in incidence by income have persisted—and for the poorest communities appear to be on the rise again. In one sense, the disparities in hospital admissions for perforated appendix are akin to the canary in the coal mine; they in essence serve as a proxy for other kinds of health care disparities that are more difficult to detect and more gradual in their emergence. However, they are also in and of themselves quite deadly in their own right, because the death rates for a perforated appendix are 10 times those for cases of appendicitis where timely intervention has occurred (Singh, 2000).

While disparities in health care *access* may be the form of health care disparities that contribute the most to higher rates of disease, disablement, and death among the poor, disparities in the *quality* of health care also play a significant causal role in disparities in health outcomes. Although the NHDR-2009 considers multiple dimensions and measures of health care quality, we will focus on just two aspects, the extent to which the poor receive care that is equitable (that does not vary quality by socioeconomic status) and effective (appropriate from an evidence-based perspective). One indicator that captures both health care equity and effectiveness is mammography screening for breast cancer for women aged over 40. Although there have been some recent scientific debates about the cost effectiveness of regular mammography screening, the prevailing view is that mammography is an effective tool in the reduction of mortality from breast cancer (AHRQ, 2009). Only about 50% of poor women report that they have had a screening mammography in the past 2 years, in contrast to a screening rate of 75% for high-income women (AHRQ, 2009). Even though this is prima facie evidence of a significant disparity in the quality of care that is clearly predictive of disparities in premature mortality among women, it should also be considered that poor women have higher concomitant risk factors for breast cancer relative to more affluent women—toxic environmental exposures, higher fat diets, and higher levels of stress.

In addition to preventive screening, clinically appropriate care for diagnosed conditions is the second area where disparities in quality of care by income are both apparent and highly determinant of disparities in health. Clinically appropriate care for diabetes includes "hemoglobin A1c (HbA1cv) testing, eye examination, foot examination, as well as appropriate influenza immunization and lipid management" (AHRQ, 2009, p. 50). According to the most recent data that compare three critical elements of clinically appropriate diabetic care by income level, only 30% of poor and near-poor adult diabetics receive appropriate diabetic care, in contrast to a rate of 50% for more affluent adults. As these findings are examined closely, it appears (intuitively enough) that insurance status plays a large role in this disparity, but it is also evident that even the poor who have public forms of health care receive lower quality of care for management of diabetes (AHRQ, 2009).

In sum, the most recent *National Healthcare Disparities Report* finds that the poor fare worse than high-income individuals on 15 of 20 measures of health care quality, and on all 6 measures used to assess health care access (AHRQ, 2009). If health care is nothing more than a commodity that (like shoes, tennis rackets, and cars) is subject only to the vicissitudes of a market economy, we should be neither surprised nor perhaps even disturbed by the failure of our largely market-based health care system to provide adequate and equitable health care for the poor. On the other hand, if we regard health care (like basic education) to be an essential element of citizenship, we must fundamentally rethink the basis upon which we have organized our health care system—and not reify what amounts to an institutionalized accident of history.[23]

SUGGESTED RESOURCES FOR POVERTY AND HEALTH

The following list of Web sites provides extensive current data that are relevant to the linkages between poverty and health, and poverty and health care. The first seven of the eight resources listed provide data on health care disparities and health care insurance coverage issues for the low income and the poor within the United States. The final resource listed, the *OECD Factbook*, provides the reader with data on economic and health inequalities that compare the United States with other modernized democracies such as the United Kingdom, Sweden, France, Australia, Japan, and Canada.

The National Health Care Disparities Report (Annual Series). The Agency for Healthcare Research and Quality
http://www.ahrq.gov/qual/measurix.htm#quality

The Henry J. Kaiser Family Foundation: Health Care Coverage and the Uninsured
http://www.kff.org/uninsured/index.cfm

The Commonwealth Fund: Health Care Disparities
http://www.commonwealthfund.org/Topics/Health-Care-Disparities.aspx

The Commonwealth Fund: Health Insurance
http://www.commonwealthfund.org/Topics/Health-Insurance.aspx

The Robert Wood Johnson Foundation: Health Care Disparities
http://www.rwjf.org/pr/topic.jsp?topicid=1180

---

[23] Journalist and social critic Malcolm Gladwell, writing for *The New Yorker* in 2005, made the point that the U.S. health care system is largely an "accident of history" that emerged in large part out of the American labor movement's exclusive reliance on collective bargaining for health care benefits as opposed to European labor's use of the political system for universal entitlements that would benefit workers as a class (Gladwell, 2005). For a full recap of this history that fully supports Gladwell's argument, see Quadagno. (2004). Why the United States has no national health insurance: Stakeholder mobilization against the welfare state, 1945–1996. *Journal of Health and Social Behavior, 45* (Extra Issue): 25–44.

The Robert Wood Johnson Foundation: Health Care Coverage and the Uninsured
http://www.rwjf.org/pr/topic.jsp?topicid=1049

Families USA: About the Insured
http://familiesusa.org/issues/uninsured/about-the-uninsured/

Organization for Economic Cooperation and Development (OECD): *Factbook 2009*
http://lysander.sourceoecd.org/vl=1231463/cl=25/nw=1/rpsv/ factbook2009/index.htm

REFERENCES

Administration for Children and Families. (2009). Estimated state median income, by family size and by state for FY 2009. Retrieved March 11, 2010, from http://www.acf.hhs.gov/programs/ocs/liheap/guidance/SMI75FY09.pdf

Agency for Healthcare Research and Quality. (2009). *National health care disparities report 2009*. Rockville, MD: U.S. Department of Health and Human Services.

Almgren, G. (2005). The ecological context of interpersonal violence: From culture to collective efficacy. *Journal of Interpersonal Violence, 20(2),* 218–224.

Almgren, G. (2007). *Health care politics, policy and services: A social justice analysis.* New York: Springer Publishing Company.

Almgren, G., & Ferguson, M. (1999). The urban ecology of hospital failure. *Journal of Sociology and Social Welfare, 26(4),* 5–26.

Amato, P., & Zuo, J. (1992). Rural poverty, urban poverty, and psychological well-being. *Sociological Quarterly, 33(2),* 229–240.

Banks, J., Marmot, M., Oldfield, Z., & Smith, J. P. (2006). The SES health gradient on both sides of the Atlantic. *NBER Working Paper Series* (No. 12674), 1–52.

Berkman, L., Glass, T., Brissette, I., & Seeman, T. (2000). From social integration to health: Durkheim in the new millennium. *Social Science and Medicine, 51,* 853–857.

Bishaw, A. (2005). *U.S. census 2000 special reports: Areas with concentrated poverty.* Washington, DC: U.S. Census Bureau.

DeNavas-Walt, C., Proctor, B. D., & Smith, J. C. (2009). *Income, poverty, and health insurance coverage in the United States: 2008.* Washington, DC: U.S. Census Bureau.

Friends of Pine Ridge Reservation. (2010). Friends of pine ridge reservation homepage. Retrieved April 16, 2010, from http://www.friendsofpineridgereservation.org

Gilens, M. (1999). *Why Americans hate welfare: Race, media, and the politics of antipoverty policy.* Chicago, IL: University of Chicago Press.

Gladwell, M. (August 29, 2005). The moral hazard myth: The bad idea behind our failed health-care system. *The New Yorker.*

Guest, A., Almgren, G., & Hussey, J. (1998). The ecology of socio-economic distress: Infant and working age mortality in Chicago. *Demography, 35(1).*

Health and Human Services. (2002). *Indicators of welfare dependence: Annual report to Congress 2002.* Washington, DC: U.S. Department of Health and Human Services, xiv

Himmelstein, D. U., Thorne, D., Warren, E., & Woolhandle, S. (2009). Medical bankruptcy in the United States, 2007: Results of a national study. *American Journal of Medicine, 122(8)*, 741–746.

Idler, E., & Benyamini, Y. (1997). Self-Rated health and mortality: A review of twenty-seven community studies. *Journal of Health and Social Behavior, 38(1)*, 21–37.

Institute of Medicine. (1993). *Access to health care in America.* Washington, DC: National Academies Press.

Krieger, N. (2001). Theories for social epidemiology in the 21st century: An ecosocial perspective. *International Journal of Epidemiology, 30(4)*, 668–677.

Krieger, N. (2002). A glossary for social epidemiology. *Epidemiol Bull, 23(1)*, 7–11.

Le, C. N. (2010). Socioeconomic statistics & demographics Asian-Nation: The landscape of Asian America. Retrieved March 11, 2010, from http:// www.asian-nation.org/

Lewis, O. (1959, 1975). *Five families: Mexican case studies in the culture of poverty.* New York: Basic Books.

Lieberman, R. (1998). *Shifting the color line: Race and the American welfare state.* Cambridge, MA: Harvard University Press.

Link, B. G., & Phelan, J. (1995). Social conditions as fundamental causes of disease. *Journal of Health and Social Behaviour, Spec No*, 80–94.

Link, B. G., & Phelan, J. (1996). Understanding sociodemographic differences in health-the role of fundamental causes. *American Journal of Public Health, 86(4)*, 471–473.

Lynch, J., Smith, G. D., Harper, S., Hillemeie, M., Ross, N., Kaplan, G., et al. (2004). Is income inequality a determinant of population health? Part 1. A systematic review. *Milbank Quarterly, 82(1)*, 5–99.

Marmot, M. (2002). The influence of income on health: Views of an epidemiologist. *Health Affairs, 21(2)*, 31–46.

Massey, D. (1995). Review essay — The bell curve: Intelligence and class structure in American life. *American Journal of Sociology, 101(3)*, 747–753.

Massey, D. (2007). *Categorically unequal: The American stratification system.* New York: Russell Sage Foundation.

Massey, D., & Denton, N. (1993). *American apartheid.* Cambridge, MA: Harvard University Press.

McCord, C., & Freeman, H. (1990). Excess mortality in Harlem. *New England Journal of Medicine, 322(3),* 173–177.

McLanahan, S. (1985). *Losing ground: A critique. institute for research on poverty special report series #38.* Madison, WI: Institute for Research on Poverty.

McLanahan, S. (2004). Diverging destinies: How children are faring under the second demographic transition. *Demography, 41(4),* 607–627.

Mead, L. (1986). *Beyond entitlement: The social obligations of citizenship.* New York: Free Press.

Mead, L. (1992). *The new politics of poverty: The non-working poor in America.* New York: Basic Books.

Moore, K. A., Redd, Z., Burkhauser, M., Mbwana, K., & Collins, A. (2009). *Children in poverty: Trends, consequences and policy options.* Washington, DC: Child Trends.

Murray, C. (1984). *Losing ground: American social policy, 1950–1980.* New York: Basic Books.

Murray, C., & Herrnstein, R. J. (1994). *The bell curve: Intelligence and class structure in American life.* New York: Free Press.

Nielsen, F., Alderson, A., & Beckfield, J. (2005). *Exactly how has income inequality changed? Patterns of distributional change in core societies.* Unpublished manuscript, The Future of World Society, University of Zurich, Zurich, Switzerland, June 23–24, 2004.

O'Connor, A. (2001). *Poverty Knowledge: Social science, social policy, and the poor in twentieth-century U.S. History.* Princeton, NJ: Princeton University Press.

OECD. (2007). Trends in income inequality and income position of different household types. *OECD Family Database.* Retrieved March 11, 2010, from http://www.oecd.org/dataoecd/52/13/43201528.pdf

OECD. (2009a). *OECD health data: Trends in health care expenditures as a percent of the GDP.* Paris, France: Organization for Economic Co-operation and Development.

OECD. (2009b). *Society at a glance: OECD social indicators.* Paris, France: Organization for Economic Co-operation and Development.

OECD. (2009c). *Trends in income inequality and income position of different household types.* Paris, France: Organization for Economic Co-operation and Development.

OECD. (2010a). Income distribution - Inequality - Country tables *OECD Stat Extracts*. Retrieved March 20, 2010, from http://stats.oecd.org/Index .aspx?QueryId=11112&QueryType=View

OECD. (2010b). Poverty rates and poverty gaps. *OECD Factbook 2009: Economic, environmental and social statistics*. Retrieved March 1, 2010, from www.oecdilibrary.org/economics/oecd-factbook-2009_factbook-2009-en

Portes, A., Fernández-Kelly, P., & Haller, T. (2009). The adaptation of the immigrant second generation in America: Theoretical overview and recent evidence. *Journal of Ethnic and Migration Studies, 35(7)*, 1077–1104.

Schott, L. (2009). *An introduction to TANF*. Washington, DC: Center on Budget and Policy Priorities.

Sen, A. (1999). *Development as freedom*. New York: Knopf.

Singh, B. (2000). An unusual presentation of ruptured appendicitis. *UCLA Department of Medicine Clinical Vignette.* Retrieved April 16, 2010, from http:// www.med.ucla.edu/modules/wfsection/article.php?articleid=121

Smith, T. W. (1987). That which we call welfare by any other name would smell sweeter: An analysis of the impact of question wording on response patterns. *Public Opinion Quarterly, 51(1)*, 75–83.

Soss, J., Schram, S. T. V., & O'Brien, E. (2001). Setting the terms of relief: Explaining state policy choices in the devolution revolution. *American Journal of Political Science, 45(2)*, 378–395.

South Dakota Department of Health. (2008). *2008 South Dakota vital statistics report: A state and county comparison of leading health indicators*. Pierre, SD: Author.

Stuber, J., Meyer, I., & Link, B. (2008). Stigma, prejudice, discrimination and health. *Social Science and Medicine, 67(3)*, 351–357.

Thornton, R. (1997). Aboriginal North American population and rates of decline, ca. A.D. 1500–1900. *Current Anthropology, 38(2)*, 300–315.

U.S. Census Bureau. (2009). *Current population survey: POV01: Age and sex of all people, family members and unrelated individuals iterated by income-to-poverty ratio and race: 2008*. Washington, DC: Author

U.S. Census Bureau. (2010a). *2006–2008 American community survey 3-year estimates: S1702. Poverty status in the past 12 months of families*. Washington, DC: Author

U.S. Census Bureau. (2010b). *2006–2008 American community survey 3-year estimates S1703. Selected characteristics of people at specified levels of poverty in the past 12 months*. Washington, DC: Author

U.S. Department of Agriculture. (2004). *Rural development research report No. 10: Rural poverty at a glance*. Washington, DC: Author

Weber, M. (1998). *The Protestant ethic and the spirit of capitalism/translated by Talcott Parsons*. Los Angeles, CA: Roxbury Publishers.

Wilson, W. J. (1987). *The truly disadvantaged: The inner city, the underclass, and public policy*. Chicago, IL: University of Chicago Press.

Wilson, W. J. (1996). *When work disappears: The world of the new urban poor*. New York: Knopf.

3

Stratification and Stigma

SOCIAL STRATIFICATION

Social Stratification Defined

Social stratification derives from the term *strata*, meaning different layers of a structure that are distinctive in their composition and order of hierarchy (Massey, 2007). We thus use the terms "bottom layer of society," "bottom strata," and "bottom of the heap" in reference to the same general thing—the persons or groups in a society that are the least advantaged in reference to some important social resource (most typically wealth, social status, and social power). The characteristics that locate persons into different strata or levels of social advantage/disadvantage are referred to as either ascribed or achieved social characteristics. Ascribed characteristics, such as gender and race, are set at birth in accordance with a given society's culturally defined "rules of ascription," whereas achieved characteristics refer to identifiers acquired in the course of living (such as wealth, education, or even criminality).

Both the ascribed and achieved social characteristics that define a person's relative position within a given social hierarchy are themselves artifacts of social construction. For example, the rules that identify a newly born infant as either "White" or "Black" have been far more determined by historical epoch, region, and even the social class of the parents than they have by the DNA of any particular child (Hirschman, 2004). Perhaps more intuitively, achieved social characteristics are also socially constructed. Being considered "wealthy" has depended upon the prevailing standard of living and distribution of material resources over different periods and across different local contexts. Similarly, the assignment of "criminal" to a person's character or identity depends not only on the prevailing rules of law defining criminal conduct, but in many instances also on the social class, race, and gender of the perpetrator.

The Function of Social Stratification Systems

Aside from the particular ascribed and achieved social characteristics that separate people into strata or levels of social hierarchy, different systems of social stratification pertain to the unequal allocation of different kinds of critical resources. Generally speaking, these critical resources may be material, symbolic, emotional, or some combination of all of them (Massey, 2007). For example, by the methodological conventions of sociology, an individual's placement on the socioeconomic status hierarchy is defined by their income, education, and occupation. It can be seen that income is particularly relevant to material resources, whereas both education and occupation have symbolic value in our society. The person holding a doctoral degree has more prestige in almost any social setting than a person with less than a high school diploma (sometimes even absent other evidence of greater genuine learning and wisdom), and doctors of medicine have higher occupational prestige than doctors of dental science—despite comparable levels of occupational selectivity and training. There are also decades of evidence that occupational status hierarchies are associated with emotional resources (Wilkinson, 1997).

Racially defined systems of social stratification also entail the unequal allocation of material, symbolic, and emotional resources. For example, the ascribed racial category of "oriental" was, for much of the 19th century, associated with poverty, disdain, and the emotional losses associated with systematic denial of human dignity.

At their essence, systems of social stratification exist to sustain the ability of some groups to advance their control over limited social and material resources to the detriment of other groups. The opposite of social stratification is egalitarianism, where a person's social characteristics or membership in a particular social group is independent of their having equal access to resources. As summarized by Massey

(2007), systems of social stratification use two basic mechanisms to advance one group's control over limited social and material resources to the disadvantage of other groups. The first, *exploitation*, refers to the various ways that one group expropriates the resources produced by another group in the absence of equal value compensation. A classic example of this is the underpriced fruit (in American supermarkets) harvested by the low-wage labor of undocumented workers through the sustainment of immigration policies designed to disadvantage migrant labor. The second, *opportunity hoarding*, entails one group's capacity to restrict another group's access to material and social resources (Massey, 2007, p. 6). There are countless examples of this, important among which has been the historical ability of the medical profession's capacity to restrict access to a medical education—and the material and symbolic rewards of a medical degree—from racial minorities and women (Starr, 1982). Both *exploitation* and *opportunity hoarding* are dependent upon the capacity of the dominant group to legitimize their claims to advantage or privilege or, alternatively, delegitimize the claims of the disadvantaged groups. Undocumented migrant labor is exploitable, in part, because amendments to immigration laws designed to legitimize the status of undocumented workers are characterized by opponents as either undermining free enterprise, posing a threat to national security, or encouraging illegal immigration. In the case of the medical profession's historic capacity to restrict access to medical education, not until the last half of the 20th century were any but White males regarded by most medical schools as intellectually or temperamentally suited for the practice of medicine (Starr, 1982).

The Social Psychology of Stratification and Stereotyping

The final critical aspect of social stratification processes to be considered is the social psychology of stratification and the intersect between social stratification and stereotyping. As synthesized by Massey (2007) in his definitive analysis of social stratification in American society, in evolutionary terms human beings are psychologically "hardwired" to classify or categorize other people in accordance with highly simplistic and generally subconscious schemas (learned memory structures). In essence, successful social existence over the ages has required that human beings develop a capacity to rapidly classify others based on small bits of information or "cues"—indicators from behavior, appearance, or the context of the encounter. These classification systems are commonly referred to as "stereotypes," and though they can be modified by informed self-reflection, they are in reality inescapable even for the most enlightened among us. According to the decades of research summarized by Massey, human beings tend to classify or stereotype people (or the groups we assume they represent) in accordance with a very simple two-dimensional Stereotype Content Model, which is defined by assumptions pertaining to *warmth* and *competence* (Massey, 2007, p. 11). People or groups that evoke perceptions of warmth and competence are those that we consider to be "like us," in essence both trustworthy and deserving of our respect. The three other combinations of these two dimensions (warm–incompetent, unwarm–competent, and unwarm–incompetent) are ways of classifying those that are unlike us. Depending on which of these three other combinations are at play, the "others" we encounter may evoke pity, contempt, or envy. Table 3.1 provides a useful summary of the ways in which humans are said to classify or stereotype others.

SOCIAL STRATIFICATION IN HEALTH CARE

The American health care system, like other major institutions of American society (the educational system, the economic system, and the justice system), is embedded with an array of structures and processes that reflect and perpetuate social stratification. We can see processes and structures of social stratification in the racial and ethnic composition of the hierarchical structure of the health care labor force, in the influence of political power and money in the financial structure of the health care industry, and in the ways in which a child's access to health care is often determined more by the education and income of the child's parents than the urgent need for medical care. We also see how stratification in the health care system segregates the hospitals and clinics serving the poor from the hospitals and clinics serving those with higher income and health insurance. Although most health care systems worldwide mirror the processes of social stratification that exist in the society as a whole, among modern societies with democratic governments, the United States stands at the extreme in its segregation of health care by race and by poverty. Rather than bringing attention to all the ways that social stratification is embedded in American health care, we will focus on the safety-net system and the ways in which it influences the context of career preparation in health care.

TABLE 3.1
Stereotype Content Model

SENTIMENTS TOWARD GROUP	PERCEPTIONS ABOUT WARMTH AND COMPETENCE	EXAMPLES OF STEREOTYPED GROUPS
Esteemed In-Group	High Warmth and High Competence	Friends, professional colleagues, those with whom we choose to associate.
Envied Out-Group	Low Warmth and High Competence	Legal immigrants and racial/ethnic minorities with perceived money and power.
Pitied Out-Group	High Warmth and Low Competence	Developmentally disabled children.
Despised Out-Group	Low Warmth and Low Competence	The poor, mentally ill, petty criminals, undocumented immigrants.

Constructed from Figure 1.1 The Stereotype Content Model, in Massey, 2001, *Categorically Unequal: The American Stratification System.* Russell Sage Foundation, New York.

Poverty, Race, and Medical Education

Medical education in the United States, as in the history of medical education in Europe, has always depended on the poor as willing fodder for medical training and the advancement of medical science. People who have no means to pay for the professional attention of a doctor when sick or injured have always been willing to subject themselves to being "cases" in the advancement of the medical education of students and apprentices in exchange for the possibility of help, if not cure. Until the end of the 1800s, medical education in the United States was dominated by an apprenticeship training model that mirrored training in the skilled trades rather than the science-based medical education that became the standard after the 1910 Flexner report that revolutionized medical education (Starr, 1982). Prior to 1900, medical students learned medicine largely under the tutelage of dubiously credentialed doctors who would teach them the "tricks of the trade" garnered more from experience and (often erroneous) belief systems— such as the use of purging for infant diarrhea (Condran & Preston, 1994). Doctors were generally reluctant to subject their fee-paying patients to the untried skills of their medical apprentices—but not so much the poor who were in desperate need of medical care they could not pay for. The 19th century clinics for the poor were called "dispensaries," a term that originated from places through which free medicines were dispensed to the poor based on medical diagnosis and clear evidence of poverty (Davis & Warner, 1918). Thus, then as now, in an effort to receive urgently needed but otherwise unaffordable medical care, the poor have maintained an enduring covenant with American medicine that entails the use of their bodies and health in the service of medical education. The dispensaries of today, while they are located in the emergency departments of safety-net hospitals and the community clinics subsidized by the federal government, are in many ways not terribly different from their 19th century precursors—with their crowded waiting rooms of poor in desperate need of medical attention, harried physicians, isolation from mainstream health care, and their social function as an essential laboratory for medical education. Also, like the dispensaries of the 19th century, these modern counterparts serve a disproportionate share of new immigrants and racial minorities.

This intersect among poverty, race, and medical education brings into vibrant play the previously discussed social psychology of stratification. Although there is often a significant social distance between providers (nurses, social workers and physcians) and the patients they treat based on professional education and role, within the safety-net hospitals and clinics serving the poor, immigrants, and disadvantaged racial minorities, the social distance is accentuated. That is, the patients health care providers encounter are much more likely to be of a different race and social class than the provider, and thus in the social cognition of the provider belong to any one of the three "out-groups" depicted in Table 3.1. Rather than being evaluated in the subconscious appraisal of the health care professional as "being like me," and accorded the default esteem and regard associated with persons who are akin to the health care professional in racial and social class background, patients encountered in safety-net settings are often cognitively relegated to alternative categories representing stereotypes that are linked to negative sentiments and perceptions—distrust, hostility, and pity.

It should be emphasized that such negative subconscious appraisals may have little to do with the professional values and individual belief systems of the health care provider, which are generally far more positive and embracing of difference. Rather, these are latent cognitive processes that merge human evolution with the deeply etched context of the individual provider's social development. Although professional education, organizational standards of professional conduct, and sincerely held personal beliefs often dominate the latent prejudicial and negative cognitive appraisals of those we are hardwired to perceive as "different," they sometimes betray themselves in very nuanced differential responses that are invisible to us—but quite transparent to those we appraise as suspect or different from us. It is also true that, under the everyday circumstances of tension, stress, and fatigue that are endemic in safety-net health care, latent negative appraisals are both more difficult to sublimate and more likely to invade patient–provider relationships and clinical judgments.

Latent Biases, Clinical Judgments, and the Role of Uncertainty

Although health care providers, and perhaps physicians in particular, are reluctant to acknowledge that their relationships with patients and clinical judgments are susceptible to various kinds of negative stereotypes, the evidence to the contrary from decades of research is quite compelling. One kind of evidence is of an indirect nature, observed as it is in disparities in the quality of health care that appear based on race, gender, and social class—even in instances where patients have access to health insurance. For example, although persons over age 65 in the United States are almost universally covered by Medicare, African American older adults are significantly less likely to have been vaccinated for pneumonia (AHRQ, 2008). With respect to latent gender biases in medicine, women are far more likely to be diagnosed in later stages of heart disease and as a result have higher age-specific death rates from myocardial infarction when hospitalized (AHRQ, 2008). One explanation for this gender disparity in the diagnosis of heart disease is that physicians may have more of a tendency to discount the somatic complaints of women that in men they might interpret as serious indicators of heart disease (Berra, 2000). This speaks to the second kind of evidence of latent biases in patient appraisals and clinical judgments, studies that more directly assess the ways in which health care professionals are likely to assign negative attributes that are based on race, gender, or social class.

The tendency of racial stereotyping to affect the clinical judgments of physicians was one of several health disparities addressed in the Institute of Medicine's (IOM's) *Unequal Treatment: Confronting Racial and Ethnic Disparities in Health Care*. This report cites multiple scientifically rigorous studies that collectively provide compelling evidence that physicians are more likely to assign negative traits to racial minorities than patients who fall within their own racial group. For example, in one study that asked physicians (N = 143) to rate their post-angiogram patients (N = 842) on such traits as intelligence, self-control, education level, pleasantness, rationality, responsibility, tendencies to exaggerate discomfort, likelihood of drug or alcohol abuse, and likelihood of complying with medical advice (van Ryn & Burke, 2000), it was found that African American patients were generally less likely to be positively perceived than White patients. Despite controls for a range of nonracial background variables, African Americans were perceived as less intelligent, less educated, more likely to abuse drugs and alcohol, and less likely to comply with medical advice (IOM, 2002). In another study that considered both race and gender biases in the clinical assessments of medical students, medical students were asked to provide a diagnosis of "definite" versus "probable" angina in videos of either a White male patient or an African American female patient identifying identical clinical symptoms (Rathore et al., 2000). While the medical students generally were more likely to rate the overall health status of the African American females lower than that of White males, they were far more likely to assign a diagnosis of "definite" angina to the White male patients (IOM, 2002, p. 165). However, and at least of equal importance, neither minority students nor the female medical students rated the health status of the African American female patients differently than that of the White male patients (p. 164).

It is fair to assume that the medical students who participated in this study would be surprised, if not aghast, that their clinical judgments were so blatantly affected by the race and gender of the patient depicted in the diagnostic video. However, it is this very disconnect between overt expressed beliefs and latent and unconscious biases that lies at the root of the most enduring and seemingly intractable health care disparities—those we prefer to attribute to factors outside of ourselves.

The IOM's *Unequal Treatment* report disputes the credibility of evidence pointing to the existence of *overt* racism among health care providers in accordance with criteria that seem torturously narrow (IOM, 2000, p. 176). However, the IOM report makes very strong and compelling evidence-based arguments pertaining to the mechanisms through which latent biases influence clinical decision making in ways that are detrimental to racial minorities, women, and persons of low income/education. Like the theories summarized by sociologist Massey (2007), the IOM points to the evolutionary-based social processes of categorization and stereotyping that are common to all human societies in the formation of biased clinical assessments and patient treatment responses. However, the IOM moves well beyond Massey with an emphasis placed on *uncertainty* in a social context that is very demanding both of information and also a definitive response. That is, in contrast to everyday casual encounters between individuals of vastly different socioeconomic and/or racial backgrounds (in such places as schools, public transportation, and in restaurants), in the clinical encounters that are typical to the high-pressure environments of safety-net hospitals and clinics, there is a high demand for definitive conclusions within a general context of limited time, a formidable array of potentially relevant information, and often great uncertainty. As pointed out by the IOM, it is under just such circumstances that deeply embedded and generally subconscious attitude and belief systems dominate the more objective forms of critical thinking that are the essence of professional education (p. 161). Although it is difficult, if not impossible, to totally eradicate deeply entrenched unconscious beliefs and ways of thinking that shape our clinical judgments and patient interactions, our own reflective awareness of their existence and their sometimes subtle power is a hallmark of genuine clinical wisdom.

STIGMA AND PROCESSES OF STIGMATIZATION

In the discussion that follows, we consider the meaning of stigma, the distinctions between stigma, prejudice, and discrimination, and the origins and social functions of stigma. We finish with a discussion of the relationships between poverty, disablement, and virtual "embodiment of stigma" as an outcome of social structural arrangements.

The Meaning of Stigma

The classic definition of *stigma*, advanced by pioneering sociologist Erving Goffman, refers to stigma as an attribute that links a person to an undesirable stereotype, leading other people to reduce the bearer from a whole and usual person to a person with a *tainted* and *discounted identity* (Goffman 1963, p. 11 [our italics]). For example, there is a certain stigma attached to being a Medicaid recipient as opposed to a person with an insurance card from Blue Cross, Blue Shield, or Medicare (Stuber & Schlesinger, 2006). In contrast to the patient with an *insurance card*, the patient on Medicaid possesses a *medical coupon*— the latter making even clearer the distinction between a patient having a claim to care based upon insurance versus a patient making a claim to care based upon his or her status as a dependent upon the tax-paying public. Although the extensive tax subsidies attached to health insurance benefits undermine the de facto legitimacy of this distinction, what matters in this comparison is the perception of relative social status and legitimacy—in the mind of the public, in the mind of the health care provider, and in the experience of care and sense of self-worth of the patient burdened with the stigma of a Medicaid coupon.

Another example of stigma, again within the context of health care, concerns the tainted identities attached to persons with particular diseases and health conditions. The history of medicine and society is replete with examples of diseases that have been attributed to so-called justly-deserved afflictions or a sign that the person is possessed by evil spirits. Epilepsy, schizophrenia, cancer, blindness, and leprosy are well-known examples of diseases or health conditions that were once commonly attributed to the consequences of witchcraft, demon possession, or divine retribution for an unclean spirit (see Exhibit 3.1 "'Ugly' Laws").

Although the last known "Ugly" Law in the United States was finally repealed over 30 years ago, persons with many forms of disease, disablements, and health conditions continue to suffer the consequences of stigma in their everyday encounters with both the public

EXHIBIT 3.1

Although these stigmatizing causal assumptions about various forms of disease have waned in many parts of the world as education and industrialization have advanced, even in the recent history of the United States, many U.S. municipalities retained so-called Ugly Laws that made it a crime for persons with some physical conditions and disabilities to appear in public spaces such as city streets, parks, and public buildings. Perhaps the most famous of such laws is the City of Chicago's public ordinance that remained in force in 1974, nearly a decade after the Voting Rights Act of 1965 and 5 years after the first astronaut walked on the moon:

> *No person who is diseased, mutilated, or in any way deformed so as to be an unsightly or disgusting object or improper person is to be allowed in or on the public ways or other public places in this city, or shall therein or thereon expose himself to public view, under penalty of not less than $1 nor more than $50 for each offense.*

—Quote of City of Chicago, Public Ordinance (repealed in 1974) from Susan Sweik, *The Ugly Laws: Disability in Public*, NYU Press, 2009.

and with health care providers. There are a host of complex reasons for this, including deeply embedded beliefs about a causal relationship between human suffering and human moral deficits, misinformation and ignorance about the noncontagious nature of many forms of disease and disablement, generalized fear and suspicion of human difference, feelings that are evoked of helplessness and vulnerability, and the very real linkages between some forms of disease or health conditions and highly stigmatized human behaviors (for example, health conditions associated with addiction, such as lung cancer and alcoholic neuropathy).

Stigma, Prejudice, and Discrimination — Important Distinctions

Stigma, prejudice, and discrimination all entail biased and pejorative judgments that are targeted toward individuals and groups. All three concepts also involve social interactions that reinforce relationships of power and dominance, in that the individuals and groups that are targets of stigma, prejudice, and discrimination are devalued and disadvantaged relative to those assigning the stigmatized identity, holding the prejudice, or engaging in discriminatory behavior. There are, however, distinctions among these concepts that are worth considering and illuminating.

Both prejudice and discrimination, more common to the general language of the health professions, in many respects are outcomes that are reinforced or sustained by stigma. That is, the essence of stigmatizing a person (or group) is to assign to them a "discounted or tainted identity" by attaching their identity to an undesirable stereotype (Goffman, 1963). Prejudice endorses and incorporates negative stereotypes into the belief systems of persons, groups, and even organizations (Pescosolido, Martin, Lang, & Olafsdottir, 2008). Discrimination, on the other hand, entails the specific motivations and actions undertaken to avoid or exclude some persons and groups (Pescosolido et al., 2008).

As an illustrative example of how stigma, prejudice, and discrimination each make their distinct and essential contributions to poor quality of care, consider the case of the young adult male who comes to a typical hospital emergency room (ER) with a physical complaint (a severe headache) who presents with the following attributes: his clothing is somewhat rumpled and inconsistent with the prevailing season and weather; while waiting to be examined he is observed whispering and mumbling to himself; his source of payment is a Medicaid coupon; and when asked about the nature of his complaint, he attributes the cause of his headache to a microchip implanted by aliens. On the basis of this description, it is reasonable to assume that most of us would readily conclude that the person is mentally ill, poor, and also delusional about the cause of his headache. It is also true that the young male patient in question carries with him the dual *stigmatized* identities of poverty and mental illness—in the everyday banter of the typical ER this patient might be referred to as a "crazy," "schizo," or a "gomer" (if you are unfamiliar with this term, "gomer" is a derogatory acronym for undesirable patients, more fully explained in a later discussion). These, of course, are pejorative terms that reflect the patient's discounted or tainted identity. It also is fair to assume that in the typical hospital ER the potential seriousness of the patient's complaint might well be discounted. Perhaps because the patient's belief that the headache is caused by an implanted microchip appears sufficiently irrational to cast doubt on anything else he claims, or because the ER staff member doing the assessment assumes the "headache" is a ploy for seeking narcotics—consistent with her stereotypical beliefs about the general characteristics of "street people." The point is that both assumptions, to the extent that they substitute *prejudice* for deliberative clinical inquiry, invariably lead to *discriminatory* health care—in this case, the failure to adequately investigate the possibility that the patient's symptoms might be secondary to a brain tumor, meningitis, or any number of serious and potentially deadly conditions.

By highlighting the distinctions between stigma, prejudice, and discrimination, we achieve a more nuanced understanding of the processes through which health disparities are generated. Mental illness and poverty are but two sources of stigma that lead to discriminatory health care practices. Other sources include sexual orientation, multiple categories of disease, race or ethnicity, substance abuse, smoking, obesity, and gender. Individuals who belong to one stigmatized group often carry the burden of more than one stigmatized identity. In the preceding example, the young male ER patient possessed two sources of discounted identity, poverty and mental illness—either of which was sufficient to lead to discriminatory health care. This social phenomenon, the possession of multiple sources of discounted identities, is sometimes referred to by social theorists as *intersectionality* or *intersecting oppressions*.

Originating from feminist theory, the idea of *intersectionality* or *intersecting oppressions* argues that unitary categories such as female, undocumented, gay, disabled, or poor fail to capture either critical within-group differences or the combined effects of multiple disadvantaged identities (Meyer, Schwartz, & Frost, 2008; Stewart & McDermott, 2004). For example, being a member of a stigmatized group often can promote a sense of solidarity or belonging within that group on the basis of shared experiences of oppression and suffering. However, groups that are stigmatized by the larger society may also exclude and isolate members who have attributes that they themselves consider negative or undesirable—as in the case of gay African American men who encounter condemnation and rejection from a significant proportion of the African American clergy despite their shared legacies of racial discrimination (Schulte & Battle, 2004). Individuals who possess intersecting sources of stigma are often among the most isolated and marginalized members of society. Whereas some groups that have suffered the consequences of stigmatized identities develop an empathetic response to members who possess other stigmatizing traits on the basis of shared suffering, others tend to be far less empathetic—often because they resist the association of their group with other negative identities and stereotypes.

The Origins and Social Functions of Stigma

The assignment of stigma to particular groups and individual attributes is a feature common to all human societies and religious traditions. Anthropology, sociology, and evolutionary biology have all sought to examine the functional basis of stigma, in essence, the social purposes that provide the basis of stigma's persistence over time and across all contexts of human society. Using evidence from these diverse literatures, Phelan, Link, and Devidio (2008) propose that both stigma and prejudice have three functions within human societies: (a) exploitation/domination, (b) the enforcement of social norms, and (c) the avoidance of disease.

Assignment of Stigma as a Means of Domination and Exploitation

In the case of exploitation and domination, both stigma and prejudice work together to provide a rationale for one segment of society's actions to advance their own power, privilege, and resources at the expense of another's. Although the American institution of slavery is an infamous historical example of this, a more contemporary example is the use of undocumented workers to sustain the cheap clothing and food prices that are essential to the high standard of living of today's middle class (Schulman, 2005). In the context of health care, there are a myriad of examples where the assignment of stigma has been employed as a means of discounting the status and worth of one group relative to another—thus advancing the power, privilege, and resources of the dominant group.

One of the most evident is the gendered history of the medical profession. Throughout the history of the U.S. medical profession, women have been presumed to lack the aptitude to practice medicine— particularly the medical subspecialties that were the most rewarding in both professional status and income. In fact, the advancement of medicine as a high-status and lucrative profession for men was to a large extent predicated upon the capacity of the American Medical Association (AMA) to organize in a way that excluded women from its membership (Starr, 1982). Due to their discounted identity and status, women were relegated to the subordinate and historically underpaid profession of nursing. Similarly, African Americans were excluded from membership in the AMA as a means of advancing the exclusive privileges of the White male medical establishment through the mechanism of racial stigma—in essence by attaching to African Americans' racial identity the negative traits of unstable temperament, inferior intelligence, and weak character (Starr, 1982).

The case can also be made that even in the contemporary organization of the U.S. health care system, stigma is employed as a means of privileging the interests of the middle-class elderly over those of the working poor. Medicare has long existed as an entitlement to health care that is based upon age, and the very structure of the Medicare program as a social insurance fund precludes the bearer of a Medicare insurance card from being stigmatized as the medical version of a welfare recipient. Although numerous proposals have been advanced over the decades that would extend Medicare to be an all-inclusive program as a way of providing care to the poor, instead Congress (in 2003) poured several hundred billion dollars into expansions of Medicare targeted at the middle-class elderly—funded in part through reductions in Medicaid—the means-tested program for the medical care of the poorest of the poor (Almgren, 2007). In this regard, it is instructive to note that the more recent attempts by the Obama Administration to expand health care coverage to include more of the poor have been widely criticized as radical socialism, while periodic expansions to the Medicare program have tended to be regarded as legitimate entitlements.

Assignment of Stigma as Means of Enforcing Social Norms

Social norms are the written and unwritten rules of conduct that govern social relationships at all levels of society. The absence of social norms is anarchy and chaos. In order to be effective, social norms require mechanisms of enforcement—the most extreme of which is capital punishment. Most social norms are enforced through informal mechanisms, typically by attaching shame or pejorative judgments to forms of conduct that violate or threaten the written and unwritten rules of any social group—including small networks, families, social clubs, tribes, professional societies, and formal organizations such as schools and hospitals.

In fact, the medical staff norms provide a useful illustration of the assignment of stigma to certain behaviors as a means of enforcing groups' unwritten rules and of establishing the boundaries of acceptable conduct—in this example substandard medical practice. Within the medical staffs of any hospital, there is a wide range of professional competency, and typically a small number of physicians known among their peers to be marginal practitioners. While there are formal organizational sanctions for cases of blatantly incompetent practice, the application of these formal sanctions comes at a high cost both to the medical staff and to the hospital as a whole. In fact, professional sanctions (such as the termination of medical staff privileges) are fraught with the risk of successful legal action in the absence of clear, unequivocal evidence of a pattern of medical incompetence. Medical staffs also have the tendency to operate as semi-closed societies as a way of maintaining group trust and solidarity, manifested in the maintenance of group secrets that if made public might threaten the power and the status of the group as a whole. As a result, medical staffs often have to rely on informal mechanisms as a means of maintaining group norms, including the assignment of a stigmatized identity to physicians that, due to their marginal levels of professional competency, threaten the status and power of the group. While harshly disparaging terms like "quack" and "ditz" might be avoided except in whispered conversations, terms like "foggy thinker" or "difficult colleague" might be more openly expressed. Whatever terms or phrases might be used, within every medical staff there are labels or code words that signify a tarnished and devalued reputation among one's peers, even if the conduct in question falls shy of formal professional sanction.

There are also social norms that extend to society as a whole, matched to the maintenance of mechanisms that assign stigma to the groups and individuals who appear to violate these norms. Homosexuality, unwed pregnancy, welfare use, producing most forms of pornography, and atheism are all examples of behaviors that, if no longer commonly sanctioned in criminal law, at least result in the attachment of stigma. Maintaining the mechanisms of shame and tarnished identity to a wide range of generally constitutionally protected activities that run contrary to established beliefs and norms of conduct is central to the social and political agenda of the religious right. By way of contrast, core to the social and political environmental groups is the attachment of stigma to forms of public consumption that are deemed a threat to the environment, such as the purchase of gas guzzling SUVs (Balaker, 1999). Another example of the application of stigma in the pursuit of a progressive social agenda can be found in the public health strategies that promote stigmatization as the means to reduce smoking (Stuber, Galea, & Link, 2008). The general point here is that stigma is often a mechanism through which social norms and the boundaries of social behavior are established—sometimes to the general benefit of a just society and often to its detriment.

Assignment of Stigma as a Means of Avoiding Disease

Stigma also appears to have origins that are connected to the containment and avoidance of disease and genetic anomalies that are associated with species survival and evolutionary disadvantage. Many of the esthetic preferences in human societies that pertain to desirable and undesirable physical traits are believed to have their origins in the evolutionary history of the human species (Phelan et al., 2008). According to this evolutionary perspective, physical traits that are associated with markers of disease and/or disadvantageous genetic conditions are "hardwired" into our evolutionary makeup in ways that evoke primitive reactions of disgust and avoidance—manifested verbally in expressions such as disgusting, nauseating, repulsive, and sickening (Phelan et al., 2008, p. 363). Mental retardation, cancer, skin disorders, and physical disabilities are all examples of diseases and hereditary conditions that have provoked intense negative reactions throughout what is known of human history—manifested in the shunning, isolation, and condemnation of persons who have the physical markers that suggest their presence (p. 363). These adverse visceral reactions to the physical traits of disease and disability are one explanation for the origins and enduring legacies of "Ugly" Laws. The critical contribution of this evolutionary line of thinking on the functions of stigma is the recognition that there are some origins of rejection and marginalization that have little to do with current mechanisms of socialization. Such adverse reactions to the physical markers of disease or disability may also be less susceptible to logic and scientific enlightenment.

Connecting the Social Functions of Stigma to the Context of Safety-Net Health Care

Safety-net hospitals are the only resort for persons and groups that are shunned and rejected by mainstream health care providers. In fact, the treatment of stigmatized populations is a defining feature of safety-net health care providers (IOM, 2000). For the bearer of a stigmatized identity, the burden of stigma is in many respects akin to carrying the daily burden of a chronic debilitating disease in its physical, social, and psychological manifestations. Although a stigmatized identity is commonly regarded as a defining trait of an individual who is captured in a range of pejorative labels ("welfare queen," "junkie," "hooker," "faggot," "retard," "gimp," and "gomer"—to name only a few), in reality the true origins of a stigmatized identity are reflective of a social process that largely lies outside the individual. That is, the selective assignment of stigmatized identities to some persons and not others serves a variety of social purposes—thus, any particular stigmatized identity is more truly a trait of a given society or social group than it is the trait of an individual.

The health care professionals who choose to practice in safety-net hospitals and clinics as a career choice often possess an uncommon capacity to separate the individuals they treat from the stigmatized identities they bear. We are socialized much differently of course, and must unlearn the tendency to accept the pejorative jargon of stigma as the legitimate or acceptable definition of the patients and groups that we seek to treat with compassion, insight, and dignity. Much of this rests with our willingness and capacity to critically deconstruct the origins of the language of stigma that we encounter daily and the social purposes served.

Poverty, Illness, Disablement, and the "Embodiment" of Social Stigma

There is a strong association between poverty, disablement, ill-health, and social stigma. Poverty, disablement, and ill-health are each by themselves stigmatizing in the sense of evoking a social response that is negative or discounting of one's worth and dignity. There is a stigma associated with being poor in American society, in large part because it is commonly assumed that poverty and being poor reflect individual deficits, weakness, and moral failure (Gilens, 1999; Murray & Herrstein, 1996). Also, as discussed previously, the worth and human capacities of disabled persons and persons in ill-health have a long history of being discounted and devalued throughout American society (Osterweis, Kleinman, & Mechanic, 1987; Schweik, 2009). However, it is also true and critically important that disabled persons and persons with various forms of chronic disease are disproportionately represented among the poor (She & Livermore, 2007).

In causal terms, the relationship between disabling conditions or chronic disease and poverty works both ways. That is, children who are in ill-health or who are disabled are at a significant disadvantage in our systems of education and employment as they age into adulthood, and persons who become disabled or who become compromised by ill-health in adulthood face escalating health care expenditures and diminished earnings potential that ultimately result in poverty. For example, a recent study funded by the Robert Wood Johnson Foundation estimates that 62% of bankruptcies in the United States during 2007 were attributable to health problems and related medical expenditures—most of which occurred in formerly middle-class households (Himmelstein, Thorne, Warren, & Woolhandler, 2009).

Persons who are both disabled (or in ill-health) and poor embody at least two stigmatizing identities. They at once embody the negative social status of being poor and the discernable negative attribute of being disabled or "diseased." The term "embodied" is used very deliberately here in the sense described by social epidemiologist Krieger (2002). That is, embodiment refers to the ways in which we as human beings incorporate into our individual biological processes and traits the material and social contexts in which we live (p. 694). This means that persons who carry with them various forms of stigma quite literally incorporate, biologically and over time, the social and psychological slings and arrows suffered daily and relentlessly as a consequence of their devalued and undesirable social identities.

Pathways to the Embodiment of Stigma: Structural Determinants

Figure 3.1 depicts the pathways through which various forms of stigma, which may once have originated in poverty, disability, or ill-health, produce secondary health consequences of their own.

Although the causal pathways between the basic sources of stigma (poverty, illness, and disablement) and their health consequences are more complex than those shown in Figure 3.1, they at least show the essentials critical to a general appreciation of the phenomenon. Stigma, because it entails the negative appraisal of a person's basic human worth and "deservedness," leads others to justify or legitimize various forms of deprivation, discriminatory treatment, and social isolation. This process of justification occurs on a large scale, as exampled by the ways in which some historically discounted groups in American society have less access to adequate health insurance and have endured legacies of racial segregation (African Americans, Native Americans), and at a microinterpersonal scale as exemplified by discriminatory health care practices toward persons who carry with them stigmatizing attributes (IOM, 2002).

FIGURE 3.1   Stigma and Pathways to Embodiment

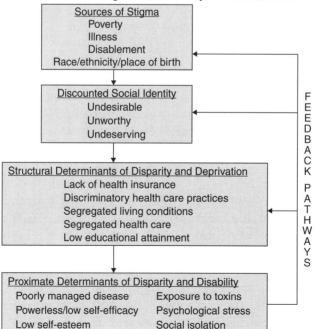

In the discussion that follows, we will focus on the bottom half of Figure 3.1—some of the *structural determinants of disparity and deprivation* that are consequent to a *discounted social identity,* and the ways in which these structural mechanisms in turn foster some of the well-established *proximate determinants of disease and disability.* It should be noted that the structural mechanisms and the proximate determinants shown in Figure 3.1 are a representative rather than an exhaustive list—the intent here is to illuminate rather than fully explain the processes through which stigmatized identities produce disease and disability.

Structural Determinants of Disparity and Deprivation

The status of *lacking health insurance* is not a randomly distributed phenomenon. The poor, most non-white Americans, and the foreign born are all historically stigmatized groups that carry a disproportionate risk of having no health insurance (Kaiser Commission on Medicaid and the Uninsured, 2008). While it might be argued that this systematic disparity in health insurance coverage is a regrettable and an unintended artifact of the employment-based health insurance system in the United States, a more considered analysis must acknowledge that the employment-based health insurance system has endured precisely because those groups least served by the employment-based health insurance system (the poor, racial minorities, and the foreign born) possess discounted (stigmatized) social identities. In this regard, it is instructive to note that the current broad political accord that the U.S. health care system must be radically reformed to expand coverage to all Americans is largely based on diminished access to health insurance coverage among White middle-class Americans.

The *discriminatory health care practices* to which various stigmatized groups are subject are well documented. For example, it has been shown that the status of being a Medicaid patient can bias both the assessment of clinical need and also the willingness of the patient to articulate his or her health care needs (Gurwitz et al., 2002; Obst, Nauenberg, & Buck, 2001). As another example pertaining to racial/ethnic stereotyping and stigmatized identities, it has been shown that elderly African Americans and Hispanics who are being treated for myocardial infarction are less likely to be prescribed the conventionally appropriate drug therapies than Whites (AHRQ,

2004). It has also been shown that patients who carry the stigma of being obese also are subject to discriminatory attitudes and practices among health care providers (Brown, 2006; Kaminsky & Gadaleta, 2002; Yancy et al., 2005).

Also prominent among the structural determinants of disparity and deprivation are *segregated living conditions.* Classic and tragic examples of this are the millions of African Americans who continue to reside in urban neighborhoods characterized by concentrated poverty, poor-quality schools, and endemic violence (Massey & Denton, 1993) and the large share of Native Americans residing on impoverished and isolated reservations (Almgren, 2007). It is well documented that populations of segregated neighborhoods, communities, and entities such as rural counties and reservations experience multiple sources of disadvantage both to their health and their access to quality health care (IOM, 2002; Rogers, Humner, & Nam, 2000).

Although distinct conceptually and in their effects on health, *segregated living conditions* and *segregated health care* are also linked in many ways—particularly to the extent that racially and economically segregated groups are dependent upon hospitals and clinics that serve a disproportionate share of poor patients living in poor neighborhoods (Almgren, 2007; Almgren & Ferguson, 1999; Sarrazin, Campbell, & Rosenthal, 2009). In this context, *segregated living conditions* refer to geographic patterns within large cities that locate racial minorities and the poor to specific neighborhoods. While the processes behind these spatial patterns are complex and embedded in history, the concentration of racially and economically disadvantaged groups within specific urban boundaries perpetuates and magnifies their disadvantage—via such mechanisms as lower quality schools, isolation from employment opportunities, exposure to endemic crime and violence, and higher levels of exposure to environmental toxins (Brulle & Pellow, 2006; Massey & Denton, 1993).

Historically, *segregated health care* in the United States was primarily an outcome of deliberate policies that created separate hospitals and clinics for racially and ethnically stigmatized groups—racial and ethnic minorities that were excluded from hospitals built to serve White Protestants of Northern European ancestry (Almgren, 2007; Rosenberg, 1987). In the decades since the U.S. Supreme Court rejected the Constitutional premise for racial segregation in the 1954 *Brown v. The Board of Education* decision, overt segregation policies among American hospitals and clinics were gradually challenged and dismantled.

EXHIBIT 3.2

Although much of the discrimination among health care providers toward stigmatized groups tends to be subtle or latent, there are often quite overt and well-institutionalized expressions, among them the so-called GOMER scale, an acronym for "Get out of my Emergency Room!" (Anonymous, 2009). Promulgated in its many versions to be a humorous insider's joke among health care professionals, the GOMER scale in its essence quantifies the level of stigma that is assigned to a given patient based on his or her particular cluster of undesirable clinical and demographic characteristics. Depending upon the version of the GOMER scale, a given patient accumulates social undesirability points by having any reference to a social (as opposed to medical) need noted in his or her record, having a possible psychiatric diagnosis, being aged and frail, being morbidly obese, having been admitted to a Veterans Hospital (often interpreted as a marker for poverty), and speaking a language other than English. A recent and typical example of a GOMER scale downloaded from the internet uses a summary scoring system that includes derogatory evaluation points for having active tuberculosis, developing a fever prior to hospital discharge, having psychiatric commitment recommendation, fracturing a hip during a hospital episode, and having an extensive and voluminous medical record (Miller, 2007). On a superficial level, it seems that all but a very few health care workers would find the scale anything but a humorous and a good example of what is often referred to as "black" or "gallows" humor. However, it should also be acknowledged and recognized that the GOMER scale in its various versions serves as an expression of disdain for patients with traits and behaviors that health care workers, for a variety of reasons, tend to resent—in particular those patients who have conditions and histories that imply an unwillingness or inability to be helped.

However, patterns of racial and ethnic segregation in American hospitals and clinics endure. In large part, this is due to two factors: (a) the suburbanization of health care that maps onto the suburbanization of White America, and (b) the financing structure of the U.S. health care system that makes it desirable and largely permissible for all but publicly owned hospitals to avoid care of the poor—who in turn are disproportionately people of color.

This phenomenon was quite recently in evidence in August of 2005, in the wake of Hurricane Katrina's flooding of the city of New Orleans. In many respects, the health care infrastructure of pre-Hurricane Katrina in New Orleans reflected the racially segregated character of the city itself. In one of the most deeply flooded areas, there were two hospitals that were quite literally across the street from one another: Tulane University Hospital and Charity Hospital of New Orleans. Charity Hospital was New Orleans' publically owned safety-net hospital serving the poor and uninsured patients of the city, who also happened to be 85% African American (Rudowitz, Rowland, & Shartzer, 2006; Stivers, 2007). Tulane University Hospital, owned by a for-profit hospital, exclusively served patients with health insurance—in fact less than 2% of the patients admitted to Tulane University Hospital were funded by Medicaid (Solucient, 2005). Whereas the patients and the staff of Tulane University Hospital were evacuated by helicopter within hours of the hospital's flooding, the staff and patients of Charity Hospital were essentially abandoned— despite the existence of a skybridge that connected the two hospitals that could have permitted the speedy evacuation of Charity Hospital's most critically ill patients (Almgren, 2007; Berggren, 2005). Instead, the poor, Black, and uninsured patients of Charity Hospital waited 5 days for evacuation—and then only after their desperate plight had been broadcast by the cable television news media to a scandalized nation. For some nine of the most critically ill patients of Charity Hospital, this belated response didn't really matter. Because they were poor, uninsured, and ergo in the wrong hospital to be rescued, they had already died (deBoisblanc, 2006).

The last example of a structural determinant that links stigma with disparity and deprivation is *low-educational attainment*. Persons with low levels of education have shorter life spans and higher levels of disease and disablement (Rogers et al., 2000). There are a variety of reasons for this, including a higher likelihood of working in low-wage and dangerous occupations, lower levels of self-efficacy and investment in personal health, and greater susceptibility to targeted marketing by the tobacco industry. The pathways to higher levels of educational attainment are often impeded for persons who for one reason or another are burdened with a stigmatized identity that leaves them discounted and devalued. Two examples of this are teenaged obesity (Gortmaker, Must, Perrin, Sobol, & Dietz, 1993) and teenaged pregnancy (Moore & Waite, 1977).

Pathways to the Embodiment of Stigma: Proximate Determinates

In contrast to the *structural* determinants of disparity and deprivation, which refer to the opportunities and resources that are reduced or constrained on the basis of a discounted social identity, the *proximate* determinants of disease and deprivation refer to the more immediate mechanisms of poorer health outcomes that arise from structural factors. For example, although the absence of a health insurance card is not a disease pathogen or a source of disablement, those without health insurance are more likely to encounter inadequate health care, *poorly managed disease*, and have worsened diseases and health conditions as a direct result (AHRQ, 2004). Similarly, living in a poor and racially segregated neighborhood does not in and of itself lead to premature death from respiratory disease, but the greater levels of *exposure to environmental toxins* that are more prevalent in poor neighborhoods does (Evans & Kantrowitz, 2002). Although *low self-esteem* and a *sense of powerlessness* are distinct psychological attributes, they are obviously closely related, often can be consequent to racism and poverty, and in effect work together to impede an individual's ability to be an effective advocate for his or her own health. Patients with low self-esteem and a sense of powerlessness are often reluctant to identify symptoms, ask questions of health care providers, expect a high level of care and attention from health care providers, or believe that they are capable of influencing their health (AHRQ, 2004; Sanders-Phillips, Settles-Reaves, Walker, & Brownlow, 2009). Finally, discriminatory health care practices (as a deeply embedded structural feature of the health care system) also negatively affect the health outcomes for women, African Americans, and persons suffering from stigmatized health conditions through the proximate mechanism *poorly managed disease*. As previously noted, it has been well established that women with cardiac disease are less likely to be diagnosed and to receive adequate treatment than men in part because physicians tend to disregard or otherwise misinterpret their somatic complaints (Berra, 2000).

CONCLUDING COMMENTS

Safety-net health care providers are asked to do the impossible. They are expected to treat some of the most problematic and difficult of health problems in the context of the most intractable of human conditions—profound and enduring poverty. Moreover, the nurses, social workers, and physicians who interact daily with the excluded, deprived, and disdained, must manage their own deeply embedded pejorative belief systems and feelings of despair and powerlessness. From an individual developmental perspective, the health care providers who do best in safety-net settings tend to have a deep reservoir of patience, empathy, and tolerance of ambiguity. We are not sure that these are capacities that can be necessarily taught or socialized in clinical training; they seem to be instead the province of family, community, life experience, and even spirituality. Treating a patient with stinking breath, rancid body odor, dirty clothes, and hostile distrust with the openness, objective competence, and humane dignity we would want for ourselves isn't something that can be "taught" in a professional school. On the other hand, even the most empathetic of practitioners can benefit from an enhanced capacity to objectify and deconstruct the attributes of patients who provoke strongly negative sentiments and reactions. Understanding the ways in which social stratification functions as a cognitive as well as social process, or the ways in which the assignment of stigma to some groups sustains and benefits others will not in and of themselves generate a more empathetic response. However, seeing and appraising the negative attributes of patients as the outcome and manifestation of very basic and enduring social structural determinants does offer the clinician a useful sense of informed perspective and an important source of critical self-evaluation. But beyond this abstract, general appreciation of the embeddedness of stereotyping and stigmatizing responses within our own cognitive processes, can we actively discern and eliminate the latent biases we harbor toward some groups or kinds of patients?

The evidence suggests that, with a high level of motivation and sustained efforts, we can at least ameliorate the impacts of embedded stereotypes on clinical practice—even if we cannot always completely eradicate their influences altogether (Burgess, Ryn, Davidio, & Saha, 2007). The beginning point for this, we believe, is the strong willingness (and courage if you will) to *interrogate our own agency* in the production of disparities in health care. By interrogating our own agency, we mean our active embracement of the evidence-based reality that stereotyping, and the discriminatory actions that sometimes follow, are both endemic in human experience and deeply embedded in our own cognitive processes.[1] Beyond our embracement of the reality that stereotyping and latent bias are endemic in human experience, there are specific evidence-based interventions that individuals and organizations can use to counter and inhibit deeply embedded processes of stereotyping.

Based on their review of decades of social cognitive psychology research on stereotyping, Burgess et al. (2007) have identified six

---

[1] We explore this topic in more depth in Chapter 4—Differences: Power, Privilege, and Disparities in Care.

evidence-based interventions that organizations and individual clinicians can use to combat stereotyping and unintentional biases among health care providers—which in essence focus on enhancing clinicians' motivation and ability to focus on the unique qualities of individuals rather than the groups to which they are assumed to belong. Briefly stated, these six interventions include (a) enhancing internal motivation and avoiding external pressure to reduce bias, (b) enhancing the understanding of the psychological basis of bias (which we identify as a major objective of this particular chapter), (c) enhancing providers' confidence in their ability to successfully interact with socially dissimilar patients, (d) enhancing emotional regulation skills specific to promoting positive emotions, (e) increasing perspective taking and affective empathy, and (f) improving the ability to build partnerships with patients.

Although the research summarized by Burgess et al. (2007) offers an optimistic portrayal of our individual and collective ability to counteract and inhibit the impact of deeply embedded stereotypes and latent biases, they present their findings with two key caveats. First, it is important to remember that genuine and enduring change, in addition to strong motivation and the right strategies, takes time and practice. Second, particularly in the initial stages of change and the development of new skills, providers must be willing to absorb a larger cognitive burden during clinical encounters. We can only suggest that although the added burdens may be formidable, the long-term rewards (for both patients and clinicians) are immense.

REFERENCES

Agency for Healthcare Research and Quality. (2004). *2004 National healthcare disparities report* (No. AHRQ No. 05-0014). Rockville, MD: U.S. Department of Health and Human Services.

Agency for Healthcare Research and Quality. (2008). *2008 National healthcare disparities report* (No. AHRQ No. 05-0014). Rockville, MD: U.S. Department of Health and Human Services.

Almgren, G. (2007). *Health care politics, policies and services: A social justice analysis*. New York, NY: Springer Publishing.

Almgren, G., & Ferguson, M. (1999). The urban ecology of hospital failure: Hospital closures in the city of Chicago, 1970–1991. *Journal of Sociology and Social Welfare, 25*(4), 5–26.

Anonymous. (2009). *The official definitive gomer rating scale*. Retrieved July 17, 2009, from http://www.lambert.net.au/med/gomerscale.pdf

Balaker, T. (1999). *What will moralists make of fuel-efficient SUVs?* Retrieved August 3, 2009, from http://reason.org/news/show/what-will-moralists-make-of-fu

Berggren, R. (2005). Unexpected necessities-inside Charity Hospital. *New England Journal of Medicine, 353*(15), 1550–1553.

Berra, K. (2000). Women, coronary heart disease, and dyslipidemia: Does gender alter detection, evaluation, or therapy? *Journal of Cardiovascular Nursing, 14*(2), 59–78.

Brown, I. (2006). Nurses' attitudes towards adult patients who are obese: Literature review. *Journal of Advanced Nursing, 53*(2), 221–232.

Brulle, R., & Pellow, D. (2006). Environmental justice: Human health and environmental inequalities. *Annual Review of Public Health, 27,* 103–124.

Burgess, D., van Ryn, M., Davidio, J., & Saha, S. (2007). Reducing racial bias among health care providers: Lessons from social-cognitive psychology. *Journal of General Internal Medicine, 22*(6), 882–887.

Condran, G., & Preston, S. (1994). Child mortality differences, personal health care practices, and medical technology: United States, 1900–1930. In L. C. Chen, A. Kleinman, & N. C. Ware (Eds.), *Health and social change in international perspective.* Boston, MA: Harvard University Press.

Davis, M. M., Jr., & Warner, A. R. (1918). *Dispensaries, their management and development : A book for administrators, public health workers, and all interested in better medical service for the people.* New York, NY: Macmillan.

deBoisblanc, B. (2006, July 25). It was heroism, not homicide, during Katrina. *Time.*

Evans, G., & Kantrowitz, E. (2002). Socioeconomic status and health: The potential role of environmental risk exposure. *Annual Review of Public Health, 23,* 303–331.

Gilens, M. (1999). *Why Americans hate welfare: Race, media, and the politics of antipoverty policy.* Chicago, IL: University of Chicago Press.

Goffman, E. (1963). *Stigma: Notes on the management of spoiled identity.* Englewood Cliffs, NJ: Prentice-Hall.

Gortmaker, S. L., Must, A., Perrin, J. M., Sobol, A. M., & Dietz, W. H. (1993). Social and economic consequences of overweight in adolescence and young adulthood. *New England Journal of Medicine, 329*(14), 1008–1012.

Gurwitz, J. H., Goldberg, R. J., Malmgren, J. A., Barron, H. V., Tiefenbrunn, A. J., Frederick, P. D., & Gore, J. M. (2002). Hospital transfer of patients with acute myocardial infarction: The effects of age, race, and insurance type. *The American Journal of Medicine, 112*(7), 528–534.

Himmelstein, D. U., Thorne, D., Warren, E., & Woolhandler, S. (2009). Medical bankruptcy in the United States, 2007: Results of a national study. *The American Journal of Medicine, 122*(8), 741–746.

Hirschman, C. (2004). The origins and demise of the concept of race. *Population and Development Review, 30*(3), 385–415.

Institute of Medicine. (2000). *Institute of Medicine-America's health care safety net: Intact but endangered*. Washington, DC: National Academies Press.

Institute of Medicine. (2002). *Unequal treatment: Confronting ethnic and racial disparities in health care*. Washington, DC: National Academies Press.

Kaiser Commission on Medicaid and the Uninsured. (2008). *The Uninsured: A primer*. Menlo Park, CA: The Henry J. Kaiser Family Foundation.

Kaminsky, J., & Gadaleta, D. (2002). A study of discrimination within the medical community as viewed by obese patients. *Obesity Surgery, 12*(1), 14–18.

Krieger, N. (2002). A glossary for social epidemiology. *Epidemiological Bulletin, 23*(1), 7–11.

Massey, D. (2007). *Categorically unequal: The American stratification system*. New York, NY: Russell Sage Foundation.

Massey, D., & Denton, N. (1993). *American apartheid: Segregation and the making of the underclass*. Cambridge, MA: Harvard University Press.

Meyer, I., Schwartz, S., & Frost, D. (2008). Social patterning of stress and coping: Does disadvantaged social statuses confer more stress and fewer coping resources. *Social Science and Medicine, 67*(3), 368–379.

Miller, I. (2007). *The back passage: And other true stories; demonstrating that laughter is best practice*. Retrieved January 11, 2010, from http://www.impactednurse.com/pics3/the_back_passage.pdf

Moore, K. A., & Waite, L. J. (1977). Early childbearing and educational attainment. *Family Planning Perspectives, 9*(5), 220–225.

Murray, C., & Herrstein, R. (1996). *The bell curve: Intelligence and class structure in American life*. New York, NY: Simon and Schuster.

Obst, T. E., Nauenberg, E., & Buck, G. M. (2001). Maternal health insurance coverage as a determinant of obstetrical anesthesia care. *Journal of Health Care Poor Underserved, 12*(2), 177–191.

Osterweis, M., Kleinman, A., & Mechanic, D. (Eds.). (1987). *Pain and disability: clinical, behavioral, and public policy perspectives*/Institute of Medicine, Committee on Pain, Disability, and Chronic Illness Behavior. Washington, DC: National Academies Press.

Pescosolido, B., Martin, J., Lang, A., & Olafsdottir, S. (2008). Rethinking theoretical approaches to stigma: A framework integrating normative influences on stigma (FINIS). *Social Science and Medicine, 67*(3), 431–440.

Phelan, J., Link, B., & Dovideo, J. (2008). Stigma and prejudice: One animal or two? *Social Science and Medicine, 67*(3), 358–367.

Rathore, S., Lenert, L., Weinfurt, K., Tinoco, A., Taleghani, C., Harless, W., & Schulman K. A. (2000). The effects of patient sex and race on medical students' ratings of quality of life. *American Journal of Medicine, 108*(7), 561–566.

Rogers, R. G., Hummer, R. A., & Nam, C. B. (2000). *Living and dying in the USA: Behavioral, health, and social differentials of adult mortality.* San Diego, CA: Academic Press.

Rosenberg, C. (1987). *The care of strangers: The rise of America's hospital system.* New York, NY: Basic Books.

Rudowitz, R., Rowland, D., & Shartzer, A. (2006). Health care in New Orleans before and after Hurricane Katrina. *Health Affairs, 25*(5), w393–w406.

Sanders-Phillips, K., Settles-Reaves, B., Walker, D., & Brownlow, J. (2009). Social inequality and racial discrimination: Risk factors for health disparities in children of color. *Pediatrics, 124*(Suppl. 3), s176–s186.

Sarrazin, M. V., Campbell, M., & Rosenthal, G. E. (2009). Racial differences in hospital use after acute myocardial infarction: Does residential segregation play a role? *Health Affairs, 28*(2), w368–w378.

Schulman, B. (2005). *The betrayal of work.* New York, NY: The New Press.

Schulte, L. J., & Battle, J. (2004). The relative importance of ethnicity and religion in predicting attitudes towards gays and lesbians. *Journal of Homosexuality, 47*(2), 127–143.

Schweik, S. (2009). *The ugly laws: Disability in public.* New York, NY: New York University.

She, P., & Livermore, G. A. (2007). Material hardship, poverty, and disability among working-age adults. *Social Science Quarterly, 88*(4), 970–990.

Solucient, L. L. C. (2005). *Profiles of U.S. hospitals.* Chicago, IL: Health Administration Press.

Starr, P. (1982). *The social transformation of American medicine.* New York, NY: Basic Books.

Stewart, A. J., & McDermott, C. (2004). Gender in psychology. *Annual Review of Psychology, 55,* 519–544.

Stivers, C. (2007). "So poor and so black": Hurricane Katrina, public administration, and the issue of race. *Public Administration Review, 67*(1), 48–56.

Stuber, J., Galea, S., & Link, B. (2008). Smoking and the emergence of a stigmatized social status. *Social Science and Medicine, 67,* 420–430.

Stuber, J., & Schlesinger, M. (2006). The sources of stigma in means-tested programs. *Social Science and Medicine, 63*(4), 933–945.

van Ryn, M., & Burke, J. (2000). The effect of patient race and socio-economic status on physicians' perceptions of patients. *Social Science and Medicine, 50,* 813–828.

Wilkinson, R. (1997). *Unhealthy societies: The afflictions of inequality.* Oxon, UK: Routledge.

Yancy, W., Olsen, M., Curtis, L., Schulman, K., Cuffe, M., & Oddone, E. (2005). Variations in coronary procedure utilization depending on body mass index. *Archives of Internal Medicine, 165*(12), 1381–1387.

4

Differences: Power, Privilege, and Disparities in Care

REVISITING THE STRUCTURAL CONTEXT OF HEALTH CARE

The Demography of the Health Care Work Force: Why This Matters

By demography of health care, we mean the social and economic characteristics of health care providers, and of the patients and communities they have a public and professional obligation to serve. Differences in social and economic characteristics of the health care provider work force, and those they serve, affect both the structural (system level) components of health care and the processes and outcomes that are generated at the level of patient–provider clinical encounters. Despite the shared ethical standards and humanitarian personal motivations common among health care providers who embrace uniformly high standards of care for all patients, there is compelling evidence from decades of research on health disparities that racial, cultural, and class differences between patients and their health care providers are a powerful source of disparities in clinical care (Institute of Medicine [IOM], 2003). There are a myriad of reasons for this, including the lack of cultural competency on the part of providers, language barriers that are both race and class based, and a (sometimes very well informed) reluctance to trust the motivations of health care providers. For example, data from a nationally representative survey of adult patients[1] reveal that although there has been some progress in removing racial barriers to patient/provider communication, non-White and Hispanic patients are much more likely to report negative communication experiences with providers. It is also very clear that social class differences negatively impact patient/provider communications. To the extent that the patients have less income and less education, they are also far less likely to report satisfactory communications with their health care provider (Agency for Healthcare Research and Quality [AHRQ], 2009). Although it might very reasonably be argued that some part of these findings may reflect the ability of more affluent patients to obtain higher-quality individualized health care, there is also strong evidence that minority health care providers tend to be more highly motivated to serve minority patients and lower-income communities (AHRQ, 2009).

Aside from the direct positive impacts that a racially and ethnically diverse health care provider labor force can produce via individual coracial or coethnic patient encounters, there are important indirect impacts on patient care. For example, it is pointed out by the Agency for Healthcare Research and Quality (AHRQ) that a more ethnically and racially diverse provider workforce can improve the cultural competence of health care organizations and the system as a whole—both through program designs and policies and through everyday collegial interactions (AHRQ, 2009).

The Racial and Ethnic Composition of the Nation's Health Care Labor Force

Table 4.1 shows the racial and ethnic composition of a broad sample of the health care professions and occupations, relative to the racial and ethnic composition of the U.S. labor force as a whole. By comparing the racial/ethnic percentages in the top row of Table 4.1 (Total Labor Force) with the percentages in specific health care professions and occupational categories, we can identify the extent to which particular racial or ethnic groups are either overrepresented or underrepresented in some professions/occupations. We first consider the more financially lucrative and high-status occupations,

---

[1] Agency for Healthcare Research and Quality, Medical Expenditure Panel Survey, 2002–2006.

TABLE 4.1
Health Care Professions and Occupations: Percentage by Race/Ethnicity 2008

	WHITE-NH	AFRICAN AMERICAN	ASIAN	HISPANIC/ LATINO	OTHER RACE(S)
Total Labor Force	68.9	10.7	4.8	14.0	1.6
Dentists	78.0	3.2	12.0	5.2	1.6
Physicians	70.4	6.1	16.6	5.8	1.2
Registered Nurse	76.1	9.9	7.8	4.7	1.5
Licensed Practical Nurse	65.2	22.0	3.6	7.1	2.1
Social Workers	61.1	24.3	2.9	10.1	1.7
Physical Therapists	78.9	3.8	13.0	3.5	0.7
Speech Therapists	85.9	2.2	4.8	6.2	0.9
Occupational Therapists	87.9	1.1	6.3	5.5	0.0
Nursing, Psychiatric, Home-Health Aides	46.1	34.2	4.3	13.1	2.2

From U.S. Bureau of Labor Statistics Division of Labor Force Statistics, from the Current Population Survey: Table 6. Employed persons by detailed occupation, race, and Hispanic or Latino ethnicity, 2008 annual averages.

NOTE: Because the Bureau of Labor Statistics did not separate White into Hispanic vs. Non-Hispanic for this table, an adjustment was made based on the 2000 population counts by race and Hispanic origin.

dentists and physicians. We immediately see that, consistent with the racial stratification that is evident in American society as a whole, non-Hispanic Whites are significantly overrepresented in these high-reward, high-status health professions, whereas African Americans and Hispanic/Latinos are significantly underrepresented. Asian Americans are also overrepresented among dentists and physicians (as well as in most of the health care professions shown), but it should be pointed out that the Bureau of Labor Statistics' decision to collapse Asian Americans into a single racial category obscures significant disparities in education and occupational status attainment among different groups of Asian Americans having distinct national origins, immigration histories, and socioeconomic distributions (Hirschman, 2001).

Non-Hispanic Whites are also overrepresented in all other professional categories shown, with the sole exception of the profession of social work, which interestingly has an overrepresentation of African Americans and at least a higher than typical representation of Hispanic/Latinos. In this light, it is worth noting that social work has a distinct professional mission toward the advancement of social justice and service on behalf of disadvantaged populations and communities (National Association of Social Workers, 2010)[2]—a characteristic of the profession that has tended to attract a higher proportion of students from historically disadvantaged racial and ethnic groups. Finally, in contrast to the health professions, the nonprofessional health care occupations shown in Table 4.1 (licensed practical nurses and nursing, psychiatric, and home-health aides) have a disproportionately high representation of African Americans—and among licensed practical nurses, a disproportionately high representation of Hispanic/Latinos.

So what does all of this mean, aside from the general correlation evident between racial and socioeconomic stratification in American society as a whole and the racial and socioeconomic stratification that is evident within the health professions? In visual symbolic terms, it means that for African Americans and Latinos (as well as many other racial/ethnic minorities) they see in the typical American hospital a stark reflection of their group's place in American society as a whole—in essence, that the persons having the highest status, privilege, and power tend to be non-Hispanic Whites. To further complete and reinforce the picture and central message, the hospital staff emptying the bedpans, changing the linens, mopping the floors, and serving food in the hospital cafeteria are disproportionately persons of color. In terms of the clinical encounter (where patient narratives are heard, bodies are inspected and invaded, and where crucial decisions and choices are made), the persons possessing the cultural and scientific power and authority are also typically non-Hispanic White. This may be comforting for White patients, but for many patients of color, this can be a troubling replication of the racially defined power relations they have experienced in other aspects of their lives (in their workplace, in their experience of public education, and even in their occasional

---

[2] That said, it should be kept in mind that the nation's first hospital social worker and pioneer of medical social work, Ida Cannon, was originally trained in the profession of nursing.

encounters with petty public officials).[3] These are issues we will explore in more depth at a later point in this chapter.

The Political Economy of Safety-Net Hospitals

By political economy, we mean the ways in which "scarce resources" (specifically in this case health care, power, status, and wealth) are allocated by political processes. The term "scarce resources" is used by economists and political philosophers to refer to things that are both highly desirable and in limited supply—thus creating dilemmas of just or at least generally accepted rules of allocation. In civil society, rules of allocation are, by definition, established through political processes, thus the term political economy. In the American system of health care, those activities and material resources that we formally regard as health care (e.g., diagnostic tests and procedures, medicines, medical equipment and supplies, and the time and advice of physicians) are treated as commodities—goods that are exchanged in the context of a market transaction between buyer and seller. This is in contrast to health care that is directly produced and allocated by government on the basis of general rules of entitlement—the latter representing the true definition of socialized medicine (despite political rhetoric to the contrary).

In contrast to countries that allocate health care on the basis of shared citizenship entitlements and medical necessity, it is a particular feature of the American health care system that considerations of power, status, and wealth drive the allocation of health care and thus have created the need for and social function of the safety-net system of health care. Were the maximization of population health and the minimization of health care disparities to become the primary determinants of the allocation of health care, the safety-net health care system would (as we progressed toward that goal) gradually wither away. This is true because the safety-net health care system serves two essential social functions that are tied to the particular political economy of American health care. The most visible function is to provide health care to the uninsured and those that have special illnesses and conditions that entail stigma and marginalization (IOM, 2000).

---

[3] As an example, in April 2010, the governor of the state of Arizona signed into law a provision that obligates local police to demand verification of immigration status of persons suspected (for whatever arbitrary reason) of being undocumented immigrants. Although the governor denied this law will result in racial profiling, this of course is a preposterous claim.

The second, less visible or "latent," social function of the safety-net system involves the allocation of power, status, and wealth in accordance with entrenched hierarchies of advantage.

Interrogating the Five Latent Functions of Safety-Net Hospitals

Our use of the term "latent function" in connection with safety-net hospitals derives from a specific theoretical tradition in American sociology, pioneered by Columbia University sociologist Robert Merton (1910–2003). Merton brought critical attention to the distinction between two kinds of institutional functions, *manifest functions* and *latent functions*. The manifest functions of the safety-net hospital system (as a type of social institution) are those that are articulated by the Institute of Medicine (IOM)—in essence, an institutional arrangement for the provision of health care to the uninsured and those who have special illnesses and conditions that entail stigma and marginalization (IOM, 2000). Latent functions, on the other hand, are those institutional functions that are neither explicitly recognized nor necessarily intended (Merton, 1936, 1957).[4] American social policy is replete with examples of latent institutional functions with unintended consequences—for example, the development of massive public housing projects that ultimately led to both the concentration and perpetuation of inner-city poverty (Massey & Denton, 1993). In the discussion that follows, we illuminate further what we see as the five key latent functions performed by the safety-net hospital system.

1. *By providing hospitals and clinics of last resort and quasi-universal accessibility for the poor,[5] the existence of this alternative health care system for the poor undermines (at least superficially) the political justification for a universal system of health care access that is organized on more egalitarian principles.*

---

[4] Robert Merton described the latent functions of institutions and institutional practices as those resulting in unforeseen or unintended consequences. We modify Merton's definition by interjecting the qualifier "necessarily" unintended, thus leaving room for the idea that there are latent functions that, although not openly acknowledged, are nonetheless recognized as beneficial for some individuals or groups.

[5] We say "quasi-universal accessibility," because safety-net hospitals and clinics are often overcrowded, understaffed, and geographically isolated from the poor populations and communities they are mandated to serve, thus undermining accessibility.

In various versions of Charles Dickens's beloved *A Christmas Carol*, the most telling declaration of Ebenezer Scrooge's hardened heart and absence of any charitable sentiment is captured in his incredulous response to a simple request for even a small contribution to the needs of the poor . . . "Are there no prisons, are there no workhouses?" Dickens's purpose in this narrative of Scrooge's reaction is to not only show readers how devoid of simple humane sympathy Scrooge had become, but more critically, also to remind British literate society of the latent social function of 19th century workhouses—to perpetuate the social tolerability of endemic poverty through the existence of workhouses as a somewhat less harsh alternative to starvation in the streets. There is a clear parallel between the latent function of Scrooge's workhouses as a way of reconciling the ruthless capitalism of the 19th century British society and Judeo-Christian morality, and the safety-net hospital systems' latent function as a means of avoiding a more critical examination of the national health care system's failure to provide an avenue of essential health care for all Americans. Although the unrepentant version of Ebenezer Scrooge would probably have considered former President George W. Bush to be a bleeding heart liberal, Bush's declaration that "[P]eople have access to health care in America. After all, you just go to an emergency room" has a very familiar Charles Dickens-like ring to it.[6] Taken at face value, Bush's declaration suggests that any of the nation's millions of uninsured could at their option show up at any nearby hospital emergency room (ER) and expect adequate and appropriate treatment for any number of health conditions. Were that the case, we would likely see no disparities in the management of conditions and diseases and health care outcomes between persons relying on hospital ERs and insured patients having access to ongoing care through a regular physician—but there is an overwhelming evidence-based consensus to the contrary (AHRQ, 2009). The other message embedded in Bush's declaration, paraphrased in its unvarnished meaning, is something akin to "Look, we already have mechanisms for the poor and uninsured to have access to health care. While it might be desirable to improve things, there is no particular urgency or moral imperative to reinvent a health care system that meets the needs of most of us."

---

[6] Public remarks by President George W. Bush made in Cleveland, Ohio (July 2007).

2. Safety-net hospitals and clinics provide a way to replicate and sustain segregation by race and social class that align with systems of racial and class segregation in the urban landscape and in the nation's educational system.

It is well established that a large share of the American urban landscape is defined by deeply embedded patterns of racial segregation, both in housing and in public education (Massey & Denton, 1993). Although efforts were made during the 1960s through the 1990s to desegregate schools through the notoriously unpopular, mandatory, and voluntary busing programs, the racial desegregation of public schools proved to be unachievable. Even modest gains in school desegregation were made unsustainable in the face of entrenched patterns of racial segregation in housing. While overt racism as a mechanism for the segregation of schools has been outlawed since the 1954 *Brown v. The Board of Education* U.S. Supreme Court ruling, the de facto racial segregation of schools endures attributable both to the persistence of racially segregated neighborhoods and the local taxation policies that impoverish the schools serving low-income neighborhoods. The safety-net hospital system in many American cities, very much like the public school system, functions as a separate and unequal system of care for African Americans (and other disadvantaged racial/ethnic groups)—not through the mechanism of overt racism, but through racial and ethnic disparities in health insurance coverage and entrenched patterns of health care access. For example, relative to White workers, the nearly two times as many African American workers lack health insurance and therefore are far more reliant on hospitals that have a specific mission to provide care for uninsured patients (Kaiser Family Foundation, 2009). This has also meant that hospitals that serve racially segregated and disadvantaged neighborhoods operate much closer to bankruptcy and have fewer dollars to invest in state-of-the art facilities and medical technology relative to private sector hospitals. This fact at last became evident to the American public in the wake of Hurricane Katrina, when the mostly White patients of the privately owned Tulane University Medical Center were evacuated by private helicopter, whereas the mostly African American patients in Charity Hospital of New Orleans languished in dreadful conditions for several days (Berggren, 2005). There is also strong evidence that African Americans living in cities where there are high levels of racial segregation are more likely to be admitted to inferior hospitals with higher mortality rates. In a very recent study that focused on hospitalization patterns among cities with high rates of racial segregation, it was found that (a) the risk of admission to such high-mortality hospitals was 35% higher for African Americans than for Whites and (b) African Americans were more likely than Whites to be admitted to high-mortality hospitals—even where lower-mortality hospitals were in closer proximity (Sarrazin, Campbell, & Rosenthal, 2009).[7] What is remarkable about this study is the fact that by focusing on African American Medicare recipients,the study speaks to the powerful and enduring influence of social factors other than health insurance on the persistence of racially segregated health care.

> 3. *As argued in Chapter 2, safety-net hospitals and clinics function as a place where the poor can trade at least limited access to health care for the professional education and future income and status benefits of the non-poor—in particular, the traditionally privileged segments of the population disproportionately represented in the high-status/high-pay health professions (see the first column of Table 4.1).*

Following the pre-Victorian era British physicians, during the late 1800s American doctors established a network of "dispensaries" in U.S. cities, which we would recognize today as community clinics for the poor. In this context, the term "dispensary" refers to the dispensing of medicine to patients who could not afford to pay the fees of a private physician. These 19th century dispensaries had three social functions: (a) They served as a mechanism for provision of essential health care to the poor, often through cooperative relationships between private physicians and local charity organization societies; (b) they enabled physicians to retain clear boundaries between the private practice of medicine consistent with a professional ethos of medical free enterprise and charity care for the poor; and (c) they functioned as a venue for the bartering of medical care and medicines in return for the lending of bodies and diseases for the purposes of medical education (Starr, 1982). Beginning with the first decades of the 1900s, these dispensaries were gradually replaced with a network of publicly financed teaching hospitals that today constitute the core of

---

[7] Although public safety-net hospitals have a much smaller profit margin (or return on equity) than private nonprofit and for-profit hospitals, these do not always translate to health care that is of lower quality. Depending on a variety of local contextual factors and the specific health condition in question, public safety-net hospitals often provide superior care. However, there is a clear general relationship between low-profit margins, antiquated facilities, out-dated technology, and lower-quality care (Shortell et al., 1994).

the nation's health care safety net. However, as we critically compare the functions of 19th century dispensaries with 21st century safety-net hospitals, it becomes readily apparent that the social functions of the 19th century dispensary endure in the contemporary safety-net hospital. That is, (a) safety-net hospitals serve a disproportionate share of poor patients (although publically financed programs like Medicaid and Medicare have largely subsumed the functions of private charity); (b) because they absorb the uninsured patients who are avoided by the mainstream not-for-profit and private sectors of the hospital industry, they enable both the modern medical profession and the hospital industry to cater to the more lucrative insured patient populations; and (c) to the extent that low-income and poor patients are dependent upon publically financed safety-net teaching hospitals for their care, there is a de facto bartering of their bodies for medical education in exchange for health care. On this last point, although it can be argued that to the extent that more insured patients also seek services at teaching hospitals, they too are subject to a similar exchange—insured patients are able to access health care at any number of nonteaching hospitals that are only too eager for their business.[8]

> 4. *The secondary beneficiaries of the health care professionals trained in safety-net hospitals include middle- and upper-class Americans, who can avoid being the training fodder of novice students, interns, and residents while eventually reaping the benefits of their experience as patients in private sector hospitals.*

America's public teaching hospitals are often the best in the world for certain kinds of specialized care and sometimes the best available for even routine care depending on the region. That said, public teaching hospitals that also function as safety-net providers, often can be characterized by a frenetic pace of activities, noisy patient care corridors, crowded clinics, and legions of students and interns from various disciplines endeavoring to gain professional confidence and competence. The patients of these places, whether they like it or not, provide the grist for medical education through their disabilities, diseases, suffering, and (if all goes well) their cure and recovery. We collectively benefit from a shared willingness to risk the errors of

---

[8] There are only very limited circumstances where insured patients are compelled to chose care at a teaching hospital over the nonteaching sector of the hospital industry such as highly specialized care or due to constraints of geographical proximity.

novices as they gradually acquire the knowledge and skills essential to competent professional practice, and a surprisingly small proportion of patients resist having students involved in their care (even student phlebotomists!). However, consistent with the arguments in the preceding paragraph, this is not a burden that is shared equally. Insured patients, because they can access private sector hospitals that don't have the large teaching mission sustained by public teaching hospitals, can reap the health care benefits delivered by competently trained health care professionals, while being less exposed to the mistakes of career novices.

5. Safety-net hospitals institutionalize, in symbolic terms, the acceptability of a two-tiered health care system.

Even among modern democratic societies, there are large differences in the extent to which an ethos of egalitarianism is prevalent across all social institutions. There is also variation in the extent to which inequality is considered acceptable in private material conditions, but deemed unacceptable in core institutions such as the public educational system and the health care system. Despite political rhetoric to the contrary, Americans have a very high tolerance of inequality both in public education and in health care, but we reconcile reality with political rhetoric by the funding of secondary systems of provision for the poor. In the case of impoverished public schools located in poor neighborhoods, we infuse targeted federal dollars that are supposed to offset the effects of endemic poverty and disparities in local funding—as an alternative to pursuing genuine parity in the funding of basic education for all students, rich and poor alike. Funding poor schools with targeted federal dollars makes it seem as if we are actively pursuing equality in education, without actually having to achieve genuine parity in the educational funding of all students. The safety-net hospital system performs a similar kind of latent function. That is, by creating a highly visible separate system of care for the poor and uninsured, we can at once (a) claim credit for making hospital care accessible for all Americans, and (b) place a beneficent halo over the institutional symbols of a two-tiered health care system. The most famous safety-net hospitals in the nation (e.g., Bellevue Hospital in New York City, Cook County Hospital in Chicago, Charity Hospital of New Orleans, and Jackson Memorial Hospital in Miami) symbolize a national commitment to hospital care for the poor, while institutionalizing the legitimacy of a two-tiered health care system.

Reconciling the Latent and Manifest Social Functions of Safety-Net Hospitals

In the 1971 movie satire, *The Hospital*,[9] Chief of Surgery Dr. Henry Bock (played brilliantly by George C. Scott) screams his rage and despair in what is remembered as one of the late George C. Scott's truly classic Hollywood rants . . . "It is all rubbish isn't it? I mean . . . transplants, antibodies, we can produce birth ectogenetically, we can clone people like carrots, and half the kids in this ghetto haven't been inoculated for polio! We have established an enormous medical entity and we're sicker than ever! We cure nothing! We heal nothing! The whole goddamn wretched world, strangulating in front of our eyes. . . ."

Like George C. Scott's anguished Dr. Henry Bock, it may seem that in our analysis of the safety-net hospital system's *latent social functions*, we have been consumed and blinded by cynicism and despair. Although we concede we have presented a fairly bleak and admittedly harsh appraisal of the latent social functions of safety-net hospitals, we will now turn our attention to the more noble purposes and crucial humanitarian social functions of safety-net hospitals—the functions that social theorist Robert Merton would describe as the *manifest social functions* of safety-net hospitals.

The *manifest social functions* of social institutions are those that are conscious, readily visible, and intended. The manifest social functions of safety-net hospitals, including those described by the IOM's (2000) *America's Health Care Safety Net: Intact but Endangered*, can be readily observed in a casual sampling of the public relations materials and mission statements from safety-net hospitals and their parent organizations. These include not only the provision of health care to patients and poor communities regardless of their ability to pay, but also their teaching and research functions. For example, Miami's Jackson Memorial Hospital makes visible its public health care, teaching, and research functions in its simple but to-the-point motto: "An academic health system with a public health care mission" (Jackson Health System, 2010). Chicago's Cook

---

[9] This dark satire of the American care system, written by Paddy Chayefsky and directed by Arthur Hiller, was both riveting and in many respects prescient in its portrayal of the complex interactions of humanitarianism, greed, power, unintended consequences, and embedded systems of oppression. The film helped spark (instead of health care system reform) the urban hospital drama genre, which in the decades since its debut has generated enormous profits for the television industry.

County Hospital[10] mission statement is directly reflective of the IOM's description of the central public purpose of safety-net hospitals: "To provide a Comprehensive Program of Quality Health Care with Respect and Dignity, to the residents of Cook County, regardless of their ability to pay" (John H. Stroger Jr. Hospital of Cook County, 2010). As a final example, the National Association of Public Hospitals and Health Systems (NAPH) speaks of the manifest social functions of safety-net hospitals as providing "high-quality health services for all patients, including the uninsured and underinsured, regardless of ability to pay . . . [and to] train many of America's doctors, nurses, and other health care providers" (NAPH, 2010).

As another manifest social function, safety-net hospitals also provide the institutional context for individual health care providers to realize what, for many, are very genuine and deeply held humanitarian and altruistic career ideals. For a large share of the nurses, social workers, physicians, and others choosing career employment in a safety-net hospital, no other setting would be likewise sufficient to fulfill their sense of professional purpose. Although it is always tempting to critically deconstruct sentiments and motivations like altruism and humanitarianism, we embrace the idea that safety-net hospitals continue to attract some of the best and the brightest for career employment—precisely because they are professionally fulfilled by serving those most in need of care, despite inferior pay, professional status, and difficult working conditions.

The manifest social functions of safety-net hospitals, although they coexist with latent social functions, sometimes directly conflict with them. Take, for example, the inherent conflict between the mission statement for Miami's Jackson Memorial Hospital ". . . to build the health of the community by *providing a single, high standard of quality care* [authors' italics] regardless of ability to pay" (Jackson Health System, 2010) and the latent social function of the safety-net hospital system that entails the institutionalization and perpetuation of the two-tiered health care system. Although Jackson Memorial Hospital has continuously strived in a myriad of deliberate ways to reduce endemic disparities in health care on the basis of ability to pay, as an organization it is embedded in a structural context that defines its place and reason for being as a component part of the financially strapped second tier of the nation's

---

[10] In 2002, rebuilt and renamed as the John H. Stroger Jr. Hospital.

two-tiered health care system. In February of 2010, this conflict between Jackson Memorial Hospital's manifest function as a high-quality provider of health care for all residents of Miami-Dade County, regardless of their ability to pay, and its latent function as the institutional manifestation of the two-tiered health care system resulted in the hospital's financial collapse. As the national economic recession imposed an ever-growing burden of uninsured patients on Jackson Memorial Hospital, the hospital's operating losses mounted—such that by February of 2010, the hospital found itself with a budget deficit of $230 million (Weaver, 2010). Even as early as 2008, the then CEO of Jackson Memorial Hospital had warned the Miami-Dade County public health commissioners that "its business model catering to the indigent, poor and uninsured was unsustainable" (Weaver, 2010). Rephrased in unvarnished prose, the former CEO of Jackson Memorial Hospital was conceding that the hospital could not sustain a business strategy that would seek to fulfill its public mission as a high-quality provider of health care for the poor and uninsured. In truth, the only path for the financial solvency of Jackson Memorial Hospital (short of achieving the single-handed overhaul of the nation's health care system) entailed a fundamental betrayal of its public mission—the discovery of ways *to avoid* the provision of high-quality health care to the indigent, poor, and uninsured.

Jackson Memorial Hospital's plight illustrates the necessity of recognizing the coexistence of the manifest and latent social functions of safety-net hospitals and the places where they conflict. By the time the leadership of Jackson Memorial Hospital recognized the irreconcilable conflict between the public mission of the hospital and its fiscal solvency, it was too late. Similarly, it may be said that George C. Scott's character in *The Hospital* sank into suicidal despair because, after a career of professional denial and self-delusion, he had arrived at a point where all he could see was his hospital's (and his own) failure to achieve the impossible—the reconciliation of his hospital's manifest humanitarian social purposes with the gritty reality of its being part and parcel of a larger system of social stratification. We suggest that somewhere between starry-eyed idealism about the nature of safety-net hospitals and safety-net health care and bitter professional cynicism, there is a healthy balance to be achieved by the deep appreciation of complexity and a willingness to interrogate all of the possible social functions of both safety-net hospitals and the professional socialization process.

THE INTERPERSONAL COMPONENT OF DISPARITIES
IN HEALTH CARE

Patient-Centered Health Care and Equity of Care: The Impacts of Race,
Class, Privilege, and Power

The AHRQ[11] identifies high quality of care as being effective, safe,
timely, patient centered, equitable, and efficient (AHRQ, 2009). In
the discussion that follows, we focus on two of these key dimensions of health care quality, patient centeredness and equitability,
and the ways each is impacted by patient and provider differences
in race, class, power, and privilege. We believe that to the extent
that health care is patient centered, it also promotes health care that
is equitable, so we will begin by considering the nature of patient-
centered care.

According to the AHRQ, patient-centered care is health care that is
"respectful of and responsive to individual patient preferences, needs,
and values and ensuring that patient values guide all clinical decisions"
(AHRQ, 2009, p. 35). Under the most optimal of circumstances, being
sensitive and truly responsive to patient preferences, needs, and values
can often be difficult to achieve. Even patients who share the same race,
class, and gender characteristics as their clinical provider, and are in a
position to pay for their care, can sometimes have a very difficult time
expressing their needs and preferences in a transparent way. However,
to the extent that the clinician shares the same social background characteristics as the patient, they are in a much better position to discern
needs and preferences, and, if not, to at least prompt expression of them.
On the other hand, differences in race, class, and ethnicity can impose
significant additional impediments, even where a common language is
shared. It is also highly relevant when these differences are hierarchical—
as is typically the case in safety-net health care settings.

Racial/Ethnic Hierarchy and the Communication of Patient
Preferences, Needs, and Values

In 2003, the IOM published *Unequal Treatment: Confronting Racial and
Ethnic Disparities in Health Care* (National Academies Press, Washington,
DC). As the title suggests, it is a comprehensive analysis of the evidence

---

[11] The AHRQ is the health services research arm for the U.S. Department of Health and
Human Services focusing on the evaluation and improvement of health care quality in the
United States.

pertaining to racial and ethnic discrimination in health care. Although this IOM report finds that there is little direct evidence that overt racism among health care professionals continues to adversely affect the quality of care for minority patients, it does concede that there are significant disparities in health care that originate in the patient–clinician encounter as a result of racial differences in both the expression and discernment of patient preferences, needs, and values. Despite our disagreement with the IOM report's interpretation of the evidence concerning the influence of overt racism on health disparities, we do believe the IOM report is correct in its conclusion that well-intended clinicians end up generating significant racial disparities in health care through very subtle subjective processes of diagnostic interpretation and assessment.[12] In fact, we believe the latter, more latent processes, are much more prevalent and also more powerful than overt prejudice in their genuine effects.

The cultural ideal of the clinical encounter is a face-to-face interaction between patient and provider that is founded upon mutual trust, honesty, empathy, objectivity, scientific knowledge, and deep concern for the patient's preferences and best interests. As noble as this sounds, a variety of factors make this ideal exceedingly difficult to accomplish. In the reality of American health care, the clinical encounter typically involves three actors: the clinician (e.g., physician, nurse practitioner, or physical therapist), the physically absent but omnipresent utilization manager, and the patient. All three actors have the capacity to exercise discretion in what is shared and offered, and all three actors bring their own very subjective orientation to the "facts," purposes, and priorities of the encounter. Moreover, all three actors are encumbered by uncertainty and specific disadvantages with respect to critical information. Thus, the clinical encounter is not typically governed by complete objectivity, science, and clarity of purpose—but rather by a fog of uncertainty and discretion. To paraphrase the IOM's *Unequal Treatment* report on this point, despite benign intent, "discretion and ambiguity create the conditions within which race and ethnicity may become salient and operative in ways that are more likely to produce disparities in health care" (IOM, 2003, p. 128). As noted in *Unequal Treatment*, there are a number of ways in which each actor in the clinical encounter

---

[12] In this report, 11 of the 13 studies cited on racial disparities in clinical care and outcomes that had the appropriate controls for confounding factors, showed distinct patterns of racial disparities in care that could not be explained by patient characteristics other than race [see *Unequal Treatment: Confronting Racial and Ethnic Disparities in Health Care* (IOM, 2003, pp. 380–383)].

introduces the potential for disparities in care—absent the distrust, malicious intent, or overt negligence that is often assumed to be the basis of disparities in health care. In fact, there is a substantial body of evidence from the literature in the behavioral and social sciences establishing that patients vary greatly in their perception of symptoms, their reporting of pain, their conceptual frameworks of health and illness, and their help-seeking behavior—and that some of this variation correlates with race and ethnicity (IOM, 2003). Differences between the patient and clinician by race, ethnicity, and social class then serve to compound the difficulties in clinical perception and interpretation.[13]

However, the genesis of health care disparities is not just about racial, class, or cultural "differences" in health beliefs, the reporting of symptoms, and help-seeking behavior—we believe that the hierarchical nature of these differences is also important. By hierarchical, we mean that both the patient and the clinician bring into the clinical encounter some legacy of intergroup domination that has effects that are at least as important as such differences as race, ethnicity, or sex. One way of thinking about this is to consider what your response would be to the following hypothetical question on a national survey:

> There are two individuals in a patient examining room, one a patient and the other a doctor. Of the two, which is the one more likely to be a White male?

The fact that most persons answering this question would readily suggest that it would be the doctor (absent any knowledge about the race and sex of the other person in the examining room) says a lot about the embeddedness of just two kinds of hierarchies common to the clinical encounter, one racial and the other sexual.

Focusing on race, non-White racial groups typically deal with two kinds of power imbalances in the clinical encounter—one racial and the other cultural. The first and most obvious, racial, is represented in overrepresentation of Whites in the physician labor force. Independent of any physician's belief system and his or her socioeconomic background, possessing the racial identity of a dominant group often encumbers the physician's ability to establish the level of mutual trust,

---

[13] A substantial part of the discussion of the origin of health disparities in the clinical encounter is taken from Almgren (2007).

empathy, and communication he or she might more readily achieve in the absence of the legacy of racial conflict and oppression that is large in American society. For example, in contrast to non-Hispanic Whites, historically disadvantaged racial groups are far less likely to report that their health care providers listen carefully, explain things clearly, respect what they say, and spend enough time with them (AHRQ, 2009). Although it may be difficult to disentangle the various factors that may be at play in these racial disparities in patient/provider communication (such as racial disparities in having a regular provider of health care, language barriers, confounding influences of social class, and subtle biases and stereotyping), it is clear that race plays a role in the extent to which patients feel respected and empowered in their relationships with their providers.

The second kind of power imbalance in the clinical encounter, specific to physicians, entails a dynamic in American medicine that is prevalent in all patient–physician encounters—the *cultural authority* of physicians in American society. Starr (1982) introduced the idea of the American physician's cultural authority in his critical history of the American health care system, *The Social Transformation of American Medicine*. By cultural authority, Starr means not only the capacity to diagnose disease and prescribe treatment (Starr defines this as *social authority*), but rather the ability to define reality . . . "cultural authority entails the construction of reality through the definitions of fact and value" (Starr, 1982, p. 13). Despite the rise of consumerism in health care, the role of the Internet in affording the public access to the worldwide medical discourse, and legions of malpractice lawyers, the physician holds a unique position in American society as the professional embodiment of wisdom, science, and humanitarian benevolence. Americans have been socialized to defer to the wisdom and benevolence of physicians, not only on medical concerns and issues, but also on all aspects of our lives that affect our well-being and our sense of coherence. The cultural authority of the medical profession in American society can be observed in a variety of ways, among them the use of physicians (or actors playing the part of physicians) in television advertising for a range of products and services that have little relationship to health.

Equitable Patient Care and Health Care Disparities

Equitable patient care is defined as providing care that does not vary in quality because of personal characteristics such as gender, race, ethnicity, geographic location, and socioeconomic factors (AHRQ, 2009).

While the IOM's (2003) *Unequal Treatment* report makes the point that disparities in health care, including variations in health care quality, do not in and of themselves provide prima facie evidence of discrimination on the part of individual health care providers, they are both highly prevalent and detrimental to health outcomes. Whether through overtly discriminatory belief systems and attitudes on the part of providers, the effects of subtle biases and stereotypes on the subjective processes of diagnostic interpretation and assessment, or institutional factors such as racial disparities in access to high-quality clinics—the disparities in health care quality by gender, race, ethnicity, and social class are both well documented and persistent. To cite just a few of the many illuminating examples of disparities in health care from the *2009 National Health Care Disparities Report* (AHRQ, 2009), we consider findings as they pertain to cancer prevention screening for women, management of diabetes, end-stage renal disease, and pneumococcal vaccination for older adults.[14]

Cancer Prevention Screening.   Income, of course, matters: As of 2005, the only groups to meet the *Healthy People 2010* target of 70% of women of age 40 and over receiving a mammogram within the past 2 years were women with high income, women with at least some college education, and women with private insurance. This compares to a screening rate of only 48.5% for poor women. Ethnicity and race also matter: Both African American and Hispanic women had significantly lower mammography rates than non-Hispanic White women.

Management of Diabetes.   According to the AHRQ, recommended care for the management of type I and type II diabetes includes three components: (a) HbA1c testing, (b) dilated eye examination, and (c) foot examination. Although only about 42% of White diabetics received all three components of diabetes care, the rates of appropriate care for both Hispanics and persons living in poverty were much lower (31.6% for Hispanics and 33.4% for the poor). Even though African American diabetics did not appear to be statistically distinct from White diabetics in their rates of receiving all three components of recommended care, their rates of hospitalization for short-term complications were more than three times those of Whites. Income is also clearly

---

[14] The findings cited by the AHRQ *2009 National Health Disparities Report* are based on data collected for the years 2005–2007, depending upon the specific measure reported.

related to the risk of diabetic complications; the rate of hospital admissions for short-term complications was almost three times as high for people living in communities with median household incomes of less than $25,000 as it was for people living in communities with median household incomes of $45,000 or more.

End-Stage Renal Disease.   One prevalent consequence of poorly managed diabetes (or hypertension as well) is kidney failure. Although it may seem that universal eligibility for renal dialysis under the Medicare program should all but eliminate significant racial, ethnic, and income disparities in the quality of care in end-stage renal disease, in fact that is not the case. When the AHRQ compared the adequacy of dialysis (measured as the urea reduction ratio equal to or greater than 65%) by race, it found dramatic disparities in rates of adequate dialysis by race—with African Americans and Hispanics disadvantaged relative to non-Hispanic Whites, and non-Hispanic Whites disadvantaged relative to Asians.[15] There are also racial and ethnic disparities evident in the likelihood of receiving kidney transplantation—with African Americans, Hispanics, and American Indian/Alaska Natives in kidney failure having significantly lower rates of registration for kidney transplantation relative to both Whites and Asians. For example, the AHRQ found that only 11.6% of American Indian/Alaska Native end stage patients were registered for transplantation, compared to 17.7% for Whites and 26.7% for Asians.

Pneumococcal Vaccination for Older Adults.   Vaccination for pneumonia is both an inexpensive and an effective means of preventing illness and premature mortality for susceptible populations, including older adults. The availability of Medicare coverage for all adults at age 65 suggests that we should not see the large racial and ethnic disparities in recommended health care that are observed in the younger age ranges, but in fact we do. Only 44% of African Americans of age 65 and older have ever had pneumococcal vaccination, relative to a figure of 60% for Whites. For Hispanic older adults, the rate of pneumococcal vaccination is only about one-half of that for non-Hispanic Whites. Notably, these racial and ethnic disparities are evident across income levels.

---

[15] It should be kept in mind that there is likely great variation within the general racial category of "Asian," which includes an array of national origins with distinct cultural and socioeconomic characteristics.

That said, there are income effects as well. Only 48.6% of poor older adults received pneumococcal vaccination compared with a vaccination rate of 61% of high-income older adults.

The Multilevel Origins of Health Care Disparities

The existence of various kinds of disparities in health care, as disturbing as they are, tells us little about their causal origins, or the paths that we should be pursuing as we seek ways to eradicate them. Although race, ethnicity, gender, income, and geography are all demographic factors that are associated with differences in the quality of health care, being at higher risk for substandard health care because you happen to be African American, poor, or a resident of rural Mississippi does not suggest that race, income, or geography are causal. They are simply risk factors that are suggestive of *complex multilevel causal processes*—by multilevel, we mean that health care disparities can be consequent to social processes at the level of the individual, at the level of the organization that delivers health care, and at the level of the social institutions that provide the fundamental structural context for the delivery of health care. It is usually the case that any particular health care disparity that is observed is consequent to processes at all three levels. To illustrate the multilevel origins of health care disparities, we will examine some potential causal processes in the generation of health care disparities in the pneumococcal vaccination for older adults. Given that health insurance coverage through Medicare is, for all practical purposes, universally available to Americans over age 65, why is it that both low-income and African American older adults are substantially less likely to receive an inexpensive, simple, and highly effective measure against premature mortality from pneumonia?

Institutional Level Causal Processes.   By institutional level we mean the fundamental social arrangements a society creates to address problems that are essential to its perpetuation. Our health care system, in this sense, is a particular kind of social institution, in essence a highly complex and enduring set of relationships and procedures that are intended to promote population health. Population health is essential to the perpetuation of society in at least two fundamental ways. The most obvious is population survival itself—human history is replete with examples of societies that have either withered away or been dramatically transformed by rampant disease and death. Population health is also essential to the survival of societies via the relationships between robust population health and such competitive imperatives as economic productivity and military strength. Societies vary in the ways in which they have organized their health care systems—and in the United States we have used a mixed public and private approach that, in various ways, favors some segments of society and disadvantages others. We see this play out in the likelihood of an elderly African American citizen receiving vaccination for pneumonia relative to a White counterpart.

Although African Americans are just as likely to be eligible for Medicare health-insurance coverage as Whites, it is far less likely that any given African American older adult will either have had health insurance or a usual source of health care during most preceding years of their life span (Corbie-Smith, Flagg, Doyle, & O'Brien, 2002). This is because the probability of having health insurance through the majority of the life span in the American health care system is tied to race—primarily through the mechanisms of income, education, and occupational status. As a result, as older adults, African Americans (even with Medicare health care insurance) are less likely to be connected to a regular provider who monitors their health risks and potential need for a vaccination against pneumonia.

Organizational Level Causal Processes. By organizational level processes, we are referring to the organizational characteristics of the clinics and hospitals that deliver health care and the quality of care delivered. African Americans, relative to Whites, are also less likely to have access to high-quality health care providers. According to the *2009 National Health Care Disparities Report*, African Americans fared worse than Whites on 15 indicators of health care quality, whereas they were favored on only 4.

There are large differences in the quality of preventive services by health care setting, in part because some health care settings are far more suited to emergency medicine and urgent care than preventive care. On this point, the IOM notes that relative to Whites, African Americans are far more likely to rely on safety-net hospital emergency rooms, outpatient departments, and publicly sponsored community clinics than Whites for their usual source of care (IOM, 2003).

Individual Level Causal Processes. When confronted by racial disparities in health care that cannot be attributed wholly to institutional factors, like racial differences in health insurance coverage, it suggests the possibility of racial discrimination on the part of individual providers. This indeed seems to be the case with the racial disparities evident in the vaccination for pneumonia in the Medicare-eligible population. Because health care is embedded in a racially stratified society, we cannot and should not wholly dismiss overt racial discrimination on the part of individual clinicians as a potential factor. Racial bigotry exists at all levels of American society and across all occupational categories—including our most prestigious professions. However, we believe it is unlikely that overt, intentional racial discrimination plays more than a minor role in the production of health disparities at the level of the clinical encounter. We believe, consistent with the evidence from dozens of rigorous studies, that far more prevalent and insidious processes of racial discrimination account for the kinds of findings illuminated by the National Health Care Disparities Report series.

It has been well established that, as a general social phenomenon, the way we interpret the behavior of others is influenced by race, class, ethnicity, and other demographic characteristics, and that the racial effect on behavioral interpretation is stronger to the extent that the behavior is ambiguous (van Ryn, 2002). This is a two-way interactive process between the patient and the provider, one that often results in race-based variations in the perception and reporting of symptoms, the expression and interpretation of preferences, and the development of patient/provider rapport—variations that can in turn produce disparities in health care absent any conscious or malicious intentions (IOM, 2003). As summarized by van Ryn (2002, p. 143), although physicians (as one example) are trained and generally expected to view each patient objectively, these expectations are unrealistic in light of deeply embedded cognitive processes and structures that enable us all to navigate a highly complex social world. Beginning from infancy, we develop beliefs and expectations about categories or groups of people and generalize these beliefs and expectations to all individuals we have mentally assigned to that group/category. These subtle and typically unconscious processes of placing individuals into categories with assumed common traits and then generalizing these traits to that individual fulfill the classic definition of stereotyping.[16]

Although physicians are cautioned against stereotyping throughout their educational careers, it is naïve to assume that physicians (any more than the rest of us) are invulnerable to the employment of

---

[16] Readers will note that van Ryn's synopsis of the stereotyping process in the context of physicians replicates the stereotyping process described in Chapter 3, Stratification and Stigma).

stereotypes in all spheres of social life—including clinical practice. Both van Ryn (2002) and the IOM's (2003) *Unequal Treatment* report cite compelling evidence substantiating the role that stereotyping plays in provider beliefs and expectations of patients. In particular, a number of studies have shown that negative stereotyping (assigning negative traits to individual patients based on their race, gender, sexual orientation, etc.) can influence diagnosis and treatment. As one example of such studies, a chief medical resident surreptitiously tracked whether and how often patient race was mentioned during staff case presentations and whether negative patient characteristics (such as low intelligence and uncooperativeness) were also noted. The investigators found that race was more often cited in cases involving African American patients than in those involving White patients, and that in African American patients with negative ascribed traits, race was always mentioned, whereas in White patients with negative traits, race was mentioned in less than half of the cases (Finucane & Carrese, 1990). In another study that used physician survey data to examine the degree to which patient race and socioeconomic status affected physicians' perceptions of patients during a postangiogram encounter (physician $N = 193$, patient $N = 618$), it was shown that physicians tended to perceive African Americans and members of low and middle socioeconomic status (SES) groups more negatively on a number of dimensions than they did Whites and upper SES patients. In particular, race was associated with physicians' assessments of patient intelligence, feelings of affiliation toward the patient, and beliefs about the patient's likelihood of risk behavior and adherence with medical advice (van Ryn & Burke, 2000).

Returning to the findings that relative to Whites, a substantially smaller proportion of Medicare-eligible African Americans receive pneumococcal vaccination, it seems reasonable to suggest that such racially influenced factors as rapport with the patient and positive beliefs about treatment adherence might promote the likelihood of aggressive preventive care. On the patient side of the interaction, we should also consider the crucial role that patient/provider rapport plays in the acceptance of medical advice and the likelihood that the patient will even make him- or herself accessible to the provider for routine preventive care. In this regard, we note that even among White older adults, there is a large share (40%) who are also not vaccinated for pneumonia—suggesting that factors such as patient/provider rapport and provider discretion may be particularly influential in the likelihood of vaccination.

Interrogating Our Own Agency in Health Care Disparities

The IOM's (2003) *Unequal Treatment: Confronting Racial and Ethnic Disparities in Health Care* is rigorous, comprehensive, illuminating, and in our view a groundbreaking acknowledgment of provider agency in the production of health care disparities on the basis of factors such as race, ethnicity, education, and income. That said, we are also struck by the extraordinarily cautious and conservative tone of the report—as if the IOM is endeavoring to convince the most skeptical of audiences that it is indeed possible, even likely, that the profession of medicine is as vulnerable to stereotyping and unconscious discrimination as the rest of society. We suggest that for a significant share of this skeptical audience, they will continue to equate their conscious beliefs and humanitarian motivations with their unconscious perceptions—despite the most rigorous and voluminous of clinical evidence to the contrary. For some clinicians, acknowledgment of the possibility of personal agency in the perpetuation of health disparities is just too painful and too threatening to abide. For others of us (hopefully the majority), we can follow the path of reason, evidence, and humility—and thus be prepared to embrace the reality that stereotyping and the discriminatory actions that sometimes follow are both endemic in human experience and deeply embedded in our own cognitive processes. Interrogating our own agency in the perpetuation of health care disparities is not an easy or comfortable process; in fact it is a life's work if we take it seriously—but in the end, we are far better prepared to engage in genuinely patient-centered, evidence-based practice. So what does interrogating our own agency entail?

Reflexivity, Positionality, and Privilege. In contrast to popular approaches to diversity training, which tend to focus on the eradication of various forms of stereotyping, interrogating our own agency entails a deeply self-reflective process—one that is centered on discerning how we ourselves fit within intersecting systems of social stratification. This form of self-reflection about one's position within the hierarchy of social relationships, and how that frames interpretations, methods of inquiry, and conclusions about "facts," is known in the social sciences as *reflexivity* (Sultana, 2007). Although the concept originates in postmodernist approaches to social science research, we believe the concept is deeply relevant to genuinely culturally competent clinical practice. To reemphasize a point made earlier in this chapter, there are a range of differences between patients and providers that represent not only differences in such cultural dimensions as language, perspective, norms, and values, but also disparities in social power and privilege. Although we may have the "privilege" of sublimating or denying the race- and class-based status and power advantages we often have over our patients and the disadvantaged communities we serve (in fact, denying one's power and privilege often feels sort of noble and altruistic), to many of our patients, these distinctions are a daily reality of their existence. For a large share of the patients and communities that rely on safety-net health care providers, theirs is a harsh social space that is built upon and saturated with various systems of stratification.

Whereas politicians, ideologues, and a large share of the public may enjoy the luxury of denying the possibility of their personal agency in the perpetuation of such outcomes as disparities in health care, we in the health professions are called to a higher standard of self-reflection and awareness. We think of this as *the process of interrogating the possibilities of our own agency in the perpetuation of health care disparities.*

Interrogating the possibilities of our own agency in the perpetuation of health thus entails two kinds of knowledge. The first is a general appreciation of the ways in which providers who generally consider themselves to be champions of equity and patient-centered care can actually play a role in the generation of health care disparities. The second kind of knowledge, which is far more difficult to acquire, entails the examination of positional privilege. We will turn to the easier task first—gaining an appreciation of the ways in which providers can, absent conscious intent, play a role in generating disparities in health care.

Figure 4.1, made available from van Ryn's (2002) summary of the evidence on provider contributions to health care disparities, presents an illuminating graphic synopsis of the nonintentional production of health care disparities by well-meaning clinicians. Although the processes described in the figure pertain to physicians, they can be extended to any health profession with diagnostic functions—including, for example, the seemingly less omnipotent professions of social work and nursing. As Figure 4.1 suggests, both the patient's help-seeking behavior and the provider's embedded and unconscious beliefs about race and ethnicity (as well as other factors such as gender and social class) can directly shape a provider's interpretation of symptoms and problems, which in turn influences treatment decisions. However, it is also suggested that the provider's interpersonal behavioral responses (participatory style, warmth, content, information sharing, and

FIGURE 4.1   Hypothesized mechanisms through which provider factors influence race/ethnicity disparities in health care received, independent of institutional and organizational level factors

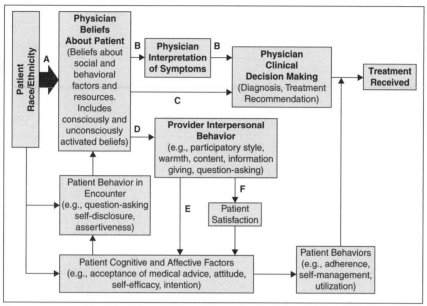

From van Ryn, M. (2002). Research on the provider contribution to race/ethnicity disparities in medical care. *Medical Care,* 40(Suppl. 1). Used with permission.

questions framing of) can also shape the patient's behavior during the encounter—in ways that can either reinforce or challenge a provider's unconscious beliefs and stereotypes. We suspect that, based on the tendency of racial and ethnic minorities to report a higher incidence of unsatisfactory communications with providers, what more often happens in the patient–provider encounter is the subtle unintended mutual reinforcement of cultural and racial stereotypes[17]— often to the completely inadvertent detriment of equitable patient care.

Positional Privilege.   The pathways to unintended disparities depicted in Figure 4.1 should resonate with most of us, at least to the extent that we do not consider ourselves immune from the unconscious processes of stereotyping that have enabled us to navigate the

---

[17] We use as our primary examples racial and ethnic stereotyping, but these same arguments apply to gender, sexual orientation, social class, and other dimensions of difference and disparities in care.

complexities of human society. The second kind of knowledge that we need to grapple with, *positional privilege*, is often less intuitive and more difficult to accept. At its essence, positional privilege acknowledges that social hierarchies of whatever type (be they race based, class based, sex based, etc.) involve not only disadvantage, but also privilege. It is axiomatic that, to the extent that a factor such as race disadvantages one group, it must advantage or "privilege" others (Massey, 2007; McIntosh, 1990). As sensible as this proposition is, we have found that even the people who are most concerned with the disadvantaged status of others often are reluctant to consider the sources of their own personal privilege—in essence, their special set of unearned advantages based on such factors as their race, class background, gender, or even their sexual orientation. Speaking of privilege in racial terms, feminist scholar McIntosh (1990) describes her White racial privilege as being like an invisible knapsack, packed with unearned assets: "I have come to see white privilege as an invisible package of unearned assets that I can count on cashing in each day, but about which I was 'meant' to remain oblivious. White privilege is like an invisible weightless knapsack of special provisions, maps, passports, codebooks, visas, clothes, tools, and blank checks" (p. 1). Among the items that McIntosh discerns in this invisible knapsack are (pp. 2–3):

- The ability to avoid spending time with people you have learned to mistrust or mistrust you.
- The ability to rent or purchase housing in areas of affordability and preference.
- The ability to protect your children from exposure to people who might not like them.
- The ability to make simple errors of etiquette without it being attributed to your race.
- When seeking to speak to the person "in charge," the assurance that you will typically be talking to a person of your own race.
- The confidence that, when seeking legal or medical help, your race will not work against you.

Although McIntosh's metaphorical knapsack is used to illuminate White racial privilege, just as she does in the balance of her insightful essay, we can think of McIntosh's invisible knapsack as extending to other forms of positional privilege—heterosexual privilege, male privilege, religious privilege, and the privileges that are commensurate with social class.

The Myth of Meritocracy.   The typical readers of this book are a group of very select people—students and health care professionals who have invested years in their professional education, excelled on highly competitive aptitude examinations, and been willing to make count-less sacrifices in pursuit of their professional credentials. Central to the criteria for selection and advancement within the ranks of the health professions is the idea of meritocracy—selection and advancement by aptitude and performance rather than by unearned personal ad-vantages. Those of us who remember grueling exams, all-night study sessions, hours in the lab, and the foregone pleasures traded for high grades understandably rebel at the idea that, to a significant extent, professional status and social power derive not from merits earned, but from a more complex interaction of aptitudes, efforts, social invest-ments, and selective unearned opportunities. We might acknowledge the partial influence of unearned opportunities and positional privi-leges in our educational achievements, but there is an overwhelming tendency to discount the magnitude of their influence relative to what we see as the justly deserved fruits of our labor.

In response to this near universal tendency to emphasize the power of meritocracy relative to positional privilege, Harvard University political philosopher Michael Sandel describes an annual experimental ritual he performs with his undergraduate classes, where he asks those that are first born in their families to raise their hands. The results, incredibly consistent, show that most of his students fall into the first-born category. Sandel does this to demonstrate to his class (most of whom believe they represent the epitome of meritorious selection) that arbitrary accidents of birth and positionality are both ingrained within seemingly privileged neutral systems of meritocracy (Sandel, 2009). There is, of course, a considerable empirical literature on the relation-ship between birth order, parental investment, and achievement to back up Sandel's anecdotal classroom experiments (Paules, Trapnell, & Chen, 1999).

In fact, were selection into the most prestigious categories of the health professions a reflection of pure meritocracy, we would then have to be prepared to embrace the argument that in our society, the "best and the brightest" are disproportionately composed of White males. In do-ing so, we would simply be replicating the (now) abhorrent founda-tional arguments of the AMA (Starr, 1982). There are two alternatives to this kind of overtly racist and sexist bigotry. The first is to acknowledge that although pure meritocracy is indeed a myth, the unearned aspects to our individual selection into our professions have little to do with our professional perspective or our interactions with less-advantaged patients. The second alternative is to more critically examine the ways in which our positionality, and the unearned privileges that accompany our place in various systems of stratification, might influence our professional perspective and clinical interpretations. We argue for the second alternative—a critical examination of our own positional privileges and their potential influences on our professional perspective, clinical interpretations, and personal motivation to change the organizational and institutional structures that perpetuate health care disparities.

The point has been well made here and elsewhere (IOM, 2003; van Ryan, 2002) that health disparities are perpetuated both through overtly oppressive institutional structures and individual practices, and through more deeply embedded processes that the members of the dominant or privileged groups are taught not to see (McIntosh, 1990). We are challenged both to recognize the places we individually occupy in various hierarchies of dominance and to appreciate the privileges we possess as a result. As well-paid and highly educated professionals, to the extent that we believe our positional privileges are purely merit based (as opposed to derivative of an arbitrary accident of birth), we are more likely to harbor a professional perspective on poverty and poor patients that is decidedly unsympathetic (Gilens, 1999). We will also be less likely to challenge social class-based disparities in health care that are embedded organizationally and institutionally. To the extent that those of us who are heterosexual are unaware of heterosexual privilege (the rights and considerations that heterosexuals can take for granted when seeking health care), we will fail to interrogate the various subtle and not-so-subtle ways in which same-sex couples and LGBT (lesbian, gay, bisexual, and transgendered) individuals are treated as second-class families in our system of health care. Finally, but not exhaustively, to the extent that those of us who are White health care providers fail to see our inherent trust in the best intentions of colleagues as a benefit of racial privilege, we will be more likely to make erroneously naïve assumptions about the trust and confidence we should expect from our non-White patients.

CONCLUDING COMMENTS

Dr. Gregory House, the enigmatic antihero of the contemporary television hospital drama series *House*, thrives on critically deconstructing and identifying the latent motivations of seemingly virtuous sentiments: romantic love, loyalty, compassion, altruism, self-sacrifice, religious faith, and even grief (especially grief it seems). In his rare moments of painful self-reflection, House recognizes that his addiction to deconstruction of all that seems virtuous comes at a high personal price—his seeming inability to experience and express unencumbered humanitarian sentiments. Except for very rare moments, the character of Dr. Gregory House exists within a world of dark rationality and merciless critique. In this sense, it may seem that this chapter has had a certain House-like quality about it.

This chapter has indeed been dedicated to a critical deconstruction of the safety-net health care organizations we rely upon for our training and our careers, and the seemingly altruistic structures and processes of professional education that reflect and perpetuate disparities in health care. We have also examined the possibilities of our personal agency in the perpetuation of health care disparities that are tied to various forms of latent, unearned privilege. In summary, we have presented a fairly grim and perhaps even pessimistic reading of the heretofore humanitarian institutions and career motivations that have served as the original inspiration of this book. We acknowledge this, but we do so with the conviction that critical early career reflection can serve as an antidote to later career disillusionment, cynicism, and professional inertia. We believe that critical consciousness, the willingness and capacity to engage in the critical interrogation of health care delivery system at all levels—most especially our own privilege and agency, are in the end personally and professionally empowering.

REFERENCES

Agency for Healthcare Research and Quality. (2009). *National Health Care Disparities Report 2009*. Rockville, MD: Author.

Almgren, G. (2007). *Health care politics, policy and services: A social justice analysis.* New York: Springer Publishing.

Berggren, R. (2005). Unexpected necessities-inside Charity Hospital. *New England Journal of Medicine, 353*(15), 1550–1553.

Corbie-Smith, G., Flagg, E., Doyle, J., & O'Brien, M. (2002). Influence of usual source of care on differences by race/ethnicity in receipt of preventive services. *Journal of General Internal Medicine, 17*(6), 458–464.

Finucane, T., & Carrese, J. (1990). Racial bias in presentation of cases. *Journal of General Internal Medicine, 5*(2), 120–121.

Gilens, M. (1999). *Why Americans hate welfare: race, media, and the politics of anti-poverty policy.* Chicago, IL: University of Chicago Press.

Hirschman, C. (2001). The educational enrollment of immigrant youth: A test of the segmented-assimilation hypothesis. *Demography, 38*(3), 317–336.

Institute of Medicine. (2000). *America's health care safety net: Intact but endangered.* Washington, DC: National Academies Press.

Institute of Medicine. (2003). *Committee on Understanding and Eliminating Racial and Ethnic Disparities in Health Care, Unequal treatment: Confronting racial and ethnic disparities in health care.* Washington, DC: National Academies Press.

Jackson Health System. (2010). Mission & vision Jackson health system. Retrieved May 1, 2010, from http://www.jhsmiami.org/body.cfm?id=143

John H. Stroger Jr. Hospital of Cook County. (2010). John H. Stroger Jr. Hospital mission statement. Retrieved May 1, 2010, from http://johnstrogerhospital.org/dom/cchmission.html

Kaiser Family Foundation. (2009). *Health insurance coverage in America 2008 data update.* Menlo Park, CA: The Henry J. Kaiser Family Foundation.

Massey, D. (2007). *Categorically unequal: The American stratification system.* New York: Russell Sage Foundation.

Massey, D., & Denton, N. (1993). *American apartheid.* Cambridge, MA: Harvard University Press.

McIntosh, P. (1990). White privilege: Unpacking the invisible knapsack. *Independent School, 49*(2), 31–35.

Merton, R. (1936). The unanticipated consequences of purposive social action. *American Sociological Review, 1*(6), 894–904.

Merton, R. (1957). *Social theory and social structure.* Glencoe, IL: Free Press.

National Association of Public Hospitals and Health Systems. (2010). About NAPH. Retrieved May 1, 2010, from http://www.naph.org/Main-Menu-Category/About-NAPH.aspx

National Association of Social Workers. (2010). *Code of ethics of the National Association of Social Workers, revised 2008 version.* Washington, DC: National Association of Social Workers.

Paules, D. L., Trapnell, P. D., & Chen, D. (1999). Birth order effects on personality and achievement within families *Psychological Science, 10*(6), 482–487.

Sandel, M. J. (2009). *Justice: What's the right thing to do?* New York: Farrar, Straus and Giroux.

Sarrazin, M. V., Campbell, M., & Rosenthal, G. E. (2009). Racial differences in hospital use after acute myocardial infarction: Does residential segregation play a role? *Health Affairs, 28*(2), w368–w378.

Shortell, S. M., Zimmerman, J. E., Rousseau, D. M., Gillies, R. R., Wagner, D. P., Draper, E. A., . . . Duffy, J. (1994). The performance of intensive care units: Does good management make a difference? *Medical Care, 32*(5), 508–525.

Starr, P. (1982). *The social transformation of American medicine.* New York: Basic Books.

Sultana, F. (2007). Reflexivity, positionality and participatory ethics: Negotiating fieldwork dilemmas in international research. *ACME: An International E-Journal for Critical Geographies, 6*(3), 374–385.

van Ryn, M. (2002). Research on the provider contribution to race/ethnicity disparities in medical care. *Medical Care, 40*(Suppl. 1), 140–151.

van Ryn, M., & Burke, J. (2000). The effect of patient race and socio-economic status on physicians' perceptions of patients. *Social Science and Medicine, 50*(6), 813–828.

Weaver, J. (2010, March 14). Warnings of crisis at Jackson Health System went unheeded. *Miami Herald.*

PART II: POPULATIONS AND PROVIDERS

5

Homelessness as a Social Phenomenon and Being Homeless

HOMELESSNESS DEFINED

Most people would think of a homeless person as a person who has no regular place to sleep that is in any way adequate or humane, or would fitthe common definition of a home. This is generally consistent with the definition of homelessness provided by the Stewart B. McKinney Act of 1994, the first major federal legislative act dealing specifically with the problem of homelessness. According to this federally sanctioned definition of homelessness, a homeless individual is defined as "(a) an individual who lacks a fixed, regular, and adequate nighttime residence, and (b) an individual who has a primary nighttime residence that is— (a) a supervised publicly or privately operated shelter designed to provide temporary living accommodations (including welfare hotels, congregate shelters, and transitional housing for the mentally ill), (b) an institution that provides a temporary residence for individuals intended to be institutionalized, or (c) a public or private place not designed for, or ordinarily used as, a regular sleeping accommodation for human beings" (Stewart B. McKinney Act of 1994). This definition of homelessness covers persons sleeping in public parks, shelters for the homeless, and in transient hotels or transitional housing. Notably, this definition of homelessness does not include runaway teenagers "couch

155

surfing" with friends or the 2.3 million persons residing in federal, state, and local prisons and jails (West Coast Poverty Center, 2009).

Although the above definition is the official definition that is used by the U.S. Department of Housing and Urban Development (HUD) and the public and private agencies that serve homeless populations, even HUD concedes the definition is in some respects incomplete. According to HUD, the people who experience homelessness can be classified into two main categories: (a) those who are literally homeless within the federal definition just cited, and (b) those who are "precariously housed"—for example, women who must seek a place to sleep with reluctant relatives, or individuals having income that is both unstable and barely sufficient for rent (HUD, 2008). It is for this reason that the National Coalition for the Homeless suggests that discussions about the prevalence of homelessness should not be focused solely on "homeless people," but rather on people who experience homelessness over time (National Coalition for the Homeless [NCH], 2009a).

The Social Characteristics of Homeless Persons

In a recent analysis of the social characteristics of the homeless, the National Coalition for the Homeless (NCH) delineated estimates of the homeless population by age, gender, families with children, race/ethnicity, victims of domestic violence, veterans, the mentally ill, persons with addictions, and employment characteristics (NCH, 2007). These illuminating findings are summarized in Table 5.1.

As shown in Table 5.1, there are a number of social characteristics of the homeless that are both nonintuitive and disquieting. In contrast to stereotypical representations of the homeless as mentally ill or addicted adults, a large share of the homeless are children (39%) and a significant number of homeless children are under age 5. Although it is more typical for homeless children to sleep in temporary shelters and transitional housing than under bridges, there is little emotional or even physical safety for children forced to seek refuge in a series of seedy motels and temporary shelters. It may be surprising to many that, although mental illness is highly prevalent among the homeless, it accounts for no more than one out of five homeless adults. Perhaps less surprising, among the 33% of homeless who are in families with children, a very large share of those (about one-half) have been victims of domestic violence. It may also be unsurprising that African Americans are significantly overrepresented among the homeless

TABLE 5.1
Selected Social Characteristics of Homeless Persons

SOCIAL CHARACTERISTIC	STATISTICAL ESTIMATE	DATA SOURCES
Age	39% Children under age 18 16% Children under age 5	National Law Center on Homeless and Poverty (2004)
Gender	17% Single women	U.S. Conference of Mayors (2003)
Families	33% Families with children	U.S. Conference of Mayors (2005)
Race/ethnicity	49% African American 35% Caucasian 13% Hispanic 2% Native American 1% Asian	U.S. Conference of Mayors (2004)
Domestic violence	50% of homeless women/children	National Coalition Against Domestic Violence (2004)
Veterans	40% of homeless men	Rosenheck et al. (1994)
Mentally Ill	16% of the single adult homeless	U.S. Conference of Mayors (2005)
Addicted persons	30%–38% of homeless	U.S. Conference of Mayors (2005) SAMHSA (2003)
Employment	13%–25% of homeless	U.S. Conference of Mayors (2005–2006)

Data from National Coalition for the Homeless. (2007). Who is homeless: NCH fact sheet. Washington, DC. National Coalition for the Homeless (2009). Substance abuse and homelessness. Washington, DC.

population—although most would be surprised at the magnitude of disparity. Despite African Americans constituting only about 12% of the U.S. population, they constitute 49% of the homeless. Some of this racial disparity in the risk of homelessness simply reflects the racial disparity in overall poverty, but it is a legacy of decades of housing discrimination that has made decent low-income housing less afford-able for African Americans. Finally, it should be noted that although veterans constitute only 34% of the adult male population, they are 40% of the homeless (NCH, 2007).

Although we have taken pains to demonstrate that the stereotypical representation of homeless persons as either drug addicted, mentally ill, or willfully living on the streets bears little resemblance to the demographic reality, it is certainly also true that mental illness and drug/alcohol addictions affect a significant minority of the homeless population. Yet, as we consider the causal pathways to homelessness in a discussion to follow, we will see that addictions and mental illness do not typically act alone as the singular cause for any individual's homelessness. That is, some of the structural factors that leave low-wage workers at high risk for homelessness also impact the mentally ill and addicted.

Estimating the Size of the Homeless Population

Among the most formidable challenges in social science is obtaining reasonably accurate estimates of the homeless population. In fact, there are a number of difficult obstacles to precise estimates of the homeless population, among which is the fact that the federal government's effort to systematically enumerate the national homeless population is actually as recent as 2004, when Congress charged HUD with providing annual assessment reports. Prior to 2004, the only estimates of the homeless population available were from individual studies, efforts by local public and private agencies, and decennial U.S. Census estimates. These efforts were typically underfunded, inconsistent in their methods of estimation, and often not appropriate as a basis for valid national estimates. Beginning in 2004, HUD has produced an *Annual Homeless Assessment Report* that is based on a combination of (a) counts of the sheltered and unsheltered homeless persons undertaken by HUD-funded agencies during the same night in any given year, and (b) and a database tracking counts of homeless over a full year from a representative sample of communities that use the same information system for tracking counts of the homeless (HUD, 2008). The single night counting method provides an estimate of the homeless population living in shelters and in unsheltered conditions at a point in time, by design a winter night, whereas the yearly tracking method is more useful as a method for tracking people who move in and out of homelessness over a year. The HUD report makes a distinction between *sheltered homeless* (persons in emergency shelters or transitional housing) and *unsheltered homeless* (persons living in places not fit for human habitation—that is, city parks, cars, abandoned buildings, stairwells, train stations, and parking garages).

According to the fourth *Annual Homeless Assessment Report* released in July of 2009, during a single night in January of 2008, there were 664,414 sheltered and unsheltered homeless persons nationwide.

Of the homeless, about 42% were unsheltered, that is living in cars, abandoned buildings, train stations, stairwells, etc. (HUD, 2008). The HUD estimates make a distinction between homeless individuals (single adults, unaccompanied youth) and homeless persons in families (at least one adult and one child in a family who is homeless). Homeless individuals formed about 60% of those enumerated, whereas about 40% of the homeless were in the company of at least one other member of their family. Although homeless persons in families are more likely to be sheltered than single individuals, it is still the case that 27% (just over one in four) were discovered living in unsheltered conditions in the middle of winter (HUD, 2008). Of homeless adults and teens not accompanied by other family members, 51% were found in unsheltered conditions. As pointed out in the HUD report (p. 9), one of the reasons that homeless individuals are more likely to be found in unsheltered conditions is that many communities have explicit policies that seek to reduce or eliminate the specter of children living in their streets and parks and thus are more likely to target shelter resources to homeless families. It is also true that families with children are less likely than individuals to transition to homelessness (as narrowly defined) because family and friends are more likely to step forward with assistance where children are involved (p. 9).

Aside from making the distinction between homeless persons who are counted as individuals and those who are in homeless families, the HUD *Annual Homeless Assessment Report* also distinguishes between persons who suffer homelessness as an isolated episode in their lives and those who are *chronically homeless*—that is either continuously homeless for a year or more or having at least four episodes of homelessness over the most recent 3 years (p. 15). Using this definition, about one in five homeless persons enumerated by the HUD were chronically homeless. Consistent with intuitive expectations, it is more likely that single adults and unaccompanied adolescents fall within the chronically homeless category than do homeless persons in families–although even a significant share of homeless families also fall within the chronically homeless category (HUD, 2008).

Trends in the Prevalence of the Homeless Population

As discussed previously, annual systematic counts of the national homeless population have only become available since 2004, thus making it difficult to arrive at a scientific consensus on the long-term growth trend in homelessness. However, it is fair to say that since the early 1980s, cities across the nation found themselves engulfed in a rising tide of the homeless population. Despite the lack of available data on national direct counts of the homeless precluding scientific consensus on the magnitude of the national crisis in homelessness, there were multiple studies in different cities using different methodologies that suggested a crisis was at hand (Levinson & Ross, 2007).

One way of capturing the magnitude of the growth in the homeless population, given the absence of adequate direct counts of the homeless, is through the growth in the number of shelters for the homeless that emerged during the 1980s throughout the urban landscape. During the 1980s, just as now, cities were financially strapped and unable to accommodate competing demands for more police and firefighters, repairs for aging public buildings, and an array of social services in the face of rising levels of poverty. Thus, it can be safely assumed that cities would only invest their limited dollars in expanding the number of shelters for the homeless in the face of greatly increased demand. This method still underestimates the growth in the homeless population because in strapped urban economies, public resources typically fall well short of actual need. Still, between 1981 and 1989, the numbers of shelter beds relative to the overall population in 182 of the largest U.S. cities tripled, in essence suggesting that by a very conservative estimate during the 1980s, the homeless population in U.S. cities at least tripled (Burt, 1997).

The significant efforts undertaken by communities across the country to combat homelessness through various housing and social service initiatives in recent decades may have had some modest impact in reducing homelessness. According to the latest HUD estimates, between 2006 and 2008, the point-in-time counts of the homeless population declined from 759,101 persons in 2006 to 664,414 persons in 2008—a reduction of some 12% (HUD, 2008). Although both homeless individuals and families benefited from this decline, the decline was somewhat more pronounced among homeless families (p. 10). Among the chronically homeless, recent trends have been somewhat more mixed. On the one hand, there has been a decline in chronic homelessness of 20% between 2006 and 2008, but the decrease in chronically homeless unable to find sheltered accommodations has only been slight (p. 16).

Despite these recent favorable trends in the prevalence of homelessness, it must be acknowledged that the estimates are based upon counts taken in January of 2008—just at the point when the national unemployment rate was beginning to show the effects of a deep recession. In the 2 years subsequent to the point-in-time count that is the basis of this most recent HUD estimate of the homeless population, the national civilian unemployment rate has grown from 7.4% to 10.0% (U.S. Bureau of Labor Statistics, 2010). Because so many individuals and families are one paycheck away from homelessness, it is likely that these favorable trends have since reversed themselves.

Causes of Homelessness

The Interplay of Structural and Individual Factors

In the everyday encounters with homeless persons that take place in hospitals and clinics across the country, the causes of homelessness would seem to be fairly self-explanatory and the homeless themselves would be categorized by quasi-diagnostic labels. In fact, that is usually how clinicians see the homeless. For example, there is the woman fleeing an abusive relationship, the person with schizophrenia going through the state hospital revolving door, the homeless inebriate brought in by the police, the addict with a leg ulcer, the street kid who is a victim of sexual assault, the disabled veteran looking for a warm bed, the mentally retarded adult who has mismanaged his or her meager Social Security check, the jobless day laborer, and so on down the long tragic list.

Every homeless person has a presentation of symptoms and a history, and by the conventions of medical model diagnosis, it is usually quite straightforward in the individual case to infer a reasonably valid chain of causality. What is less straightforward is to appreciate the extent to which each homeless person's story reflects larger *structural* causal processes. Structural factors are those aspects of any individual's social context that are beyond his or her control; for example, the functioning of labor and housing markets, federal and local social policies as they apply to particular populations (e.g., abused and neglected children, disabled workers, the chronically mentally ill, drug and alcohol addicts, and victims of domestic violence), and even major demographic trends such as changes in the age structure of the population.

Among the structural factors cited in a recent review of the now large literature on homelessness are deindustrialization and the subsequent low-wage economy for workers of limited education, declines in the "real dollar" value of Social Security and public assistance funds for poor individuals and families, the deinstitutionalization of mentally ill and developmentally disabled adults in the wake of both innovations in medication and more restrictive civil commitment laws, the "decriminalization" of public intoxication that emptied local jails of impoverished alcoholics, and the loss of large zones of low-rent and transient housing in the wake of urban gentrification (Kogel, 2007).

Another structural factor, specific to adolescent homelessness, entailed sweeping changes in juvenile delinquency laws, which afford adolescent runaways many of the same civil rights as adults— meaning that in many communities, police can only arrest and detain a "street kid" in connection with criminal conduct as opposed to arrest and detention for protective reasons.

Kogel (2007) argues that homelessness is a phenomenon that reflects the interaction of two kinds of factors: individual vulnerabilities and structural conditions, rather than specifically one set of factors to the exclusion or deemphasis of another. At the *individual level*, the common vulnerabilities include physical or mental disabilities, being addicted, having limited education and job skills, being in a single female parent household, being raised in poverty, having an unstable and disrupted family history, being gay/lesbian/bisexual/transgender (GLBT), and having a limited network of family and friends. These are some of the individual vulnerabilities that increase the probability of homelessness to the extent that there are escalating disadvantages at the *structural level*, for example reductions in available low-income housing, economic downturns, further "real dollar" declines in wages for low-wage workers, and further reductions in the social safety net for populations living at the margins (Kogel, 2007, p. 255).

Public Beliefs About the Causes of Homelessness and Characteristics of the Homeless Population

It is probably fair to say that the doctors, nurses, social workers, and other health care professionals who work in the clinics and hospitals serving the poor tend (at least in the abstract) to be more empathetic and informed about the homeless population than the general public. However, it is also likely that the health care professionals serving on the front lines of poverty and despair are not wholly immune from the prevailing beliefs and stereotypes about the homeless that are reinforced by media and the general political discourse on poverty and the poorest of the poor. For this reason, it is helpful to consider more deeply and critically the nature of public beliefs about both the causes of homelessness and the characteristics of homeless persons.

The foremost expert on public attitudes about the causes of homelessness and the characteristics of homeless persons is sociologist Barrett Lee. As Lee notes, public beliefs about the characteristics of the poor in general are tied to their beliefs about poverty and also their own social characteristics (Lee, Jones, & Lewis, 1990). That is, to the extent that people tend to see the causes of poverty as arising from individual characteristics and the behavioral choices made by individuals, they tend to view the poor in negative and pejorative ways. Because the individualistic orientation has been the dominant social and political philosophy in America since colonial times, popular and anecdotal portrayals of the homeless have reinforced such behaviors as laziness, drunkenness, immorality, and wanderlust as the principal causes of homelessness (Lee et al., 1990, p. 254).

Of equal importance, it is also true that beliefs in the individualistic causes of poverty are tied to relative social position. That is, the more advantaged in society tend to attribute the causes of wealth and poverty to individual initiative and moral character, whereas less affluent persons tend to see the poor as victims of unfavorable structural conditions (Gilens, 1999). In large part, this is because people who are located farther down the scale of income and assets are more likely to have direct encounters with the poor and personal experiences of poverty (Gilens, 1999). Persons having a more structural orientation toward poverty and homelessness are thus not only likely to have had more direct encounters with human despair, they are also more likely to support structural solutions to poverty and homelessness (e.g., a higher minimum wage structure, more government investment in housing subsidies, and expansion of social services targeted at the homeless).

Although this dichotomized public belief system about the causes of poverty and homelessness has decades of empirical support and self-evident political discourse in support of its validity, Lee argues that individuals and the public in general may have a much more complex and nuanced orientation toward the causes of homelessness than they do toward poverty in general. In his seminal investigation on this issue (Lee et al., 1990), Lee and his coinvestigators found that (a) people tend to harbor beliefs about the causes of homelessness that incorporate both individual and structural factors; (b) consistent with the structure of public attitudes toward poverty in general, the more advantaged in society (in terms of race, education, and income) tend to place higher emphasis on individual deficits as the principal causes of homelessness; and (c) beliefs about the causes of homelessness and the characteristics of the homeless are also influenced by the nature of contacts with the homeless (e.g., being panhandled as opposed to having a direct conversation with a homeless person that is not about money). This third finding is a reflection of the so-called contact hypothesis that predicts that contacts between members of in-groups and out-groups tend to help develop more positive attitudes toward previously distrusted or disparaged out-groups through the substitution of direct experience for ignorance and stereotypes (Lee, Farrell, & Link, 2004).

The Contact Hypothesis: Implications for Provider Beliefs About Homelessness and the Homeless

The applicability of the "contact hypothesis" to the homeless population has not only been replicated in more recent studies (Knechta & Martinez, 2009), but it also has important implications for the health care professionals working in settings where there is a high proportion of homeless persons. In essence, to the extent that interpersonal contacts with homeless persons tend to illuminate the complete context of their social circumstances, health care providers will tend to harbor more favorable attitudes toward the homeless and thereby be more capable of the kinds of compassionate, nonjudgmental, and empathetic responses that are common to the ethos of all the health professions. On the other hand, to the extent that contacts with homeless persons are centered on difficult demands and frustrating exchanges, negative stereotypes and attitudes will be reinforced rather than dispelled.

The likelihood of either a positive or a negative encounter between a health care provider and a homeless person can turn on a variety of contextual factors apart from the provider's general knowledge, beliefs, and attitudes about the homeless; these include the presentation of the homeless person as sympathetic versus alienating, the nature of the demands being made on the provider by the homeless person, and the provider's immediate state of either energy or stress/exhaustion at the point of encounter.

With respect to the first contextual factor that shapes the outcome of an encounter with a homeless person, the presentation of the homeless person as either sympathetic or alienating, it is easy to see how a cleanly attired woman fleeing an abusive relationship garners more sympathy than a scruffily clad and smelly inebriate who appears to be choosing to live on the street. However, even the nicely dressed woman fleeing an abusive relationship can evoke a negative reaction from a health care provider if, for example, the provider has a personal history of abuse that evokes discomfort, anger, or even rage at what he or she perceives as the victim's "learned helplessness." As counterintuitive as it may seem, that same provider may actually be able to garner more sympathy for the street drunk. The point being made here is that the presentations of homeless persons as either sympathetic or alienating are in large part determined not only by the prevailing social norms that influence the criteria of a sympathetic response, but also by the provider's unique personal history, belief systems, and vulnerabilities.

The second contextual factor that may influence the positive or negative direction of the encounter, the nature of the demands being made on the provider, often has everything to do with demands that are either inherently burdensome or cause the provider to feel powerless. Inherently burdensome demands include those that are time consuming, introduce a significant degree of diagnostic doubt and difficulty, or entail tolerating something that is stressful or disagreeable. For example, a homeless person complaining of excruciating pain to an emergency room physician may be in agony for a variety of legitimate reasons—or he or she may be drug seeking. Sometimes, there is just no way to be sure. This leaves the emergency department (ED) doctor in significant doubt as to the correctness of his or her judgment, whether or not he or she elects to provide the homeless person with pain medication. As much as ER staff are accustomed to dealing with the difficult and disagreeable, few ER staff are totally inured against the effects of caked-on feces or reeking breath from rotting teeth.

Along similar lines, a homeless person in need of shelter on a frigid winter night when homeless shelters are filled to capacity can leave the ER staff with an ethically excruciating choice—of either concocting a medical diagnosis that places the homeless patient in a hospital bed for the night or sending the homeless person away from light and warmth into darkness and cold. In the context of providing health care, power is about the ability to do things that are clinically appropriate and efficacious. Powerlessness derives from the sense that one is forced to take actions that are experienced as dishonest, cruel, or futile (we will return to a discussion of moral distress in the final chapter). Homelessness and encounters with homeless persons have an incredible capacity to evoke a profound sense of powerlessness and professional futility.

Although Table 5.2 is a greatly reduced and simplified version of complex processes, it at least illuminates the ways in which the presenting characteristics and needs/demands of individual homeless

TABLE 5.2
**Contextual Factors Influencing Provider Encounters
with Homeless Persons**

	SYMPATHETIC PRESENTATION	ALIENATING PRESENTATION
Routine demands	Positive encounter	Neutral encounter
Burdensome demands	Neutral encounter	Negative encounter

persons can shape the health care provider's perceptions of the homeless population as a whole. As shown in Table 5.2, there are three kinds of outcomes to clinical encounters with homeless persons: (a) Those that are neutral and therefore unlikely to change the health care provider's preencounter perceptions of homeless persons; (b) those encounters that are negative and likely to reinforce pejorative stereotypes of the homeless; and (c) encounters that are more positive and therefore more likely to engender empathetic sentiments toward homeless persons (Lee et al., 2004).

The third and final contextual factor that influences the outcome of an encounter with a homeless person has to do with the state of stress/exhaustion carried into the encounter by the health care provider. Optimal patient care entails the merger of the skillful application of clinical objectivity with human empathy. Mixing clinical objectivity with empathy, although it expresses the essence of the healer's gift, is not something that comes easily or naturally to most of us under all circumstances. In fact, it requires a robust and resilient state of mind and a deep reserve of professional perspective. The ER nurse, physician, or social worker at the tail end of a long shift or feeling professionally pummeled by a series of taxing patient encounters is unlikely to have many reserves available to both make the empathetic link to a frightened and delusional person with schizophrenia (or hostile street kid) and at the same time apply clinical objectivity to his or her assessment and response.

The purpose of the preceding review of the "contact hypothesis" and its applicability to clinical encounters with homeless persons is to encourage critical deconstruction of our individual beliefs and sentiments in connection with this profoundly vulnerable and difficult-to-serve population. One way of gaining a foothold on the complex nature of homelessness and our own agency in either perpetuating or alleviating despair (the despair of the homeless as well as our own) is to critically debrief our encounters with the homeless. That is, to consider what it is about the homeless person's presentation that evoked our sympathy or aversion, the nature of the demands/needs and their fit with our sense of professional efficacy, and finally, the psychoemotional resources (or burdens) we were bringing into the encounter. In the end, those patients who are most like us and are least disconcerting to our particular sensibilities also have the least to teach us.

THE HEALTH CARE NEEDS OF THE HOMELESS POPULATION

In many respects, the homeless are the most disadvantaged of all Americans—not only in terms of material needs, but also in terms of health and health care as well. The homeless are among the least likely to have any kind of health insurance, yet several times more likely than the general population to become ill (NCH, 2009b). In a comprehensive review of the literature on premature mortality and homelessness, O'Connell (2005) found that death rates among homeless persons were 3–4 times higher for the homeless population than the general population—not only in the United States, but also in Canada, Europe, Asia, and Australia (O'Connell, 2005, p. 13).

Among the most illuminating studies cited in this literature review was a study done in Boston of 17,292 homeless adults seen in Boston Health Care for the Homeless Program between 1988 and 1993. Although it is commonly assumed that drug and alcohol overdoses and hypothermia would be leading causes of death for this population, in fact the leading causes of death both differed by the age range of the homeless persons, and (other than homicides among the 18–24 age group) deaths were largely attributable to chronic diseases (AIDS, heart disease, and cancer). The median age of death for this population was 44 years, and among homeless persons aged 24–45 years, death from heart disease alone was three times that of the general population. Remarkably, the death rates among homeless persons did not vary by season of the year and there were only six deaths from hypothermia—thus dispelling the myth that acute exposure is a leading cause of death among homeless persons.

Among the general findings illuminated in O'Connell's review of the literature on the relationships between premature mortality and homelessness are (a) the most dramatic disparities in mortality among the homeless are seen in the younger (18–54) age range; (b) in contrast to the general population, homeless women do not have a mortality advantage over men; and (c) deaths from acute and chronic disease are far more prevalent than deaths from exposure, drug/alcohol abuse, or in association with mental illness.

Although research shows that the premature death rates among the homeless are a result of a complex relationship between the absence of stable housing in combination with poorly managed chronic disease, it does not suggest there is some kind of consistent progression from poverty to homelessness to unmanaged disease and ultimately to early death. In fact, for an unknown but likely significant share of the homeless population, illnesses and injuries precede homelessness in the causal chain—because for many low-income workers and families, health insurance is unattainable (NCH, 2009b). In fact, in the United States, about one-half of all family bankruptcies arise from unaffordable health care costs (Himmelstein, Warren, Thorne, & Woolhandler, 2005).

It must therefore be concluded that the relationships between homelessness and premature death must be tackled both "downstream and upstream" rather than at one point in the causal flow to the exclusion of the other. Upstream strategies must address such causal factors as the relationships between low-wage work and the affordability of stable housing, early detection of debilitating illnesses that can result in job loss and poverty, and health insurance for low-income persons and families. Downstream strategies must then consider the adequacy of health care services targeted to homeless populations. It is to that issue we now turn.

Health Care Services and the Homeless Populations: General Considerations

In various segments of this chapter, we have switched back and forth between references to "the homeless population" (meaning all homeless individuals and families) and "homeless populations" (meaning subgroups of the general homeless population). When considering the structure of health care services and the homeless, it is far more helpful and even essential to think in terms of specific "homeless populations" with distinct defining characteristics and different kinds of health care needs. However, there are some general health care needs among the homeless that transcend differences among the different segments of the homeless population because they arise from the shared consequences of homelessness: poor nutrition and personal hygiene, exposure-related conditions that arise from extremes of heat and cold as well as wet conditions, exposure to infectious diseases as a result of living in crowded and unsanitary shelter conditions, untreated acute injuries and illnesses, and chronic illnesses (such as HIV/AIDS, chronic obstructive pulmonary disease, and tuberculosis) that are allowed to worsen in the absence of access to consistent and appropriate treatment (NCH, 2009b). Thus diseases that are common across subgroups representing the homeless population include "heart disease, cancer, liver disease, kidney disease, skin infections, HIV/AIDS, pneumonia, and tuberculosis" (NCH, 2009b, p. 2).

Although it might easily be assumed that the prevalence of liver and kidney disease among the homeless is consequential to stereotypical drug and alcohol addiction, in fact both liver failure and kidney disease can also arise from chronic exposure to poor nutrition, untreated infections, rotting teeth, and of course unmanaged diabetes. Finally, a common etiological factor that cuts across all segments of the homeless population is exposure to chronic stress: everyday uncertainty about the next meal or place to sleep, lack of privacy, continuous exposure to violence and never feeling safe, and the stress that arises from social exclusion, isolation, and stigma (Daiski, 2007). In particular, the chronic stress that comes with sustained social isolation has long been implicated in premature mortality from cardiovascular disease, a broad range of cancers, and susceptibility to infectious diseases as well (House, Landis, & Umberson, 1988).

These findings suggest that the *general* health care needs of the homeless population must entail a comprehensive approach to health care that includes not only emergency care and routine primary health care, but also substance abuse services, dental care, and a range of social services, including housing placement assistance (National Coalition for the Homeless [NCH], 2009b). Toward that end, the U.S. Congress has passed amendments to the Social Security Act (specifically the sections pertaining to Medicare and Medicaid) and the Public Health Service Act that fund specialized Community Health Centers (CHCs) structured to serve special populations: migrant workers, persons living in public housing projects, and the homeless (Health Resources and Services Administration [HRSA], 2010). To qualify for federal funding, Health Care for the Homeless (HCH) centers are required (at minimum) to provide routine primary health care, emergency care, substance abuse services, outreach and housing placement assistance—and many also provide dental care, mental health care, and a range of other essential services (NCH, 2009b, p. 2). By the most recent estimates available, the 143 federally funded CHCs (including HCH centers) served at least 934,000 persons experiencing homelessness (HRSA, 2010; National Home Health Care [NHHC], 2010). As impressive as this number is, it should be kept in mind that 2–3 million persons experience at least one episode of homelessness over the course of the year (HRSA, 2010). It remains the situation that in communities across the United States, homeless persons in need of health care either go without, or must be dependent upon the overburdened EDs of hospitals that are ill-suited to treat chronic health conditions.

According to McMurray-Avila, Gelberg, and Breakey (1999), the outcome goals of clinical interventions with the homeless cover two broad categories, *system level outcomes* and *client level outcomes*. The system level outcomes include access to a range of comprehensive services, continuity of care within an integrated system both to help contain costs and prevent new or recurring problems, and facilitation of client involvement at each step of the care process. The client level outcomes include improved health status, improved level of functioning, improved quality of life, involvement in treatment, disease self-management, client choice, and client satisfaction (p. 3).

Achieving these system level and individual level outcomes with a complex, heterogeneous, and impoverished population is a formidable endeavor. Based on their evaluation of research demonstration programs that provided health and social services to homeless populations, as well as their analysis of the experiences of frontline workers in health care programs, McMurray-Avila et al. (1999) formulated nine general principles intended to serve as a guide for health care practitioners caring for the homeless. Some of these nine principles pertain to critical aspects of the patient–provider relationship, and others address larger structural resources that practitioners should help to promote through collective action and public policy advocacy (McMurray-Avila et al., 1999).

1. The importance of outreach to the engagement of clients in treatment.

   Many of the homeless persons in dire need of health care assume that they will be either denied help or be forced to endure disparaging looks and remarks in the few places where health care might be available. Sadly, these beliefs tend to be well informed by direct experience. Additionally, some homeless persons may not know they are becoming dangerously ill and are in need of prompt care. Outreach to the enclaves and individual refuges of the homeless by community health workers and clinically savvy social service providers is therefore essential.

2. Respect for the individuality of each person.

The narrator in Ralph Ellison's *Invisible Man* speaks of his existence in society as being an invisible one, because of powerful forces that conspire to deny and ultimately make invisible his essential humanity and individuality. While the source of the "invisible existence" of Ellison's character is racial subjugation, the experiences of being seen, yet unseen, can be extended to the homeless as well. Just as Ellison's character found himself being typecast and categorized as some specific type of Black man (as opposed to simply a man or individual) throughout his journey into adulthood, the homeless themselves are typically well aware of the various ways they too are being stereotyped, depreciated, and ultimately denied their essential humanity. In part, this is because they exist within degrading and dehumanizing circumstances and often see themselves and their demeaning circumstances through the eyes of others. The homeless also experience the reality of their invisible existence through the sometimes subtle, and often very direct, ways they are treated disparagingly by clinic and hospital staff who resent their presence and dubious claims on the status of "patient." Respecting the individuality of the homeless patient, aside from being an ethical obligation, is good medicine—because both the patient and the practitioner become more invested in the ultimate therapeutic purpose of the clinical encounter.

3. Cultivation of trust and rapport between service provider and client.

This particular principle speaks both to individual clinical skills and capacities of the care provider, and the structural context of therapeutic intervention. By *skills* we mean the listening skills that are basic and essential to the education of all health care providers and, for that matter, most management training programs (such as maintaining eye contact, not interrupting, giving body language or verbal cues that you are listening, and providing paraphrased feedback), and the strategic use of questions and feedback comments to guide the patient/client toward clinically relevant information. By *capacities*, we mean primarily the ability to make what some refer to as the "empathetic leap"; in essence, the ability to put yourself in the place of another person and see the encounter and the clinical situation through the eyes and perspective of the patient/client. Although the vast majority of clinical practitioners genuinely see themselves as empathetic people, and in fact routinely endeavor to see clinical situations through the lens of their patients, the "empathetic leap" in the typical clinical encounter is a small one. Most of us can imagine in ourselves the terror and confusion of a middle-aged woman with a lump in her breast, the ambivalence of a smoker being confronted with health concerns, and the anger of an adolescent facing a long and difficult recovery from an injury. In contrast, the capacity to generate genuine empathy for a large share of the homeless population is less common. This may be because they represent stereotypes that we abhor, disdain, or pity (the street drunk, drug addict, and ambulatory schizophrenic), or because they present or behave in ways that are offensive or frightening to us.

Another barrier to genuine empathy is our usually healthy aversion to emotional pain and profound despair. Seeing and experiencing the world through the lens of a person living at the extreme margins of society, feeling at any level their daily sense of despair, hopelessness, or invisibility, comes at a cost most of us find ways to avoid. All that said and acknowledged, a compelling case can be made that the *capacity* to make these kinds of difficult empathetic leaps can be fostered and embraced in ways that build upon rather than undermine our resources and resilience as health care practitioners (Kleinman, 1988).

Beyond the skills and capacities of the individual practitioner, the cultivation of trust and rapport between the service provider is heavily dependent upon the structural context of care. No matter how skilled and motivated an ER nurse, physician, or social worker might be, it is difficult and often even impossible to cultivate trust and rapport in the context of the typical ER. Although trust and rapport can sometimes be cultivated over multiple encounters with some individual homeless patients in ways that may ultimately lead to effective long-term intervention, there are obvious structural barriers to this being anything but the rare exception. This is in fact the central point of McMurray-Avila et al.'s (1999) fourth principle that should guide health care services to the homeless.

4. Flexibility in service provision, including location and hours of service, as well as flexibility in treatment approaches.

Many of the homeless populations that are in most dire need of health care are located in urban enclaves that are a far physical or social distance away from hospitals and clinics. Although safety-net hospitals and clinics are more likely to be located near the street refuges and shelters serving a large share of the homeless, there are segments of the homeless population that may well be geographically isolated from even safety-net health care providers (for example, homeless teenagers may tend to congregate near an urban university campus where there are other young people). For the homeless, even a distance of several blocks may be too formidable a barrier to seeking health care—particularly if the distance entails leaving urban environs that are familiar and "safer feeling" to homeless persons for neighborhoods that are experienced as threatening or intolerant. It is also the case that for many groups of homeless persons, the typical daytime clinic hours don't coincide with their hours of wakefulness and mobility.

Finally, treatment approaches need to be realistic and flexible. For example, prescribing and even furnishing an oral antibiotic to a homeless mentally ill patient may be futile and even harmful to his or her health, unless structured with some means of monitoring adherence (e.g., choosing a once daily antibiotic that can then be dispensed on a daily basis with a free meal).

5. The need to attend to the basic survival needs of homeless people and to recognize that until those needs are met, health care may not be an individual's priority.

Health care practitioners are generally frustrated by patients who fail to adhere to even seemingly simple regimes of treatment that if ignored have dire health consequences. The classic example is hypertensive patients, who can often manage their disease with relatively inexpensive daily medication and a few very basic behavioral adjustments. Yet, even well-off people die every day from unmanaged hypertensive disease due to their unwillingness to make seemingly modest adjustments to their lifestyles. In the situation of many of the homeless, the motivational impediments to essential health care are not trivial preferences, but often daily omnipresent survival needs that trump the more distant concerns of health and health care. For the homeless person in search of money for a small meal or a safe place to sleep for a few nights, even the modest co-pay required for an antibiotic or seizure medication may be of low priority.

6. The importance of integrated service provision and case management to coordinate needed services.

The health care service and financing literature has long argued for better integration and coordination of services through case management strategies for a broad array of chronic conditions (Flet-Lisk & Mays, 2002). Although we have said that the homeless are made up of many distinct subpopulations, all share a high prevalence of chronic illnesses and disabling conditions (O'Connell, 2005). For this reason alone, integrated service provision and coordination of care through case management services would seem to be essential. Added to this should be the consideration that for most groups of homeless, many of the services that are most crucial to their well-being are located outside the health care system in complex and often fragmented community social services.

7. Clinical expertise to address complex clinical problems, including access to specialized care.

As one consequence of poverty and homelessness, very treatable diseases are allowed to progress to chronic conditions (NCH, 2009b; O'Connell, 2005). In addition, the homeless carry a disproportionate share of multiple debilitating health conditions. As a result, homeless populations have a particular need for access to clinicians able to manage multiple advanced comorbid conditions and specialists who are trained to manage diseases such as drug-resistant tuberculosis.

8. Need for a range of housing options, including programs combining housing with services.

In a recent article that summarized the perspectives of a sample of homeless persons on their health needs and priorities (Daiski, 2007), there is a quote from a 19-year-old homeless girl that captures the tragic irony of thinking about personal health while living under a bridge:

> I get sick a lot more down here . . . a lot of the kids have bronchitis and stuff like that. Especially us living under the bridge, with all those toxins. Everyone is coughing, the dogs are coughing too. And in the summer there is the smog and they say, "Everyone stay inside today, ha ha . . ." (p. 275).

By this same irony and brutal logic, it can also be concluded that living in crowded shelters in close quarters with all varieties of infectious diseases and under the chronic stress that goes with homelessness makes ultimately futile the narrowly construed notions of health care that fail to address the full context of diseases and susceptibility. For the homeless, access to decent and stable housing is as much essential for health care as is an antibiotic for a debilitating infection. It is for this reason that community clinics that are funded by the federal Health Care for the Homeless Program are required to provide assistance in qualifying for housing (NCH, 2009b). However, these kinds of clinic-based social services will themselves be of limited value without local and national efforts to increase affordable housing resources for the homeless.

9. A longitudinal perspective that ensures continuing care until the person's life situation is stabilized.

The prevalence of homelessness is typically reported on the basis of a single night count. However, these estimates do not capture the distinction between persons and families who experience homelessness as a rare or one-time episode in their lives and the chronically homeless who either live on the streets or shelters continuously or cycle in and out of homelessness (HUD, 2009). For this latter segment of the homeless population, the chronically homeless, interrupting and ultimately breaking the pattern of homelessness requires a holistically oriented and sustained effort to address the factors that are most crucial to placing the person at risk for homelessness in a stable situation.

Although considered collectively these nine principles seem well beyond the individual agency of any health care provider or even community clinic, they do frame the way to think about the general health care needs of the homeless population in a holistic, comprehensive, and ultimately meaningful way—as opposed to the atomistic, episodic encounter-based paradigm that is based on a population that is both healthy and sheltered from the extremes of poverty and social isolation.

Health Care Services and the Homeless Populations: General Clinical Practice Considerations

In 2004, the Health Resources and Services Administration (HRSA) published *Adapting Your Practice: General Recommendations for the Care of Homeless Patients,* a groundbreaking guide to targeting primary care physicians caring for homeless persons (Bonin et al., 2004). While reading the complete 45-page monograph is highly recommended for physicians practicing in clinics and hospitals serving a large share of the homeless population, we highlight some crucial recommendations and cite some of the major special considerations/fundamental issues for clinicians that were advanced by the panel preparing this report. These special considerations include:

- **Limited access to food and water.** It is noted that the homeless eat where and what they can, not what they should. Meals served in shelters tend to be high in fat, starch, and sugar—all of which complicate cardiovascular disease and diabetes. Sanitary water sources are often problematic, creating the risk of dehydration and also making it more difficult for the homeless to take oral medications as they should.
- **Developmental discrepancies.** Homeless children, adolescents, and young adults often manifest developmental deficits originating from exposure to physical and/or drug abuse, chronic ear infections, insufficient opportunities to practice fine and gross motor skills, and chronic stress.
- **Higher risk for communicable diseases.** The HRSA report also notes that one out of every four homeless persons has an infectious or communicable disease (in particular, disproportionate incidence of HIV, STDs, infestations, and skin diseases). Crowded shelters and the lack of hygienic facilities further exacerbate both the management and the communicability of many diseases.

The summary recommendations of the HRSA report also address diagnosis and evaluation (history taking, physical evaluation, and diagnostic tests/screens), and plan and management considerations (e.g., addressing patient needs, patient goals and priorities, special patient education considerations). Some of the clinical recommendations that are particularly worth highlighting include:

- **Special attention to living conditions.** Medical providers in developed countries are not accustomed to asking their patients about when they sleep and where, when and how they get food and water, and where they store their possessions and medication. Yet, in the context of providing effective health care to a homeless patient, these questions are critical.

- **Mental illness/cognitive deficits.** Symptoms that are consistent with mental illness and cognitive deficits are common among the homeless, but also are neither universal nor even manifested in the majority of the homeless population. While they are risk factors for transition into chronic homelessness, they are also consequent to all of the detrimental exposures and conditions that are entailed in homelessness. Differential diagnosis is key in this domain to discern chronic from acute situational impairments.

- **Dental assessment.** Homeless persons are at least twice as likely to have serious dental pathologies than the general population and far less likely to have access to dental care. In one study of the population of homeless adults in Boston shelters, over 90% were found to have untreated dental caries (HCH Clinicians' Network, 2003b). Aside from its effects on self-esteem, daily suffering, and even prospects for employment, untreated dental disease in its advanced stages is implicated in cardiovascular and lung disease, and among women the risk of low birthweight and premature infants (HCH Clinicians' Network, 2003b).

- **Work history.** Health care providers who delve into the work histories (longest job held, vocational interests and skills, and occupational injuries) of homeless patients often find themselves surprised by the discrepancies between stereotypes of homeless persons as indolent or unskilled, and their actual work histories. In fact, there are a high proportion of homeless persons with long periods of stable employment in their lives and marketable job skills. By *not* asking a homeless person questions about their past episodes of employment, and their vocational interests and skills, health care workers in fact subtly and unintentionally reinforce stereotypes and risk discounting the aspirations and capacities of many homeless patients that may be important motivators for treatment adherence.

- **Focus on strengths.** One legacy of the traditional medical model of diagnosis and intervention is the focus on symptoms, pathologies, and deficits to the exclusion of the assessment of coping skills, abilities, and interests. A deliberative strengths-based assessment is essential to the recognition of patient capacities and motivations that can be used as leverage points for the pursuit of positive health status and social functioning outcomes. By contrast, a deficits-based assessment can lead both the clinician and the patient toward a distorted sense of powerlessness and intractability.

■ **Serial rather than first-encounter comprehensive physical exams.** Even patients with a high level of confidence and trust in physicians typically find comprehensive exams to be anxiety provoking. By contrast, many homeless persons tend to approach the clinical encounter with reactions of distrust, fear, and even shame. For many of the homeless, the comprehensive exam can only be accomplished in serial, incremental steps over time as bridges of trust and confidence are built.

■ **Diagnostic tests.** There are diagnostic scales for interpersonal violence, mental health screening, and substance abuse screening instruments, and cognitive assessment tools that are specific to the social and behavioral risk factors that are prevalent in the homeless population. These should be used in conjunction with baseline lab tests (for specific recommendations, see Bonin et al., 2004).

■ **Sensitivity to patient goals and priorities.** Even among more affluent patient groups with fewer barriers to care, there is a yawning gap between the intervention priorities that the clinician believes are in the patient's best interests and the patient's own goals and priorities. Although physicians and other health providers are becoming more attuned to exploring the goals and priorities of everyday mainstream adult patients, it is often taken for granted that there are other groups of patients for whom their goals and priorities are of less concern (children, older adults with cognitive deficits, persons with mental retardation, and homeless persons). However, aside from ethical considerations, being attuned to the goals and priorities of any patient increases the likelihood of adherence to an effective plan of intervention. Often, the dialogue between a homeless patient and a clinician about treatment goals and priorities can be a fruitful and trust-building negotiation that over time ultimately achieves all the essentials.

■ **Action plans.** The action steps that a homeless patient needs to take to achieve clinical outcomes need to be reduced to very limited reminders/instructions in simple language. Optimally, these should be put on a portable and durable pocket-sized card. It is also important to review each action step with the homeless patient in his or her language to ensure both clarity and reinforcement of the benefits to be achieved.

- **Understanding behavior change.** Sustained behavioral change entails thorough assessment of the individual and contextual factors that either impede behavioral change or might help motivate and sustain it. Successful behavioral change typically entails the reduction of contextual impediments to change, the development of new skills, and use of techniques such as motivational interviewing (Miller & Rollnick, 2002).[1]

- **Education of key service providers/supporting persons.** Clinicians who are able to gain general knowledge on special problems/needs of homeless patients through their clinical encounters with the homeless are a crucial resource of expertise to other clinicians and social service providers. At the individual level, it is also critical to educate the service providers and others providing social support on the specific problems/needs of the patient. If, for example, curing a potentially serious respiratory infection entails rigorous adherence to a regime of oral antibiotics for several days, it may be essential to enlist the assistance of shelter staff to cue the patient to take the medication appropriately and for as long as prescribed to avoid the development of drug-resistant strains of the infection.

It should be obvious that most of the above HRSA recommendations are not achievable in the context of the typical hospital ER, although the rates of ER utilization among the homeless greatly exceed those of the general population, and the homeless are among the highest repeat visitors (Pearson, Bruggman, & Haukoos, 2007). However, there is some evidence to suggest that ERs that invest in more attentive and compassionate care for the homeless can achieve dramatically lower levels of recidivism (Redelmeier, Molin, & Tibshirani, 1995). While to some this may seem counterintuitive, in the sense that generally "unwelcome" patients are "welcomed" by an empathetic and attentive staff, it is speculated that for a large segment of the homeless patient population, they tend to frequent an ER *until* they are satisfied with their treatment rather than *because* they are satisfied with their treatment (Redelmeier et al., 1995). Without the local availability of a community clinic with comprehensive services for homeless persons, the most effective and ultimately resource-efficient practices

---

[1] These issues are addressed in more depth in Chapter 9 on adherence to care.

with homeless patients may be an individualized care plan that sanctions a series of repeat visits to the ER for care until the acute problem is resolved.

Health Care Services and the Homeless Populations: Subgroup Clinical Practice Considerations

The Mentally Ill

As mentioned previously, about 16% of single adult homeless persons are mentally ill. In addition to their cognitive and emotional impairments, the mentally ill homeless (like other segments of the homeless population) manifest a disproportionate share of chronic diseases and a high prevalence of premature mortality (HCH Clinicians' Network, 2009). In fact, as a subset of the general homeless population, they have more chronic disease risk factors such as long-term psychotropic drug use (associated with weight gain, diabetes, and hypertension), the predisposition toward glucose intolerance that is associated with some psychiatric disorders, higher rates of tobacco addiction and use, reduced physical activity, and limited motivation/capacity to attend to personal health (HCH Clinicians' Network, 2009). The research to date suggests that at least three general clinical strategies are effective in reducing the prevalence of chronic disease among the mentally ill homeless or at least ameliorating the effects of chronic disease: The first entails the formation of collaborative partnerships between primary care providers and mental health specialists; the second, more fundamental strategy entails a focus on homelessness itself as the primary risk factor; and the third places an emphasis on an incremental approach to an ultimately comprehensive clinical intervention. Strategies 1 and 2 can be conceptualized as system-level public health strategies. The third general clinical strategy is more purely at the individual level.

Pertaining to this third "individual incremental" strategy, McMurray-Avila et al. (1999) suggest that there is a hierarchy of objectives that can be constructed for clinical interventions for homeless persons who are mentally ill, which begins with the most basic and moves incrementally toward the more ambitious and ultimately transformative. They provide the following example as an illustration (p. 4):

1. Accepts sandwich from outreach worker
2. Maintains eye contact with outreach worker

3. Accepts clean clothing
4. Accepts housing/shelter assistance
5. Permits interview with clinician
6. Accepts medication
7. Spontaneously attends to personal hygiene
8. If dangerous, is brought to ED facility
9. Attends clinic regularly
10. Manifests reduction in symptoms
11. Improvement in self-care ability
12. Adjusts satisfactorily to sheltered living program
13. Participates in social activities
14. Maintains mutually satisfactory relationship
15. Transfers from homeless program to generic program
16. Participates in vocational rehabilitation program
17. Able to live independently
18. Sustains competitive employment

Although there might be some disagreement among experts about the specific ordering of some objectives or even the inclusion of others, the take-home point of this illustration is its emphasis on incremental steps toward a higher level of self-care and social functioning. It should also be pointed out that there should be "stopping points" for individual clients who represent their particular optimal level of functioning given the limits of their capacities. For example, insisting under all individual circumstances that the achievement of sustained mainstream labor market employment is the ultimate benchmark of success is more of a political objective than a clinical or humanitarian one.

Homeless Veterans

As shown in Table 5.1, it is estimated that about 40% of homeless adult men are veterans. In contrast to the general population of homeless persons, homeless veterans tend to be older (44% are middle aged), and they are more likely to have been married and to be better educated (McMurray-Avila, 2001). There are a number of public myths pertaining to the relationship between veterans' status and homelessness and the characteristics of homeless veterans, chief among them being the belief that being a veteran leads to homelessness. In fact, there is little evidence that this is the case. The most comprehensive study of homeless veterans (Rosenheck, Frisman, & Chung, 1994) suggests that whereas different age cohorts of veterans may be at disproportionately high risk for homelessness, other age cohorts of veterans are actually at lower risk. The age cohort of veterans who had the highest risk of homelessness, well in excess of the risk of homelessness for nonveterans, were veterans who served from the mid-1970s and to the early 1980s—the final stage of the Vietnam War period and the early era of the nation's all volunteer military force policy. Based on their analysis of different age cohorts of veterans, Rosenheck et al. (1994) concluded that the higher rates of mental illness and substance abuse within this cohort (due to period-specific military service selection effects), in combination with the early 1980s recession and declining availability of affordable housing, accounted for the higher risk of homelessness for this particular age cohort of veterans.

Other than the effects of older average age and some age cohort differences in the higher prevalence of mental health and substance abuse issues, there is actually little evidence to suggest that there are remarkable health status differences between veterans and nonveterans. However, for veterans who were exposed to particular risks during the Vietnam War and the Gulf War, there are health conditions that may be of higher prevalence in these subgroups of homeless veterans. For combat-exposed veterans of both wars, there is the higher risk of post-traumatic stress disorder (PTSD); for the Vietnam War combat veterans, there are a variety of health conditions that are implicated from exposure to the herbicide "Agent Orange"; and for veterans stationed in the Persian Gulf, there is the possibility of "Gulf War Syndrome,"which makes its appearance in a range of unexplained illnesses (McMurray-Avila, 2001). For homeless veterans who have served during the Iraq and Afghanistan Wars, there is far less research currently available. However, the relationships between repeated exposures to combat conditions and PTSD, and the disturbingly higher rates of depression and suicide among the more recent cohorts of veterans, strongly suggest that mental health screening and access to mental health care are essential considerations for more recent veterans.

In contrast to the general population of homeless persons, a large proportion of homeless veterans may have access to a range of medical and social services through the U.S. Department of Veterans Affairs (a.k.a. the VA). It is often the case that the most beneficial intervention that a community health care provider can offer a homeless veteran is access to the VA health and social services that he/she is entitled to based on military service. Sometimes this takes an artful combination of engagement and trust building with the homeless veteran and aggressive sustained advocacy within the VA system. For this reason, it is essential that providers who work with homeless veterans have at least basic familiarity with the VA's eligibility criteria. In general, eligibility for VA veterans benefits requires discharge from active military service under "other than dishonorable conditions" (a dishonorable discharge is a sanction that denies VA benefits for veterans who have been discharged for serious violations of military regulations). Many homeless veterans may have been discharged from the military for problems related to mental health and substance abuse issues, but this does not necessarily entail a dishonorable discharge that would result in a denial of benefits. Aside from this general criteria for VA benefit eligibility, the VA has a different set of entitled benefits depending upon service during periods of war, whether health problems and disabilities have been connected by the VA to military service, and the effects of health problems/disabilities on employability. Finally, access to services through the VA health care system is determined by a priority ranking system that considers the extent of disablement, whether or not the health conditions/disabilities are service connected, period of military service, and level of income (Department of Veterans Affairs, 2010).[2]

Homeless Families With Children

Although the years from 2005 through 2007 showed some decline in the proportion of the homeless population that comprised families with children, there is growing evidence that much if not all the recent progress in reducing family homelessness may have been halted by the national economic downturn that emerged during the final years of the Bush Administration. It remains the situation that well over a third of the homeless population comprises families with children, with tens of thousands living in unsheltered conditions (Homelessness Research Institute, 2009). Racial minority families, particularly African American families, are more than three times more likely to

---

[2] While the VA provides the public and health care providers with an array of conveniently accessible documents pertaining to VA benefits and eligibility criteria, see McMurray-Avila (2001) *Homeless Veterans and Health Care: A Resource Guide for Providers* (available for download at no cost at http://www.nhchc.org/Publications/HomelessVetsHealthCare.pdf). Section 3 of this resource guide includes an extraordinarily clinician-friendly and detailed summary of the VA's complex eligibility criteria.

be counted among the homeless than White families, and the typical homeless family is a young single mother with two or more preschool aged children (HCH Clinicians' Network, 1998). While family violence is a significant cause of homelessness among families with children, the principal causes are the disproportionate rates of poverty among families with children and the lack of affordable housing for low-income families (NCH, 2009c). Since 2008, low-income families with children have been the first to be affected by rising levels of unemployment and poverty rates, and more middle-income families appear to be transitioning to homelessness through the mechanism of home mortgage foreclosures. Between April of 2008, when rising levels of unemployment and the crisis in the home mortgage market began to ensnare middle-income families, and April of 2009 (when the crisis in the home mortgage market was fully blown), home foreclosure filings had increased by 32% (NCH, 2009d). Although it may seem that families that lose their homes to foreclosure have the option of moving to rental housing, that is often only an option for families that have managed to maintain a household income that is close to the local median. For families whose income is no more than 30% of the local median income level, there are far fewer rental options—particularly for families with younger children (NCH, 2009d).

Families with children who lose their homes engage in a variety of strategies to try to minimize the impact of homelessness on their children, and as much as possible ensure that their children are safe. These strategies include seeking transitional housing, living with relatives, and choosing to have the older boys and the father of the family live elsewhere due to restrictive homeless shelter policies (NCH, 2009c). However, even though the parents and social service providers may be more successful in keeping homeless children in warm and safe environs, the loss of stable housing can have serious long-term effects on children. Mental health problems such as anxiety, depression, and withdrawal are much more prevalent among homeless children, and compared to other children, they have twice as many ear infections, four times the number of asthma attacks, a high prevalence of speech and other developmental delays, and a much higher rate of hospitalizations (National Policy and Advocacy Council on Homelessness, 2009; NCH, 2009c). Despite a national policy to expand Medicaid and State Children's Health Insurance Program (SCHIP) coverage to a larger share of low-income and poor families, proof of citizenship policies put in place to prevent the enrollment of undocumented immigrants on publicly sponsored health care coverage programs have placed significant barriers to the Medicaid/SCHIP enrollment of all homeless children—not just those specifically targeted by pejorative immigration policies (NHHC, 2009).

Aside from the health problems mentioned previously (the high prevalence of poorly controlled asthma, ear infections, and developmental delay markers), homeless children tend to have much higher rates of exposure to domestic violence (NCH, 2009c). Despite the high prevalence of health problems and various risk factors, homeless children are far less likely to have even routine preventive health care. Even relative to other poor children, they have fewer routine health screenings, fewer basic and essential immunizations, and inadequate dental care (HCH Clinicians' Network, 1998; NHHC, 2009). Finally, because homeless children also face significant barriers to enrollment and attendance in school (transportation problems, restrictive residency requirements, and the lack of school supplies and clean/appropriate clothing), even for primary grade school-aged homeless children, rates of enrollment in schools are low relative to children in stable housing (NCH, 2009e).

All of these findings have important implications for health care providers. In addition to the *General Clinical Practice Considerations* that were summarized in the preceding section, children who are in homeless families require sensitivity to their health and mental health risks, specialized assessment questions, and special screenings for mental health problems and developmental delays. Fortunately, over the past decade, a number of organizations have worked cooperatively to develop clinical practice guidelines and other resources for clinicians that are specific to providing health care to homeless families—including, in particular, the Health Resources and Services Agency (HRSA), the National Coalition for the Homeless, the National Alliance to End Homelessness, and the National Health Care for the Homeless Council.[3]

Homeless Youth

Homeless youth are generally defined as adolescents under the age of 18 who lack parental, foster, or institutional care (NCH, 2008). However, many consider persons in their late teens (18–19 years old) to be included among this population. Homeless youth are equally divided between

---

[3] See the List of Resources at end of the chapter for information on the array of clinical practice resources that these organizations have developed. For children in homeless families, see in particular the National Health Care for the Homeless Council's *Homeless Children: What Every Health Provider Should Know* (available at http://www.nhchc.org/Children/).

males and females, and it is estimated that 5% to 7% of American youths become at least temporarily homeless in a typical year (National Alliance to End Homelessness, 2007).

The factors that lead to youth homelessness are found at multiple levels. At the macrostructural level, the same factors that lead to adult homelessness also affect youth: poverty, unemployment, and the lack of affordable housing. At the institutional level, a particular engine of homelessness among young people in late adolescence is the foster care system; every year, it is estimated that between 20,000 and 25,000 youths "age out" of the foster care system—meaning that at age 18 in many states, they become ineligible for either shelter or supervision under the foster care system (National Alliance to End Homelessness, 2007). At the family level, the same family dysfunctions that populate the foster care system (abuse, neglect, and unmanaged conflict) cause youth to run away from home. Youth who are GLBT and fail to find acceptance and support from their family and community are also at risk for homelessness. Finally, at the individual level, there are the risks and vulnerabilities that also lead to homelessness in adulthood: impaired coping skills, mental illness, and substance abuse (NCH, 2008).

In addition to the health risks that are general to all homeless persons (exposure to infectious disease, lack of preventive medical and dental care, poor nutrition, stress, and social isolation), there are some health risks that are more specific to homeless youth. For example, because many homeless youth have few job skills or have the legal documentation needed to obtain conventional employment, it is not uncommon for either boys or girls to trade sex for food, clothing, and shelter. As a result of unprotected sex and also exposure to IV drug abuse, the prevalence of HIV in homeless youth is from 2 to 10 times higher than that of the general youth population (NCH, 2008). Other areas of specific risk include violence victimization, injuries due to risky behavior, and suicide (National Alliance to End Homelessness, 2007). However, in contrast to older groups of homeless persons, there is some evidence that homeless adolescents are more likely to have health insurance coverage through their status as students or dependents on parental policies (Barkin, Balkrishnan, Manuel, Andersen, & Gelberg, 2003).

Based on extensive experience in clinical practice with homeless youth, Akers (2009) suggests there are several factors and considerations that clinicians should keep in mind as they grapple with the unique challenges of providing health care to homeless youth, most of which we summarize in the points that follow. First, clinicians should be aware that homeless youth have typically had a number of negative encounters with the health care system, the child welfare system, and juvenile courts, and as a result, they tend to distrust traditional health care providers. The building of trust can begin with being open to differences in appearance (tattoos, piercings, and dramatic hair styles), in sexual orientation, and in language and demeanor. Transparency about the nature and limits of confidentiality is critical, as is consistency of follow-through on all matters, both large and small. Akers also makes the point that, for both boys and girls, clinic encounters (for whatever original reason) are an important opportunity to discuss STDs, safe sex, and birth control knowledge and resources. Because for both boys and girls there are often histories of sexual abuse and exploitation, genital exams should always be chaperoned by another staff member. Finally, should referrals to specialists be required, the probability of follow-through and adherence is greatly enhanced if another trusted figure (e.g., a caseworker) accompanies the youth (Akers, 2009).

Insights from more systematic qualitative research with homeless youth (Darbyshire, Fereday, & Drummond, 2006; Haldenby, Berman, & Forchuk, 2007) confirm Akers's (2009) observations that homeless youth are particularly sensitive to being labeled, and acutely aware of being judged. Other pervasive alienating encounters with the health care system included the sense of being "processed" as opposed to cared for. Examples include hasty "drive-by" assessments with no attempts by clinicians to connect with or engage the youth; the lack of explanations for procedures, tests, and referrals; the lack of any sense of personal say, control, or agency in their health care; and approaches to health care that are fragmented and fragmentizing, thus further undermining the youth's search for coherence, safety, and predictability (Darbyshire et al., 2006).

In contrast to the common perception that homeless youth are apathetic to health and indifferent to effects of life in the street on their health, researchers have found that homeless youth tend to be very worried about their health, and also the ironic contrast between their marginalized daily existence and the health care system's monotonic emphasis on healthy nutrition, avoidance of health risks, and timely preventive health care (Haldenby et al., 2007). It is not at all lost to the homeless youth that the essential requisite to good health and long life is having a suitable place to call home.

Homeless Persons With Addictions

Although substance abuse is a fact of life on the streets, as discussed at the beginning of the chapter, only about 38% of the homeless population are addicted to alcohol and only about 26% abuse other drugs

(NCH, 2007). However, the prevalence of addiction is much higher among the chronically homeless (defined previously as persons continuously homeless for a year or more or having at least four episodes of homelessness over the most recent 3 years). Point-in-time estimates of addictions can also understate the problem of addictions among the homeless population; researchers estimate that as many as half of all people who are homeless have or will have diagnosable substance use disorders at some point over the course of their lives (HCH Clinicians' Network, 2003a).

The relationship between addictions and homelessness is a complicated one. On the one hand, there is clear evidence from a range of studies that confirm the public perception that the principal causes of homelessness include drug and alcohol addictions. On the other hand, homelessness itself can be a factor in either causing or further exacerbating substance abuse and addictions. The harshness of life on the streets, the daily experiences of disdain and stigmatization, isolation from social supports, and the use of drugs or alcohol as a path to acceptance in some homeless communities are all factors that identify homelessness as a cause of addiction as well as an effect (NCH, 2007). It is also true that homeless persons with untreated mental illness often use street drugs and alcohol as a form of self-medication (NCH, 2007).

According to a summary of research on homelessness and addictions by the HCH Clinicians' Network (2003a), alcohol addiction is the most common form of addiction among the homeless, occurring in almost half of all homeless, single adults, while drug abuse occurs in approximately one-third of this group. It is also noted that "increasingly, individuals who are homeless and have substance use disorders are younger and include women, minorities, poly-drug users, and individuals with cooccurring mental disorders" (p. 1). In another summary of the research on homelessness and addictions that was developed by the National Health Care for the Homeless Council,[4] gender and race are also associated with different risks for and forms of substance abuse. For example, homeless males are more likely to report drug and alcohol problems than homeless women (who in turn are more likely to report mental health problems), whereas crack cocaine addiction is more prevalent among African American homeless (Zerger, 2002).

---

[4] The parent organization for the HCH Clinicians' Network.

For homeless persons who are addicted, the treatment problem is much more formidable and complex than simply focusing on the addiction. Even if it can be determined in the individual case that the addiction problem preceded homelessness in the causal chain, the challenge is to then break the vicious cycle that has been established between homelessness and addiction. There are a range of approaches for the treatment of addictions with homeless persons, and some of the major distinctions between them are as follows:

- Voluntary treatment versus mandated treatment
- Short-term versus long-term programs
- Addiction-focused versus holistically framed approaches
- Total abstinence versus reduced harm models
- Medical model treatment programs versus social model treatment programs

The definition of "success" also can vary substantially from one treatment program or clinician to the next. For example, in Zerger's (2002) summary of a hierarchy of "successful" treatment outcomes for homeless persons addicted to alcohol, there were seven levels of success defined:

1. Complete sobriety and abstinence as advocated by 12-step programs
2. Graduation from the treatment program, or at least engagement in the program for a lengthy period of time
3. Attainment of life skills objectives such as sobriety, employment, enrollment in school, ability to handle money, and housing
4. Change in psychological and emotional realms
5. Interpersonal improvements in terms of better relationships with family and friends
6. Ability to cope with problems and stress
7. Existential/phenomenological improvement—a global, subjective sense of improving one's life that depends on the client's idiosyncratic life and drug history, patterns of residential instability, motivational state, and prior functioning

However success is defined, the evidence concerning the efficacy of alternative approaches to the treatment of addictions in the homeless is difficult to sort out. There are some broad conclusions, though, that pertain to the characteristics of the programs that have the most success in breaking the cycle between addictions and homelessness. These are summarized by the HCH Clinicians' Network as "Common Themes in Effective Substance Abuse Programs" (HCH Clinician's Network, 2003a).

- **Comprehensive Services.** Offering a rich blend of services that address the client's safety, health, social, and material needs, through formal and informal relationships with other service organizations.
- **Integrated Services.** Use of multidisciplinary clinical teams to provide simultaneous, well-coordinated treatment of co-occurring conditions at the same service site, with an emphasis on housing as an essential component of treatment.
- **Client-Centered Care.** An individualized plan of care based on the client's needs, wishes, capacities, and readiness for treatment, rather than on the program's predetermined benchmarks for treatment outcomes.
- **Uniquely Qualified Staff.** Caregivers with compassion, empathy, patience, flexibility, and a sense of humor who are able to handle difficult situations rationally and calmly and who reflect the diversity of their clients.
- **Access to Housing.** A stable living situation, especially early in the treatment process, that is not necessarily contingent upon sobriety.

As critical as it is to fully understand the characteristics of successful approaches to the treatment of the drug and alcohol addictions that create and sustain homelessness, these considerations should be framed by the powerful point made by Zerger at the conclusion of her comprehensive review of the research on addictions and homelessness (Zerger, 2002, p. 44):

> Much of this research begins with the premise that homelessness is a static variable. Researchers examine the efficacy of specific treatment modalities and techniques to engage or retain homeless individuals in treatment with the understanding that outcome "success" resides in the individual. This underlying assumption obscures the social and economic causes of homelessness, drawing our attention away from structural solutions.

In our own analysis of the literature on addictions and homelessness, we too have been struck by the general tendency to deemphasize the social and economic factors that promote and sustain the linkages between addictions and homelessness. Although clinicians and clinical researchers may be more at home with an individualistic orientation to addictions and homelessness, making genuine in-roads to the reduction of risk and prevalence of the homelessness addiction syndrome entails a strong focus on the social and economic causes of homelessness that lie outside of the scope of individual agency.

CONCLUSION

The central purpose of this chapter is to enable clinicians from all health care disciplines to be more informed and effective practitioners with patients who happen, for any number of reasons, to be homeless. Toward that end, we have endeavored to provide a helpful synopsis of the structural and individual factors that produce homelessness, knowledge about the prevalence of homelessness and the characteristics of different subpopulations of homeless persons, and summary information about the diseases and risk factors found to be associated with homelessness. We have also discussed what is known about best practices with different subpopulations of homeless persons and how the organization of health services should be adapted to promote optimal outcomes for homeless persons. To accomplish all of this, we have drawn upon two decades of social and clinical research on the nature of homelessness and its impacts on health and health care as well as the experience-based wisdom of dedicated frontline clinicians in social work, nursing, and medicine. In doing the background research for this chapter, we have been deeply impressed and gratified by the innovative clinical practice and social policy interventions that have created a vibrant network of clinics and practitioners who specialize in health care for homeless persons. As a nation, we are far, far ahead of where we were even a decade ago in adapting clinical practices and the organization of health care services to the unique challenges imposed by endemic homelessness.

That said and celebrated, the adaptation of clinical practice and health services to achieve better outcomes for homeless patients really should not be the end goal of any health care clinician or administrator. If only one thing can be gleaned from the collective wisdom summarized in this chapter, it is that homelessness is not a clinical complication, so much as it is the disease itself. While health care clinicians are in a leveraged position with respect to their potential impact on the health and lives of individual homeless families and persons, they also hold a leveraged position at the social policy level. Because of their encompassing daily knowledge of the health and mental health consequences of homelessness, health care clinicians from all disciplines can be (and must be) a powerful and authoritative voice in the promotion of policies essential to the elimination of homelessness as a defining social problem of our time. Such social policies as affordable housing for low-wage workers, adequate income subsidies for the disabled, well-integrated community mental health services (including supported housing for the mentally ill), and transitional housing for families in crisis are not social policies so much as they are highly effective public health strategies. In truth, such strategies target the containment and ultimate eradication of a societal epidemic that disables and kills thousands every year.

SUGGESTED RESOURCES FOR HEALTH CARE AND HOMELESS POPULATIONS

National Alliance to End Homelessness
http://www.endhomelessness.org/

National Coalition for the Homeless
http://www.nationalhomeless.org

National Health Care for the Homeless Council: Clinicians' Network
http://www.nhchc.org/network.html

Clinical Practice Resources
http://www.nhchc.org/clinicalresources.html

Adapted Clinical Guidelines
http://www.nhchc.org/practiceadaptations.html

Healing Hands Newsletters
http://www.nhchc.org/healinghands.html

Homeless Children: What Every Health Provider Should Know
http://www.nhchc.org/Children/

Homeless Veterans
http://www.nhchc.org/Publications/HomelessVetsHealthCare.pdf
http://www.va.gov/health/homeless/

Motivational Interviewing Techniques, (brief review) see:
http://homelessness.samhsa.gov/resource/motivational-interviewing-assumptions-and-principles—a-broad framework-32839.aspx.

REFERENCES

Akers, P. (2009). Pearls of wisdom: Serving homeless youth and adolescents. Retrieved February 21, 2010, from http://www.nhchc.org/2009conference/workshops/W79/Peggy_Pearls_of_Wisdom.ppt#258,8,What We Know

Barkin, S., Balkrishnan, R., Manuel, J., Andersen, R., & Gelberg, L. (2003). Health care utilization among homeless adolescents and young adults. *Journal of Adolescent Health, 32*(4), 253–256.

Bonin, E., Brehove, T., Kline, S., Misgen, M., Post, P., Strehlow, A. J., Yungman J. (2004). *Adapting your practice: General recommendations for the care of homeless patients.* Nashville, TN: National Health Care for the Homeless Council.

Burt, M. (1997). Causes of the growth of homelessness during the 1980s. In Fannie Mae Foundation (Ed.), *Understanding homelessness: New policy research perspectives.* Washington, DC: Fannie Mae Foundation.

Daiski, I. (2007). Perspectives of homeless people on their health and health care needs priorities. *Journal of Advanced Nursing, 58*(3), 273–281.

Darbyshire, P., Fereday, J., & Drummond, A. (2006). Engagement with health and social care services: Perceptions of homeless young people with mental health problems. *Health and Social Care in the Community, 14*(6), 553–562.

Department of Veterans Affairs. (2010). *VA health care enrollment priority groups fact sheet No. 164-2.* Washington, DC: Author.

Flet-Lisk, S., & Mays, G. (2002). Back to the drawing board: New directions in health plans' care management strategies. *Health Affairs, 21*(5), 210–217.

Gilens, M. (1999). *Why Americans hate welfare: Race, media, and the politics of antipoverty policy.* Chicago, IL: University of Chicago Press.

Haldenby, A. M., Berman, H., & Forchuk, C. (2007). Homelessness and health in adolescents. *Qualitative Health Research, 17*(9), 1232–1244.

Health Care for the Homeless Clinicians' Network. (1998). Health care for homeless children: A clinician's perspective. *Healing Hands, 2*(6), 1–4.

Health Care for the Homeless Clinicians' Network. (2003a). A comprehensive approach to substance abuse and homelessnes. *Healing Hands, 7*(5), 1–6.

Health Care for the Homeless Clinicians' Network. (2003b). Filling the gaps in dental care. *Healing Hands, 7*(3), 1–6.

Health Care for the Homeless Clinicians' Network. (2009). Caring for clients with comorbid psychiatric & mental illnesses. *Healing Hands, 13*(6), 1–6.

Health Resources and Services Administration. (2010). The health center program: What is a health center? Retrieved February 12, 2010, from http://bphc.hrsa.gov/about/

Himmelstein, D. U., Warren, E., Thorne, D., & Woolhandler, S. (2005). Market Watch: Illness and injury as contributors to bankruptcy. *Health Affairs, 63*(5), 1377–1386.

Homelessness Research Institute. (2009). *Homelessness counts: Changes in homelessness 2005–2007.* Washington, DC: National Alliance to End Homelessness.

House, J., Landis, K., & Umberson, D. (1988). Social relationships and health. *Science, 241*(4865), 540–545.

Kleinman, A. (1988). *The illness narratives: Suffering, healing, and the human condition.* New York, NY: Basic Books.

Knechta, T., & Martinez, L. M. (2009). Humanizing the homeless: Does contact erode stereotypes? *Social Science Research, 38*(3), 521–534.

Kogel, P. (2007). Causes of homelessness. In D. Levinson & M. Ross (Eds.), *Homelessness handbook.* Great Barrington, MA: Berkshire Publishing Group.

Lee, B., Farrell, C., & Link, B. (2004). Revisiting the contact hypothesis: The case of public exposure to homelessness. *American Sociological Review, 69*, 40–63.

Lee, B. A., Jones, S. H., & Lewis, D. W. (1990). Public beliefs about the causes of homelessness. *Social Forces, 69*(1), 253–265.

Levinson, D., & Ross, M. (Eds.). (2007). *Homelessness handbook.* Great Barrington, MA: Berkshire Publishing Group.

McMurray-Avila, M. (2001). *Homeless veterans and health care: A resource guide for providers.* Nashville, TN: National Health Care for the Homeless Council.

McMurray-Avila, M., Gelberg, L., & Breakey, W. R. (1999). Balancing act: Clinical practices that respond to the needs of homeless people. In L. B. Fosburg & D. L. Dennis (Eds.), *In practical lessons: The 1998 National Symposium on Homelessness Research.* Washington, DC: U.S. Department of Housing and Urban Development and U.S. Department of Health and Human Services.

Miller, W., & Rollnick, S. (2002). *Motivational interviewing: Preparing people to change addictive behavior* (2nd ed.). New York, NY: Guilford Press.

National Alliance to End Homelessness. (2007). *Youth homelessness.* Washington, DC: Author.

National Policy and Advocacy Council on Homelessness. (2009). Helping homeless families: The role of health care. Retrieved February 19th, 2009, from http://npach.org/facts-health.pdf

National Coalition for the Homeless. (2007). *Who is homeless: NCH fact sheet #3.* Washington, DC: Author.

National Coalition for the Homeless. (2008). *Homeless youth.* Washington, DC: Author.

National Coalition for the Homeless. (2009a). *How many people experience homelessness.* Washington, DC: Author.

National Coalition for the Homeless. (2009b). *Health care and homelessness.* Washington, DC: Author.

National Coalition for the Homeless. (2009c). *Homeless families with children.* Washington, DC: Author.

National Coalition for the Homeless. (2009d). *Foreclosures to homelessness: The forgotten victims of the subprime crisis.* Washington, DC: Author.

National Coalition for the Homeless. (2009e). *Education of homeless children and youth.* Washington, DC: Author.

National Health Care for the Homeless Council. (2010). The basics of homelessness. Retrieved February 12, 2010, from http://www.nhchc.org/Publications/basics_of_homelessness.html

National Health Care for the Homeless Council. (2009). *Medicaid, SCHIP, and homelessness.* Nashville, TN: Author.

O'Connell J. J. (2005). *Premature Mortality in Homeless Populations: A Review of the Literature,* 19 pages. Nashville, TN: National Health Care for the Homeless Council.

Pearson, D., Bruggman, A., & Haukoos, J. (2007). Out-of-hospital and emergency department utilization by adult homeless patients. *Annals of Emergency Medicine, 50*(6), 646–652.

Redelmeier, D., Molin, J., & Tibshirani, R. (1995). A randomised trial of compassionate care for the homeless in an emergency department. *Lancet, 345*(8958), 1131–1134.

Rosenheck, R., Frisman, L., & Chung, A. (1994). The proportion of veterans among homeless men. *American Journal of Public Health, 84*(3), 466–468.

Stewart B. McKinney Act of 1994. U.S. Code: Title 42: § 11302.

U.S. Bureau of Labor Statistics. (2010). *Employment situation summary.* Washington, DC: Author.

U.S. Department of Housing and Urban Development, Office of Community Planning and Development. (2008). *The 2007 annual homeless assessment report: A summary of findings.* Washington, DC: Author.

U.S. Department of Housing and Urban Development, Office of Community Planning and Development. (2009). *The 2008 annual homeless assessment report: A summary of findings.* Washington, DC: Author.

West Coast Poverty Center. (2009). *Poverty news flash no. 2009-10, Enumerating inequality.* Seattle: University of Washington.

Zerger, S. (2002). *Substance abuse treatment: What works for homeless people? A review of the literature.* Nashville, TN: National Health Care for the Homeless Council.

6

Substance Abuse and Addiction

INTRODUCTION

Definitions

Among the general public, the definitional boundaries between *substance abuse, drug dependence,* and *addiction* tend to be fuzzy and the terms are often used interchangeably. Although there are ongoing interdisciplinary debates about the most precise definition of each, there is clear consensus that *substance abuse* refers to a category of risky health behaviors, rather than a health condition. On the other hand, both *drug dependence* and *addiction* are health conditions. More specifically, the National Library of Medicine Encyclopedia refers to *drug abuse* as the use of illegal drugs or the misuse of prescription or over-the-counter drugs for at least a year with negative consequences; whereas, it defines *drug dependence* as an individual needing a drug (illicit or otherwise) to function normally. *Addiction,* distinct from dependence, entails the compulsive use of a drug, despite its negative or dangerous effects (Dugdale, 2010a, 2010b). According to the National Institute of Drug Abuse (NIDA), *addiction* is specifically defined as a chronic relapsing disease that is characterized both by compulsive drug seeking and by long-lasting chemical changes in the brain (NIDA, 2010).

Whereas drug abuse, dependence, and addiction are conceptually distinct, for a small but significant share of the U.S. population they are linked together in progressive stages from abuse to dependence and to addiction. That said, whether or not an individual progresses from drug abuse to dependence and addiction is contingent on a variety of risk and protective factors that pertain to the specific properties of the drugs used, genetic history, psychological strengths and vulnerabilities, and the interaction of individual traits and social context (Brook, Pahl, & Rubenstone, 2008).

Data on Prevalence

There is no single optimal source for data on the prevalence of drug abuse and addiction. Although the National Survey of Drug Use and Health (NSDUH) provides the most comprehensive and current estimates of drug abuse and addiction among persons living in U.S. households, the NSDUH does not sample the homeless, military, and institutionalized segments of the populations. For these populations, as well as some other special populations, we need to rely on an array of other special sample surveys and smaller scale studies. Although the substances that entail abuse and addiction include tobacco, alcohol, and prescribed and illicit drugs, in this chapter, we focus on the categories of drug abuse and addiction that are most specific to the mission of safety-net hospitals—abuse and addictions that entail alcohol and illicit drugs.

We will begin with a review of the most recently available illicit drug and alcohol abuse data from the NSDUH. The way to think about the NSDUH estimates is as a nationally representative sample of U.S. residents, aged 12 years and older, residing in either individual or family households—rather than atypical populations such as the military, institutionalized, or homeless populations. Although illicit drug use occurs among children younger than 12 years of age, the risk of illicit drug use escalates dramatically after age 12 and for this reason (as well as the validity of estimates), the NSDUH data are limited to the 12 and older population.

Illicit Drug Use

According to the NSDUH survey data, in 2008 an estimated 20.1 million Americans aged 12 or older (or about 8% of the 12 and older population) are current illicit drug users, meaning that they had used an illicit drug defined as marijuana/hashish, cocaine, heroin, hallucinogens, inhalants, or prescription-type psychotherapeutics used nonmedically (Substance Abuse and Mental Health Services Administration [SAMHSA], 2009). Marijuana was the most commonly used illicit drug (6.1% of the 12 and older population), followed by prescription-type psychotherapeutic drugs used nonmedically in the past month (2.5%), methamphetamine (1.3%), cocaine (0.7%), and hallucinogens (0.4%) (SAMHSA, 2009).

The Age Distribution of Illicit Drug Use. Although it is important to have some grasp of the general prevalence of illicit drug use among the 12 and older population, prevalence varies dramatically by age, gender, race, ethnicity, and socioeconomic factors. We will begin with a graphical depiction of the age distribution of illicit drug use.

As Figure 6.1 suggests, illicit drug use has a low incidence (about 3.5%) among children until about age 14, when it begins to escalate dramatically until it peaks to a 22% prevalence by about age 19—at which point, the prevalence of illicit drug use undertakes an almost equally dramatic decline. That said, it is also apparent that the prevalence of illicit drug use remains modestly high (in excess of 10%) throughout the 20s and does not reach the low-preadolescent level, until about age 60. It should also be kept in mind that there is a great deal going on in the age distribution of illicit drug use that is not captured in a simple linear graph such as Figure 6.1. For example, while it is true that in the life of any one individual, the probability of drug use over the life course escalates in adolescence and then begins to decline with the initiation of adulthood, it is also true that those continuing to use illicit drugs beyond the early 20s are more likely to represent the drug dependent and addicted as opposed to those who are experimenting with drugs. For the dabblers and experimenters, the decline in regular use after age 20 is much sharper than the general picture depicted in Figure 6.1 It is also true that the age trajectories for illicit drug use, dependency, and addiction also vary significantly by the type of drug. For example, the highest risk for meeting the *Diagnostic and Statistical Manual of Mental Disorders*, third edition, revised, criteria for dependency for marijuana occurs between 17 and 18 years of age, whereas for cocaine dependence the high-risk range falls between 24 and 26 years of age (Brook et al., 2008).

Gender and Illicit Drug Use. The rate of current illicit drug use among persons aged 12 and older is higher for males than for females; as of 2008, the prevalence of current drug use was 9.9% for males versus 6.3% for females (SAMHSA, 2009). However, gender disparities in

FIGURE 6.1 Prevalence of Current Illicit Drug Use by Age; U.S. Population
Age 12 and Older

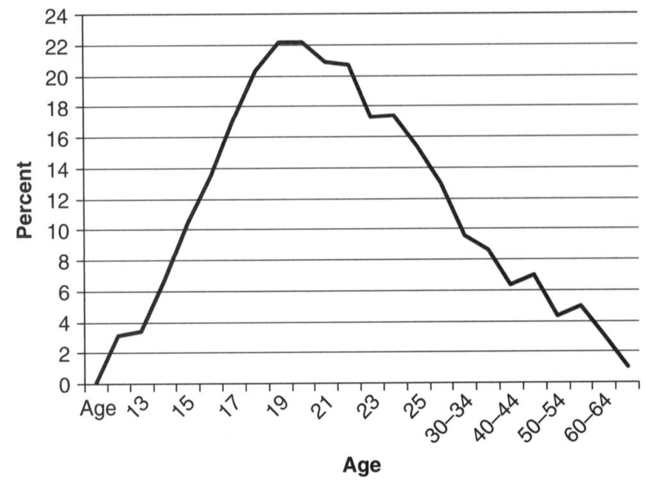

From Substance Abuse and Mental Health Services Administration (2009). *Results from the 2008
National Survey on Drug Use and Health: National Findings (Office of Applied Studies, NSDUH
Series H-36, HHS Publication No. SMA 09-4434)*. Rockville, MD: U.S. Department of Health and
Human Services. Table G.10 Illicit Drug Use in Lifetime, Past Year, and Past Month, by Detailed
Age Category: Percentages, 2007 and 2008.

illicit drug use vary by the specific drug. For example, whereas males
have a higher incidence of marijuana use (7.9% vs. 4.4%), for the nonmedical use of psychotherapeutic drugs, pain relievers, tranquilizers,
stimulants, methamphetamine, and sedatives, the prevalences are
nearly identical.

There are two gender-related trends in illicit drug abuse that are
worrisome from a public health perspective. The first concerns what
appears to be recent rise in illicit drug use among females, in contrast
to a stable and even declining trend among males. According to the
most recently released NSDUH survey, the rate of current illicit drug
use among females aged 12 or older increased from 5.8% in 2007 to
6.3% in 2008, whereas for males, illicit drug use declined from 10.4%
to 9.9% during the same period. Current marijuana use also increased
among females during the most recent year, but for males, there was
no significant change (SAMHSA, 2009).

The second gender-related trend that is worrisome is illicit drug
use during pregnancy. On the one hand, it is reassuring to note that
the rate of illicit drug use among pregnant women aged 15 to 44 years

is only about half of that of non-pregnant women of the childbearing age range (5.1% for pregnant women age 15 to 44 vs. 9.8% for non-pregnant women 15 to 44). On the other hand, the more dismal statistic is that among women aged 15 to 17, the rate of illicit drug use is much higher among those who are pregnant than those who are not pregnant—respectively, 21.6% versus 12.9% (SAMHSA, 2009).

Race, Ethnicity, and Illicit Drug Use.   There are dramatic racial disparities in illicit drug use that are generally consistent with the racial/ethnic disparities in an array of other health risks and health conditions that are by-products of a racially and ethnically stratified society. As Figure 6.2 shows, the highest incidence of current illicit drug use is reported by NSDUH survey respondents who identify themselves as multiracial (14.7%), whereas the lowest incidence of illicit drug use is reported among Asians (although it should be noted that incidence of illicit drug use varies dramatically among the different subpopulations of Asian Americans). Native American respondents (such as American Indian/Alaska Natives) have a somewhat higher prevalence of illicit drug use than Whites, but these disparities are not as dramatic as those depicted by the popular media and the television crime genre—or as would be expected given the racial disproportionality in imprisonment rates for drug-related offenses.[1] In reference to American Indians/Alaska Natives, although the NSDUH sampling design includes residents of tribal reservations, it does not provide separate estimates for American Indians/Alaska Natives living on tribal reservations (J. Colliver, Substance Abuse and Mental Health Services Administration statistician, personal communication, July 20, 2010). As another caution, it should be emphasized that racial and ethnic differences in illicit drug use, as with other health disparities, represent the confounding influences of socioeconomic disparities by race and ethnicity.

Socioeconomic Characteristics and Illicit Drug Use.   As discussed in Chapter 3, Stratification and Stigma, socioeconomic characteristics refer to income, education, and occupation. The NSDUH survey data report illicit drug use by education, which of course highly

---

[1] That said, it can be argued that the disproportionate imprisonment rates for African Americans for drug related offenses, relative to Whites, suppress the racial differences in illicit drug use in the NSDUH estimates, because the NSDUH excludes institutionalized populations. We are not aware of any studies that address this possibility, but we believe it is a plausible argument.

FIGURE 6.2 Current Illicit Drug Use by Race and Ethnicity for Persons Aged 12 and Older; U.S. Population 2008

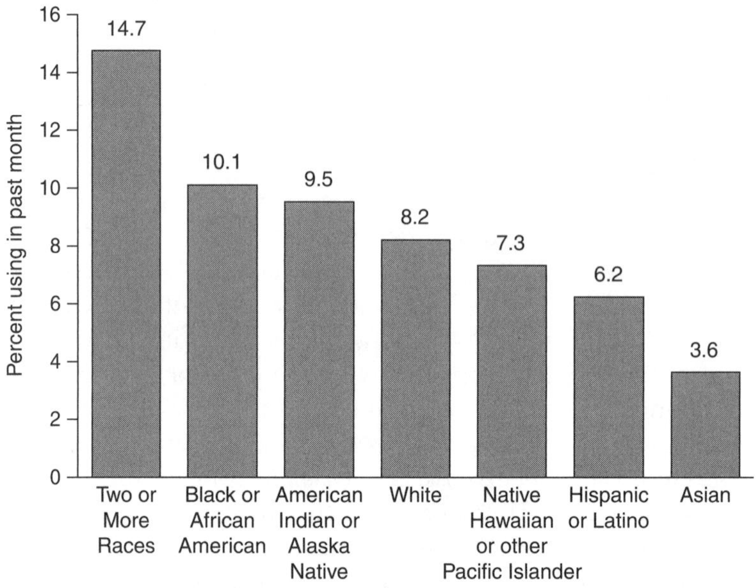

From Substance Abuse and Mental Health Services Administration (2009). *Results from the 2008 National Survey on Drug Use and Health: National Findings (Office of Applied Studies, NSDUH Series H-36, HHS Publication No. SMA 09-4434).* Rockville, MD: U.S. Department of Health and Human Services. Figure 2.9 Past Month Illicit Drug Use among Persons Aged 12 or Older, by Race/Ethnicity: 2008.

correlates with occupation. Education has an interesting relationship with illicit drug use that is captured in the distinction between *lifetime* illicit drug use and *current* illicit drug use. In essence, individuals who have higher levels of education are more likely to have experimented with illicit drugs than persons with less than a high school education, but the prevalence of current illicit drug use is significantly lower among college graduates (5.7%) than for those of lesser educational attainment: those who did not graduate from high school (8.1%), high school graduates (8.6%), and those with some college (9.4%) (SAMHSA, 2009). It might be said that exposure to college is a risk factor for illicit drug experimentation (noting that the current illicit drug use rates are highest among the "some college" category), but the completion of college is a protective factor against illicit drug dependency and addiction.

Intuitively enough, there is a strong relationship between employment status and illicit drug use. Among the unemployed, the prevalence of illicit drug use during 2008 was 19.6%, whereas for those employed full time, the prevalence was 8.0%. Even part-time employment brings with it dramatically lower rates of illicit drug use at not more than 10.2% (SAMHSA, 2009). The causal relationship between employment and illicit drug use obviously goes in both directions; that is, regular substance abuse and dependency reduces the likelihood of sustained, stable employment, and employment serves as a protective factor against a range of health risks—including substance abuse and addiction.

The Geography of Illicit Drug Use.   The prevalence of use varies both regionally across the United States and also by the degree of urbanization. Regionally, the highest rates of illicit drug use occur in Western states (9.8%), followed by the Northeast (8.2%), the Midwest (8.2%), and finally the Southern states at 7.1% (SAMHSA, 2009). With respect to urbanization, the highest rate of illicit drug use occurs in large metropolitan counties (8.5%), followed by small metropolitan counties (8.1%). The lowest rates of illicit drug use are found in modestly urbanized counties that are not a part of metropolitan areas (5.6%), whereas in completely rural counties, the rates of illicit drug use is slightly higher (6.1%) (SAMHSA, 2009).

Alcohol Abuse, Dependency, and Addiction

The NSDUH reports three categories of current alcohol use: *current use* (meaning at least one drink in the past 30 days, *binge drinking* (defined as 5 or more drinks on the same occasion on at least 1 day in the past 30 days), and *heavy use* (defined as 5 or more drinks on the same occasion on each of 5 or more days in the past 30 days). Obviously, these are not mutually exclusive or exhaustive categories of alcohol use, but they do provide a reasonable estimate of the prevalence of problematic drinking patterns. In our summary of the NSDUH data, we will focus on the prevalence of *binge drinking* and *heavy use* of alcohol as imperfect proxies for the relative prevalences of alcohol dependence and addiction—using the term *high-risk alcohol consumption* to represent either binge drinking or heavy alcohol use. Although reporting at least one episode of binge drinking or at least one 5-day spell of heavy alcohol use during the past 30 days does not translate to the definition of alcohol dependence or addiction, both are high-risk health behaviors that entail the use of alcohol to excess that at the population level correlate with alcohol addiction rates. By some conventions, drinking alcohol to excess is by itself sufficient to meet the definition of alcohol abuse. However, the American Psychiatric Association's *DSM-IV* definition of alcohol abuse requires evidence of problems with the recurrent use of alcohol in fulfilling major role obligations (in the workplace, school, or home), or recurrent use in situations where use is physically hazardous (e.g., driving, operating machinery), or where recurrent use of alcohol creates relational or legal problems (Hasin, 2003).

For this reason, we choose to use the term high-risk alcohol consumption as opposed to alcohol abuse—but, we emphasize that high-risk consumption serves as a useful proxy for the relative prevalence of alcohol abuse, dependence, and addiction in comparisons by gender, race, ethnicity, and socioeconomic position.[2]

The Age Distribution of High-Risk Alcohol Consumption. Figure 6.3 provides a highly useful summary of both the age-specific prevalences of binge drinking and heavy alcohol use during different points in the life course. For example, the prevalence of alcohol use rapidly escalates in adolescence, and throughout the 20s, the patterns of alcohol use are dominated by the high-risk patterns of binge drinking and heavy use. Although high-risk drinking patterns begin to recede at about age 25 (coinciding with the average age at first birth for women in the United States), it is only after the early 30s that the high-risk patterns of alcohol use recede to being the less normative forms of alcohol consumption—and even then, the retreat is quite gradual. It is not until the mid-40s that the pattern of alcohol consumption is reduced from being two-thirds high risk (as it is in the early 20s) to about one-third high risk. Indeed, it is fair to say that high-risk drinking in American society appears to only become markedly deviant (such that only about 10% or less engage in this behavior) after age 65.

---

[2] An alternative approach to the definition of alcohol abuse frames the definition of alcohol abuse in terms of the adverse consequences of alcohol use (e.g., property damage, drunk driving injuries, and deaths). For example, a report on the national economic costs of alcohol abuse for the National Institute of Alcohol Abuse and Alcoholism (Harwick, 2000) defines alcohol abuse as "any cost-generating aspect of alcohol consumption" (p. 1).

FIGURE 6.3 Current, Binge, and Heavy Alcohol Use Among Persons Aged 12 or Older, by Age: 2008

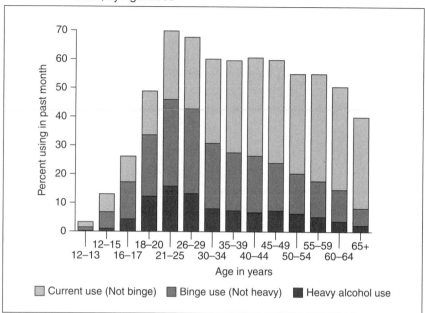

From Substance Abuse and Mental Health Services Administration (2009). *Results from the 2008 National Survey on Drug Use and Health: National Findings (Office of Applied Studies, NSDUH Series H-36, HHS Publication No. SMA 09-4434).* Rockville, MD: U.S. Department of Health and Human Services. Figure 3.1 Current, Binge, and Heavy Alcohol Use among Persons Aged 12 or Older, by Age: 2008.

Gender and High-Risk Alcohol Consumption. Females have rates of alcohol use during adolescence that are similar to males (respectively, 15.0% and 14.2%), and then sustain somewhat lower rates of alcohol use through the remainder of the life course. According to the most recent NSDUH data, 57% of males 12 or older identified themselves as current drinkers, while 46% of females do so (SAMHSA, 2009). Although there is a modest (11%) gender disparity in the general rate of alcohol use, the gender differences in high-risk drinking patterns are more pronounced. The male rate of binge drinking is 48% relative to a female binge drinking rate of 34%, and the male rate of heavy alcohol use is 20% relative to a female heavy alcohol usage rate of 9%.

Another way of assessing gender disparities in high-risk drinking is to examine gender disparities in arrests for driving under the influence (DUIs) where traffic fatalities are involved. DUI arrests where there are fatalities involved are more reliable then general

DUI arrests because fatality-involved DUI arrests are less likely to entail law enforcement discretion in the evaluation of intoxication. The male rate for fatality-involved DUIs is about 10 per 100,000 men, whereas the female fatality-involved DUI rate is 1.7 per 100,000 women (Schwartz, 2008). These data suggest that men, although being only moderately more likely to engage in binge and heavy drinking than women, are significantly more likely to engage in riskiest use of alcohol—DUI.

There is, however, a particular form of very high-risk drinking that is specific to women during the childbearing age range—drinking during pregnancy. Any level of alcohol consumption during pregnancy places the normal development of the fetus at serious risk for a range of alcohol-associated anomalies—most notably, fetal alcohol syndrome. The NSDUH estimates for alcohol consumption among pregnant women aged 15–44 are 10.6% for current alcohol use, 4.5% for binge drinking, and .8% for heavy drinking (SAMHSA, 2009). As disturbing as these rates of alcohol use during pregnancy are, they are likely to be well below those of the actual prevalences, since the NSDUH estimates are based on the self-reporting of behavior that is generally condemned as reckless and irresponsible.

Race, Ethnicity, and Alcohol Use.   Figure 6.4 provides a general summary of the NSDUH estimates for alcohol consumption patterns by race and ethnicity in the United States. We caution that racial and ethnic differences in alcohol use, as with other health disparities, represent the confounding influences of socioeconomic disparities by race and ethnicity.

As Figure 6.4 shows, there is significant racial and ethnic variation in both the prevalence of current alcohol use and in the prevalence of high-risk alcohol use. White Americans have the highest rate of current alcohol consumption, but are second only to Asian Americans in having a lower proportion of alcohol use that is of high risk (binge drinking or heavy alcohol use). Among Whites, about 43% of alcohol users report high-risk drinking behaviors, whereas among Asians, only 33% of alcohol users report high-risk drinking behaviors. Among African Americans and persons reporting themselves as being multiracial, slightly less than 50% of alcohol users report high-risk alcohol use. Among Latinos and Native Americans, however, most alcohol users report either binge or heavy alcohol use (respectively, 58% and 56%). These high-risk alcohol use rates also correspond to the higher proportion of DUI

FIGURE 6.4 Current, Binge, and Heavy Alcohol Use Among Persons Aged 12 or Older, by Race/Ethnicity: 2008

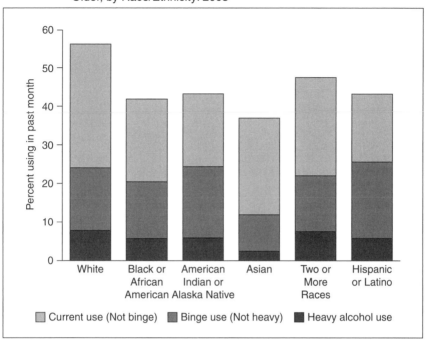

From Substance Abuse and Mental Health Services Administration (2009). *Results from the 2008 National Survey on Drug Use and Health: National Findings (Office of Applied Studies, NSDUH Series H-36, HHS Publication No. SMA 09-4434).* Rockville, MD: U.S. Department of Health and Human Services. Figure 3.2 Current, Binge, and Heavy Alcohol Use among Persons Aged 12 or Older, by Race/Ethnicity: 2008.

arrests among Latinos and Native Americans relative to other racial/ethnic groups. While the national rate of DUI arrests among drivers aged 21 and older is slightly less than 1 per 100 (.6/100), among Latino drivers the DUI arrest rate is 1.3 per 100 drivers aged 21 and over, and for American Indian/Alaska Natives, the DUI arrest rate is 2.5 per 100 drivers aged 21 and over (SAMHSA, 2005).[3]

Socioeconomic Characteristics and Alcohol Use. Whereas the prevalence of alcohol use increases with the level of education, the prevalence of high-risk drinking declines with the level of education.

---

[3] Arrests for DUIs involve some amount of law enforcement discretion, and racial/ethnic discrimination may account for some of the disparities noted. However, the magnitude of the disparities correspond to the high-risk alcohol consumption patterns among Latinos and Native American/Alaska Natives shown in Figure 6.4.

Among high-school graduates aged 26 or older, the prevalences of binge and heavy alcohol use are, respectively, 23.2% and 7%, while for college graduates, these high-risk drinking prevalences are 19.5% and 4.6%, respectively (SAMHSA, 2009). Employment, like education, is also associated with higher rates of alcohol use, but with lower prevalence of high-risk drinking. Among persons who are employed full time, the rate for heavy alcohol use is 8.8%, whereas for unemployed persons, the rate of heavy alcohol use is 12.8%. Interestingly, employment status does not appear to have a clear relationship with the prevalence of binge drinking—about 30% of adults employed full time and the unemployed report a recent episode of binge drinking (SAMHSA, 2009). As with illicit drug abuse, the relationship between employment status and the prevalence of high-risk drinking reflects both selection effects (persons who do not engage in high-risk drinking are more likely to secure and retain full-time employment) and protective effects (employment reduces the propensity to engage in high-risk drinking).

The Geography of High-Risk Alcohol Use. There is some amount of regional variation in the use of alcohol (e.g., in the South only 47.3% of persons report current alcohol use, while in the Northeast, the current alcohol use rate is 56.8%). There is also slight variation in current alcohol use by metropolitan/nonmetropolitan status, with large metropolitan areas having higher rates of current alcohol use than nonmetropolitan areas (respectively, 53.6% and 45.8%). Interestingly, rates of high-risk alcohol use (specifically, binge drinking) appear unrelated to metropolitan status (SAMHSA, 2009).

Illicit Drug-Related Emergency Department Visits

The NSDUH, because it is based on self-report data from persons residing in households, does not provide information on the prevalence of drug and alcohol abuse and addiction among homeless persons and other groups living at the margins of society. Self-report data also have significant limitations that are related to the accurate disclosure of illicit drug use. Another avenue of gaining knowledge about the prevalence of substance abuse and addiction is through data that are collected via the Drug Abuse Warning Network (DAWN), a federally sponsored public health surveillance system of Emergency Department (ED) visits that employs a national sample of non-federal hospitals operating 24-hour EDs.[4]

There are several features of DAWN data that yield critical information on the prevalence of substance abuse and dependence among the patient populations that are most dependent on safety-net hospitals. The first advantageous feature has to do with the social function of 24-hour EDs as one of the few general social welfare institutions that are mandated by law to provide professional, social, and medical assistance to all comers—regardless of the social status, presenting problems, or ability to pay (Gordon, 1999). In effect, this means that the ED is perhaps the only context where the prevalence of drug and alcohol use among otherwise "invisible" populations (e.g., homeless persons, undocumented immigrants) can be observed. In fact, the DAWN estimates directly assess the prevalence of substance use/abuse issues among the populations that regularly use safety-net hospitals. As another distinct advantage, the DAWN data are based on retrospective analysis of clinical records in accordance with strict diagnostic criteria, rather than either solely patient self-reports or subjective judgments by clinicians. Finally, the DAWN prevalence estimates are quite detailed with respect to the types of substances used/abused.

In the discussion that follows, we highlight prevalence findings from the most recent DAWN surveillance estimates (published May, 2010) and based on analysis of ED records for the year 2007 (SAMHSA, 2010). During 2007, there were 116 million ED visits, of which DAWN data estimate that 1.9 million involved drug use or misuse. Of these 1.9 million ED visits involving drug use/misuse, 52% involved the use of illicit drugs—either alone (28%) or in combination with pharmaceuticals or alcohol. The most prevalent illicit drug was cocaine, followed by marijuana, heroin, stimulants, and then a residual category of miscellaneous illicit drugs that is inclusive of PCP, Ecstasy, and GHB.

Table 6.1 provides population estimates of ED visit rates (per 100,000 persons) by the type of illicit drug involved. These rates are

---

[4] The DAWN surveillance system is administered by the Substance Abuse and Mental Health Services Administration (SAMHSA), and its estimates pertain to the entire United States, including Alaska, Hawaii, and the District of Columbia. ED medical records from DAWN-participating hospitals are reviewed retrospectively to find the ED visits that involved recent drug use and abuse of all types—illegal drugs, prescription drugs, and over-the-counter pharmaceuticals. Alcohol is considered a reportable drug when consumed by ED patients under the age of 21.

TABLE 6.1
Rates of ED Visits per 100,000 Population Involving Illicit Drugs

Total ED visits, drug misuse/abuse	618.5
Total ED visits, illicit drugs	320.0
Cocaine	181.8
Heroin	61.8
Marijuana	101.3
Stimulants	27.9
Amphetamines	7.1
Methamphetamine	22.3
MDMA (Ecstasy)	4.2
GHB	0.7
Ketamine	0.1
LSD	1.2
PCP	9.2
Miscellaneous hallucinogens	1.6
Inhalants	2.6

From Drug Abuse Warning Network (2007). *National Estimates of Drug-Related Emergency Department Visits.* Rockville, MD: U.S. Department of Health and Human Services. Table 4. Rates of ED visits per 100,000 population involving illicit drugs, 2007.

NOTE: All rates are ED visits per 100,000 population. Estimates of ED visits are based on a representative sample of non-federal, short-stay hospitals with 24-hr EDs in the United States. Population estimates are drawn from the 2007 U.S. Census Bureau Postcensal Resident Population National Population Dataset as of July 1, 2007. ED visits often involve multiple drugs, thus, visits will appear multiple times in this table (e.g., a visit involving both cocaine and marijuana will appear twice). The sum of visits or rates by drug will be greater than the total, and the sum of percentages by drug will be greater than 100.

the most useful metric for gauging the general population impact of different kinds of illicit drugs. It should be noted that the overall rate for illicit drug visits (320 visits per 100,000 U.S. residents) often entails a combination of different illicit drugs and is not the simple additive sum of different types of illicit drugs. The rate of cocaine-involved ED visits (181.8 per 100,000) is 1.8 times that of the next nearest prevalence rate, that of marijuana (101.3), and 2.9 times that of heroin. Among stimulants, the ED visit rate for methamphetamine is clearly dominant. Among the less frequent illicit drugs, the rate for PCP is highest—but even so is only about 5% of the rate observed for cocaine.

ED Visits Involving Illicit Drugs by Age, Sex, and Race.   There are large differences in illicit drug usage preferences by age and sex, reflected in the rate of ED visits involving each type of drug by age and sex. As shown in Figure 6.5, cocaine usage has an older age distribution than other types of illicit drugs, with the peak cocaine usage occurring in the 35–44 age range. In contrast, both marijuana and stimulant usage peak in early adulthood and heroin usage rates tend to be fairly stable at their highest rates from early adulthood through most of the middle age years. No matter what type of illicit drug is considered, males use illicit drugs more than females—always by a ratio of almost 2:1 or more. For the four types of drugs shown in Figure 6.5, the male usage ratios by type of drug used are as follows: cocaine (1.8:1), heroin (2.4:1), marijuana (2.0:1), and stimulants (1.8:1).

The DAWN data estimates of illicit drug-related ED visits by race and ethnicity are quite limited, largely because ED records have missing or very limited racial/ethnic information. Based on the limited racial/ethnic categories that are available from DAWN data, it is estimated that 46% of illicit drug using patients are White, 32% Black, 13% Hispanic, and 1% are identified as multiracial—with the remaining 9% of unknown race/ethnicity (SAMHSA, 2010).

Illicit Drug Usage Trends.   The most recent *Drug Abuse Warning Network* data tracked illicit drug-related ED visits from 2004 through 2007. During this period, the overall level of ED visits involving illicit drugs remained stable for three of the four major illicit drug categories (cocaine, marijuana, and heroin). Stimulants, the fourth major illicit drug category, showed a significant decline in usage related with ED visits—with 75,000 fewer visits between 2004 and 2007. Among the less frequently encountered illicit drugs, there were significant declines in ED visits related to usage of PCP and Ecstasy (SAMHSA, 2010).

Alcohol-Related Emergency Department Visits

Estimates from the DAWN data for 2007 (as made available in 2010) suggest that about one-half million of the 116 million ED visits made that year involved the use of alcohol with other drugs (both illicit and pharmaceuticals). This was about 26% of all of the ED visits that involved drug misuse/abuse in 2007 (SAMHSA, 2010). DAWN data do not report alcohol-involved ED visits for persons aged 21 or older, unless it is related to the abuse/misuse of other drugs—but among

FIGURE 6.5 Rates of ED Visits per 100,000 Population Involving Illicit Drugs, by Selected Drugs, Age, and Gender, 2007

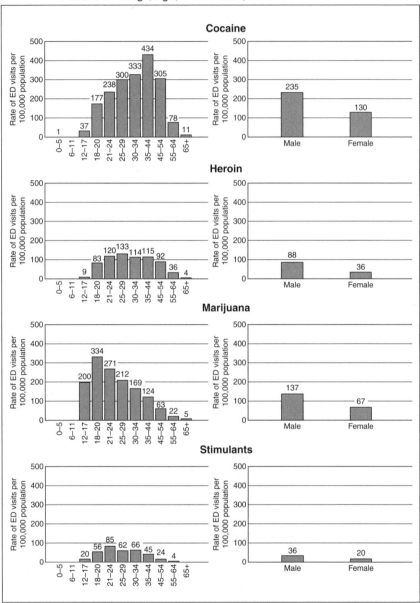

From Drug Abuse Warning Network (2007). *National Estimates of Drug-Related Emergency Department Visits.* Rockville, MD: U.S. Department of Health and Human Services. Figure 2. Rates of ED visits per 100,000 population involving illicit drugs, by selected drugs, age, and gender, 2007.

persons under age 21, about 7% of ED visits were related to the use of alcohol alone (SAMHSA, 2010).

Of particular concern to health care providers and public health professionals is the use of alcohol in combination with illicit drugs and pharmaceuticals. Drug combinations and interactions can be fatal, and it is important to identify the most frequent combinations encountered. Toward that end, Table 6.2 shows the prevalences of specific drug/alcohol combinations according to ED visits per 100,000 persons—based on the DAWN data from 2007. Drug/alcohol combinations involve more illicit

TABLE 6.2
Rates of ED Visits Per 100,000 Population Involving
Drugs and Alcohol Taken Together

Total ED visits, drugs with alcohol	163.3
Illicit drugs	101.1
Cocaine	63.8
Marijuana	38.5
Heroin	12.3
Stimulants	5.9
Pharmaceuticals	85.2
Psychotherapeutic agents	43.1
Antidepressants	9.6
Benzodiazepines	27.9
Alprazolam	10.5
Clonazepam	4.9
Central nervous system agents	37.6
Opioid/opiate pain medications	23.4
Hydrocodone	7.1
Oxycodone	6.8
Miscellaneous pain medications	7.0
Muscle relaxants	3.7

From Drug Abuse Warning Network (2007). *National Estimates of Drug-Related Emergency Department Visits*. Rockville, MD: U.S. Department of Health and Human Services. Table 5 ED visits involving drugs and alcohol taken together, by most frequent combinations, 2007.

NOTE: All rates are ED visits per 100,000 population. Estimates of ED visits are based on a representative sample of non-Federal, short-stay hospitals with 24-hr EDs in the United States. Population estimates are drawn from the 2007 U.S. Census Bureau Postcensal Resident Population National Population Dataset as of July 1, 2007. ED visits often involve multiple drugs, thus, visits will appear multiple times in this table (e.g., a visit involving both cocaine and marijuana will appear twice). The sum of visits or rates by drug will be greater than the total, and the sum of percentages by drug will be greater than 100.

drugs than pharmaceuticals, and among the illicit drugs used in combination with alcohol, cocaine tops the list (with an ED visit rate/100,000 persons of 63.8). Among pharmaceutical products, psychotherapeutic drugs have a somewhat higher prevalence rate of being used in combination with alcohol than central nervous system agents—with antidepressants being the most frequently misused/abused in combination with alcohol. Opioids prescribed for pain management is the class of central nervous system pharmaceuticals that is most often combined with alcohol.

The Demography of Drug/Alcohol-Combined Misuse/Abuse. DAWN also provides estimates of the proportion of ED visits involving combined usage of drugs and alcohol by sex, age, and gender. We have transformed these data to three simple graphs, shown together in Figure 6.6. The first graph depicts the age distribution of combined drug/alcohol use visits, which is considerably older than that for use of illicit drugs (see Figure 6.1 for the age distribution of illicit drug use). Illicit drug use peaks in early adulthood, whereas the highest risk behavior (combined use of drugs and alcohol) rapidly climbs in mature adulthood and then peaks in the 35 to 44 age range. As the second graph shows, consistent with use of illicit drugs in general, ED visits that involve combined drug and alcohol use overrepresent males by a wide margin (males comprise 67% more of such ED visits). Finally, as shown in the third graph, whereas Whites are somewhat underrepresented in the combined drug and alcohols usage prevalence, African Americans are overrepresented by a significant margin (23% of combined drug/alcohol use ED visits, relative to a U.S. population percentage of about 13%). Interestingly, although Hispanics have a higher prevalence of high-risk alcohol use than the U.S. population as a whole (see previous discussion under *Race, Ethnicity, and Alcohol Use*), they are underrepresented in the combined usage of drugs and alcohol. However (as noted previously), the racial identification in ED records is limited to a small number of very general categories, and there is evidence that minority racial identification is more salient where negative behaviors are encountered (Finucane & Carrese, 1990; van Ryn, 2002). For these reasons, there are no precise national estimates of the relationships between race and ethnic identification and combined drug/alcohol usage available from DAWN data.

Alcohol/Drug-Related Emergency Department Visits by Type of Case. The final DAWN findings we will summarize provide a glimpse of the types of cases that are involved in drug- and alcohol-involved ED visits. These data, summarized in Table 6.3, are national

FIGURE 6.6 ED Visits Involving Combined Use of Drugs and Alcohol by Sex, Age and Race/Ethnicity, 2007

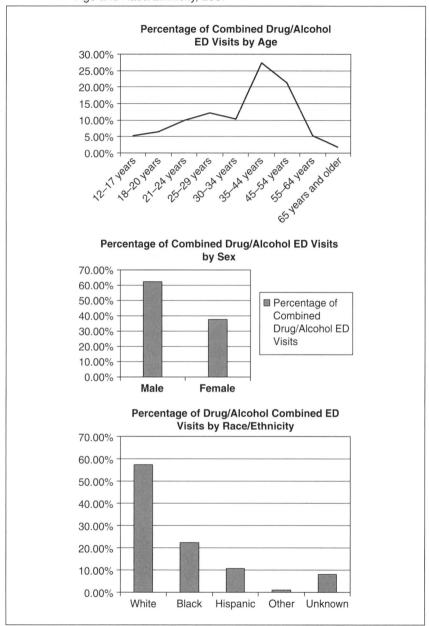

From Drug Abuse Warning Network (2007). *National Estimates of Drug-Related Emergency Department Visits.* Rockville, MD: U.S. Department of Health and Human Services. Table 11. ED visits involving drugs and alcohol taken together, by patient demographics, 2007.

prevalence estimates that are based on the records of the 24-hour EDs sampled in the DAWN system. Of the 116 million ED visits made during 2007, analysis of DAWN data estimates that 3,998,228 visits (3.4% of all ED visits) involved misuse/abuse of drugs and/or alcohol. The most common categories of such cases entailed adverse reactions (47.7%) and overmedication (8.28%). About 3.5% of drug/alcohol-related ED visits pertain to the seeking of detoxification treatment, and a similar percentage of cases involve suicide attempts.

Prevalence of Drug and Alcohol Abuse in Homeless Populations

In the previous chapter (Chapter 5, Homelessness as a Social Phenomenon and Being Homeless), we discussed the prevalence rates of drug and alcohol addiction among the homeless at some length. Unlike the NSDUH and DAWN data, the prevalence rates of addictions among the homeless are based specifically on surveys of homeless persons and the agencies serving them. To briefly recap, it is estimated that (despite public perceptions to the contrary), only about 38% of the homeless population are addicted to alcohol and only about 26%

TABLE 6.3
Alcohol/Drug-Related Emergency Department Visits by Type of Case, 2007

	ED VISITS	PERCENT
Suicide attempt	197,053	3.50
Seeking detox	139,908	3.40
Alcohol only (age <21)	135,900	3.40
Adverse reaction	1,908,928	47.74
Overmedication	331,134	8.28
Malicious poisoning	12,563	0.31
Accidental ingestion	91,632	2.29
Other	1,181,110	29.54
Total drug-related ED visits	**3,998,228**	**100.00**

From Drug Abuse Warning Network (2007). *National Estimates of Drug-Related Emergency Department Visits*. Rockville, MD: U.S. Department of Health and Human Services. Table 5 ED visits involving drugs and alcohol taken together, by most frequent combinations, 2007. Table C2 Drug-related ED visits and drugs, by type of case, 2007.

NOTE: All rates are ED visits per 100,000 population. Estimates of ED visits are based on a representative sample of non-federal, short-stay hospitals with 24-hr EDs in the United States. Population estimates are drawn from the 2007 U.S. Census Bureau Postcensal Resident Population National Population Dataset as of July 1, 2007.

abuse other drugs (National Coalition for the Homeless, 2007). That is to say that drug and alcohol addiction, although endemic among the homeless populations and certainly a causal factor of homelessness, is not universal. The prevalence rates also differ between persons who are temporarily homeless and those who are chronically homeless—defined by the U.S. Department of Housing and Urban Development as continuously homeless for a year or more or having at least four episodes of homelessness over the most recent 3 years. However, in contrast to the general population, the lifetime risks of either drug or alcohol addictions among the homeless are very high—a 62% lifetime prevalence for alcohol and a 58% lifetime prevalence for other drugs (Zerger, 2002). Among the homeless population in particular, drug and alcohol abuse/addiction often originates in mental illness as a means of self-medication (Zerger, 2002).

THE ETIOLOGY OF DRUG AND ALCOHOL ADDICTION

The General Picture—The Interplay of Risk and Protective Factors

Safety-net health care providers encounter particularly difficult challenges in treating persons who are addicted to drugs and alcohol. Historically, theories of addiction tend to be discipline specific. For example, sociological theories of addiction tend to emphasize social structures and social processes—such as the relationship between socioeconomic disadvantage and addiction prevalence or the role of deviant identity formation in sustaining deviant behavior patterns. On the other hand, psychological theories of addiction have placed emphasis on behavioral reinforcement and personality traits that are linked to susceptibility to addiction. There are also cultural theories of addiction that place emphasis on cultural norms that either promote or impede addictive behavioral patterns. More recently, advances in neurobiology and genetics have implicated both the malleability of brain structures and the role of hereditary factors in propensities toward addiction. An enduring question that cuts across all theories of addiction pertains to the role of individual agency and culpability in the progression toward addiction, the consequences of addictive behavior, and recovery from addiction.

Although there is no consensus on a comprehensive omnibus theory of addiction, there is broad agreement that addiction is a phenomenon that entails a complex interplay of individual characteristics, developmental influences (both genetic and social), and social context (Brook et al., 2008). Rather than invoking overly deterministic language of "causal determinants," addiction theorists emphasize the role of risk and protective factors that influence the probability of an individual becoming addicted. Risk factors are those that increase the probability of addiction, whereas protective factors reduce the likelihood of addiction. Protective factors, aside from offsetting the negative effects of risk factors, can also augment each other (Brook et al., 2008). There are risk and protective factors that are specific to individual characteristics (such as the propensity toward or against engaging in risky behavior), developmental influences (such as having either strong or weak connections with supportive parents), and social context (living in a neighborhood with either low or high rates of methamphetamine experimentation among teenagers). It should also be emphasized that the relative influence and interplay of risk and protective factors may vary by the type of substance considered (e.g., a local youth culture of substance experimentation may be a more powerful risk factor where there is easy access to highly addictive opioids). What follows is our synopsis of the findings from a recent review of the literature on the epidemiology of addiction by Brooks et al. (2008), in a standard reference text on addictions.[5]

The *individual characteristics* that have been found to be related to substance use, abuse, and dependence involve three dimensions: an orientation toward risk-taking and sensation-/novelty-seeking behavior, a relative lack of emotional control, and interpersonal relatedness—meaning that people who have difficulty forming and sustaining relationships are at elevated risk for substance abuse and addiction (Brooks et al., 2008, p. 34). *Developmental influences* on the risk of substance abuse and addiction encompass (a) the interplay between genetic characteristics and the social environment, (b) family factors, (c) peer influences, (d) marital/partner relationship factors, and (e) risk trajectories that may differ depending upon such factors as the age of exposure to substance use/abuse and the cluster of risk and protective factors at play at the point of exposure (Brooks et al., 2008, pp. 34–35). *Social context influences* on the risk of dependence include such factors as residence in neighborhoods with high levels of concentrated poverty and endemic drug

---

[5] Galanter, M., & Kleber, H. D. (Eds.). *Textbook of substance abuse treatment* (4th ed.). Arlington, VA: American Psychiatric Publishing.

and alcohol abuse, and exposure to racial and ethnic discrimination (Brooks et al., 2008, pp. 35–36). Brooks et al. (2008) make the point that the majority of risk and protective factors that influence the likelihood of substance abuse and addiction do not appear to differ appreciably across ethnic/racial groups—at least in terms of their causal influences on substance abuse and addiction (p. 36). However, we add our own point that both race and ethnicity have been shown to play a very large role in determining the likelihood of accumulating particular clusters of risk and protective factors. For example, race and ethnicity very much influence the likelihood of growing up in neighborhoods typified by high levels of concentrated poverty and endemic substance abuse and addiction (Massey & Denton, 1993).

Advances in the Neurobiology and Genetics of Addiction

Over the past two decades, advances in neurobiology and genetic science have led the field of addiction studies to move from a *psychosocial* theoretical paradigm of addiction to *biopsychosocial* theories of addiction— meaning that knowledge about the specific biological determinants and mechanisms of addiction can now be directly incorporated into theories of addiction that consider the interplay of psychological, sociological, *and* biological structures and processes. Until roughly two decades ago, although it was recognized that there were neurological and genetic influences on the likelihood of addiction risk, limited information of the precise biological mechanisms impeded our ability to advance the biological components of addiction to theoretical specificity—and ultimately to application in clinical practice. Although it is well beyond the scope of this chapter to summarize the formidable literatures on the neurobiology and genetics of addiction, we can provide a glimpse of the directions being undertaken in both of these crucial arenas of scientific inquiry.

Advances in the Neurobiology of Addiction

For this glimpse of the research on the Neurobiology of Addiction, we rely on the recently published review of this literature by Koop (2008). In essence, as drug use for some individuals moves from occasional use or experimentation to loss of behavioral control and chronic drug dependence, an addictive drug-taking cycle emerges that involves three distinct stages: binge/intoxication, withdrawal/negative effect, and preoccupation/anticipation (Koop, 2008). Each of these three stages has been successfully replicated in animal models of addiction that have led to the identification of neurological mechanisms that are specific to each stage. For example, the withdrawal/negative effect stage involves neuroadaptations (chemical changes in the neurotransmitter system) that are manifested in decreases in dopaminergic and serotonergic transmission—in behavioral terms, contributing to the negative motivational state associated with drug/alcohol abstinence (Koop, 2008, pp. 5–6). In fact, advancements in neurobiological research have shown there is a "neurocircuitry of addiction" that has three distinct neurobiological circuits, each one corresponding to one of the three stages of the addiction cycle (Koop, 2008, p. 9). Perhaps most critically, animal model neurobiological research has shown that there are specific brain cell genetic changes that result from chronic drug exposure that appear to be common to all abused drugs (Koop, 2008, p. 9). These kinds of advancements in the neurobiology of addiction hold great promise for preventive, diagnostic, and concomitant pharmaceutical and psychosocial interventions.[6]

Advances in the Genetics of Addiction

As with the neurobiology of addiction, we are providing a basic glimpse of the state of knowledge in the genetics of addiction, rather than the full synopsis of a highly complex and evolving field.[7] As noted by Galanter and Kranzler (2008), although the genetic influences on addiction are substantial, they are both complex and also not wholly determinant. That is, in contrast to some hereditary conditions (such as schizophrenia) that do not require specific environmental exposure, the genetic determinants of addiction act in concert with environmental influences (Galanter & Kranzler, 2008, p. 17). Speaking broadly, there are two general forms of scientific evidence that bridge genetic composition and processes to addictions. The first form of evidence comes from familial studies of prevalence and concordance involving comparisons of monozygotic (MZ) and dizygotic (DZ)

---

[6] For readers interested in a detailed synopsis of recent advances in the neurobiology of addiction, as opposed to the mere "glimpse" we have offered, we suggest Koop's (2008) essay.
[7] For this brief section as well, we are drawing on a recent literature review from the *Textbook of Substance Abuse Treatment* (American Psychiatric Publishing, 2008)—specifically the literature review on the "Genetics of Addiction" by Galanter and Kranzler.

twins and from studies of adopted children. Evidence of this type is most useful in giving us an understanding of the general genetic contribution to the risk of addiction relative to that of the social environment. The second form of evidence is focused on specific genetic linkages to various forms of substance abuse and addiction. This form of evidence holds particular promise for a better understanding of the exact environmental–gene interactions that result in addiction—with implications for prevention, early identification, and treatment (Galanter & Kranzler, 2008).

Focusing first on familial studies of addiction, at least in the case of addiction to alcohol, the largest twin studies have established that the hereditary component of addiction accounts for 50% to 60% of the overall risk (Galanter & Kranzler, 2008, p. 18). In particular, a series of studies based on multiple cohorts of Swedish twins who were born between 1902 and 1949 (*N* = 9,000) show that the hereditary contribution to alcohol addiction is not only substantial and very possibly dominant, but also stable over time (Galanter & Kranzler, 2008, p. 18).[8] Although less numerous than the familial studies on the hereditary contributions to alcoholism, other large scales studies of twins have shown that there is a hereditary component implicated in the abuse and dependence risks for a range of illicit drugs, including marijuana, stimulants, cocaine, and opiates (Galanter & Kranzler, 2008, p. 18).[9] In a study of 3,372 pairs of twins who served in the U.S. military during the Vietnam War era, results of biometrical modeling from prevalence and concordance rates among MZ and DZ twins suggested that genetics accounted for 34% of the variance in risk, whereas the environmental influences accounted for the remaining 66% of the risk (Tsuang et al., 1996).

Studies that provide evidence pertaining to specific genetic linkages and mechanisms in addiction fall into two general categories: genome-wide linkage and association studies, and candidate gene studies (Galanter & Kranzler, 2008) Genome-wide studies have the advantage of being able to identify specific genes that are associated with risk, without precise *a priori* knowledge of the risk mechanisms. The most well-established, genome-based approach, genome-wide linkage studies, has produced studies

---

[8] For interested readers, see Kendler, K. S., Prescott, C. A., & Neale, M. C., et al. (1997). Temperance board registration for alcohol abuse in a national sample of Swedish male twins, born between 1902 and 1949. *Archives of General Psychiatry, 54,* 178–184.
[9] See Tsuang et al. (1996).

of alcohol, cocaine, opiate, and nicotine dependence (Galanter & Kranzler, 2008, p. 19). Another promising and essential avenue of genetics research on substance abuse and addictions is "gene-by-environmental interaction research," which focuses on how the environmental impacts on the risk of substance abuse and addiction differ depending upon the underlying phenotype (Galanter & Kranzler, 2008, p. 23).

Neurobiology, Heredity, Social Environment, Social Stigma, and Individual Agency in Addictions

The diagnosis and treatment of substance abuse and addiction has evolved over time from a "character-based" orientation that defined addiction as a personality deficit, to a period that focused on enabling or otherwise destructive social environments, to a more recent era that identifies specific biological components of addiction that challenge long-held assumptions pertaining to the degree of genuine human agency in alcohol and drug addiction. Although it is now very clear that (a) there is a strong, if not dominant, genetic component to addiction susceptibility, and (b) addiction itself produces profound neurological changes that impede the capacity for abstinence and recovery, addiction still brings with it great stigma and ostracism. In part, this is no doubt due to the fact that addiction usually results in behavior that is unacceptable, if not reprehensible and often a threat to the community as a whole. Perhaps less obvious is the fact that most of us have experienced first hand the suffering caused by the behavior of addicted patients, colleagues, or even our own family members. These twin realities work together to undermine our ability to objectify addiction as a complex process that involves both biology and environment as well as individual agency or choice. When it comes to addictions in particular (as opposed to most other forms of chronic disease), the human agency of the addicted individual is generally what is most salient and grasped upon as the primary determinant cause. Yet, in purely scientific terms, a singular focus on the personality and behavioral choices of the addicted patient remains an erroneous basis for either an understanding of the causal factors or an effective plan of treatment. Addiction is a chronic disease with a complex cluster of biobehavioral risk factors and disease processes—not a characterological trait (Brook et al., 2008; NIDA, 2009).

TREATMENT APPROACHES TO DRUG AND ALCOHOL ADDICTION

A Holistic Perspective on the Treatment of Drug and Alcohol Addiction

To summarize what has been said so far: addiction is a chronic disease that entails both genetic and psychosocial susceptibilities; there is a progression from initial exposure to a three-stage cycle of compulsive drug taking that is consistent across a range of drugs; over time addiction affects multiple brain circuits (including those involved in reward and motivation, learning, memory, and inhibitory control); and addiction brings with it a range of dysfunctional behaviors and diminished capacities that interfere with normal functioning in all spheres of social existence—family, work, friendships, and the broader community (NIDA, 2009). For these reasons, the road to sustained abstinence and recovery to normal psychosocial functioning requires treatment programs that are both long term and inclusive of components that are specific to the multiple dimensions of an individual's life that are affected by addiction (NIDA, 2009).

General Categories of Drug and Alcohol Addiction Treatment Programs

Although there is a large range of treatment modalities that use various combinations of social, behavioral, and pharmacological interventions, there are four major categories of treatment programs:

- Detoxification and Medically Managed Withdrawal
- Long-Term Residential Treatment
- Short-Term Residential Treatment
- Outpatient Treatment Programs

The choice of program and its relative effectiveness in affecting sustained abstinence and recovery vary both by the type of substance addiction, the treatment modalities used within programs, and the psychosocial characteristics of the individual person. In particular, it is common to use a combination of these four major program categories at different stages of the abstinence and recovery process (NIDA, 2009). After briefly describing the defining characteristics of the four major categories of treatment programs, we will turn to a discussion of the treatment approaches that are specific to the major categories of addictive substances (alcohol, stimulants, hallucinogens, and opioids).

Detoxification and Medically Managed Withdrawal Programs. Detoxification is the first stage of abstinence and recovery, and is typically characterized by uncomfortable and even agonizing side effects that can sometimes be fatal. Depending on the individual circumstances, detoxification requires either direct medical management or, at the very least, close medical supervision and the availability of medical consultation (NIDA, 2009). Detoxification settings can be hospitals, correctional facilities, or special detoxification facilities. Because detoxification treatment does not address the psychosocial and behavioral issues that are consequent to addiction, it is critical that the detoxification process be linked with a longer-term and more comprehensive treatment program that addresses all aspects of addiction. Without linkage to a comprehensive treatment program, detoxification treatment programs function only as a revolving door for the addicted. Also, a clear distinction needs to be made between a detoxification treatment program that addresses the potentially dangerous side effects of withdrawal, and places where detoxification often occurs because the addicted individual is denied access to the drug(s) he or she is addicted to (e.g., county jails).

Long-Term Residential Treatment Programs.   Long-term residential treatment programs provide 7 days a week/24 hours per day care and supervision within a non-hospital residential setting over an extended period— typically 6 to 12 months rather than days or weeks. The most common approach used in long-term residential treatment programs is the "therapeutic community" approach, where residents, staff, and context are all active components of the individual's treatment (NIDA, 2009). Long-term residential treatment programs are often the optimal and perhaps the only path to sustained abstinence and recovery for individuals who have deeply entrenched social and behavioral deficits and few social and economic resources available to them (e.g., homeless persons, persons significantly involved with the criminal justice system, and adolescents enmeshed in destructive peer networks).

Short-Term Residential Treatment Programs.   These programs entail a 3–6 week intensive immersion approach that is typically based on a version of the "12-step approach" used by Alcoholics Anonymous (NIDA, 2009).[10]

---

[10] See Miller, M. M. (1998). Traditional approaches to the treatment of addiction. In A. W. Graham, & T. K. Schultz (Eds.), *Principles of addiction medicine* (2nd ed.). Washington, DC: American Society of Addiction Medicine.

Although short-term residential treatment programs were originally developed for the treatment of alcoholism in community hospital settings, the increased prevalence of other forms of addiction over the last three decades, including polydrug addictions, led to the development and proliferation of short-term residential programs targeted at other common forms of drug addiction. These short-term intensive programs place a strong emphasis on the transition to outpatient treatment programs modeled along the same treatment principles, and tend to be a preferred treatment option for addicted individuals who have intact (albeit often damaged) familial, community, and employment connections.

Outpatient Treatment Programs. Outpatient treatment programs have a high degree of variability, particularly in their level of intensity. They range from treatment programs that involve little more than structured drug and alcohol abuse education to programs that require intense daily immersion over a specified period, with the level of intensity calibrated to the individual's stage of recovery. Outpatient programs, because they do not involve 24-hour monitoring within a controlled therapeutic milieu, are more suitable for addicted individuals with solid social supports and a strong motivation to abstain (NIDA, 2009).

Drug-Specific Treatment Approaches

Although it is beyond the purpose and scope of this chapter to cover the myriad of treatment approaches that are specific to different types of drugs, we do want to provide at least a glimpse into the conventional evidence-based approaches for the treatment of the general categories of addictive drugs: alcohol, stimulants, hallucinogens, and opioids.

Evidence-Based Approaches to the Treatment of Alcoholism. Treatment of alcoholism entails two distinct components: treatment of acute alcohol withdrawal and relapse prevention (Myrick & Wright, 2008). Treatment of acute alcohol withdrawal can occur on either an inpatient or outpatient basis, depending on several risk and protective factors. Based on an extensive review of the literature on alcohol withdrawal, Myrick and Wright (2008) suggest that outpatient alcohol detoxification may be indicated where there are mild to moderate withdrawal symptoms, there are no (medical, neurological, or psychiatric) complications, there is no history of delirium tremens, and there is reliable support and monitoring available (Myrick & Wright, 2008, p. 133). Because nutritional deficits are common to persons with alcoholism, it is important that detoxification includes multivitamin therapy. In particular, thiamine replacement therapy is essential throughout the withdrawal period to avert the precipitation of Wernicke's encephalopathy (Myrick & Wright, 2008, p. 132). Relapse prevention includes pharmacological approaches, psychosocial/behavioral interventions, or combinations of both. Among the pharmacological approaches, the clinical objectives include deterrence (disulfiram), impeding the neurological reward mechanisms of alcohol consumption (nalrexone), and decreasing the negative symptoms associated with the acute post withdrawal period in recently detoxified alcoholics (acamprosate) (Myrick & Wright, 2008, p. 135). There is a large range of non-pharmacological treatment alternatives used to reduce the likelihood of relapse into alcohol consumption, including individually based psychotherapeutic interventions such as psychodynamic therapy and cognitive behavioral therapy; therapies targeted at support networks crucial to abstinence (group therapy, family therapy); variations of the traditional Alcoholics Anonymous 12-step facilitation (TSF) programs; and more recently various forms of motivation enhancement therapy (motivational interviewing techniques or MET). Interestingly, evidence from a multisite longitudinal study that compared abstinence and reduced consumption results across different psychosocial/psychotherapeutic treatment regimes found (a) that outpatient programs that use the TSF program had higher rates of sustained abstinence than other approaches, and (b) that the level of anger was a critical individual patient characteristic influencing the relative effectiveness of different programs (Myrick & Wright, 2008, pp. 136–137).

Evidence-Based Treatment Approaches for Stimulant Addiction. As with treatment for alcohol addiction, both pharmacological and behavioral interventions have been used to treat stimulant abuse and addiction. Because withdrawal from stimulants (most prevalently cocaine and amphetamines) can produce a wide range of dysphoric symptoms that negatively reinforce addictive use (e.g., depression, anxiety, agitation, and craving), pharmacological interventions that target dysphoric symptoms are suggested as an important adjunct to behavioral interventions such as cognitive behavioral therapy and positive contingency management (Kosten, Sofuoglu, & Gardner, 2008). These include agents that either mimic or block stimulant effects, agents that decrease the neurological reinforcement mechanisms of stimulants, and agents that treat the dysphoric symptoms associated with stimulant withdrawal. Because psychiatric disorders are implicated in the risk of stimulant abuse and addiction, psychopharmacological agents may be indicated for the management of psychiatric comorbidities (Kosten et al., 2008, p. 163). As important as these pharmacological interventions are, the most recent comprehensive summary of the evidence suggests that the most crucial component of stimulant addiction treatment involves the use of behavioral therapies as a means of engaging the patient in treatment and facilitating long-term changes (Kosten et al., 2008, p. 162). Along these lines, both cognitive behavioral and positive contingency management therapies have shown promising results in the treatment of cocaine and amphetamine addictions (Kosten et al., 2008, p. 162).

With respect to methamphetamine addiction, an increasingly prevalent form of stimulant addiction, the evidence suggests that behavioral therapies—for example, cognitive behavioral and contingency management—are the most effective (NIDA, 2006). In particular, evidence suggests that "the Matrix model, a comprehensive behavioral treatment approach that combines behavioral therapy, family education, individual counseling, 12-Step support, drug testing, and encouragement for nondrug-related activities, has been shown to be effective in reducing methamphetamine abuse" (NIDA, 2006, p. 1).

Evidence-Based Treatment of Hallucinogen Addiction. Hallucinogens include a wide range of both naturally occurring and synthetic drugs, the former including such agents as mescaline (a.k.a. peyote) and psilocybin (a.k.a. magic mushrooms), and the latter including LSD and PCP. Although hallucinogens do not appear to involve the addictive neurological pathways found in such drugs as cocaine and alcohol, the use of hallucinogens is often a component of polydrug addiction (Weaver & Schnoll, 2008). As with other drug addictions, there are therapeutic interventions that are specific to acute intoxication, acute withdrawal, and the maintenance of long-term abstinence. However, with hallucinogens there are sometimes long-term consequences that include flashbacks (acute episodes that replicate aspects of the original hallucinogenic experience) and elevated risk for psychiatric disorders in the form of chronic anxiety, depression, and psychosis (NIDA, 2001; Weaver & Schnoll, 2008). With respect to the treatment of prolonged psychiatric disorders that result from hallucinogenic use, the treatment is the same as that for non-hallucinogenic-related psychiatric disorders. Regarding treatment approaches targeted at sustained abstinence, although there are as yet no known pharmacological agents that have proven more effective than placebos, the psychosocial and behavioral approaches that have been effective for other types of illicit drug abuse and addiction appear to be appropriate for hallucinogens (Weaver & Schnoll, 2008).

Evidence-Based Treatment Approaches for Opioid Addiction.   The term *opioids* refers to the entire class of drugs that bind to the neurological system's opioid receptors, while the term *opiates* refers to opioids that are derived or synthesized from natural products such as the poppy plant (Hahn, 2010). Synthetic opioids include such drugs as codeine, oxycodone, meperidine, and methadone, while opiates include opium, morphine, and heroin (Hahn, 2010). For purposes of simplicity, we will refer to opioids as inclusive of both natural opioids and synthetic opiates. As with treatment for other drugs that entail physiological dependence such as alcohol and cocaine, there are treatment approaches to opioid addiction that are specific to acute detoxification, and treatment approaches that are targeted at the achievement and maintenance of sustained abstinence and recovery.

Detoxification from opioids occurs in progression with symptoms that are fairly specific to each phase of the withdrawal process. However, both the speed of the progression and the severity of symptoms are influenced by factors such as the specific drug used, the daily amount used, and the duration and regularity of use (Polydorou & Kleber, 2008). Until fairly recently, the conventional method of detoxification from opioids was methadone substitution and tapering; however, buprenorphine (approved by the FDA in 2002) appears to have some distinct advantages over methadone. Specifically, buprenorphine is long acting, it can suppress withdrawal symptoms at least as well as methadone, it appears to cause less severe withdrawal symptoms than methadone when abruptly stopped, it is appropriate for outpatient use, and it has been shown to be safe when used by experienced physicians (p. 283). Because buprenorphine acts as both an opioid agonist (it has some morphine-like action) and an opioid antagonist (it blocks the effects of additional opioids), it has been shown to be effective both for detoxification and long-term treatment of opioid addiction (Hahn, 2010; Polydorou & Kleber, 2008).

Treatment approaches for the maintenance of illicit opioid abstinence include long-term methadone maintenance, the use of opioid agonist and antagonist drugs to gradually achieve total opioid abstinence, drug-free residential and outpatient treatment centers, individual drug counseling, and self-help groups such as Narcotics Anonymous (Hahn, 2010). The relative effectiveness of different approaches varies by individual patient characteristics, in particular the addiction history of the patient and the availability of social supports. For persons with long-term opioid addiction, pharmacological maintenance treatments in combination with behavioral and psychosocial supports have been shown to be the most effective (Schottentfeld, 2008). When used in combination, behavioral and pharmacological treatments help restore normal brain function and behavior, with higher rates of employment and lower rates of high-risk behavior (NIDA, 2005).

However, it should be noted that opioid agonist and opioid antagonist compound drugs have not been FDA approved for use where addiction is complicated by pregnancy (Polydorou & Kleber, 2008). Although methadone maintenance remains the standard approach where addiction is accompanied by pregnancy and no known birth defects are associated with prenatal methadone exposure where prenatal care is adequate, dosage during pregnancy poses special challenges. In addition, the newborn will need to be withdrawn from prenatal methadone-induced dependence (Polydorou & Kleber, 2008).

Screening, Referral, and Placement

Drug abuse and addiction is disproportionately prevalent among patients who depend upon safety-net hospitals as their primarily source of health care (Gordon, 1999; Institute of Medicine, 2000). While drug abuse (both illicit drug use and misuse of prescribed drugs) introduces the risk of addiction, drug abuse does not by itself constitute drug addiction. Although this may seem obvious, it not uncommon for clinicians to confuse the behaviors of illicit drug use with the condition of drug addiction. In addition, it is also easy for clinicians to overlook drug addiction in patients that do not fit the stereotype associated with drug abuse and addiction. The awareness of indicators of substance abuse combined with the routine use of standardized screening instruments to identify addictive behavioral patterns in clinical practice is the best way of avoiding these twin pitfalls.

Common Indicators of Drug and Alcohol Abuse

The common indicators of drug and alcohol abuse can be categorized by patient history, physical signs and symptoms, and laboratory tests. Patient history indicators include factors such as a history of referrals to substance abuse treatment programs, legal problems, job loss and downward occupational mobility, legal problems, relationship problems, and a history of psychiatric symptoms—in particular, affective disorders (NYSDPH, 2007). Physical signs and symptoms that are common indicators of drug and alcohol abuse include hypertension (associated with alcohol, cocaine, methamphetamine), resting tachycardia (alcohol, cocaine, marijuana, methamphetamine), tremors (alcohol withdrawal or stimulant intoxication), alcohol on breath, dilated pupils (stimulant use or sedative withdrawal), small pupils (opiate use), needle marks/tracks, bruises, and healed fractures (especially of the ribs, puffy facies and heptomegaly; alcohol), and weight loss (cocaine, methamphetamine) (NYSDPH, 2007). Laboratory test indicators of drug and alcohol abuse include elevated mean cell volume (MCV) if not taking zidovudine, elevated GGT, the AST>ALT, decreased serum B12, and (with the patient's consent usually required) urine drug screens and blood alcohol levels (NYSDPH, 2007).[11]

Standardized Screening Instruments

There are a range of standardized screening instruments for substance abuse and addiction that have been validated for use for adults as well as standardized instruments that have been validated for use with special populations (Greenfield & Hennessy, 2008). Screening instruments with a small number of items that take less than 3 minutes to administer are particularly appropriate for use in general medical settings. Examples of instruments that meet these criteria that are used for adult populations include the CAGE (alcohol addiction), the DAST (drug abuse), and the NIDA Quick Screen (drug and alcohol abuse). Examples of brief standardized instruments for special populations include the TWEAK (alcohol abuse and dependence for pregnant women and older adults) and the CRAFFT (alcohol or drug abuse in adolescents).[12] Although

---

[11] The source of this list of common indicators of drug and alcohol abuse is the New York State Department of Health AIDS Institute's Clinical Guidelines Development Program, specifically the guidelines for the *Screening and Ongoing Assessment for Substance Use* (Copyright © New York State Department of Health AIDS Institute, 2000–2010. All Rights Reserved). Although these guidelines were developed for clinicians serving HIV-positive patients, they are applicable to the general population and are used here with permission.

[12] For an excellent summary of the substance abuse and assessment process and a review of recommended standardized screening instruments appropriate for medical settings, see Greenfield, S. F., & Hennessy, G. (2008). Assessment of the patient. In M. Galanter & H. D. Kleber (Eds.), *Textbook of substance abuse treatment* (4th ed., pp. 55–78). Arlington, VA: American Psychiatric Publishing.

standardized screening instruments are a highly useful aid to the assessment of substance abuse and addiction, their accuracy is sensitive to the context of their administration. That is, their accuracy is facilitated when the clinician is able to interview the patient in a setting that offers privacy and confidentiality, and questions are posed in a frank, respectful, and non-judgmental manner (Greenfield & Hennessy, 2008; NYSDPH, 2007).

Referral and Placement

In general use, the term *referral* applies to the exchange of information that is intended to facilitate the utilization of a service. *Placement*, on the other hand, entails a series of actions on the part of the clinician that actively locates the patient into the treatment setting. In the world of addictions in particular, the distinction is an important one—often the difference between life and death. When a clinician merely refers an addicted patient to a treatment program, the onus for the facilitation of addiction treatment is placed entirely on the patient and/or his or her natural support system, often if not generally with little expectation of follow through. Placement of a patient in treatment, or at least serious attempts to do so, entails intensive collaborative efforts and deliberative diagnostic decision making about the most appropriate treatment setting and modalities. As stated by Mee-Lee and Gasfriend (2008, p. 81), ". . . in clinical practice, the placement decision is the last step in a multidimensional assessment that guides the variety of and intensity of services needed in an individualized treatment plan."

There are two diagnostic dimensions that are critical to placement in pursuit of optimally effective addiction treatment. The first, *placement matching*, refers to the identification of the treatment settings with the appropriate level of resource intensity. The second, *modality matching*, refers to the selection of the clinical approach or theoretical model of treatment that most closely fits with the patient's cluster of problems (Mee-Lee & Gasfriend, 2008). In the field of addictions, there is now a systematic criteria-based approach to placement into treatment that has been in effect and periodically updated since the early 1990s, referred to as the Patient Placement Criteria for the Treatment of Substance-Related Disorders of the American Society of Addiction Medicine (or ASAM PPC).[13]

---

[13] For a thorough review of the ASAM PPC principles and placement criteria, see Mee-Lee, D., & Gasfriend, D. R. (2008). Patient placement criteria. In M. Galanter & H. D. Kleber (Eds.), *Textbook of substance abuse treatment* (4th ed., pp. 79–91). Arlington, VA: American Psychiatric Publishing.

Special Populations in Substance Abuse and Addictions

There are special subpopulations of addicted persons that introduce particular and challenging complications, such as: persons with HIV/AIDS, pregnant substance abusing/addicted women and their drug exposed infants, persons with active tuberculosis, older adults, adolescents, and persons involved with the criminal justice system. Although it is well beyond the scope and purpose of this already lengthy chapter to delve into the array of issues represented within these special populations of addicted persons, we suggest and encourage the use of an excellent and easily accessed resource—known generally among addictions experts as the Treatment Improvement Protocols (TIPs). As an aid to effective

TABLE 6.4
Selected Examples of SAMHSA Treatment Improvement Protocols
(TIP Guidelines) for Special Populations and Issues in Substance
Abuse and Addictions

TIP #	POPULATION/ISSUE ADDRESSED
TIP 51	Substance Abuse Treatment: Addressing the Specific Needs of Women
TIP 44	Substance Abuse Treatment for Adults in the Criminal Justice System
TIP 42	Substance Abuse Treatment for Persons With Co-Occurring Disorders
TIP 37	Substance Abuse Treatment for Persons With HIV/AIDS
TIP 36	Substance Abuse Treatment for Persons With Child Abuse/ Neglect Issues
TIP 32	Treatment of Adolescents With Substance Use Disorders
TIP 29	Substance Use Disorder Treatment for People With Physical and Cognitive Disabilities
TIP 26	Substance Abuse Among Older Adults
TIP 25	Substance Abuse Treatment and Domestic Violence
TIP 18	The Tuberculosis Epidemic: Legal and Ethical Issues for Alcohol and Other Drug Treatment Providers
TIP 9	Assessment and Treatment of Patients With Coexisting Mental Illness and Alcohol and Other Drug Abuse
TIP 5	Improving Treatment for Drug-Exposed Infants
TIP 2	Pregnant, Substance-Using Women: Treatment Improvement Protocol

NOTE: For a complete list of the Substance Abuse and Mental Health Services Administration (SAMHSA) Treatment Improvement Protocols, see: http://www.ncbi.nlm.nih.gov/bookshelf/br.fcgi?book=hssamhsatip

practice in the addictions field, the SAMHSA (an agency within the U.S. Department of Health and Human Services) has developed this extensive array of evidence-based "best-practice guidelines" for the treatment of substance use disorders which are available for download at no cost. These guidelines incorporate cutting-edge knowledge of clinical, research, and administrative experts on drug abuse and addictions, and help clinicians ident ify the most appropriate practice approaches for special populations (Center for Substance Abuse Treatment, 2005). In Table 6.4, we show a subset of these SAMHSA TIPs that we have selected as particularly useful exemplars of the kind of support available to clinicians seeking to achieve the most optimal outcomes in the diagnosis and treatment of addictions.

SUGGESTED RESOURCES FOR SUBSTANCE ABUSE AND ADDICTION

Drug Abuse Warning Network Publications
https://dawninfo.samhsa.gov/pubs/

Detailed Tables
https://dawninfo.samhsa.gov/data/

National Survey of Drug Abuse and Health
http://oas.samhsa.gov/nsduh/2k8nsduh/2k8Results.pdf

National Institute on Drug Abuse (NIDA)
Homepage
http://www.nida.nih.gov/

Resources for Medical and Health Professionals
http://www.nida.nih.gov/nidamed/

Principles of Drug Addiction Treatment: A Research-Based Guide (Second Edition)
http://www.nida.nih.gov/PODAT/PODATIndex.html

The NIDA Clinical Toolbox: Science-Based Materials for Drug Abuse Treatment
www.nida.nih.gov/TB/Clinical/ClinicalToolbox.html

NIDA Clinician's Screening Tool
http://www.drugabuse.gov/nidamed/screening/

Substance Abuse and Mental Health Services Administration (SAMHSA)

SAMHSA Homepage
http://www.samhsa.gov/

Evidence-Based Practices Web Guide
http://www.samhsa.gov/ebpwebguide/index.asp

Office of Applied Statistics
http://www.oas.samhsa.gov/

SAMHSA/CSAT Treatment Improvement Protocols
http://www.ncbi.nlm.nih.gov/bookshelf/br.fcgi?book =hssamhsatip

REFERENCES

Brook, J. S., Pahl, K., & Rubenstone, E. (2008). Epidemiology of Addiction. In M. Galanter & H. D. Kleber (Eds.), *Textbook of Substance Abuse Treatment* (Fourth ed., pp. 29–44). Arlington, VA: American Psychiatric Publishing.

Center for Substance Abuse Treatment. (2005). *Substance abuse treatment for persons with co-occurring disorders. Treatment improvement protocol (TIP) series 42* (No. DHHS (SMA) 05-3922). Rockville, MD: U.S. Department of Health and Human Services.

Dugdale, D. (2010a). Drug abuse. *Medline Plus Encyclopedia*. Retrieved June 11, 2010, from http://www.nlm.nih.gov/medlineplus/ency/article/001945.htm

Dugdale, D. (2010b). Drug dependence. *Medline Plus Encyclopedia*. Retrieved June 11, 2010, from http://www.nlm.nih.gov/medlineplus/ency/article/001522.htm

Finucane, T., & Carrese, J. (1990). Racial bias in presentation of cases. *Journal of General Internal Medicine, 5*(2), 120–121.

Galanter, M., & Kleber, H. D. (Eds.). *Textbook of substance abuse treatment* (4th ed.). Arlington, VA: American Psychiatric Publishing.

Galanter, J., & Kranzler, H. R. (2008). Genetics of addiction. In M. Galanter & H. D. Kleber (Eds.), *Textbook of substance abuse treatment* (4th ed., pp. 17–27). Arlington, VA: American Psychiatric Publishing.

Gordon, J. A. (1999). The Hospital Emergency Department as a Social Welfare Institution. *Annals of Emergency Medicine, 33*(3), 321–325.

Greenfield, S. F., & Hennessy, G. (2008). Assessment of the patient. In M. Galanter & H. D. Kleber (Eds.), *Textbook of substance abuse treatment* (4th ed., pp. 55–78). Arlington, VA: American Psychiatric Publishing.

Hahn, J. (2010). Opioids and related disorders. *Encyclopedia of Mental Disorders*. Retrieved July 16, 2010, from http://www.minddisorders.com/Ob-Ps/Opioids-and-related-disorders.html

Harwick, H. (2000). *Updating estimates of the economic costs of alcohol abuse in the United States: Estimates, update methods, and data.* Report prepared by The

Lewin Group for the National Institute on Alcohol Abuse and Alcoholism. Rockville, MD: National Institutes of Health, U.S. Department of Health and Human Services.

Hasin D. (2003). *Classification of alcohol use disorders.* Bethesda, MD: National Institute on Alcohol Abuse and Alcoholism.

Institute of Medicine. (2000). *Institute of Medicine—America's Health Care Safety Net: Intact but endangered.* Washington, DC: National Academies Press.

Kendler, K. S., Prescott, C. A., & Neale, M. C., et al. (1997). Temperance board registration for alcohol abuse in a national sample of Swedish male twins, born between 1902 and 1949. *Archives of General Psychiatry, 54,* 178–184.

Koop, G. F. (2008). Neurobiology of addiction. In M. Galanter & H. D. Kleber (Eds.), *Textbook of substance abuse treatment* (4th ed., pp. 3–16). Arlington, VA: American Psychiatric Publishing.

Kosten, T., Sofuoglu, M., & Gardner, T. (2008). Clinical Management: Cocaine. In M. Galanter & H. D. Kleber (Eds.), *Textbook of substance abuse treatment* (4th ed., pp. 29–44). Arlington, VA: American Psychiatric Publishing.

Massey, D., & Denton, N. (1993). *American apartheid: Segregation and the making of the underclass.* Cambridge, MA: Harvard University Press.

Mee-Lee, D., & Gasfriend, D. R. (2008). Patient placement criteria. In M. Galanter & H. D. Kleber (Eds.), *Textbook of substance abuse treatment* (4th ed., pp. 79–91). Arlington, VA: American Psychiatric Publishing.

Miller, M. M. (1998). Traditional approaches to the treatment of addiction. In A. W. Graham, & T. K. Schultz (Eds.), *Principles of addiction medicine* (2nd ed.). Washington, DC: American Society of Addiction Medicine.

Myrick, H., & Wright, T. (2008). Clinical management of alcohol abuse and dependence. In M. Galanter & H. D. Kleber (Eds.), *Textbook of substance abuse treatment* (4th ed., pp. 129–142). Arlington, VA: American Psychiatric Publishing.

National Coalition for the Homeless. (2007). *Who is homeless: NCH Fact Sheet #3.* Washington, DC: Author.

National Institute of Drug Abuse. (2001). *Research report series-Hallucinogens and Dissociative Drugs.* Retrieved June 6, 2011, from http://www.nida.nih.gov/ResearchReports/Hallucinogens/Hallucinogens.html

National Institute of Drug Abuse. (2005). *Research report series—Heroin Abuse and Addiction.* Retrieved June 6, 2011, from: http://www.nida.nih.gov/ResearchReports/Heroin/Heroin.html

National Institute of Drug Abuse. (2006). *Research report series—Methamphetamine Abuse and Addiction.* Retrieved June 6, 2011, from http://www.drugabuse.gov/ResearchReports/methamph/methamph5.html#treatment

National Institute of Drug Abuse. (2009). *Principles of drug addiction treatment: A research-based guide second edition (No. NIH 09-4180).* Retrieved from http://www.drugabuse.gov/ScienceofAddiction/addiction.html

National Institute of Drug Abuse. (2010) *Drugs, Brains, and Behavior— The Science of Addiction.* Retrieved June 6, 2011, from http://www .drugabuse.gov/ScienceofAddiction/addiction.html

New York State Department of Public Health. (2007). *New York State Department of Health AIDS Institute's Clinical Guidelines Development Program: Screening and ongoing assessment for substance abuse.* Retrieved June 11, 2010, from http://www.hivguidelines.org

Polydorou, S., & Kleber, H. D. (2008). Detoxification of opioids. In M. Galanter & H. D. Kleber (Eds.), *Textbook of substance abuse treatment* (4th ed., pp. 265–287). Arlington, VA: American Psychiatric Publishing.

Schottenfeld, R. S. (2008). Opioid maintenance treatment. In M. Galanter & H. D. Kleber (Eds.), *Textbook of substance abuse treatment* (4th ed., pp. 289–308). Arlington, VA: American Psychiatric Publishing.

Schwartz, J. (2008). Gender differences in drunk driving prevalence rates and trends: A 20 year assessment using multiple sources of evidence. *Addictive Behaviors, 33*(9), 1217–1222.

Substance Abuse and Mental Health Services Administration. (2005). *Arrests for driving under the influence among adult drivers.* Rockville, MD: U.S. Department of Health and Human Services.

Substance Abuse and Mental Health Services Administration. (2009). *Results from the 2008 National Survey on Drug Use and Health: National Findings (Office of Applied Studies, NSDUH Series H-36, HHS Publication No. SMA 09-4434).* Rockville, MD: U.S. Department of Health and Human Services.

Substance Abuse and Mental Health Services Administration. (2010). *Drug Abuse Warning Network, 2007: National Estimates of Drug-Related Emergency Department Visits.* Rockville, MD: U.S. Department of Health and Human Services.

Tsuang MT, Lyons MJ, Eisen SA, Goldberg J, True W, Lin N, … Eaves L. (1996). Genetic influences on DSM-III-R drug abuse and dependence: A study of 3,372 twin pairs. *American Journal of Medical Genetics, 67*(5), 473–477.

van Ryn, M. (2002). Research on the provider contribution to race/ethnicity disparities in medical care. *Medical Care, 40*(1 Supplement), 140–151.

Weaver, M. F., & Schnoll, S. H. (2008). Hallucinogens and club drugs. In M. Galanter & H. D. Kleber (Eds.), *Textbook of substance abuse treatment* (4th ed., pp. 191–200). Arlington, VA: American Psychiatric Publishing.

Zerger, S. (2002). *Substance abuse treatment: What works for homeless people? A review of the literature.* Nashville, TN: National Health Care for the Homeless Council.

7

Interpersonal Violence, Injury, and Trauma

INTRODUCTION

> Some people's lives seem to flow in a narrative; mine had many stops and starts. That's what trauma does. It interrupts the plot. You can't process it because it doesn't fit with what came before or what comes afterward. A friend of mine, a soldier, put it this way. In most of our lives, most of the time, you have a sense of what is to come. There is a steady narrative, a feeling of "lights, camera, action" when big events are imminent. But trauma isn't like that. It just happens, and then life goes on. No one prepares you for it. (Stern, 2010)

Violence, injury, and trauma are ubiquitous parts of American life. Thousands of people are killed every year through car accidents, suicides, and homicides; hundreds of thousands more live with the injuries sustained from these incidents; and effects ripple beyond the victim, altering the lives of their families and friends. These events by their very nature are sudden and destabilizing to survivors.[1] As Jessica Stern,

---

[1] Several arguments have been made for the use of the term "survivor" versus "victim." People who have been victimized or injured often resist being labeled as a victim because of the word's negative connotations, particularly of powerlessness and the focus on the negative event(s) rather than the positive strengths exhibited by the survivor. We use the term survivor in this chapter to highlight this strength orientation.

237

a survivor of sexual assault and an expert on terrorism noted, there is no preparation for trauma, and its disruptive effects can go on indefinitely. The experience of traumatic injury doesn't end with discharge from the hospital; having been traumatized or victimized increases the chance that a person will be retraumatized or revictimized again later in his or her life. Understanding the physical and psychological toll of injury is important for professionals working in safety-net settings because safety-net hospitals, in particular, often are the primary providers of intensive trauma services for their community.

Just as the problems of homelessness and substance use are not equally distributed among all populations (we are not all at equal risk, although anyone may experience these troubles), violence and traumatic injury are not found equally among all groups. Although injury can happen to anyone, depending on the type of victimization or injury investigated, different demographic factors put a person at higher risk. For instance, in terms of child abuse, boys are slightly more likely to experience severe physical abuse, whereas girls are at higher risk for sexual abuse and incest; lower socioeconomic status children are at higher risk of all forms of child maltreatment (Barnett, Miller-Perrin, & Perrin, 2005). In general, the risk for exposure to unintentional injury is more prevalent among people with lower incomes, particularly young males (Cubbin & Smith, 2002). As a result of the confluence of poverty and injury, clinicians in safety net settings will see more injured clients both for patient-related and system of care-related reasons.

The focus of this chapter is on the role of injury, trauma, and interpersonal violence in the safety-net health care system. We briefly review national statistics related to injury, including basic information on the three most common causes of injury-related death: accidents, homicide, and suicide. We explore why safety-net patients are at higher risk for injury exposure, the role of safety-net hospitals in the provision of trauma services, the effects of victimization and trauma on health, and two forms of family violence (child maltreatment and intimate partner violence) that health care providers are in a particularly critical position to recognize and address.

Injury as a Leading Cause of Mortality and Morbidity

Injury can be defined as either intentional (homicide, suicide, or violent altercations) or unintentional (accidental). Sometimes, injuries are classified as either penetrating (usually injuries caused by guns, knives, or shrapnel in wars) or blunt (caused by impact with an object or as a result of force). Thirty years ago, the Centers for Disease Control and Prevention (CDC) began a study of injury-related death and disability after a report issued by the Surgeon General. This report stressed the need to "reduce these tragic and avoidable deaths . . . [through] better Federal, State, and local actions to foster more careful behavior and provide safer environments" (Richmond, 1979, pp. 1–9). In 1992, the CDC created the main federal entity in charge of violence and injury prevention, the National Center for Injury Prevention and Control (NCIPC). Since then, the NCIPC has conducted research on intentional and unintentional injury prevention. According to its most recent summary of data on injury,

> In 2004, more than 167,000 deaths—7% of all deaths in the United States—resulted from injury. In addition, 1.9 million hospitalizations and 31 million initial visits to emergency departments were attributable to injury and accounted for 6% of all hospital discharges and almost one-third of all initial emergency department visits. Another 35 million initial visits to physicians' offices and outpatient clinics were for the treatment of injuries (Bergen, Chen, Warner, & Fingerhut, 2008, p. 1).

These statistics make clear the human cost of intentional and unintentional injury in terms of its direct effects within the health care system. The CDC estimates that almost $80 billion dollars were spent in 2000 on costs associated with hospitalization, emergency department (ED) services, and outpatient visits for the physical consequences of injury alone (Bergen et al., 2008). No estimate is currently available of the associated mental health costs, disability payments, or financial burden experienced by families as a result of injuries. These costs would be even higher than the direct costs of patient care.

Next, we briefly review information about deaths caused by unintentional and intentional injuries. Although our focus in the next subsections is on mortality, we use this as an indicator of the extent of nonfatal injury. For instance, there are five times as many hospitalizations for motor vehicle-involved accidents as there are fatalities, and 80 times as many ED admissions than fatalities (Naumann, Dellinger, Zaloshnja, Lawrence, & Miller, 2010). Another way to understand the relationship of mortality and morbidity is to consider disability-adjusted life years. This figure, used by the World Health Organization, provides information on both mortality and the number of *healthy* life years lost as a result of injury or disease. Projections of the number of disability-adjusted life years lost because of injury worldwide show that motor vehicle accidents, suicide, war, and violence will all take an increasing toll on the human population. By 2020, traffic accidents will be the third leading cause of death and disability worldwide; in developing countries, war will be eighth, whereas in developed countries, suicide will be tenth (Murray & Lopez, 1997).

Accidents

Unintentional injuries include motor vehicle accidents, drowning, fires, poisoning, falls, and brain injury from sports or recreational activity. In the United States, two-thirds of all injury-related deaths are from unintentional injuries; motor vehicle accidents are by far the most common form of injury that causes death (Bergen et al., 2008). Accidents have been among the top 10 causes of death since 1900,[2] and they continue to be a primary cause of death a century later (National Center for Health Statistics, n.d.a). The second leading cause of injury-related death is poisoning; however, for those aged 35 to 54, poisoning surpasses motor vehicle accidents as the leading cause of injury-related death. The vast majority of poisonings are drug-related overdoses from methadone, oxycontin, and other opioid analgesics (Warner, Chen, & Mackuc, 2009).

Table 7.1 shows the leading causes of death from age 5 to over 65 for the U.S. population. From ages 5 to 44, accidental injury, mainly in the form of motor vehicle accidents, is the leading cause of death. Only after age 65 are all forms of preventable injury no longer a major cause of death. Native American children and youth are at particularly high risk for death from preventable injury—their rate of injury-related fatality is twice as high as youth of other races (NCIPC, 2006). However, after the age of 65, the most common cause of fatal injury is falls. When falls do not lead to death, the most serious consequence is hip fracture. Almost three-quarters of hip fractures are among women; 20% of the people who have a hip fracture will die within the following year (NCIPC, 2006).

Suicide

Each year, the number of people who die by suicide is twice the number of people who die from homicides; only in adolescence and early adulthood is homicide a larger cause of death than suicide. Although

---

[2] Motor vehicle accidents began to be tracked as a separate category of accidental death in 1926.

TABLE 7.1
Five Leading Causes of Death for Various Age Groupings, 2009

RANK	AGE				
	5–14	15–24	25–44	45–64[a]	65+[b]
1	Accidents	Accidents	Accidents	Malignant neoplasm	Diseases of heart
2	Malignant neoplasm	Homicide	Malignant neoplasm	Diseases of heart	Malignant neoplasm
3	Congenital malformations	Suicide	Diseases of heart	Accidents	Chronic lower respiratory disease
4	Homicide	Malignant neoplasm	Suicide	Chronic lower respiratory disease	Cerebro-vascular diseases
5	Suicide	Diseases of heart	Homicide	Chronic liver diseases	Alzheimer's disease

NOTE: Based on data from "Deaths: Preliminary data for 2009," by Kochanek, Xu, Murphy, Miniño, and Kung, 2011, *National Vital Statistics Reports, 59*. Shaded areas denote injury-related causes of death.

[a] Suicide is the eighth-ranked cause of death in this age range; homicide is no longer in the top 10.

[b] Accidents are the ninth-ranked cause of death in this age range; neither suicide nor homicide is in the top 10.

suicide is not a leading cause of death after age 65; if looking only at data on people who completed suicide, those over 65, particularly White men, have the highest rate of death from suicide (National Center for Health Statistics, n.d.b). Men of all ages are more likely to complete suicide, even though women attempt suicide at much higher rates (NCIPC, 2006). Men's increased risk for death may be related to the frequency of their use of firearms, the most immediately lethal form of suicide. Firearms are used in over half of all completed suicides (NCIPC, 2006).

Table 7.2 lists factors related to suicide that increase risk and those that are protective, that is, things that promote health and well-being. Ninety percent of all people who die from suicide have a mental disorder, whereas effective treatment availability and social support are consistent protective factors that prevent suicide (NCIPC, 2006). Epidemiological research has identified particular groups at higher risk of suicide. In terms of race and ethnicity, American Indian/Alaska Natives and Whites have twice the rate of completed suicide compared to African Americans, Asian/Pacific Islanders, and Hispanics. However,

TABLE 7.2
Risk and Protective Factors for Suicide Prevention

RISK FACTORS	PROTECTIVE FACTORS
Mental disorder (including depression, schizophrenia, alcohol or drug abuse, post-traumatic stress disorder [PTSD])	Effective mental health, substance use, and physical care
Prior history of suicide attempt	Skills in problem solving, conflict resolution, impulse control
Family history of suicide	Family and community support
Self-harming behaviors	Cultural and religious beliefs that discourage suicide and promote self-care
Family violence	Easily available services (mental health, violence intervention, drug and alcohol treatment)
Access to firearms	

Compiled from NIH Publication No. 06-4594, Suicide in the United States, Statistics and Prevention and "CDC Injury fact book," by NCIPC, 2006, Atlanta, GA: Centers for Disease Control and Prevention.

these statistics sometimes obscure important subgroup differences. For instance, although Asian Americans have lower reported levels of suicidal ideation and attempts, when Asian Americans are analyzed in terms of gender and nativity (whether they were born in the United States or are immigrants), United States-born Asian American women have a much higher percentage for both suicidal ideation and attempts than the national estimates (Duldulao, Takeuchi, & Hong, 2009).

Suicide risk is also higher among lesbian, gay, and bisexual (LGB) people (King et al., 2009).[3] In data from the National Longitudinal Study of Adolescent Health (Add Health), youth who reported either same-sex romantic attraction or relationships were more likely to report suicidal thoughts and attempts. Although the mechanisms linking sexual orientation to suicide risk appear similar between same-sex attracted and other-sex attracted youth (i.e., same sex-oriented youth had higher rates of mental disorders such as depression and alcohol use, and reported more suicide attempts or completions by family members), LGB youth were more likely to report victimization than heterosexual youth, and this experience was

---

[3] Information on gender identity (i.e., transgender) has not been included in most studies of suicide; Almeida, Johnson, Corliss, Molnar, and Azrael (2009) is one of the few.

TABLE 7.3
Excerpt From President Obama's Message to Lesbian, Gay, Bisexual, or Transgender (LGBT) Youth

Like all of you, I was shocked and saddened by the deaths of several young people who were bullied and taunted for being gay, and who ultimately took their own lives . . . . I don't know what it's like to be picked on for being gay. But I do know what it's like to grow up feeling that sometimes you don't belong. It's tough. And for a lot of kids, the sense of being alone or apart, I know can just wear on you . . . .

But what I want to say is this. You are not alone. You didn't do anything wrong . . . . And there is a whole world waiting for you, filled with possibilities. There are people out there who love and care about you just the way you are . . . .

The other thing you need to know is: Things will get better. And more than that, with time you're going to see that your differences are a source of pride and a source of strength. You'll look back on the struggles you faced with compassion and wisdom. And that's not just going to serve you, but it will help you get involved and make this country a better place. It will mean that you'll be more likely to help fight discrimination—not just against LGBT Americans, but discrimination in all its forms. . . .

Every day, it gets better.

Excerpt from "It gets better: Coming out, overcoming bullying and creating a life worth living," by Savage and Miller, 2011, New York, NY: Dutton.

strongly linked to suicide risk.[4] Access to people who are supportive of sexual minority status is an important protective factor in suicide risk. In 2010, as a result of the publicity surrounding a number of suicides by young gay men, the It Gets Better Project[5] was started. See Table 7.3 for an excerpt from President Barack Obama providing support to lesbian, gay, bisexual, or transgender (LGBT) youth.

Homicide

Homicide is in the top five causes of death from childhood through middle age. According to the U.S. Bureau of Justice Statistics (Fox & Zawitz, 2007), the most likely profile for a victim of homicide is a young, African American male. Most victims of homicide in the United States are in their

---

[4] The Add Health Study did not ask youth if they identified as LGBT, but instead focused on same-sex attraction and one aspect of behavior, being in a relationship. (Other studies that include sexual minorities also ask about sexual behavior, not just relationship behavior.) As a result, the results of this study may differ among people who have "come out" and experienced greater chances for victimization as a result, but who also may be able to access increased support from members of the LGBT community.

[5] Videos from the It Gets Better Project can be found at itgetsbetter.org or on YouTube.

20s and 30s, most are killed by guns, and most live in cities with more than 100,000 residents. African Americans experience a disproportionate amount of homicide—they are six times as likely to be a victim as someone who is White, and while the population of 15- to 24-year-old African American males represents just 1% of the total U.S. population, they accounted for 15% or more of victims of homicide from 1975 to 2005.

In trying to understand risk and protective factors related to homicide, researchers have turned to studies of youth violence, given the disproportionate burden of homicide that happens during adolescence and young adulthood. Table 7.4 presents empirically identified factors that promote and inhibit youth violence. For African American youth, these factors, combined with issues of racism and structural poverty, appear to be primary risk factors for youth violence. For instance, 50% of African American children live in neighborhoods characterized by high crime, poverty, and unemployment; only 2% of White youth live in similar neighborhoods (Farrington, Loeber, & Stouthamer-Loeber, 2003). African American youths with racial pride, strong spiritual values, and commitment to family and community have lower rates of involvement in youth violence (Williams, Bright, & Petersen, 2011).

Women are at risk for a different form of homicide and intentional injury—namely, assault by an intimate partner. Women are twice as likely as men to be killed by an intimate partner (husband/ex-husband or boyfriend/ex-boyfriend) (Fox & Zawitz, 2007). Among women reporting victimization by an intimate partner in the U.S.

TABLE 7.4
Risk and Protective Factors Related to Youth Violence

RISK FACTORS	PROTECTIVE FACTORS
Living in poverty	Strong external support
Living in a high-crime neighborhood	Prosocial orientation
Inadequate parental supervision	Strong attachment to parents
Low-academic attainment	Positive parental discipline, monitoring, and supervision
	Commitment to school
	Higher level of school bonding
	Problem-solving skills
	Social problem-solving skills

Adapted from Williams et al. (2011), "Racial and ethnic differences in risk and protective factors associated with youth violence."

National Crime Victims Survey, low-income and American Indian/ Alaska Native women reported the highest levels of violence (Bureau of Justice Statistics, 2011). Intimate partner homicide of women is strongly associated with separation from the abusive partner and his access to a gun (Campbell et al., 2003). Later in this chapter, we discuss factors associated with intimate partner violence in more detail.

Clearly, injury creates a substantial burden for individuals, their families, and society. The disproportionate burden of injury borne by people living in poverty has direct implications for safety-net settings, as we discuss next.

Risk for Violence and Injury Exposure Among Safety-Net Patients

Certain populations are more vulnerable to violence and injury. People living in poverty are disproportionately represented among those who are victims of violent crime. According to the U.S. Department of Justice, the rate of assault among people age 12 and older whose income is less than $7,500 is 44.1, compared to a rate of 12.4 for people whose income is $75,000 or more. Overall, the rate of any crime of violence is five times higher for people in the lowest income group compared to the highest income group (Bureau of Justice Statistics, 2010). A similar pattern in which income exerts a strong protective influence has been found in national studies of pediatric nonfatal injury (Danseco, Miller, & Spicer, 2000) and intentional and unintentional injury among adults (Cubbin & Smith, 2002; Gilbride, Wild, Wilson, Svenson, & Spady, 2006). Poverty increases the risk for injury and it appears that the reverse may also be true—that injury interferes with the ability to work and can lead to financial impoverishment (Zatzick et al., 2008).

As we have discussed in the chapter on poverty, certain groups are disproportionately represented among those who are poor, including African Americans, Latinos, and American Indian/Alaska Natives, single mothers, and children. The relationships among poverty, race, gender, age, and injury are complex, but it is clear that these demographic factors are related to the risk of certain forms of intentional and unintentional injury. The pathways through which poverty creates the risk for injury are multiple and complex (Cubbin & Smith, 2002). For example, at an environmental level, poverty restricts access to decent housing, which is then implicated in burn injuries caused by unsafe heating devices. People in poorer neighborhoods may also have less access to preventive and intervention-oriented fire and police services, escalating the possibility of injury from violence or accident. People with low-socioeconomic status are more likely to work in "3-D jobs"—work that is dangerous, demeaning, or dirty (Law, 2003) such as construction, prostitution and agriculture all have higher rates of injury. Poverty also increases psychosocial stress, which may create more risk for injury or victimization, but the mechanisms by which stress and injury may be related have not yet been identified.

Another characteristic of safety-net patients is their lack of health insurance. Health insurance status has dramatic effects on survival after injury—patients who were uninsured at the time of injury were more likely to die than their insured counterparts (Haider et al., 2008). Being uninsured and African American or Latino increased the chances of death even more in comparison to insured White trauma patients (Haider et al., 2008). These findings are particularly concerning because as many as 40% of trauma patients in some studies have no health insurance (Selzer et al., 2001). For safety-net hospital trauma centers, the number of uninsured appears even higher—information on almost 350,000 severely injured patients enrolled in the National Trauma Data Bank indicated that over 60% of safety-net trauma patients were uninsured.[6] In addition to the immediate issues associated with hospitalization from injury, many trauma patients will be unable to access beneficial rehabilitation services if they do not have access to health insurance, further increasing health disparities for this group.

One of the most frequently noted correlates of injury is substance use. In fact, alcohol use is one of the largest risk factors for fatal injury of any kind. Almost half of all drivers between 21 and 30 who died in car accidents were legally intoxicated at the time of their accident (Bergen et al., 2008); one-third of the people who committed suicide in 2007 had been drinking prior to death and almost 20% had used some kind of opiate (CDC, 2010); and one-third of all homicide victims were legally intoxicated at their death (Kuhns, Wilson, Clodfelter, Maguire, & Ainsworth, 2011). Substance use, as we noted in Chapter 6, is associated with poverty and has been seen as an effort to self-medicate the distress associated with the psychosocial stressors of poverty.

---

[6] In this study, a safety-net trauma center was defined as an institution in the highest 10% in terms of the percentage of uninsured among all hospitals treating trauma patients. This resulted in a study sample that included 46 safety net and 413 non-safety-net trauma centers.

The issues of poverty, substance use, and injury are deeply intertwined—it is difficult to tease apart these co-occurring risks. The proportion of patients with multiple comorbidities is higher in safety-net health care settings than hospitals or clinics in more affluent communities. For instance, in one of the few studies that assesses intentional injury among safety-net clients, Boccellari et al. (2007) found that the majority of crime victims in a San Francisco public hospital were young, unemployed, African American men living in poverty. A remarkable 36% of victims were homeless at the time they presented to the ED for treatment.[7] In this study, 70% of crime victims used alcohol weekly, and 58% used other drugs weekly; 43% were diagnosed with Alcohol Abuse Disorder. These figures suggest that the victims who seek treatment in safety-net settings are "distinct" from other crime victim samples in the number of psychosocial stressors, and the burden of physical and mental health symptoms that they experience as a result of the victimization (Boccellari et al., 2007, p. 241).

SAFETY-NET HOSPITALS AND TRAUMA

Since the 1970s, various medical groups have advocated for the creation of regional trauma systems to provide emergency medical treatment to the injured and to develop capacity to respond to mass casualties or terrorist attacks (Champion, Mabee, & Meredith, 2006). In large metropolitan areas that have public (i.e., safety net) hospitals, these hospitals are often the leading (Level I) trauma treatment providers. In addition to trauma center-designated hospitals, EDs in all hospitals serve injured clients, and for legal reasons, are safety-net providers, even if the larger hospital is not a safety-net service. In this section, we describe the development of regional trauma systems and the role of safety-net hospitals within these systems as well as the issues of safety-net service provision in EDs.

Trauma Centers

Centralizing injury treatment minimizes preventable deaths by ensuring that medical professionals with the greatest level of expertise in emergency medicine are immediately available to injured patients

---

[7] Homelessness increases the risk for victimization because of a person's lack of safe surroundings. It is also true that injury can lead to homelessness, as in the case of victims of domestic violence who may flee their homes when experiencing severe abuse.

24 hours a day (MacKenzie et al., 2003). This level of expertise is more important overall than being taken to the nearest hospital after traumatic injury (Branas et al., 2005). As a result of the centralization of services, trauma centers accounted for a 15% decrease in death when compared to injured patients treated in nontrauma center hospitals (Celso et al., 2006). Safety-net hospitals have equivalent rates of mortality when compared to private sector trauma centers, but they also see the highest proportion of uninsured patients (Vettukattil et al., 2011).

The designation as a Level I trauma center recognizes the increased level of knowledge and skill among the variety of health professionals which are needed to treat injured patients. To be certified as a trauma center, hospitals have to meet certain requirements (Table 7.5). As of 2010, all states in the country have at least a Level II trauma center, with over 90% of Level I and II centers being located in metropolitan areas (MacKenzie et al., 2003). Hospitals with trauma centers account for only 8% of the hospitals nationwide (Champion et al., 2006). The largest number of Level I and II trauma centers are located in the Northeast, Midwest, and California. Because of the geographic distances involved, particularly in the West, almost 50 million Americans cannot reach a Level I or II trauma center within an hour, even by helicopter (Branas et al., 2005). This situation is particularly severe in Alaska, which has only one Level II trauma center in Anchorage for the entire state.[8] Currently, there are almost 200 Level I trauma centers in the United States and over 250 Level II centers (MacKenzie et al., 2003).

Hospitals with trauma centers are more likely to be publicly owned (i.e., safety-net hospitals), and most are associated with university medical schools, another safety-net characteristic (MacKenzie et al., 2003). Almost all Level I, II, and III trauma centers have intensive care units, but only Level I centers are likely to have burn care and organ transplantation services available. Because of the noncompensated expenses associated with trauma-related medical care, trauma centers report substantial financial losses (Selzer et al., 2001). Trauma centers face a number of financial threats to survival, including the increasing number of uninsured patients, and declining reimbursement, especially through Medicaid programs (MacKenzie et al., 2003). Financial pressures associated with trauma care may drive hospitals to

---

[8] According to American College of Surgeons listing of trauma centers (available at: http://www.facs.org/trauma/verified.html), six other states also have only one trauma center, but they are all smaller than Alaska: Alabama, Arkansas, New Mexico, Rhode Island, Vermont, and Wyoming.

TABLE 7.5
Definitions of Trauma Center Classification

TRAUMA LEVEL	REQUIREMENTS
Level I	Provides comprehensive, regional care. Must have immediately available trauma surgeons, anesthesiologists, physician specialists, nurses, and resuscitation equipment. Must treat at least 1,200 admissions per year, or 240 major trauma patients per year, or an average of 35 major trauma patients per surgeon
Level II	Provides comprehensive care, usually in a more suburban or rural area. Must meet the same criteria for immediately available specialists as Level I, but does not need to serve the same volume of patients
Level III	Provides prompt assessment, resuscitation, emergency surgery, and stabilization with transfer to Level I or II
Level IV[a]	Provides trauma life support to stabilize patients with transfer to nearest trauma center. These facilities are usually found in rural, remote areas without access to higher levels of trauma care

From " Resources for optimal care of the injured patient," by American College of Surgeons, Committee on Trauma Classification System,1999, Chicago, IL: Author.

[a] Some state systems define a Level V trauma center, but this is not in standard use across the country.

specialize in more profitable services and close unprofitable ones (Shen, Hsia, & Kuzma, 2009). Although the number of hospitals being certified as trauma centers has increased in the last two decades, the pace of closure has also grown, with 339 centers shutting down between 1990 and 2005 (Shen et al., 2009). Hospitals in areas with larger percentages of minorities were at higher risk for closure (Shen et al., 2009), whereas those serving a higher proportion of people with blunt injuries were generally more profitable than those seeing patients with penetrating injuries (Selzer et al., 2001). In other words, centers that mainly treat accident victims are more financially stable than those (primarily urban safety-net centers) that treat a larger number of patients with injuries from violence. As Selzer et al. note,

> Changes in health care management recently have led to decreased [trauma treatment] funds . . . with further cuts anticipated. Without these funds, Level I trauma centers at public urban hospitals will continue to work at a significant loss, risking the financial solvency of these institutions. (2001, p. 307)

Americans have recognized through policy and funding streams the importance of access to high-quality trauma care regardless of a person's ability to pay. As a country, we believe it is wrong for someone to die of an injury that could be treated, solely as a consequence of their socioeconomic status. Despite this ideological commitment, diminishing funding streams are encroaching on access to trauma care, particularly among those living in poverty. Decreased access to trauma services may be an underlying mechanism that explains some of the racial disparities found in health outcomes, given the increased risk of injury, particularly among African American and Latino young men. The loss of safety net trauma centers would further exacerbate racial health disparities, given the disproportionate share of uninsured clients served in these institutions, and the fact that they see a higher number of African American and Latino patients (Vettukattil et al., 2011). In response to the financial exigencies faced by emergency trauma services, the Trauma Center Association of America and other injury treatment groups have advocated to the U.S. Congress for increased federal financial assistance to trauma centers, but to date these efforts have not been successful.[9]

Emergency Departments and Safety-Net Services

For the past 30 years, U.S. EDs have been required to act as safety-net providers for critically ill or injured patients—they must provide treatment regardless of the patient's insurance status as a condition of receiving financial reimbursement from federal programs (Medicare and Medicaid). This requirement applies to for-profit and nonprofit hospitals as well as safety-net health care settings. In the early 1980s, researchers at Cook County Hospital in Chicago published a report about patient "dumping," or the transfer of patients for financial rather than medical reasons. The authors found that 87% of patients transferred from other hospital EDs were sent to Cook County because they didn't have health insurance; 89% were African American or Hispanic (Schiff et al., 1986). Patients who were transferred for financial reasons were almost three times as likely to die compared to patients who came directly to Cook County, largely, the authors contended, because their urgent need for care was delayed by the transfer from the other

---

[9] The National Trauma Center Stabilization Act would provide grants directly to trauma centers to reimburse them for uncompensated trauma care and provide emergency assistance to centers at risk of closure.

TABLE 7.6
Provisions of the Emergency Medical Treatment and Active Labor Act (EMTALA)

A. *Medical Screening*

In the case of a hospital that has a hospital emergency department (ED), if any individual. . . . comes to the ED and a request is made . . . for examination or treatment for a medical condition, the hospital must provide an appropriate medical screening examination within the capability of the hospital's ED, including ancillary services routinely available to the ED to determine if an emergency medical condition exists.

B. *Necessary Stabilizing Treatment for Emergency Medical Conditions and Labor*

In general, the hospital must provide (a) within the staff and facilities available at the hospital, for such further medical examination and such treatment as may be required to stabilize the medical condition, or (b) for [appropriate] transfer of the individual to another medical facility.

C. *Restricting Transfers Until the Patient is Stabilized*

An appropriate transfer to a medical facility is a transfer— (a) in which the transferring hospital provides the medical treatment within its capacity, which minimizes the risks to the individual's health and, in the case of a woman in labor, the health of the unborn child; (b) in which the receiving facility—(a) has available space and qualified personnel for the treatment of the individual, and (b) has agreed to accept transfer of the individual and to provide appropriate medical treatment.

From EMTALA statute, **42 USC 1395dd**.

hospital (Schiff et al., 1986). As a result of stories such as these, the U.S. Congress passed the Emergency Medical Treatment and Active Labor Act (EMTALA) in 1983 (see Table 7.6 for specific language of the act). The law was seen as a remedy to patient dumping, and through successive court cases, has been broadly applied in ED settings (Zibulewsky, 2001). It requires that (a) hospitals screen and treat patients who have presented with urgent conditions, and (b) transfers can be made to another hospital only if a higher level of care is needed, not because of the patient's insurance status.

Level I trauma centers are, by definition, the highest level of care available, and according to EMTALA, must accept transfer of patients from other hospital EDs if a greater level of care is required. In 2003, the U.S. Department of Health and Human Services clarified guidelines on EMTALA on-call coverage resulting in a larger number of EDs no longer having specialty surgeons on call (Spain et al., 2007). As a result, concerns exist that ". . . many patients are transferred to Level I trauma centers not because [a higher level of] care is required but rather because of a lack of specialty physician coverage at the initial hospital or lack of insurance" (Spain et al., 2007, p. 64). Research has been mixed as to whether patients continue to be more likely to be referred to Level I trauma centers ("dumped") if they have no health insurance coverage. Some have found that uninsured patients were more likely to be transferred to safety-net trauma centers than their insured counterparts, and went so far as to describe insurance as an "unspoken triage criterion" (Nathans, Maier, Copass, & Jurkovich, 2001). In contrast, Spain et al. (2007) did not find that uninsured patients were transferred more frequently to an academic trauma center; however, transferred patients often had more complex medical issues than those who presented directly to the trauma center.

The issue of ED crowding has become more urgent as EDs have closed at the same time that an increasing number of patients are seeking ED services (Sklar et al., 2010). In 2005, an estimated 41,000 patients were seen in EDs for nonfatal injuries, primarily related to accidents and falls (Owens et al., 2010). Visits to EDs have increased at a rate of about 3% per year, but more EDs are closing (Sklar et al., 2010), in significant part because of similar financial pressures as trauma centers—namely, the requirement that all EDs provide emergency services to patients regardless of their ability to pay. Due to the increasing numbers of Americans without health insurance, EDs can end up providing a substantial portion of uncompensated care in their communities. Regionally, the South has more high-volume EDs because of a heavier reliance on safety-net hospitals than the rest of the country; most small volume EDs (less than a visit per hour each day) are likely to be in rural areas, more often in the Midwest (Sullivan et al., 2006).

Crowding of EDs has serious consequences for patient care—the more crowded an ED, the greater the risk of mortality (Bernstein et al., 2008). A number of assumptions have come to be accepted as "common knowledge" in discussions about overcrowding in EDs. One of these assumptions is that EDs are clogged with uninsured patients seeking treatment for nonurgent conditions. Approximately 17% of annual ED visits are made by people without health insurance (Owens et al., 2010). However (as can be seen in Table 7.7), research on ED utilization does not clearly support the contention that uninsured patients are presenting to EDs with nonurgent problems (Newton, Keirns, Cunningham, Hayward, & Stanley, 2008). What is clear from the review of research about uninsured adults in EDs is that they wait longer to seek care, present with more acute conditions, but generally

TABLE 7.7
Level of Research Support for Common Beliefs About Emergency Department Patients

ASSUMPTION	RESEARCH SUPPORT
Uninsured patients present with nonurgent problems	Not clearly supported
Uninsured patients cause ED crowding	Not clearly supported
Uninsured patients present to EDs more often	Not clearly supported
Uninsured patients lack access to primary care	Supported
It is more expensive for uninsured patients to be seen in the ED than elsewhere	Supported
Uninsured patients present more acutely	Supported
Uninsured patients delay seeking care	Supported
Uninsured patients receive less care	Supported
Increasing numbers of uninsured patients are coming to EDs	Partially supported

Adapted from "Uninsured adults presenting to U.S. emergency departments: Assumptions vs. data," by Newton et al., 2008, *Journal of the American Medical Association, 300,* 1914–1924.

receive less treatment. Uninsured patients have no other access to medical care other than an ED, but even insured clients find barriers to accessing primary care in the community. As Newton et al. noted,

> If patients—including privately insured, publicly insured, and uninsured patients—are unable to find primary care clinicians who accept new patients or accept insurance or cash payments; if patients are forced to wait weeks for an appointment; if the hours or location of primary care make it inaccessible; or if patients perceive the care to be substandard compared with care received in the ED, they will continue to come to the ED. (2008, p. 1921)

ED crowding is more prevalent among hospitals in large urban areas and located in poorer neighborhoods (Sullivan et al., 2006), in other words, the types of hospitals that belong to the safety-net health care system. Because poor people and people of color are more likely to have their primary hospital be one in which ED crowding occurs, they will be disproportionately affected by overcrowding issues (Bernstein et al., 2008). As we consider the complex nature of racial/ethnic- and class-based health disparities, some portion of these inequities may be explained by the services patients receive in hospital EDs.

THE RELATIONSHIP OF TRAUMA, INJURY, HEALTH, AND MENTAL HEALTH

We turn now to the issue of cause and consequences among trauma, injury, health, and mental health. A body of research indicates that physical injury causes serious mental health problems for some people. These mental health conditions (primarily post-traumatic stress disorder [PTSD], alcohol abuse, and depression) appear to increase the risk for repeated injury exposure—people who have been injured (whether intentionally or unintentionally) are at higher risk of reinjury (Zatzick et al., 2004). At the same time, childhood exposure to adverse or traumatic events creates a number of risks to adult health, including risk of injury (Felitti et al., 1998). In the next section, we explore the physical and psychological effects of physical injury and the effect of adverse childhood experiences (ACEs) on health.

The Physical and Psychological Effects of Injury

It is challenging for people who have not been injured or victimized to imagine the terror and trauma associated with the event. As noted in the opening quote for this chapter, assaults, accidents, and the like are traumatic precisely because they happen suddenly and cannot be anticipated. The following clinical case report of a husband and wife involved in a serious motor vehicle accident gives some sense of the shock and traumatization that can be elicited by injury.

> Mr. A, the husband, was a 48-year-old professional who was completely healthy until the accident. He reported feeling extremely aroused during the accident and was actively involved, both cognitively and behaviorally, in rescuing himself and his wife, ultimately breaking the windshield to allow their escape. The next day, he began experiencing flashbacks and nightmares, and his re-experiencing symptoms often included feeling as if the accident were recurring. . . . He avoided driving on the highway where the accident occurred, as well as thoughts and conversations about it. His sleep was very poor and his concentration severely impaired, rendering him unable to function at work. . . . Ms. A, the wife, was a 55-year-old professional who was healthy until the accident. She described being "in shock" during the accident and, although trapped but not pinned in the car, reported, "I could hardly move because I was completely frozen." Like her husband, she began

experiencing flashbacks and nightmares the next day and often felt as if it were recurring, although for her, this involved feeling "numb" and "frozen." She avoided driving and reading newspaper stories about the accident. Her sleep was extremely poor, her concentration was significantly impaired, and she was highly irritable and easily angered. Her work functioning was completely impaired (she sold her business several months after the accident). (Lanius, Hopper, & Mennon, 2003, p. 667)

Although this couple had strikingly different responses to an event that both felt could have ended their life, their reports are consistent with the symptoms people describe with PTSD. In studies of patients who have been hospitalized as a result of injury, more than half report a mental disorder such as PTSD or depression (Zatzick et al., 2004). Developing mental health problems is more strongly associated with unmet psychosocial needs (food, housing, etc.) (Boccellari et al., 2007) and level of disability at discharge (Ryb, Soderstrom, Kufera, & Dischinger, 2006) than the severity of the initial injury. Injury-related mental health disorders may continue for years after the event (Cameron, Purdie, Kliewer, & McClure, 2006). As a result of this heightened level of mental health symptomatology, injured people have three times the rate of suicide as compared to the general population (Ryb et al., 2006). Suicide risk in injured clients was most closely tied to alcohol use (Ryb et al., 2006). These figures make clear that people who have been injured are at high risk for serious mental health problems that may put them at risk for reinjury through self-harming behaviors.

Often, major injuries are associated with new chronic pain syndromes, disabling physical and psychological symptoms and increased fatigue. Like the couple in the case study, almost half of injured persons who were employed prior to the event are unable to return to work in the year following their hospitalization (Zatzick et al., 2008). Those patients with higher levels of PTSD and depression symptoms had the highest levels of functional impairment a year after their injury (Zatzick et al., 2008). Losing access to employment in the United States can mean loss of health insurance and entrance (or increased reliance) on the safety-net health care system. Although emergency treatment services are available for injured patients, access to rehabilitation and mental health assistance post hospitalization is difficult for people without insurance (Boccellari et al., 2007).

Unfortunately for some patients, injury is not a one-time event. The majority of patients who had experienced intentional injury reported both previous assaults and life-threatening accidents (Zatzick et al., 2004). Patients hospitalized for accidents are more likely to have been assaulted than someone in the general population (Ramstad, Russo, & Zatzick, 2004). In general, injured patients report multiple major traumas in their past at a rate that is three to six times higher than Americans who have not served in the military (Kessler, Sonnega, Bromet, Hughs, & Nelson, 1995; Zatzick et al., 2004). The risk for re-injury is heightened by psychological traits, psychiatric conditions, demographic factors, socioeconomic risk, social support, coping style, and substance abuse issues (Ryb et al., 2006). In particular, alcohol use is strongly associated with injury-related hospitalization and the risk of reinjury (Cameron et al., 2006). It is clear that, "Acute care patients carry a substantial burden of prior trauma before the injury event that brings them to the hospital" (Ramstad et al., 2004, p. 533). Poverty and injury are locked in a vicious cycle—living in poverty increases the risk for injury, and patients who are injured are at increased risk for reinjury after hospitalization, which increases the risk for poverty.

These findings suggest the need for routine mental health screening and the provision of brief treatments that have shown positive effects (Zatzick et al., 2004; see the chapter on substance abuse for a discussion of treatment approaches for the problem of drinking and the chapter on adherence for a discussion of motivational interviewing to help clients change behavior). Because the use of alcohol is so prevalent in unintentional and intentional injuries, the American College of Surgeons Committee on Trauma (ASC-COT) now requires all Level I and II trauma centers to have in place a process for screening patients for alcohol abuse and to provide treatment to those identified with an alcohol problem. Direct intervention at the time of injury may prevent reinjury in half of hospitalized patients (ACS-COT, n.d.)

Adverse Childhood Experiences and Health

Up to this point, we have focused primarily on how injury increases mental health disorders and the risk for new physical injuries. We turn our attention now farther "upstream" to psychosocial harm experienced in childhood and the risks this creates for health problems, including injury, among adults. In the 1990s, researchers at the CDC and Kaiser Permanente in San Diego began work on the adverse childhood experiences (ACE) study. Several thousand people who were patients at the Kaiser Permanente San Diego Health Appraisal Clinic participated in a survey to determine the level of exposure to child abuse and household dysfunction and the relationship of these ACEs

TABLE 7.8
Adverse Childhood Experiences

CATEGORY	DEFINITION
Psychological abuse	Swore at, insulted, or put down the person Acted in a way that made person afraid he or she would be physically hurt
Physical abuse	Pushed, grabbed, shoved, or slapped the person Hit person so hard he or she had marks or was injured
Sexual abuse[a]	Touched or fondled the person in a sexual way Touched adult's body in a sexual way Attempted oral, anal, or vaginal intercourse with person Actually had oral, anal, or vaginal intercourse with person
Substance abuse	Lived with anyone who was a problem drinker or alcoholic Lived with anyone who used street drugs
Mental illness	Had a household member who was depressed or mentally ill Had a household member attempt suicide
Domestic violence	The person's mother was sometimes, often or very often Pushed, hit, grabbed, slapped, or had something thrown at him or her Kicked, bitten, hit with a fist, or hit with something hard Ever repeatedly hit for at least a few minutes Ever threatened with, or hurt by, a knife or gun
Criminal behavior	Had a household member who went to prison

From "Relationship of childhood abuse and household dysfunction to many of the leading causes of death in adults." by Felitti et al., 1998, *American Journal of Preventive Medicine, 14*, 245–258.

[a] Sexual abuse was defined as sexual contact with an adult or a person at least 5 years older than the victim during childhood.

to health outcomes in adulthood (Felitti et al., 1998).[10] See Table 7.8 for a listing of the experiences that were assessed with participants.

Over half of all respondents reported at least one ACE (Felliti et al., 1998). More importantly, if a person was exposed to any category of adverse experience, the probability of exposure to another traumatic event was 65% to 93%. In a similar study of childhood traumatic events among a diverse sample of high school seniors, the authors reported on race and gender differences in ACEs exposure: White youths were more likely to have a parent with a drug or alcohol problem, Hispanic

---

[10] The ACE study is an observational study, and so cannot rule out possible alternative explanations for adult health problems, as Felitti et al. (1998) note in their discussion. ACEs cannot be investigated through traditional randomized controlled trials for ethical reasons, so observational evidence provides the current best evidence on the linkages between early childhood risks and adult health outcomes.

children were more likely to have been sexually abused or threatened with violence, and African American and Hispanic participants were more likely to have witnessed someone being seriously injured or murdered. Boys experienced more physical assault, whereas girls were more likely to be seriously neglected (Schilling, Aseltine, & Gore, 2007).

A strong dose–response relationship has been observed between ACEs, mortality, and morbidity—more adversity was associated with higher numbers of risky health behaviors and poor health outcome (Felitti et al., 1998). The higher the number of ACEs reported, the higher the prevalence of diseases such as cancer, stroke, diabetes, emphysema, and heart disease (see Table 7.9 for a listing of health conditions and behaviors associated with ACEs). By analyzing four age cohorts of people at the Kaiser Permanente site, Dube, Felitti, Dong, Giles, and Anda (2003) were able to show that the negative health effects of ACEs occurred regardless of birth cohort (i.e., being born in the 1930s vs. the 1950s or 1970s, etc.). Although dramatic social shifts occurred between the different birth cohorts, the relationship of ACEs to poor health remained unchanged. This finding suggests that ACEs may result in physical, brain-related changes and psychosocial damage to self-esteem and relationships in highly stressed children that persist into adulthood regardless of social influences.

Figure 7.1 describes a conceptual model of how ACEs may be linked to mortality. One possible mechanism through which ACEs affect later physical health outcomes may be through the effects of

TABLE 7.9
Health Conditions and Behaviors Associated
With Adverse Childhood Experiences

Health conditions	Autoimmune disease
	Chronic obstructive pulmonary disease
	Headaches
	Ischemic heart disease
	Liver disease
	Lung cancer
	Fetal death
	Sexually transmitted disease
	Adolescent pregnancy
	Suicide attempt
Health behaviors	Alcohol abuse
	Drug abuse
	Obesity
	Smoking

From "Adverse childhood experiences: Publications by health outcomes," by Centers for Disease Control, 2011, retrieved from http://www.cdc.gov/ace/outcomes.htm.

FIGURE 7.1 Potential Influences Throughout the Lifespan of Adverse
Childhood Experiences

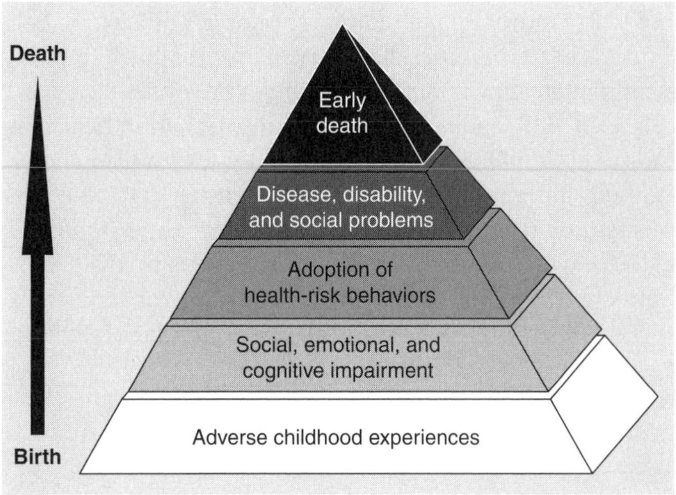

Reprinted with permission from, "Relationship of childhood abuse and household dysfunction
to many of the leading causes of death in adults," by Felitti et al., 1998, *American Journal of
Preventive Medicine, 14*, 245–258.

adversity on social, emotional, and cognitive processes, including the
increased risk for mental disorder. For example, researchers found a
strong effect of ACEs on young adult levels of depression, drug use,
and antisocial behavior (Schilling et al., 2007). A substantial portion
of adult psychiatric illness may be attributed to the presence of early
childhood abuse and household dysfunction. Afifi et al. report that,

> Approximately 1 in 4 women with a mood disorder, 1 in 5
> women with an anxiety disorder and 1 in 3 women with a sub-
> stance use disorder may not have had the disorder if the child-
> hood physical abuse, childhood sexual abuse and witnessing
> domestic violence had not occurred. Among men . . . if the
> physical abuse, sexual abuse and witnessing domestic violence
> in childhood did not occur, the prevalence of assessed psychi-
> atric disorders among men in the general population might
> have been reduced by approximately 24%. (2008, p. 950)

These forms of early childhood abuse cast long shadows into adulthood. For example, heart disease is a problem with a complex, multi-
decade developmental process. Studies have clearly shown the

relationship of traditional risk factors such as smoking, physical inactivity, obesity, depression, and anger to the likelihood of developing heart disease (Dong et al., 2004)—with all of these adverse health behaviors being more prevalent among people with ACEs (Felitti et al., 1998). Underlying proximal risks for behaviors such as smoking are the distal events related to adverse early life experiences—each additional ACE increased the likelihood of reporting ischemic heart disease by 20% (Dong et al., 2004), even after controlling for traditional risk factors. Efforts to help patients change smoking, obesity, and other risks show that these behaviors are often very difficult to change. It may be that the struggle to change these ingrained patterns exists because these behaviors are effective in helping people cope with the consequences of early childhood dysfunction. As Felitti et al. argue in relation to smoking,

> We found that exposure to higher numbers of categories of adverse childhood experiences increased the likelihood of smoking by the age of 14, chronic smoking as adults, and the presence of smoking-related diseases. Thus, smoking, which is medically and socially viewed as a "problem" may, from the perspective of the user, represent an effective immediate solution that leads to chronic use. Decades later, when this "solution" manifests as emphysema, cardiovascular disease, or malignancy, time and the tendency to ignore psychological issues in the management of organic disease make improbable any full understanding of the original causes of adult disease. Thus, incomplete understanding of the possible benefits of health risk behaviors leads them to be viewed as irrational and having solely negative consequences. (1998, p. 254)

While prevention of child abuse, domestic violence, mental illness, and substance abuse have been long-standing goals in their own rights, research on ACEs indicates that prevention of these harmful experiences could substantially reduce mortality and the morbidity associated with chronic serious illnesses. In addition to primary prevention of ACEs, secondary prevention programs aimed at stopping at-risk youth from adopting risky behaviors in adolescence and tertiary prevention in terms of changing health risk behaviors are all viable avenues of prevention of adult chronic illness (Dong et al., 2004). Health professionals need to recognize the long-term effects of ACEs on health behaviors and outcomes, particularly among the patients who use safety-net health care services as they are at higher risk for abuse and household dysfunction because of poverty.

TABLE 7.10
Examples of Screening Questions to Identify Child Adversity Risks

Child Abuse

Do you often feel your child is difficult to take care of?
Do you sometimes find you need to hit/spank your child?
Do you wish you had more help with your child?

Domestic Violence

Have you ever been in a relationship in which you were physically hurt or threatened by a partner?
In the past year, have you been afraid of a partner?
In the past year, have you thought of getting a court order for protection?

Substance Use/Mental Illness

In the past year, have you or your partner felt the need to cut back on alcohol?
Lately, do you often feel down, depressed or hopeless?
During the past month, have you felt little interest or pleasure in the things you used to enjoy?

Excerpted from Parenting Screening Questionnaire (Screening for depression in an urban pediatric primary care clinic," by Dubowitz et al., 2007, *Pediatrics, 119*, 435–443.)

Screening for Adverse Childhood Experiences

Health care providers have an opportunity and a responsibility to identify ACEs that could be prevented or treated. In particular, clinicians who are in pediatric settings, the ED, or working with injured patients should be particularly aware of the interrelationships between intentional and unintentional injury, mental health issues, and ACEs.[11] Several brief screening instruments have been developed for common problems such as depression and alcohol misuse. For example, the Patient Health Questionnaire has been validated for use in identifying common symptoms of anxiety and depression (Spitzer, Kroenke, Williams, & The Patient Health Questionnaire Primary Care Study Group, 1999). The Patient Health Questionnaire has nine questions and can be administered in just a few minutes. For alcohol problems, the World Health Organization developed the Alcohol Use Disorders Identification Test that uses 10 items to identify patients with problematic drinking patterns (World Health Organization, 2001).

In Table 7.10, we present examples that have been suggested as possible screening questions for child abuse, domestic violence, substance

---

[11] Although it may seem unrealistic to routinely perform screenings for ACEs in ED settings, when used in combination with referral to mental health and/or social services, addressing underlying ACEs can be effective in lessening the high ED utilization of those patients with a history of atypical ED use for repeated injuries and other personal crises.

use, and mental illness (Dubowitz et al., 2007). The American Academy of Pediatrics (Flaherty, Stirling, & The Committee on Child Abuse and Neglect, 2010) and other medical organizations recommend routine screening of women and children for child abuse and intimate partner violence. From the ACEs study and other research, we know that child abuse and intimate partner violence often co-occur (Dube, Anda, Felitti, Edwards, & Williamson, 2002). As Dube et al. note, "Identification of victims of [domestic violence] must include screening of their children for abuse, neglect and other types of adverse exposures, as well as recognition that substance abuse and depressed affect are likely consequences of witnessing [domestic violence]" (2002, p. 3). In particular, depression is a long-term outcome of abuse for women (Lindhorst & Beadnell, 2011), highlighting the multiple, overlapping ways in which these negative experiences can create more adversity.

It has been particularly difficult to engage health professionals in asking women about domestic violence. Clinicians may feel uninformed about or unable to respond to domestic violence, may not see abuse as relevant to health care practice, may fear that patients will be upset if asked about violence, or may feel that there is insufficient time to ask these questions in the midst of busy ED or primary care visits (Hamberger & Phelan, 2004). Consistently, women have reported that they feel it *is* appropriate for health care practitioners to ask about abuse, as long as the clinician ensures the woman's safety in the process and asks about potential abuse in a respectful, nonjudgmental manner (Lindhorst, Meyers, & Casey, 2008). In both health care and other social services settings, disclosure rates of abuse are much lower than the rate of abuse reported to survey researchers (Hamberger & Phelan, 2004; Lindhorst & Padgett, 2005) indicating that women will respond to these questions when asked, but are unlikely to volunteer this information. Table 7.11 lists other behaviors that researchers have identified as effective strategies for health care practitioners to use that encourage abused women to disclose abuse. In the additional resources section, we direct interested readers to resources for safety planning with domestic violence victims.

CONCLUDING COMMENTS

Safety net health care providers are more likely to work with patients who have survived intentional and unintentional injury, and who are living with the consequences of traumas of many kinds. The institutions we work in are more likely to be identified as centers for trauma

TABLE 7.11
Summary of Professional Screening Practices That Support
Disclosure of Abuse

1. Build rapport through active listening and empathetic reflection.
2. Ensure that any disclosure of abuse is confidential.
3. Explain the reasons why disclosure would be beneficial.
4. Ask clients directly about abuse.
5. Define abuse broadly, with physical, sexual, and emotional components.
6. Use both open-ended probes and behaviorally anchored questions.
7. Avoid questions that force a woman to identify with a stigmatized status, i.e., "are you a victim?"
8. Provide multiple opportunities for disclosure within interviews and over time.

Reprinted with permission from "Screening for domestic violence in public welfare offices: An analysis of case manager and client interactions," by Lindhorst et al., 2008, Violence against Women, 14(5), 5–28.

care, and the patients we work with are at higher risk for injuries and victimization by others. Being injured in an accident, by another person, or by oneself puts a survivor at increased risk for being reinjured, through unintentional and intentional events. In reviewing the physical and psychosocial consequences of injury, it becomes clear that trauma and violence are primary mechanisms for health disparities in the United States.

Responding to trauma in our patients requires a revisioning of our role as health professionals. Most health care practitioners are familiar and comfortable with their role as care providers, but an understanding of injury and trauma necessitates a commitment to preventive care through multiple avenues. For instance, when we ask a survivor of a car accident how he or she is coping and if he or she has any distressing feelings, we are engaging in activities that can help prevent PTSD. By asking women about the possibility that they are being abused, we are opening an opportunity for an abuse survivor to reach out for help. If she has a child we may be helping to minimize that child's exposure to adversity by asking the mother about domestic violence. When we are working with a patient with emphysema who continues to smoke, or another patient who seems propelled from one abusive relationship to another, we can manage any feelings of futility and judgment we might have by reminding ourselves that many people with chronic health behavior-related illness have experienced serious adversities in childhood that may never have been recognized as a factor in their current illness—and that our identification of these linkages can be the first crucial step toward more effective health care.

ADDITIONAL RESOURCES

Suicide Prevention

The U.S. Department of Health and Human Services funds the National Suicide Prevention Lifeline. Information on suicide and patient-related educational materials are available for free.
http://www.suicidepreventionlifeline.org/

Youth Violence Prevention

The CDC provides online training, information, and resources on a public health approach to preventing youth violence.
http://www.safeyouth.gov/Pages/Home.aspx

Child Abuse Prevention

The American Academy of Pediatrics sponsors Bright Futures, prevention and health promotion for infants, children, adolescents, and their families. The website has resources on a number of injury prevention initiatives, including child abuse prevention.
http://brightfutures.aap.org/

Prevent Child Abuse provides information on research and resources to help with child abuse prevention campaigns.
http://www.preventchildabuse.org/index.shtml

Domestic Violence Resource

The National Domestic Violence Hotline provides information on recognizing abuse and how to help a survivor plan for safety.
http://www.thehotline.org/get-help/safety-planning/

Futures without Violence (formerly the Family Violence Prevention Fund) provides information on domestic violence and sponsors a national conference on health and domestic violence concerns.
http://www.futureswithoutviolence.org/

REFERENCES

Afifi, T. O., Enns, M. W., Cox, B. J., Asmundson, G. J. G., Stein, M. B., & Sareen, J. (2008). Population attributable fractions of psychiatric disorders and suicide ideation and attempts associated with adverse childhood experiences. *American Journal of Public Health, 98*, 946–952.

Almeida, J., Johnson, R. M., Corliss, H. L., Molnar, B. E., & Azrael, D. (2009). Emotional distress among LGBT youth: The influence of perceived discrimination based on sexual orientation. *Journal of Youth and Adolescence, 38*, 1001–1014.

American College of Surgeons Committee on Trauma. (n.d.). *Alcohol screening and brief interventions for trauma patients.* Retrieved from http://www.facs.org/trauma/publications/sbirtguide.pdf.

American College of Surgeons Committee on Trauma. (1999). *Resources for optimal care of the injured patient.* Chicago, IL: Author.

Barnett, O., Miller-Perrin, C. L., & Perrin, R. D. (2005). *Family violence across the lifespan: An introduction* (2nd ed.). Thousand Oaks, CA: Sage.

Bergen, G., Chen, L. H., Warner, M., & Fingerhut, L. A. (2008). *Injury in the United States: 2007 chartbook.* Hyattsville, MD: National Center for Health Statistics.

Bernstein, S. L., Aronsky, D., Duseja, R., Epstein, S., Handel, D., Hwang, U., . . . Aspin, B. R. (2008). The effect of emergency department crowding on clinically oriented outcomes. *Academic Emergency Medicine, 16,* 1–10.

Boccellari, A., Alvidrez, J., Shumway, M., Kelly, V., Merrill, G., Gelb, . . . Okin, R. L. (2007). Characteristics and psychosocial needs of victims of violent crime identified at a public-sector hospital: Data from a large clinical trial. *General Hospital Psychiatry, 29,* 236–243.

Branas, C. C., MacKenzie, E. J., Williams, J. C., Schwab, C. W., Teter, H. M., Flanigan, M. C., . . . ReVelle, C. S. (2005). Access to trauma centers in the United States. *Journal of the American Medical Association, 293,* 2626–2633.

Bureau of Justice Statistics. (2010). *Criminal victimization in the United States, 2007—Statistical Tables.* NCJ 227669. Washington, DC: Department of Justice.

Bureau of Justice Statistics. (2011). *Intimate partner violence in the U.S.* Retrieved from http://bjs.ojp.usdoj.gov/content/intimate/victims.cfm

Cameron, C. M., Purdie, D. M., Kliewer, E. V., & McClure, R. J. (2006). Mental health: A cause or consequence of injury? A population-based matched cohort study. *BMC Public Health, 6,* 114–123.

Campbell, J. C., Webster, D., Koziol-McLain, J., Block, C., Campbell, D., Curry, M. A., . . . Laughon, K. (2003). Risk factors for femicide in abusive relationships: Results from a multisite case control study. *American Journal of Public Health, 93,* 1089–1097.

Celso, B., Tepas, J., Langland-Orban, B., Pracht, E., Papa, L., Lottenberg, L., & Flint, L. (2006). A systematic review and meta-analysis comparing outcome of severely injured patients treated in trauma centers following the establishment of trauma systems. *Journal of Trauma, Injury, Infection and Critical Care, 60,* 371–378.

Centers for Disease Control. (2010). *Suicide: Facts at a glance.* Retrieved from http://www.cdc.gov/violenceprevention/pdf/Suicide_DataSheet-a.pdf

Centers for Disease Control. (2011). *Adverse childhood experiences: Publications by health outcomes.* Retrieved from http://www.cdc.gov/ace/outcomes.htm

Champion, H. R., Mabee, M. S., & Meredith, J. W. (2006). The state of U.S. trauma systems: Public perceptions versus reality—Implications for U.S. response to terrorism and mass casualty events. *Journal of the American College of Surgeons, 203,* 951–961.

Cubbin, C., & Smith, G. S. (2002). Socioeconomic inequalities in injury: Critical issues in design and analysis. *Annual Review of Public Health, 23,* 349–375.

Danseco, E. R., Miller, T. R., & Spicer, R. S. (2000). Incidence and costs of 1987–1994 Childhood injuries: Demographic breakdowns. *Pediatrics, 105(2),* e27–e35.

Dong, M., Giles, W. H., Felitti, V. J., Dube, S. R., Williams, J. E., Chapman, D. P., & Anda, R. F. (2004). Insights into causal pathways for ischemic heart disease. *Circulation,* 110, 1761–1766.

Dube, S. R., Anda, R. F., Felitti, V. J., Edwards, V. J., & Williamson, D. F. (2002). Exposure to abuse, neglect and household dysfunction among adults who witnessed intimate partner violence as children: Implications for health and social services. *Violence & Victims, 17,* 3–17.

Dube, S. R., Felitti, V. J., Dong, M., Giles, W. H., & Anda, R. F. (2003). The impact of adverse childhood experiences on health problems: Evidence from four birth cohorts dating back to 1900. *Preventive Medicine, 37,* 268–277.

Dubowitz, H., Feigelman, S., Lane, W., Prescott, L., Blackman, K., Grube, L., . . . Tracy, J. K. (2007). Screening for depression in an urban pediatric primary care clinic. *Pediatrics, 119,* 435–443.

Duldulao, A. A., Takeuchi, D. T., & Hong, S. (2009). Correlates of suicidal behaviors among Asian Americans. *Archives of Suicide Research, 13,* 277–290.

Farrington, D. P., Loeber, R., & Stouthamer-Loeber, M. (2003). How can the relationship between race and violence be explained? In D. F. Hawkins (Ed.), *Violent crime: Assessing race and ethnic differences* (pp. 213–237). New York, NY: Cambridge University Press.

Felitti, V. J., Anda, R. F., Nordenberg, D., Williamson, D. F., Spitz, A. M., Edwards, V., . . . Marks, J. S. (1998). Relationship of childhood abuse and household dysfunction to many of the leading causes of death in adults. *American Journal of Preventive Medicine, 14,* 245–258.

Flaherty, E. G., Stirling, J., & The Committee on Child Abuse and Neglect. (2010). Clinical report—The pediatrician's role in child maltreatment prevention. *Pediatrics, 126,* 833–841.

Fox, J. A., & Zawitz, M. W. (2007). *Homicide trends in the United States.* Washington, DC: Bureau of Justice Statistics.

Gilbride, S. J., Wild, C., Wilson, D. R., Svenson, L. W., & Spady, D. W. (2006). Socio-economic status and types of childhood injury in Alberta: A population based study. *BMC Pediatrics, 6,* 30. Retrieved from http://www .biomedcentral.com/content/pdf/1471-2431-6-30.pdf

Haider, A. H., Chang, D. C., Efron, D. T., Haut, E. R., Crandall, M., & Cornwell, E. E. (2008). Race and insurance as risk factors for trauma mortality. *Archives of Surgery, 143,* 945–949.

Hamberger, L. K., & Phelan, M. B. (2004). *Domestic violence screening and intervention in medical and mental healthcare settings.* New York, NY: Springer Publishing.

Kessler, R. C., Sonnega, A., Bromet, E., Hughs, M., & Nelson, C. B. (1995). Posttraumatic stress disorder in the National Comorbidity Survey. *Archives of General Psychiatry, 52,* 1048–1060.

King, M., Semlyen, J., Tai, S. S., Killaspy, H., Osborn, D., Popelyuk, D., & Nazareth, I. (2009). A systematic review of mental disorder, suicide and deliberate self harm in lesbian, gay and bisexual people. *BMC Psychiatry, 8,* 70–87.

Kochanek, K. D., Xu, J., Murphy, S. L., Miniño, A. M., & Kung, H. C. (2011). Deaths: Preliminary data for 2009. *National Vital Statistics Reports, 59,* 1–51.

Kuhns, J. B., Wilson, D. B., Clodfelter, T. A., Maguire, E. R., & Ainsworth, S. A. (2011). A meta-analysis of alcohol toxicology study findings among homicide victims. *Addiction, 106,* 62–72.

Lanius, R.A., Hopper, J. W., & Menon, R. S. (2003). Individual differences in a husband and wife who developed PTSD after a motor vehicle accident: A functional MRI case study. *American Journal of Psychiatry, 160,* 667–669.

Law, L. (2003). Transnational cyberpublics: New political spaces for labour migrants in Asia. *Ethnic and Racial Studies, 26,* 234–252.

Lindhorst, T., & Beadnell, B. (2011). The long arc of recovery: Characterizing intimate partner violence and its psychosocial effects across seventeen years. *Violence against Women, 17,* 480–499.

Lindhorst, T., Meyers, M., & Casey, E. (2008). Screening for domestic violence in public welfare offices: An analysis of case manager and client interactions. *Violence against Women, 14*(5), 5–28.

Lindhorst, T., & Padgett, J. (2005). Disjunctures for women and frontline workers: Implementation of the Family Violence Option. *Social Service Review, 79*(3), 405–29.

MacKenzie, E. J., Hoyt, D. B., Sacra, J. C., Jurkovich, G. J., Carlini, A. R., Teitelbaum, S. D., & Teter, H. (2003). National inventory of hospital trauma centers. *Journal of the American Medical Association, 289,* 1515–1522.

Murray, C. J. L., & Lopez, A. D. (1997). Alternative projections of mortality and disability by cause 1990–2020: Global burden of disease study. *The Lancet, 349,* 1498–1504.

Nathens, A. B., Maier, R. V., Copass, M. K., & Jurkovich, G. J. (2001). Payer status: The unspoken triage criterion. *Journal of Trauma, Injury, Infection and Critical Care, 50*, 776–783.

National Center for Health Statistics. (n.d.a). *Leading causes of death 1900–1998.* Retrieved from http://www.cdc.gov/nchs/data/dvs/lead1900_98.pdf

National Center for Health Statistics. (n.d.b). *10 leading causes of injury deaths by age group highlighting violence-related injury deaths, United States—2007.* Retrieved from http://www.cdc.gov/injury/wisqars/pdf/Violence_2007-a.pdf

National Center for Injury Prevention and Control. (2006). *CDC Injury fact book.* Atlanta, GA: Centers for Disease Control and Prevention.

Naumann, R. B., Dellinger, A. M., Zaloshnja, E., Lawrence, B. A., & Miller, T. R. (2010). Incidence and total lifetime costs of motor vehicle-related fatal and nonfatal injuries by road user type, United States, 2005. *Traffic Injury Prevention, 11*, 353–360.

Newton, M. F., Keirns, C. C., Cunningham, R., Hayward, R. A., & Stanley, R. (2008). Uninsured adults presenting to U.S. emergency departments: Assumptions vs. data. *Journal of the American Medical Association, 300*, 1914–1924.

Owens, P. L., Barrett, M. L., Gibson, T. B., Andrews, R. M., Weinick, R. M., & Mutter, R. L. (2010). Emergency department care in the United States: A profile of national data sources. *Annals of Emergency Medicine, 56*, 150–165.

Ramstad, S. M., Russo, J., & Zatzick, D. F. (2004). Is it an accident? Recurrent traumatic life events in Level I trauma center patients compared to the general population. *Journal of Traumatic Stress, 17*, 529–534.

Richmond, J. B. (1979). *Healthy people: The Surgeon General's report on health promotion and disease prevention.* Washington, DC: U. S. Department of Health, Education and Welfare.

Ryb, G. E., Soderstrom, C. A., Kufera, J. A., & Dischinger, P. (2006). Longitudinal study of suicide after traumatic injury. *Journal of Trauma, Injury, Infection and Critical Care, 61*, 799–804.

Savage, D., & Miller, T. (2011). *It gets better: Coming out, overcoming bullying and creating a life worth living.* New York, NY: Dutton.

Schiff, R. L., Ansell, D. A., Schlosser, J. E., Idris, A. H., Morrison, A., & Whitman, S. (1986). Transfers to a public hospital: A prospective study of 467 patients. *New England Journal of Medicine, 314*, 552–557.

Schilling, E. A., Aseltine, R. H., & Gore, S. (2007). Adverse childhood experiences and mental health in young adults: A longitudinal survey. *BMC Public Health, 7*, 30–40.

Selzer, D., Gomez, G., Jacobson, L., Wischmeyer, T., Sood, R., & Broadie, T. (2001). Public hospital-based Level I trauma centers: Financial survival in the new millennium. *Journal of Trauma, Injury, Infection and Critical Care, 51,* 301–307.

Shen, Y. C., Hsia, R. Y., & Kuzma, K. (2009). Understand the risk factors of trauma center closures: Do financial pressure and community characteristics matter? *Medical Care, 47,* 968–978.

Sklar, D. P., Handel, D. A., Hoekstra, J., Baren, J. M., Zink, B., & Hedges, J. R. (2010). The future of emergency medicine: An evolutionary perspective. *Academic Medicine, 85,* 490–495.

Spain, D. A., Bellino, M., Kopelman, A., Chang, J., Park, J., Gregg, D. L., & Brundage, S. I. (2007). Requests for 692 transfers to an academic Level I trauma center: Implications of the Emergency Medical Treatment and Active Labor Act. *Journal of Trauma, Injury, Infection and Critical Care, 62,* 63–68.

Spitzer, R. L., Kroenke, K., Williams, J. B. W., & The Patient Health Questionnaire Primary Care Study Group. (1999). Validation and utility of a self-report version of PRIME-MD: The PHQ primary care study. *Journal of the American Medical Association, 282,* 1737–1744.

Stern, J. (2010). *Denial: A memoir of terror.* New York, NY: Ecco/Harper-Collins.

Sullivan, A. F., Richman, I. B., Ahn, C. J., Auerbach, B. S., Pallin, D. J., Scafermeyer, R. W., . . . Camargo, C. A. (2006). A profile of U.S. emergency departments in 2001. *Annals of Emergency Medicine, 48,* 694–701.

Vettukattil, A. S., Haider, A. H., Haut, E. R., Chang, D. C., Oyetunji, T., Cornwell, E. E., . . . Efron, D. T. (2011). Do trauma safety-net hospitals deliver truly safe trauma care? A multilevel analysis of the National Trauma Data Bank. *Journal of Trauma, Injury, Infection and Critical Care, 70,* 978–984.

Warner, M., Chen, L. H., & Mackuc, D. M. (2009). Increase in fatal poisonings involving opioid analgesics in the United States, 1999–2006. *National Center for Health Statistics Data Brief, 22,* 1–8.

Williams, J. H., Bright, C. L., & Petersen, G. (2011). Racial and ethnic differences in risk and protective factors associated with youth violence. In T. I. Herrenkohl, E. Aisenberg, J. H. Williams, & J. M. Jenson (Eds.), *Violence in context: Current evidence on risk, protection and prevention* (pp. 27–48). New York, NY: Oxford University Press.

World Health Organization. (2001). *AUDIT: The Alcohol Use Disorders Identification Test: Guidelines for use in primary care.* Geneva, Switzerland: Author.

Zatzick, D., Jurkovich, G. J., Rivara, F. P., Wang, J., Fan, M. Y., Joesch, J., & MacKenzie, E. (2008). A national U.S. study of Posttraumatic Stress Disorder, depression and work and functional outcomes after hospitalization for traumatic injury. *Annals of Surgery, 248,* 429–437.

Zatzick, D., Jurkovich, G., Russo, J., Roy-Byrne, P., Katon, W., Wagner, A., . . . Rivara, F. (2004). Posttraumatic distress, alcohol disorders, and recurrent trauma across Level I trauma centers. *Journal of Trauma, Injury, Infection and Critical Care, 57,* 360–366.

Zibulewsky, J. (2001). The Emergency Medical Treatment and Active Labor Act: What it is and what it means for physicians. *Proceedings (Baylor University Medical Center), 14,* 339–346.

8

Difficult Patients, Difficult Health Conditions

INTRODUCTION

The range of what we think and do is limited by what we fail to notice. And
because we fail to notice that we fail to notice there is little we can do to
change until we notice how failing to notice shapes our thoughts and deeds.
— (Goleman, 1985)

Some patients are frustrating to treat. Hang out in a hospital long
enough, and you will hear patients referred to as "black holes," "time
suckage devices," "frequent flyers," or "Velcro patients," all synonyms for the "difficult"[1] patient. In the preceding chapters, we have
explored in great detail some typical patient conditions and behaviors that are especially challenging for health care providers. To sum
up these chapters, we present here a more general discussion about
the difficulty in clinical work and its linkages to social exclusion and

---

[1]For ease of reading, we will remove the quotes from "difficult" in the rest of the chapter,
but as we will demonstrate, we feel this label is inaccurate and unnecessarily blaming of
patients, which is what the quotes in their initial usage signify.

marginalization. In particular, we focus on characteristics of patient health care provider interactions, and how some conditions come to be seen as stigmatizing in their own right. Ultimately, though, our purpose is to illustrate the structural underpinnings of the labeling of patients as difficult, the way this label represents a *transaction* between patient and clinician, and the implications this has for work in safety-net health care settings. As one author notes (echoing the thoughts of Daniel Goleman above), "As long as difficulty is perceived to be within the patient, nothing else gets examined or remedied" (Macdonald, 2007, p. 79).

Safety-net systems primarily provide services for the indigent, yet many of the practitioners who work within these settings have little personal experience or exposure to the lived experience and social pain of poverty[2] (Williams, 2004). In particular, most health care professionals have limited understanding of the scrutiny that comes with being poor (Bhabha, 1994)[3] or with being a "patient" (Macdonald & Murray, 2007).[4] When a person of even minimal means pays to see a provider for health or mental health care, there is a sense of entitlement to certain things—an assumption that the story of the "problem" will be accepted at face value, and not interpreted through a lens of suspicion or questioning of the person's knowledge or motives. Middle-class patients expect to be treated as valued consumers who have the capacity to understand and make decisions about health needs, not as people who need to be monitored or "managed." These unrecognized expectations are some of the privileges of class status (as discussed in the previous chapter on power and privilege). Sometimes, patients in safety-net settings experience a reverse entitlement—some health professionals may make it clear that the patient should feel lucky to receive any help since they are not paying

---

[2]We are referring here to the fact that most health care professionals are of middle-class backgrounds, but we understand that some practitioners grew up in poverty and have first-hand knowledge of its effects.

[3]Bhabha presents an insightful discussion of being "overlooked"—both *not* seen and watched over—when one lives outside established social norms. In Bhabha's case, he was discussing the role of colonization in creating the colonized "other," a status in which the colonial subject is both ignored as being irrelevant to the dominant society and in need of surveillance to prevent efforts to undo the established order. Bhabha's argument has relevance for understanding the social positioning of other marginalized groups.

[4]Macdonald and Murray take up the way "the clinician's gaze, in assessing the normal and the pathological, objectifies the patient, and reducing the patient to a body, masks the intersubjectivity of the clinical encounter, increasing the power imbalance" (2007, p. 69).

for the service. People who do not have insurance or large incomes have to seek treatment wherever they can find it, without the protection of class privilege to insulate them from others' overt or unspoken judgments about their behavior (Freund & McGuire, 2002).

The provision of services to low-income patients by primarily middle-class practitioners is one structural component that contributes to labeling of some patients as difficult. In the following sections of this chapter, we examine other structural issues at the level of patients, providers, and processes that explain some of the dynamics related to labeling patients as difficult. In the final section of the chapter, we turn to two examples of how societal beliefs and values contribute to the creation of difficult patients.

STRUCTURAL ISSUES IN THE CREATION OF DIFFICULTY

What makes a "good" patient versus a "difficult" patient? As we illustrate in Figure 8.1, good patients have a medical, not a psychosocial problem; their diagnosis is clear and easily made; and their problem has an effective, available treatment. An example of a good patient would be someone who has broken his or her leg in an accident, presents to the emergency department for acute treatment, and cooperates with staff. In contrast, a difficult patient has medically unexplained symptoms that are ambiguous and without a clearly identifiable etiology, may display distressing interpersonal behaviors, or have a condition that frustrates health care practitioners in terms of its chronicity or the lack of a readily accessible or acceptable treatment. Patients with soft tissue chronic pain syndromes are often seen as examples of difficult patients—there is no radiological verification of underlying disease; people in chronic pain are often demoralized and angry in their interactions; and treatment with narcotic pain relievers, although easily accessible, can lead to other unacceptable problems such as addiction, thus stymying provider's efforts to be effective helpers (Tait, Chibnall, & Kalauokalani, 2009).

Labeling patients, rather than encounters, as difficult may result in providing patients with suboptimal care (Caldicott, Dunn, & Frankel, 2005; Stevens, 2010) as clinicians "secretly hope that their challenging patients will not return" (An et al., 2009, p. 410). Patients' legitimate concerns may be masked by the label of being a difficult patient. For example, homeless people may present multiple times to an emergency department before they are discovered to have a serious condition, in part because their symptoms are overlooked because

FIGURE 8.1 Characteristics of "Good" and "Difficult" Patients

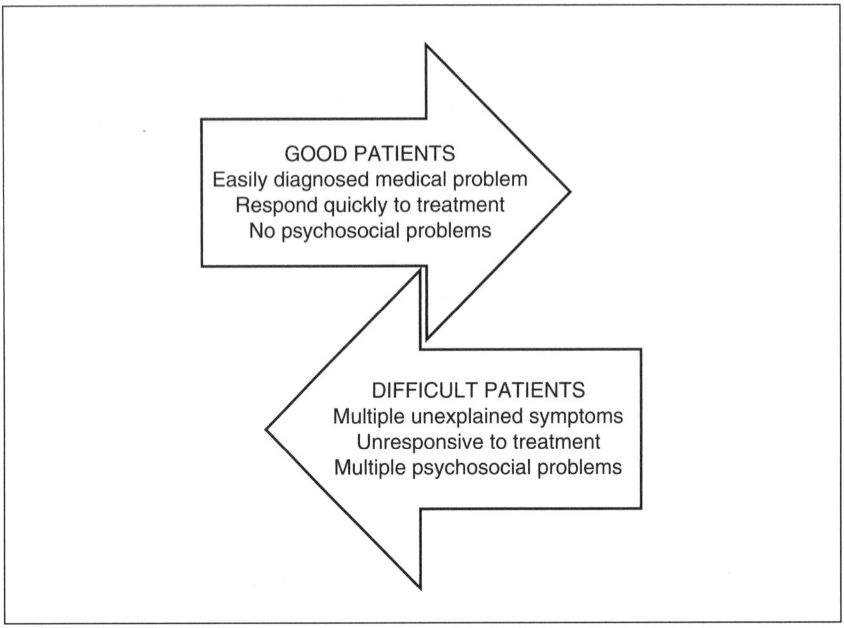

GOOD PATIENTS
Easily diagnosed medical problem
Respond quickly to treatment
No psychosocial problems

DIFFICULT PATIENTS
Multiple unexplained symptoms
Unresponsive to treatment
Multiple psychosocial problems

Based on Lorber (1975) as described in Hinchey and Jackson (2011).

they are perceived as difficult patients. A similar discounting process may explain some portion of the disparities seen between men and women in the treatment of cardiac conditions (Adams et al., 2008; Chiaramonte & Friend, 2006).[5] Women's symptoms may be interpreted as psychogenic—arising from a mental health condition—rather than perceived as physically derived. Women have historically been positioned as the prototype of the difficult patient, as Smith (1995) notes when he says that difficult patients "are more often women, [who] complain of ill-defined somatic symptoms that fluctuate over time and seem to have no organic basis" (1995, p. 653). These examples point to one possible way in which stereotyping (as we have discussed in

---

[5]Chiaramonte and Friend (2006) suggest that the discounting of women's cardiac symptoms is likely a more subtle process than purely relying on stereotyping. In vignettes where gender and stress levels were changed, only women who concomitantly presented coronary heart disease symptoms with discussion of life stress or anxiety were more likely to have their symptoms attributed to psychogenic causes. Women and men who presented with classic symptoms of heart problems (chest pain, shortness of breath, heart rate irregularities), but without statements of stress or anxiety were equally likely to be seen as having a physical problem.

relation to stigma and marginalization previously) operates—namely, through the labeling of a patient as difficult without fully exploring the biological, psychological, and social aspects of the patient's problem. This label may have serious consequences in terms of patient care.

For safety-net health care providers, there is no escape from difficult patients. As locations of "last resort" for patient care, safety net settings have no place else to send difficult patients. They can't be "turfed" (referred to another provider because of problematic behavior), except within the safety-net setting itself, and that practice is frowned upon by the receiving clinical service (Caldicott, 2007). Health providers are aware of how safety-net settings provide the context for labeling patients and avoiding their care. This resident describes how the financing of care differentially affects clinicians' willingness to work with difficult patients:

> [Turfing] only happens really at a university type institution or a VA [Veterans Administration] . . . where there's no incentive to do any extra work. In a private hospital where . . . doctors are paid for every consult or patient they get, they . . . don't mind doing extra stuff and this kind of problem doesn't go on. You only see it here. It's a money thing. (Medical resident as quoted in Caldicott, 2007, p. 138)

Although difficult patients may be found in any setting, the nature of the safety-net health care system is such that a higher proportion of difficult clinical encounters occur in these locations. Difficult encounters are distressing to both the clinician and the patient (Caldicott et al., 2005; Kroenke, 2009). Structural reasons exist for these undercurrents in patient care and are reflected in the types of patients most likely to be seen as difficult in clinical contexts and the process invoked to arrive at this label, as well as the characteristics of providers who tend to experience patients as difficult, issues we turn to next.

"Difficult" Patients

As summarized in Table 8.1, research on difficult patients has identified a number of traits that clinicians associate with challenging encounters. These characteristics most often include interpersonal behaviors such as patients who are demanding, rude, mistrustful, or threatening. Research with medical providers indicates that 15% to 18% of clinical encounters are perceived as difficult (An et al., 2009; Hinchey & Jackson, 2011). When patients have more somatic and more severe symptoms, poorer functional status, and experience psychosocial stressors, they are more likely to be labeled as difficult by practitioners (Hinchey & Jackson, 2011). Providers consistently report that it is not necessarily the complexity of the patient's medical problems that results in a determination that they are difficult, but rather the co-occurrence of medical problems with complicated psychosocial issues such as poverty, substance abuse, or mental illness (Krebs, Garrett, & Konrad, 2006).

TABLE 8.1
Conditions Associated With and Terms Used to Describe "Difficult" Patients

Psychiatric Conditions

Personality disorders

Substance abuse

Somatizing

Medical Conditions

Multiple unexplained physical symptoms

Poor functional status

Greater symptom severity

Interpersonal Behaviors

Abrasive personality traits

Angry

Demanding

Rude

Unlikeable

Hateful

Argumentative

Mistrustful

Violent

Aggressive

Threatening

Intimidating

Skeptical of professionals' expertise

Service Use

High utilizers of health care services

Dissatisfied with medical care

Threaten lawsuits

File complaints

NOTE. Compiled from articles referenced in this chapter.

Mental illness and difficulty are bidirectional—many difficult patients are assigned a psychiatric label of some sort, and patients with mental disorders are more likely to be perceived as difficult (Koekkoek, Hutschemaekers, van Meijel, & Schene, 2011). The psychiatric diagnosis may be as a hypochondriac (a person who believes he or she is ill when there is no physical evidence of illness), as a somatization disorder (people whose mental illness manifests as physical symptoms), or as a personality disorder (people with deeply ingrained, maladaptive patterns of behavior). Psychiatrist James Groves provided an early classification of "hateful" patients: the "dependent clinger," "entitled demander," "help-rejecting complainer," and "self-destructive denier" (Groves, 1978), a formulation that still resonates with clinical providers today (Arciniegas & Beresford, 2010; Stevens, 2010). Difficult patients are identified as such, in part, through the pathologizing and medicalizing[6] of their behavior—they have something wrong with them and since there is no easily discernable physical explanation for that difficulty, it is assigned to the realm of mental disorders. In clinical jargon, these patients might be referred to as the "Axis II" disorder[7] in the exam room. An approach that situates difficulty as solely a problem within the patient leads to a failure to notice important factors about the dyadic interaction and situation that are also occurring (Kroenke, 2009).

Patients are deemed difficult based on the degree to which others perceive them as having control over their behavior (Koekkoek et al., 2011).[8] The same patient behavior (i.e., shouting) is perceived differently by clinicians depending on what they think is the underlying cause. If a practitioner sees the reason for the behavior as being a neurobiological process—for instance, the patient is in a psychotic state attributable to schizophrenia—then the patient is not held responsible for the behavior (Koekkoek et al., 2011). However, if the patient is

---

[6]We recognize that certain behaviors are indicative of mental health conditions that should be treated. Other behaviors need strict limit setting to ensure the safety and well-being of staff and other patients, particularly those behaviors that are threatening, intimidating, or violent. As we will discuss later, however, these behaviors are manifested in the context of an *interaction* between provider and patient. Pathologizing patient behavior, that is, ascribing it to mental illness, allows providers to sidestep reflection on their own behaviors that may contribute to a challenging encounter.

[7]Axis II is the location for noting a personality disorder in a psychiatric diagnosis, as opposed to Axis I disorders (such as schizophrenia, depression, and organic mental disorders) that are commonly considered to be "true" mental illnesses.

[8]We return to the idea of responsibility for behavior in the discussion of compassion in the final chapter of the book.

shouting for reasons the provider attributes to social, psychological, or moral reasons, then this patient is more likely to be seen as difficult.

Being labeled as difficult is an interactive process controlled by clinicians, in response to the patient's actions and behaviors. In their in-depth examination of how patients come to be labeled as difficult within mental health settings, Koekkoek et al. (2011) depict a transactional model in which ineffective illness behavior on the part of the patient interacts with ineffective professional behavior. Patients initially present with needs of some kind, but their interpersonal behavior or other psychosocial factors (isolation, poverty, etc.) lead to the patient being labeled as difficult in the absence of a neurobiological explanation for their actions, resulting in patient needs not being met. Constructing the patient in this way changes the professional's treatment behavior—providers become more pessimistic about the possibility of patient improvement and adopt a more passive treatment approach. Patients usually know when they are not wanted (Caldicott et al., 2005) and respond to these professional behaviors as evidence of a lack of caring. Patients then exhibit more problematic behavior, reinforcing the professional's tendency to blame the patient for being difficult.

Although it may be tempting to see difficulty as an attribute that rests solely in the patient, information about the kinds of patients who are typically labeled as difficult suggests that these designations are not randomly or idiosyncratically achieved by the individual—there are discoverable processes at play. Certain medical and psychological factors are more likely to give rise to the difficult patient label, and being classified as difficult is a transactional process determined, in part, by what clinicians view as the underlying reason for the behavior.

"Difficult" Providers

Recent studies[9] have begun to focus on characteristics of providers that are associated with reports of larger numbers of difficult patients in one's practice. Clinicians vary substantially in how many patients they describe as difficult or frustrating. Consistently, physicians who

---

[9]Most of these studies are cross-sectional in design, so the question of directionality between provider characteristics and the number of difficult patients is unclear. Certain practitioner characteristics may lower the clinician's tolerance for challenging patients; on the other hand, encountering more difficult clients may lead to changes in practice or provider characteristics (An et al., 2009; Krebs, Garrett, & Konrad, 2006).

report high concentrations of difficult patients tend to be younger and less experienced (An et al., 2009; Hinchey & Jackson, 2011; Krebs et al., 2006). This finding may indicate that professionals new to health care practices require some time to acquire the skills to work effectively with various kinds of clients, or as one doctor noted in a discussion of difficult clinical encounters, "Much of what I really need to practice I learned after medical school" (Kroenke, 2009, p. 333). As many safety-net systems are associated with teaching institutions, the age and experience of practitioners is lower than in other sectors of the health care field. This fact raises the possibility that some of the burden of "difficult patients" encountered in safety-net settings may actually be related to the relative level of experience of the practitioners within these settings.

The psychosocial orientation of the clinician is frequently associated with the percentage of difficult clients in one's practice. A psychosocial orientation focuses attention on the interaction between biological, psychological, and social features of the patient's condition. Physicians with a stronger psychosocial orientation have a "more open, communicative style and have lower rates of liability claims" (Hinchey & Jackson, 2011, p. 592). Certain medical specialties such as family medicine are more holistic in their model of clinical care, and as a result, family medicine practitioners tend to report lower numbers of difficult patients (Krebs et al., 2006). One of the most common elements identified in adversarial relationships is failed communication (Strous, Ullman, & Kottler, 2006). Certain kinds of health care practice place a higher premium on communication than others, so this characteristic of the clinician may also determine which patients are labeled as difficult.

Adopting a psychosocial orientation implies that environmental resources are available to allow its implementation. For instance, in her study of harmony and difficulty in nursing relationships, Macdonald (2007) found that knowing a patient was a precondition for a harmonious relationship. Knowledge of a patient was contingent, however, on having the time, equipment, and staffing levels necessary to support quality patient care. When nurses were short-staffed while being responsible for complex client care or when they had to interrupt providing treatment to obtain needed supplies, medications, or equipment, psychosocially oriented care suffered. In her reflection on the effects of these environmental factors, Macdonald noted, "Difficulty is constructed in the encounter and that the encounter is influenced by what is happening in the context of care" (2007, p. 79).

SOCIAL POWER AND DIFFICULT SITUATIONS

Labeling a patient as difficult is an action of the clinician, not the patient, and as such it represents the power health professionals have to define and set the rules of the clinical encounter (Hinchey & Jackson, 2011; Kroenke, 2009; Macdonald, 2007). The power invested in the ability to define what is "appropriate" (Macdonald & Murray, 2007) and what is "difficult" is reflected in the fact that most discussions of difficulty in health care literature focus on patients, not providers, and more specifically on what the clinician perceives as the psychopathology of the patient, ignoring the social and contextual factors that might underlie the patient's behavior (Koekkoek et al., 2011). The social power of health care practitioners to define the parameters of illness and treatment is an underlying and unspoken truth in the humanitarian endeavor of health care.

In this section, we look at two situations that illustrate the power, health professionals have to enact societal values that may contribute to the production of difficulty in clinical encounters: their function as social gatekeepers of the "sick role" and their ability to define appropriate treatment as people approach death.

Sanctioning Sickness

Disease is a biological concept; illness is the personal experience of disease, but sickness is a social role, meaning that to be judged as legitimately sick requires agreement that a genuine health problem has occurred (Winkelman, 2009). Health and mental health providers have been given the responsibility in U.S. society to determine whether or not a claim of sickness is legitimate. Half a century ago, Talcott Parsons, a sociologist interested in social systems and how they coped with deviance,[10] formulated the concept of the "sick role."[11] According to Parson's theory, the following were true:

1. Sickness is a ground for exemption from usual social roles and tasks.

2. This exemption is only given if the sick person actively intends on getting well.

---

[10]Deviance is defined in sociology as actions that violate cultural norms or expectations. Here, Parsons construes sickness as deviance because it allows the sick person to escape cultural norms and expectations around work and productivity.

[11]Parsons's original formulation has since been updated and expanded by multiple theoreticians. See Freund and McGuire (2002) for an extended discussion of the sick role.

3. Getting well requires a person to seek out and cooperate with medical providers in the treatment of the condition (Parsons in Freund & McGuire, 2002).

In order to prevent social disorder from people who are malingering, self-perceived illness is not a sufficient justification to assume the sick role. Health care practitioners are in the position of sanctioning whether or not someone "deserves" to be considered sick, and to be relieved of ordinary social responsibilities. In the absence of detectable disease, it is the health professional who decides whether the person is sick or not. This role also requires practitioners to make judgments about whether or not the person is complying with his or her duty to get well. Some patients,

> . . . do not appear to do their very best to get better. Instead, they seem to obstruct their own, and their clinicians' efforts towards, recovery. They may regularly miss appointments or fail to comply with even the most modest of life style suggestions, apparently on purpose. Even those that do try hard to get better but to no success and relapse often, may be considered "difficult." (Koekkoek et al., 2011, p. 505)

Patients who don't cooperate with professionals (and even those who do cooperate, but don't get well) are labeled as difficult because they are not fulfilling the responsibilities of the sick role. This discussion of the sick role clarifies the importance of understanding difficult patients from a transactional perspective, rather than an individualistic one. Health care practitioners need to thoughtfully consider their reasons for deciding a patient is difficult and when they use the power invested in their social role to contest the patient's presentation of disease and illness.

Setting the Terms for Dying: Defining Appropriate Treatment at the End of Life

Despite efforts to offer home-based alternatives, over half of all people in the United States die in the hospital; in particular, African American, less educated, and more functionally impaired people are more likely to die in a hospital or nursing home (Weitzen, Teno, Fennell, & Mor, 2003). Death moved out of family homes into hospitals in the middle of the 20th century, and has been increasingly medicalized as a result (Silverman, 2004). Health care practitioners have exerted increasing control over the process of dying, extending life through the application of technologies such as intubation, cardiopulmonary resuscitation, and intravenous administration of fluid and nutritional support. Instead of death being something that families and patients wait to happen, death increasingly requires choice on the part of families and health care clinicians (Kaufman, 2005). These choices include decisions like whether to continue aggressive chemotherapy in the face of cancer progression, whether to turn off a respirator that is breathing for someone who cannot breathe on his or her own, or whether to opt for surgical interventions such as the placement of a ventricular assist device when a person's heart is failing.

Sharon Kaufman, an anthropologist who studies American medicine, conducted research on death in American hospitals for several years. She found that families were generally unaware of the "hidden knowledge" that health care practitioners shared about hospital procedures and routines surrounding care of the dying patient, yet they keenly felt the control exerted by health professionals during the dying process.

> The doctors are unreachable for conversation. There is constant change among the nurses, and you try to ingratiate yourself by bringing candy for them. You want to show that you know something, so you bring questions, an agenda. But there are control issues and you're made to feel that you shouldn't show that you know too much. . . . The family is under surveillance, even while trying to show solidarity with the patient. And everything takes place in public. You're put on your best behavior. . . . In this disorienting space the family has to make decisions. How can they? Decision-making doesn't happen in the hospital. It happens at home. Somehow you're there all the time, but decisions are still made when you're not there. . . . Social workers, case managers, have the script—which you don't know ahead of time. They know what the trajectory is. . . . Where do you sit when the patient is not in the room, when the patient is in surgery? Whose room is it? The propriety of it. The problem of it. (Daughter-in-law of patient in Kaufman, 2005, pp. 85–86)

This quote demonstrates some of the ways families struggle to figure out the rules of engagement in hospital culture. Unless they have been through someone else's death by a progressive disease, people are generally unaware of the realities of the dying process. Medical

professionals share a knowledge of the expected progression of an illness ("they know what the trajectory is"), but often clinicians avoid
or delay sharing this information with patients or families until very
close to the end of life (Freund & McGuire, 2002). As a result of the
high stakes involved, conflict in hospital settings around end of life
decision making is common, with families frequently reporting high
levels of conflict, particularly around communication with the medical
team (Azoulay et al., 2000; Studdert et al., 2003). These communication
conflicts can result in estrangement between patients, families, and
health care practitioners.

Poor people and people of color have an increased risk of terminal
illness and early death as diseases that do not have their onset until
elderhood among affluent groups are diagnosed at younger ages in
lower socioeconomic groups (Rosenblatt & Wallace, 2005; Williams,
2004). Poor people facing death feared "being subjected to negative
assessments of others" (Williams, 2004, p. 31) based on their previous
experiences of stigma and the blame that may be assigned to people
if their death is attributable to their behavior (i.e., smoking, obesity,
etc.). In particular, the confluence of poverty, addiction, and dying can
raise many conflicts within the health care team and among clinicians,
patients, and families (Bushfield & DeFord, 2010).

Since the 1980s, efforts have been made to provide patients
and families with more control over dying and better quality time
through the creation of hospice programs. As people have continued to die in the hospital despite these home-based alternatives,
new models of in-hospital care and facilitated decision making have
been established by palliative care programs (see Table 8.2 for definitions of hospice and palliative care services). Unfortunately, many
poor people and people of color, particularly African Americans, do
not or cannot access these services (Elioff, 2003; Reese, Ahern, Nair,
O'Faire, & Warren, 1999). Because of earlier death, some low-income
people are not eligible for Medicare and, as a result, have difficulty paying for services (Williams, 2004). Another barrier to care,
particularly for the homeless or addicted people, is the absence of
family support for caregiving at the end of life (Bushfield & DeFord,
2010). In Table 8.3, we present an excerpt of a case study of a homeless man who was dying of cancer. This case illustrates some of the
ways that care providers can (if they choose) reach across the barriers erected by poverty to provide compassionate care at the end of
life (Kirchhoff, 2003).

TABLE 8.2
Definitions of Hospice and Palliative Care

Hospice

Hospice focuses on caring, not curing and, in most cases, care is provided in the patient's home. Typically, a family member serves as the primary caregiver and, when appropriate, helps make decisions for the terminally ill individual. Members of the hospice staff make regular visits to assess the patient and provide additional care or other services. Hospice staff is on call 24 hours a day, 7 days a week. Among its major responsibilities, the interdisciplinary hospice team:

- manages the patient's pain and symptoms;
- assists the patient with the emotional and psychosocial and spiritual aspects of dying;
- provides needed drugs, medical supplies, and equipment;
- coaches the family on how to care for the patient;
- delivers special services such as speech and physical therapy when needed;
- makes short-term in-patient care available when pain or symptoms become too difficult to manage at home, or the caregiver needs respite time; and
- provides bereavement care and counseling to surviving family and friends.

Palliative Care

Palliative care is an approach that improves the quality of life of patients and their families facing the problems associated with life-threatening illness, through the prevention and relief of suffering by means of early identification and impeccable assessment and treatment of pain and other problems—physical, psychosocial, and spiritual. Palliative care:

- provides relief from pain and other distressing symptoms;
- affirms life and regards dying as a normal process;
- intends neither to hasten or postpone death;
- integrates the psychological and spiritual aspects of patient care;
- offers a support system to help patients live as actively as possible until death;
- offers a support system to help the family cope during the patients illness and their own bereavement;
- uses a team approach to address the needs of patients and their families, including bereavement counseling, if indicated;
- enhances quality of life, and may also positively influence the course of illness;
- is applicable early in the course of illness, in conjunction with other therapies that are intended to prolong life, such as chemotherapy or radiation therapy, and includes those investigations needed to better understand and manage distressing clinical complications.

NOTE. Hospice definition from the National Hospice and Palliative Care Organization (n.d.); palliative care definition from the World Health Organization (2011), www.who.int/cancer/palliative/definition/en/.

TABLE 8.3
"Case Study of Milton, 'The Cowboy'": A Palliative Care Patient

[Milton was] a young-looking 73-year-old African American gentleman who had an impish grin and piercing brown eyes. . . He [said] that he lived under a bridge in the inner city and I would not need a key. He affectionately called his home "The Cave." He told me the best place to get cheap food, and that afternoon I went with my boss, Dr. G., to feed [Milton's] dog.

We saw the most amazing sight. Milton's home did look like a cave. We entered through the front door, a bright blue tarp. There were several areas filled with furniture as well as a mattress. In the middle of the room was a huge tree limb decorated with pieces of metal and material. There were many bins, a shopping cart, and some chairs. . . . His dog, Cowgirl, came out to eat as we were leaving. She was a tan German shepherd mix pup about 6 months old, frightened of us, because she had been abused before Milton found her.

. . . After his hospital discharge, Dr. M. . . . and I picked up Milton to take him to the radiation oncologist. Milt scurried inside the cave to shave, change his clothes, and put on aftershave. . . . The following week we sat with him while he told us the tale of his life. . . . His father was Greek. . . . His mother abused him both verbally and physically. He was taunted at school for being a "half-breed" and "a bastard."

. . . Milton told of a life of many women, many jobs, and a great deal of drinking and gambling. . . . He served in Texas during the Korean War as a military clerk. He garnered much respect by helping officers get home on leave. . . . He was discharged honorably. I believe this was the first time in Milton's life that he was treated with respect. . . .

[He had] three failed marriages. He had one child by each marriage. He had not participated in raising any of his children, although he did see them from time to time. He stated that he had not seen his oldest son. . . for 20 years, or [his other two children] in 3 years.

. . . He told me that he had lived under the bridge for the past 3 years as he had been evicted from an apartment for seniors. "They said I played my music too loud." He got tired of following the rules so he moved to the cave. He was not homeless based on a lack of funds as he received Social Security and veteran benefits.

. . . In the 5 months I knew Milt, he was in the county hospital 10 times because of pneumonia, myocardial infarction, and pain [secondary to cancer]. . . . On December 23, he was admitted to the hospital. . . . He was in such pain that he could only sit in a chair. The cancer had spread to his spine. . . . [His aunt] called both his sons, [but] she could not find [his daughter]. . . . As they had been estranged from their father, both sons paid one visit and did not come again. After radiation to his spine, Milt's pain improved and he could no longer be a hospital patient. He was transferred to the nursing home next door to the hospital.

. . . Milton loved his dog, Cowgirl. . . . In January, he asked to see her as he knew his condition was worsening. . . . Once Cowgirl smelled Milton, she jumped on the bed arousing him. Cowboy stirred and smiling he put his arm around her saying, "Cowgirl is here." The two reunited best friends lay together for 2 hours. . . . Milton died [2 days later].

From Kirchhoff, L. S. (2003). Case Study of Milton "The Cowboy." *Smith College Studies in Social Work, 73*. 463–478. http://www.informaworld.com. With permission of Taylor & Francis.

THINKING DIFFERENTLY ABOUT DIFFICULTY

This discussion has so far highlighted the structural underpinnings of the classification of some patients as difficult, and the role health care providers have as gatekeepers to resources patients are trying to claim. We conclude this chapter with reflection on two strategies that can assist practitioners to be as effective as possible in transactions with patients: recognizing countertransference issues and adapting the care they provide in the context of difficult patient encounters.

Recognizing and Working With Countertransference

Countertransference refers to the "totality of feelings experienced by the clinician toward the patient—whether conscious or unconscious, whether prompted by the client's dynamics or by issues or events in the clinician's own life" (Katz, 2006a, p. 4). When providers share similar experiences, emotions, or stressors with patients, it can remind the clinician (whether they are aware of it or not) of his or her own past losses or failures (Stevens, 2010). Table 8.4 provides examples of the kinds of feelings that are elicited in difficult encounters with patients. Although countertransference is understood as a natural and inevitable response, especially to suffering, when health care providers remain unaware of their own personal reactions, they can engage in difficult behaviors of their own. These behaviors span a spectrum from overidentification with the patient, or, at the other extreme, inappropriate withdrawal from patient care (Bernhardt, Silver, Rushton, Micco, & Geller, 2010). The following excerpt from a geneticist working with a mother with four developmentally disabled children illustrates some of these issues.

> It is one of those situations where she calls all the time. So, you are sort of wanting to avoid talking to her because when she gets on the phone, she goes on for an hour, and again, she's like, "What are you going to do to make it better for me?" I guess in some ways I feel a little guilty, as well, because I know how difficult it must be for this mom. That makes me feel guilty that I feel ill feelings toward her. I want to be able to help them but I know that I really am not going to be able to do anything. Again, I feel for this mom because I am a mom too. To see what she has to deal with is extremely difficult, but at the same time you are like "get them off my back." (Bernhardt et al., 2010, p. 293)

TABLE 8.4
Possible Countertransference Responses to Suffering

Helplessness
Shame and embarrassment
Denial and the wish for it to go away
Anger, frustration, and hostility
Sorrow or sadness
Unresolved grief
Restlessness
Anxiety and fearfulness
Guilt

Adapted from Arbore, Katz, and Johnson (2006).

This quote illustrates several dynamics related to countertransference and the assignment of difficulty to a patient. First, the patient is identified as difficult by her behavior—she both requests extended contact with the geneticist and has unrealistic expectations of what this practitioner can do for her—she implores her for help. Second, the intensity of this mom's needs, coupled with the clinician's inability to provide any meaningful help for the patient, results in strong emotions on the geneticist's part of guilt and "ill feelings" (most likely anger or irritation) toward the patient. Third, the geneticist has a similar experience to this patient—they are both moms. From being a mom, the practitioner knows the difficulty in raising (one presumes her own healthy) children, and she acknowledges the extremeness of this mother's situation with four disabled children. But even this recognition does not shift the practitioner's fundamental ambivalence toward the mother, her assessment that the mother is difficult. The geneticist wants to avoid talking to the patient and wants her "off my back," both indications of a tendency to withdraw from this patient.

The situation of this geneticist and mother illustrates an important countertransference issue in health care, namely that, "Clinicians perceive patients as difficult when they feel denied in their best intentions and obstructed in their curative actions" (Koekkoek et al., 2011, p. 505). Some situations become distressing for providers because they cannot change the effect of the news they deliver and have to cope with the resulting feelings of helplessness (Bernhardt et al., 2010). In reorienting our understanding of difficult patients to considering the role of health care professionals in these situations, it becomes clear that those practitioners who invest in reflection on their own practice are likely to be the clinicians least prone to react in an unconscious fashion to difficult clinical encounters (Browning, 2002). If we embrace the idea that countertransference is a normal, expectable part of patient-centered clinical care, this understanding will move us toward integrating self-reflection into our daily work, especially when we are triggered by a patient or family we label as difficult (even if only in our own minds). Sometimes, personal reflection is helped along by collegial consultation. Table 8.5 presents some potential countertransference issues that would indicate that talk with a trusted, empathic colleague might be of benefit.

Adapting Care in the Context of Difficulty

To date, no intervention studies are available that provide evidence-based suggestions for transforming difficult encounters, but based on the review presented in this chapter, four recommendations may promote more constructive clinical engagement. These ideas may also help practitioners to not take difficult encounters personally, but to use them as opportunities to learn new skills and adjust course when confronted with challenging patients.

First, several authors make clear that the foundation for working through difficult clinical care situations is to focus on empathic listening and communication skills (An et al., 2009; Katz, 2006a, 2006b; Strous et al., 2006). Empathic listening and communication emphasizes a nonjudgmental orientation toward understanding the patient's underlying concerns and emotional state. Effective communication

---

TABLE 8.5
Reasons to Consider Collegial Consultation Regarding Countertransference

1. If you are feeling dissatisfied with your work or having thoughts of leaving your profession because of your response to patient care.
2. If you find yourself giving rote answers or relating to patients in "fixed" ways that do not reflect curiosity about the patient or creativity in your response (i.e., "going through the motions").
3. If you find you are treating your patients as "cases" rather than people (perhaps by referring to them by diagnosis rather than name).
4. If your patients complain about you or if several decide they do not want your services.
5. If you find yourself feeling indispensable, or feeling unusual amounts of resentment, cynicism, or anger.

Adapted from Katz (2006b).

is more likely when a practitioner can fluidly move between his or her role as an expert and his or her position as a "novice" in learning about the patient (Browning, 2002). In many clinical situations, the focus of care is highly technical and abstract (i.e., review of laboratory results, radiologic findings, or physical exams). Difficult encounters can be mitigated by using clear communication strategies as outlined in Table 8.6. When meeting with families, it is important for clinicians to monitor the amount of time they are talking—families report more satisfaction with care when health care practitioners listen more (McDonagh et al., 2004), but often health care providers spend more time talking and setting the agenda for conversation with patients rather than supporting the patient and family's questions (Fine, Reid, Shengelia, & Adelman, 2010).[12] Asking about and listening to patients' fears and concerns about their conditions can demonstrate the professional's empathy and commitment to the patient's care as well as identify issues that need further attention. In many cases, involvement of disciplines that focus on patients' emotional coping and material resources (social work, psychology, or psychiatry) can be helpful.

As we have indicated, patients who are interpreted as difficult often present with highly complex, and often chronic conditions affecting multiple domains of their lives. Psychosocially oriented care recognizes that the illness/sickness experience transcends the biomedical problem the patient has (Kroenke, 2009). As Kroenke notes in his discussion of ways to unburden difficult encounters, attention to psychosocial needs of patients is not just an issue for generalists or family medicine practitioners—specialists also need to learn to pay attention to aspects of their patient's lives that affect the diagnosis and treatment of health conditions. Chronic conditions require "work" on the part of patients in terms of all the ways they have to learn to manage the consequences of their health problems in other domains of their lives (Wasan, Wootton, & Jamison, 2005). Practitioners are reminded to ask about other arenas of the patient's experience that might contribute to patient stress and the creation of a difficult encounter (Strous et al., 2006).

Institutional resources are vital to efforts to prevent difficult client encounters before they occur (Macdonald, 2007). It is unsurprising that

---

[12]It should be also noted that the tendency of the clinician to do more talking than listening is often a form of avoidance behavior, in essence a means of avoiding a patient's expression of sentiments and experiences that the clinician feels ill-prepared to address.

TABLE 8.6
Strategies for Clear Communication

1. *Assess Prior Knowledge*
   Ask about what people already know or believe about their situation.
2. *Use Simple Language*
   Slow down, avoid jargon, provide information in digestible chunks.
3. *Encourage Questioning*
   Assume patients have question and ask what they are.
4. *Ask Patients to Restate Their Understanding*
   Put the onus for patient understanding on the clinician—I want to make
   sure I did a good job explaining, can you tell me what we talked about in
   your own words?

Adapted from Smith, Sudore, and Perez-Stable (2009).

practitioners in overstressed safety-net health care systems frequently experience difficult clinical interactions. Safety-net settings often face chronic shortages in staff time, necessary supplies, and available space for patients. These environmental barriers to high-quality patient care can promote difficult interactions as patients struggle for the attention and respect that are fundamental to harmonious relationships (Macdonald, 2007). Awareness of environmental constraints and institutional planning to adapt to resource limitations may help proactively address some of these issues.

Finally, certain clinical practices may help to prevent or work through difficult encounters. For instance, when it is possible to identify high-intensity patients ahead of time, they can be scheduled for longer clinical appointments that offer the opportunity for enough "talk time" to identify patient concerns (Kroenke, 2009). Alternatively, practitioners can also work with patients to establish more frequent regular clinical visits rather than treating problems in an ad hoc fashion as they arise until a situation has stabilized sufficiently (Wasan et al., 2005). Identifying patient expectations at the beginning of the clinical visit can aid in establishing a collaborative framework for patient care (Kroenke, 2009). When problems do occur, communicating directly with the patient about concerns of the clinician is also a valuable intervention (An et al., 2009).

CONCLUDING COMMENTS

We hope this discussion has led the reader to the conclusion that difficult patients are created, not born—and clinicians themselves often have significant agency in the origination of undesirable patient encounters. Ultimately, we would advocate for no longer validating the idea of "difficult patients," especially since being labeled as difficult promotes different behaviors among clinicians that can lead to poorer clinical outcomes (Koekkoek et al., 2011). Our contention in this chapter has been that there are difficult clinical encounters, far more than there are difficult patients (Kroenke, 2009).

This discussion has also returned to the idea of power and privilege in the context of health care provision. The relationships between safety-net health care providers and patients are asymmetrical—the clinician has the power to define what is considered appropriate or difficult behavior, can confer (or withhold) the status of being sick, and is the dominant player in decision making at the end of life. These powerful roles require equally vigorous efforts to engage in self-reflective practice and to adapt our care so that we are effective in even the most difficult situations in safety-net health care settings.

REFERENCES

Adams, A., Buckingham, C. D., Lindenmeyer, A., McKinlay, J. B., Link, C., Marceau, L., & Arber, S. (2008). The influence of patient and doctor gender on diagnosing coronary heart disease. *Sociology of Health & Illness, 30,* 1–18.

An, P. G., Rabatin, J. S., Manwell, L. B., Linzer, M., Brown, R. L., Schwartz, M. D., for The MEMO investigators. (2009). Burden of difficult encounters in primary care: Data from the Minimizing Error, Maximizing Outcomes study. *Archives of Internal Medicine, 169,* 410–414.

Arbore, P., Katz, R. S., & Johnson, T. A. (2006). Suffering and the caring professional. In R. S. Katz & T. A. Johnson (Eds.), *When professionals weep: Emotional and countertransference responses in end-of-life care* (pp. 13–26). New York, NY: Routledge.

Arciniegas, D. B., & Beresford, T. P. (2010). Managing difficult interactions with patients in neurology practices: A practical approach. *Neurology, 75,* s39–s44.

Azoulay, E., Chevret, S., Leleu, G., Pochard, F., Barboteu, M., Adrie, C., . . . Schlemmer, B. (2000). Half the families of intensive care unit patients experience inadequate communication with physicians. *Critical Care Medicine, 28,* 3044–3049.

Bernhardt, B. A., Silver, R., Rushton, C. H., Micco, E., & Geller, G. (2010). What keeps you up at night? Genetics professionals' distressing experiences in patient care. *Genetics in Medicine, 12,* 289–297.

Bhabha, H. K. (1994). *The location of culture.* New York: Routledge.

Browning, D. (2002). To show our humanness—Relational and communicative competence in pediatric palliative care. *Bioethics Forum, 18,* 23–28.

Bushfield, S. Y., & DeFord, B. (2010). *End-of-life care & addiction: A family systems approach.* New York, NY: Springer Publishing.

Caldicott, C. V. (2007). "Sweeping up after the parade": Professional, ethical and patient care implications of "turfing." *Perspectives in Biology and Medicine, 50,* 136–149.

Caldicott, C. V., Dunn, K. A., & Frankel, R. M. (2005). Can patients tell when they are unwanted? "Turfing" in residency training. *Patient Education and Counseling, 56,* 104–111.

Chiaramonte, G. R., & Friend, R. (2006). Medical students' and residents' gender bias in the diagnosis, treatment and interpretation of coronary heart disease symptoms. *Health Psychology, 25,* 255–266.

Elioff, C. (2003). Accepting hospice care: Issues for the African American community. *Smith College Studies in Social Work, 73,* 375–384.

Fine, E., Reid, M. C., Shengelia, R., & Adelman, R. D. (2010). Directly observed patient–physician discussions in palliative and end-of-life care: A systematic review of the literature. *Journal of Palliative Medicine, 13,* 595–603.

Freund, P. E. S., & McGuire, M. B. (2002). *Health, illness and the social body: A critical sociology* (4th ed.). Englewood Cliffs, NJ: Prentice Hall.

Goleman, D. (1985). *Vital lies, simple truths.* New York, NY: Simon & Schuster.

Groves, J. E. (1978). Taking care of the hateful patient. *New England Journal of Medicine, 298,* 883–887.

Hinchey, S. A., & Jackson, J. L. (2011). A cohort study assessing difficult patient encounters in a walk-in primary care clinic, predictors and outcomes. *Journal of General Internal Medicine, 26,* 588–594.

Katz, R. S. (2006a). When our personal selves influence our professional work: An introduction to emotions and countertransference in end-of-life care. In R. S. Katz & T. A. Johnson (Eds.), *When professionals weep: Emotional and countertransference responses in end-of-life care* (pp. 3–12). New York, NY: Routledge.

Katz, R. S. (2006b). The journey inside: Examining countertransference and its implications for practice in end-of-life care. In R. S. Katz & T. A. Johnson (Eds.), *When professionals weep: Emotional and countertransference responses in end-of-life care* (pp. 269–283). New York, NY: Routledge.

Kaufman, S. R. (2005). *. . . . and a time to die: How American hospitals shape the end of life.* Chicago, IL: University of Chicago Press.

Kirchhoff, L. S. (2003). Case study of Milton, "The Cowboy." *Smith College Studies in Social Work, 73,* 463–478.

Koekkoek, B., Hutschemaekers, G., van Meijel, B., & Schene, A. (2011). How do patients come to be seen as "difficult"?: A mixed-methods study in community mental health care. *Social Science & Medicine, 72,* 504–512.

Krebs, E. E., Garrett, J. M., & Konrad, T. R. (2006). The difficult doctor? Characteristics of physicians who report frustration with patients: An analysis of survey data. *BMC Health Services Research, 6,* 128–136.

Kroenke, K. (2009). Unburdening the difficult clinical encounter. *Archives of Internal Medicine, 169,* 333–334.

Macdonald, M. T. (2007). Nurse—patient encounters: Constructing harmony and difficulty. *Advanced Emergency Nursing Journal, 29,* 73–81.

Macdonald, M. E., & Murray, M. A. (2007). The appropriateness of *appropriate*: Smuggling values into clinical practice. *Canadian Journal of Nursing Research, 39,* 58–73.

McDonagh, J. R., Elliott, T. B., Engelberg, R. A., Treece, P. D., Shannon, S. E., Rubenfeld, G. D., ... Curtis J. R. (2004). Family satisfaction with family conferences about end-of-life care in the ICU: Increased proportion of family speech is associated with increased satisfaction. *Critical Care Medicine, 32,* 1484–1488.

National Hospice and Palliative Care Organization (n.d.). What is hospice and palliative care? Retrieved from http://www.nhpco.org/i4a/pages/index.cfm?pageid=4648

Reese, D. J., Ahern, R. E., Nair, S., O'Faire, J. D., & Warrren, C. (1999). Hospice access and use by African Americans: Addressing cultural and institutional barriers through participatory action research. *Social Work, 44,* 549–559.

Rosenblatt, P. C., & Wallace, B. R. (2005). *African American grief.* New York, NY: Routledge.

Silverman, P. R. (2004). Dying and bereavement in historical perspective. In J. Berzoff & P. R. Silverman (Eds.), *Living with dying: A handbook for end-of-life healthcare practitioners* (pp. 128–149). New York, NY: Columbia University Press.

Smith, S. (1995). Dealing with the difficult patient. *Postgraduate Medicine Journal, 71,* 653–657.

Smith, A. K., Sudore, R. L., & Perez-Stable, E. J. (2009). Palliative care for Latino patients and their families: Whenever we prayed, she wept. *Journal of the American Medical Association, 301,* 1047–1057.

Stevens, L. A. (2010). Responding to the difficult patient. *Bulletin of the American College of Surgeons, 95,* 12–15.

Strous, R. D., Ulman, A. M., & Kotler, M. (2006). The hateful patient revisited: Relevance for 21st century medicine. *European Journal of Internal Medicine, 17,* 387–393.

Studdert, D. M., Mello, M. M., Burns, J. P., Puopolo, A. L., Galper, B. Z., Truog, R. D., & Brennan, T. A. (2003). Conflict in the care of patients with prolonged stays in the ICU: Types, sources and predictors. *Intensive Care Medicine, 29,* 1489–1497.

Tait, R. C., Chibnall, J. T., & Kalauokalani, D. (2009). Provider judgments of patients in pain: Seeking symptom certainty. *Pain Medicine, 10,* 11–34.

Wasan, A. D., Wootton, J., & Jamison, R. N. (2005). Dealing with difficult patients in your pain practice. *Regional Anesthesia and Pain Medicine, 30,* 184–192.

Weitzen, S., Teno, J. M., Fennell, M., & Mor, V. (2003). Factors associated with site of death: A national study of where people die. *Medical Care, 41,* 323–335.

World Health Organization (2011). WHO definition of palliative care. Retrieved from http://www.who.int/cancer/palliative/definition/en/

Williams, B. R. (2004). Dying young, dying poor: A sociological examination of existential suffering among low-socioeconomic status patients. *Journal of Palliative Medicine, 7,* 27–37.

Winkelman, M. (2009). *Culture and health: Applying medical anthropology.* San Francisco, CA: Jossey-Bass.

9

Adherence to Care

INTRODUCTION

Why had the Lees always insisted on doing everything their way? Why—this was still the worst sin—had the Lees been noncompliant?
—Anne Fadiman (1997)

Attending to the patient's story clarifies how the "technological task" of medicine is irremediably framed within social relations.
—Jack Clark & Elliot Mishler (1992)

Medical care in the past century has been characterized by its emphasis on the technical expertise of the physician, enacted within a paternalistic relationship in which doctors had the social sanction to tell people what to do and to expect their compliance with the prescribed treatment plan. It is tempting to see any deviation of the patient from the prescribed treatment approach solely as a problem with the patient. Since the 1960s, this paradigm of health care has been challenged by movements that focused on patient empowerment (such as feminism's approach to teaching women about their bodies)[1] and the development of a more egalitarian "patient-centered"[2] style of care. In the resulting decades, patient empowerment movements, the expansion of

---

[1] Good examples of these approaches are the multiple editions of *Our Bodies, Ourselves* by the Boston Women's Health Collective (2005), *Living Well . . . Despite Catchin' Hell* by Melody T. McCloud (2010), or *Women's Bodies, Women's Wisdom* by Christiane Northrup (2010).

[2] Patient-centered care shifts from a focus on disease or provider-driven practices to one in which the patient's values, experience, and understanding of illness become more predominant. For foundational information on patient-centered practice, see Laine and Davidoff (1996) and the Committee on Quality Health Care in America, Institute of Medicine (2001).

Internet-based medical information, and the focus on "consumers" and "customers" rather than patients have all pushed the boundaries regarding the nature of the relationship and expectations between health care providers and their clients. In this context, treatment plans are more likely to be thought of as collaborations with patients, rather than dictates, but ongoing evidence suggests that this transformation is incomplete and that health care consultations continue to be dominated by providers' agendas (Sparks & Villagran, 2010). When patients make intentional decisions not to engage in a treatment plan, or when they don't "follow through," health care providers often struggle with how to interpret and respond to these actions. For reasons that we will explore in this chapter, issues surrounding adherence to health care treatment plans are magnified in safety-net settings.

Adherence or "the extent to which patients follow the instructions they are given for a prescribed treatment" (Haynes, McDonald, Garg, & Montesqieu, 2002, p. 2) is a complex, multidetermined process. Research consistently suggests that 30% to 50% of patients do not follow the health care provider's treatment plan (Bosworth, Weinberger, & Oddone, 2006; Haynes, McKibbon, & Kanani, 1996). To examine adherence is to immediately confront issues around terminology that reflect underlying assumptions about the nature of the health care provider–patient relationship. For instance, "compliance" is a term that is commonly used in clinical practice, but it implies that patients should obey or submit to the plan developed by the provider. This term has been abandoned in the research literature in favor of "adherence" because of the emphasis of "compliance" on the paternalism of the relationship, and the efforts to use a term that has fewer authoritarian implications. Like similar discussions around the use of the term "patient" (Scott, 2010), the word "adherence" has linguistic overtones that continue to prioritize the alignment of the patient to the health care provider's plan over the sense of collaboration between partners. As a result, other authors, in accord with a more patient-centered philosophy of care, have advocated that the term "adherence" be dropped altogether in favor of purely descriptive terms such as medication taking (Goldstein, DePue, & Kazura, 2006). We have adopted the term adherence in this chapter, even though it does not completely capture the complicated calculus that is invoked whenever change in behavior is required.

Regardless of the complex philosophical realities associated with terminology, any casual observer of informal conversations of health personnel will hear patient "noncompliance" as a frequent topic. Even though common, nonadherence has decidedly negative connotations for providers, and clinicians may misinterpret nonadherence as an indication of a patient's fundamental unwillingness to take responsibility for his or her health experiences. These clinician beliefs can result in "provider and patient frustration, anger, and hopelessness" (Bosworth et al., 2006, p. 5). Providers may feel that their expertise is being ignored; patients may feel that their "lifeworld" (i.e., individual needs and experiences) is unrecognized or undervalued (Clark & Mishler, 1992).

Although adherence is usually framed as a problem of the patient, here, as in the previous chapter, we advance the argument that nonadherence is a transactional process between health care providers and patients, which is influenced by the environment of the health care system. When nonadherence is understood as a transactional process rather than solely as a troubling patient behavior, factors that influence adherence can be examined at different system levels. Table 9.1 provides examples of research findings on factors related to nonadherence at the health care system, provider–patient relationship, and patient and treatment regimen levels. Seeing adherence as a transactional process that is influenced by patient, provider, and health system factors supports an orientation toward nonadherence as a normative, intriguing problem that has many avenues for intervention.

Adherence as an Individual and Societal Concern

When care is required for a health condition, even one as transient as a typical upper respiratory infection (i.e., head cold), the person who is ill must change a number of behaviors. In the case of a head cold, the patient has to decide whether to take symptom-relieving medications such as fever reducers or sinus treatments. He or she has to decide whether to attend to daily activities such as family responsibilities, school, or work. If the symptoms linger and are worrisome, the patient has to decide when to seek out additional consultation from a health care provider. If the provider prescribes medications, one has to have the resources to obtain these drugs, remember to take them, cope with side effects, and decide whether to continue taking the prescription once he or she begins to feel better. Patients are most likely to follow a health care provider's advice when acutely ill. However, studies of adherence to treatment regimens for acute illnesses indicate that somewhere between 20% and 40% of patients do not adhere to their prescribed treatment plan; a substantial number of patients never fill their prescriptions (Levensky & O'Donohue, 2006).

TABLE 9.1
Examples of Factors at Different System Levels Related to Nonadherence

At the Health Care System Level

    Poor accessibility of services

    Lack of continuity in care

    Unfriendly or unhelpful staff

    Uninviting setting

Between the Health Care Provider and Patient

    Poor communication

    Provider does not assess problems with the treatment plan and/or adherence

    Patient lacks trust and/or comfort with the provider

    Patient and provider have different beliefs about the problem and/or treatment

Patient Related

    Information deficits related to the health condition and/or treatment

    Lack of tangible resources (finances, housing, transportation, etc.)

    Inadequate social support for adherence

    Mental health problems

    Stressful life events

    Lack of symptoms related to the health condition

    Low motivation for treatment or pessimism about the future

Treatment Regimen

    Highly complex or demanding

    Poor fit between treatment requirements and patient's lifestyle

    Severity of side effects

Adapted from Levensky and O'Donohue (2006).

Patients who do not adhere to a prescribed treatment plan can incur devastating personal costs—almost 125,000 deaths in the United States each year may be related specifically to nonadherence to prescribed medication for people with heart disease (Peterson, Takiya, & Finley, 2003). Intentional nonadherence can also raise legal issues such as the situation in which a mother fled with her 13-year-old son to avoid chemotherapy for her son's Hodgkin's lymphoma, a form of cancer typically thought of as very treatable with a high percentage of patients achieving complete remission (Merck, 2008). The family had a religious orientation to alternative health approaches and did not concur with the medical treatment plan. The mother and son eventually returned to Minnesota, where the courts ordered the son to receive the chemotherapy (Wolfe, 2009).

Adherence to medication is only one type of treatment aimed at reducing morbidity and mortality. The Surgeon General estimates that 40% of all variation in health outcomes is related to personal health behaviors such as smoking, drug use, physical inactivity, poor nutritional habits, and difficulties in coping with stress (Satcher & Higginbotham, 2008).[3] The three leading causes of death in the United States—heart disease, cancer, and stroke (Centers for Disease Control, 2010)—are associated with high-risk behaviors of individuals such as smoking and excessive alcohol use. Changing these behaviors is difficult, and adherence research shows that 50% to 80% of people who have been "prescribed" a prevention approach (such as stopping smoking) are unable to adhere to these recommendations (Levensky & O'Donohue, 2006).

Given the severity of health, social, and financial costs of nonadherence, many research studies have been conducted to understand and improve patient adherence to treatment. Enough studies of patient adherence are now available so that it is possible to conduct meta-analyses of results across studies. Table 9.2 provides recent examples from the Cochrane Collaboration of reviews of adherence-related research. Founded in 1993, the Cochrane Collaboration is an international network of researchers recognized by the World Health Organization that provides meta-analyses of published medical intervention studies to direct clinical treatment guideline development. The table shows a range of conclusions from these reviews—many approaches have some, albeit limited, effect on improving patient adherence. For example although patient education alone was not effective in increasing adherence to antihypertensive medications (Schroeder, Fahey, & Ebrahim, 2004), it was successful in helping patients follow diabetes treatment recommendations (Vermeire, Wens, Van Royen, Biot, Hearnshaw, & Lindenmeyer, 2005).

Nonadherence not only contributes to increased suffering and death for individuals, it also poses a problem at societal levels. For example, multidrug resistant tuberculosis (MDR-TB) and methicillin-resistant

---

[3] An additional 20% of variation stems from genetic/biological differences, 20% to 25% from physical environment issues (such as exposure to toxic waste or violence), and 15% to 20% from issues related to access to quality health care (Satcher & Higginbotham, 2008).

TABLE 9.2
Recent Cochrane Collaboration Reviews Related to Patient Adherence

HEALTH PROBLEM AREA	REVIEW CONCLUSIONS
Cardiac rehabilitation[a]	Targeting patient identified barriers improves uptake and adherence
High-blood pressure[b]	Simplifying regimens, motivational strategies improve adherence, but patient education alone does not
Taking lipid-lowering medications[c]	Patient reinforcement and reminding strategies, simplification of regimen, patient information, and education all improve adherence
Diabetes treatment recommendations[d]	Nurse- and pharmacy-led interventions, home aids, and diabetes education had a small positive effect on blood glucose control
Diabetes care provided by health care practitioner[e]	Multifaceted professional interventions improve performance of care providers, but effects on patient outcomes were unclear
Directly observed therapy for tuberculosis[f]	Direct observation of medication taking did not improve tuberculosis cure rates
HIV/AIDS[g]	Interventions targeting practical medication management skills, and skills teaching to individuals versus groups provide at least 12 weeks improved medication adherence
Exercise for chronic musculoskeletal pain[h]	Supervised or individualized exercise therapy and self-management techniques improve adherence to exercise
Hormonal methods of contraception[i]	No strategies were found to improve adherence
Shared decision making for people with mental health conditions[j]	No evidence of harm from shared decision-making experiments, but no clear evidence that this intervention improves adherence to treatment
Contracts between patients and health care providers to promote adherence[k]	Limited evidence that contracts can contribute to adherence, but insufficient evidence to routinely recommend their use.

[a] From Davies, Taylor, Beswick, Wise, Moxham, Rees, and Ebrahim (2010).

[b] From Schroeder et al. (2004).

[c] From Schedlbauer, Davies, and Fahey (2010).

[d] From Vermeire et al. (2005).

[e] From Renders, Valk, Griffin, Wagner, van Eijk, and Assendelft (2000).

[f] From Volmink and Garner (2007).

[g] From Rueda, Park-Wyllie, Bayoumi, Tynan, Antoniou, Rourke, and Glazier (2009).

[h] From Jordan, Holden, Mason, and Foster (2010).

[i] From Halpern, Grimes, Lopez, and Gallo (2006).

[j] From Duncan, Best, and Hagen (2010).

[k] From Bosch-Capblanch, Abba, Prictor, and Garner (2007).

Staphylococcus aureus (MRSA) have evolved, in part, because persons with these illnesses did not take their medications as prescribed for as long as was needed (Gibbons, 1992).[4] As a result, bacteria that were able to withstand initial exposure to antibiotics survived and passed on treatment resistance at increasing cost to people now exposed to resistant strains of these illnesses. MRSA is one of the leading hospital-acquired infections, and treatment costs can range in the tens of thousands for each individual, with estimates that $3 to $4 billion per year are spent on treatment across the health care system as a whole (Infection Control Today, 2005).

In addition to the issues related to treatment resistance, nonadherence also has other societal costs. As much as one-quarter of nursing home admissions may be related to nonadherence to treatment and the subsequent inability of the person to care for themselves (Peterson et al., 2003). Nonadherence also creates issues with interpreting clinical research depending on the degree to which patients in the studies did not take the medications as instructed (Anstrom, Weinfurt, & Allen, 2006). The personal, social, and institutional costs of nonadherence are so high, and the problem is so widespread that some have wondered if it should be treated as a form of "medical error" that requires new tracking systems, theoretical models, and intervention techniques (Barber, 2002). Within the medical error framework, nonadherence would receive heightened attention by redefining it as a preventable event.

Adherence as a Clash Between Worldviews

In most conversations about culture within health care settings, an implicit assumption exists that "culture" is possessed by patients, and that, more narrowly, it refers specifically to differences associated with race and ethnicity. Although this conceptualization prevents our recognition of other cultures such as those based on age (youth culture), generational cohort, sexual identity, and others, what is more important here is the fact that this assumption makes invisible the culture of biomedicine. Medical care has its own worldview, language, rituals, and hierarchy, all of which make any interaction between the biomedical culture and a person who is not a member a cross-cultural interaction.

---

[4] Other causes for the development of drug-resistant bacteria include the inappropriate prescription of antibiotics for respiratory (often viral) illnesses (Peleg & Paterson, 2006) and their widespread use in animal food-raising operations (Shryock & Richwine, 2010).

Perhaps one of the most compelling accounts of this conflict of worldviews was the situation of Lia Lee, a Hmong child, who in the world of biomedicine was diagnosed with epilepsy at the age of 3 months. As recounted in the award-winning book, *The Spirit Catches You and You Fall Down* (Fadiman, 1997), Lia's parents were refugees from Laos after the Vietnam War. From the worldview of Lia's parents, her seizures resulted after her soul was stolen by a spirit because she was frightened by a loud sound as an infant. In Lia's culture, a seizure disorder, although potentially dangerous, was also a sign of spiritual calling, in sharp contrast to the medical worldview of epilepsy as a disabling diagnosis that required consistent daily treatment and frequent monitoring by health providers.

For the next several years, Lia was cared for within a small, rural safety-net hospital in California. The hospital saw patients regardless of their ability to pay, but as a safety-net provider, the hospital's finances were uncertain and they were unable to sustain programs such as interpreters for the large Hmong community the hospital served. Frequently, other family members or extended community members who spoke English would interpret conversations with the medical providers for the family, but the cultural concerns of Lia's parents were not a focus of these conversations. More often the communication between providers and family members was even more problematic when no interpreter was available. Conflicts erupted between the medical providers and Lia's parents as they were "noncompliant" with Lia's treatment plan.

Lia's parents did not follow the complex medication regimen prescribed by the physicians for a variety of reasons. As one example, the prescribed antiseizure medication had to be taken at very specific times throughout the day, and the family was instructed on this timing based on Western timekeeping practices (i.e., clocks with numbers) that were not relevant to the family's orientation to time (based on activities that happened throughout the day). Despite the family's devoted care of Lia, as was consistent with the family's cultural beliefs, Lia was removed by child protective services to a supervised foster care setting to ensure that she was given medical treatment as prescribed by the physicians. After being returned to her parents, Lia became ill with sepsis, and the septic shock caused a brain-damaging seizure, after which Lia was no longer responsive to external stimuli. Fadiman questions whether this outcome could have been avoided if the medical care provided to Lia had been responsive to the differences in worldviews between the culture of medicine and the culture of the family.

The situation of Lia Lee's family reflects that of many non-English speakers within the United States who seek care within the health care safety-net system—when interpreter services are limited, communication between health care providers and patients is limited or likely to be misinterpreted; even if interpreters are available, care providers may be unfamiliar with the cultural beliefs and *reasons* patients have for the health care choices they make that appear to be at odds with the prescription of the medical provider; and, systems of care may be more intent on enforcing compliance with treatment than understanding what is happening in the family.

The experience of the Lees is also indicative of the larger issue of competing worldviews in the interactions between health care providers and patients, even if overt language and/or cultural barriers appear to be absent. People who are not a part of the biomedical worldview may arrive at different conclusions about the nature of their health problem and how it should be treated than their medical providers, even if they share in every other way the same social background as their clinicians. For example, two older, English-speaking White men may share an ethnic culture, but one believes that diabetes is caused by overeating, and the other believes that fate or bad luck is the real reason people become diabetic. In this example, these two men may have entirely different responses to the same disease and health treatment plan, despite their similarities in cultural and language backgrounds. We will return to this idea of worldview later in this chapter when we discuss ways to improve adherence in treatment.

CHALLENGES TO ADHERENCE IN SAFETY-NET SETTINGS

As we have noted, adherence is a transactional process between patients and health care providers. To implement a behavior change (taking a medication, changing a habit, and carrying out a new action) requires the *motivation* and *capacity* to carry out the change (Martin, Haskard-Zolnierek, & DiMatteo, 2010). Motivation suggests an internal recognition that change is required, while capacity includes both the internal and external resources necessary to take action. For example, when a person is diagnosed with HIV, they often start on a complex medication regimen. Some people who start on multiple medications may not feel ill and may not believe that the medicines are important for their health; in other words, they may lack motivation to adhere. Other people may believe they need the medication to maintain their health, but are unable to take their medications on the correct schedule, may not have the understanding of how to take their medications, or may lack the financial resources to obtain all their medications on a consistent basis. They lack the capacity to adhere. Health care providers have many opportunities to help patients understand, plan for, and adjust their adherence to prescribed changes, but, for reasons we will discuss, they may not be able to assist the patient in developing adherence.

Acceptance of therapeutic interventions and adherence to plans of care is an issue that cuts across all sectors of the health care system, and is not confined to hospitals and clinics serving the poor and other marginalized populations. Rich and poor patients alike misunderstand, evade, and undermine the best intentions of care providers. Health care professionals, both intentionally and unintentionally, may engage in practices that diminish patient trust and willingness to divulge the difficulties they are experiencing in coping with their health conditions. Health systems make more or less effort to serve challenging patient populations. Some reasons for nonadherence are common across groups, but sometimes adherence issues arise for reasons that are distinctly reflective of poverty, marginalization, and social position.

Although adherence is an issue that is felt across the health care system, it is particularly prominent in safety-net settings. By virtue of their status as providers of "last resort," practitioners in health care safety-net settings are more likely to see clients who are poor, and therefore may not have the financial or other resources needed to comply with treatment plans; who have limited English communication skills and are within institutions that sometimes do not have cultural interpreter resources; are members of racial and ethnic minority groups who have historic reasons for distrusting what are usually seen as "White" service systems; or who have conditions such as serious mental illness or substance abuse where adherence to health treatment plans may be more problematic. As a result, the issue of adherence is a central one within the health care safety-net.

In addition, because of their unstable funding situation (as discussed in Chapter 1), institutions within the health care safety-net are often themselves resource poor. Access to the newest technology, such as patient information management systems that automatically produce reminders for patients to promote adherence to treatment, may not be available. Given their shortage of financial resources, many safety-net systems may not be able to offer health care providers the time or support services necessary to work effectively with patients and families. Next, we look more closely at patient and provider factors that affect adherence within safety-net systems.

Patient-Related Factors

As has been discussed in previous chapters, adverse conditions such as poverty are unequally distributed in society and constitute "fundamental causes" of illness (Link & Phelan, 1995). More advantaged groups have access to resources such as money, knowledge, prestige, and social connections that protect their health (Phelan, Link, & Tehranifar, 2010), all of which are forms of "capital," or something symbolic or material that has value to human life. The idea of cultural health capital draws on the larger theory of capital as articulated by French sociologist Pierre Bourdieu. He describes three forms of capital: economic capital or material resources such as money and property; social capital, the networks of people and social relationships that provide both material and intangible resources (such as social connections); and cultural capital, the knowledge, values, and attitudes that are associated with various social statuses (Bourdieu, 1986). For example, hospitals constitute a "field," which is a "set of objective, historical relations between positions anchored in certain forms of power" (Bourdieu & Wacquant, 1992, p. 16). Hospitals operate with certain financial resources (economic capital), employ networks of individuals of varying levels of power within the institution (social capital), and who have levels of knowledge that have differing value within the system (cultural capital). Being able to diagnose a medical problem is more highly valued (and monetarily rewarded) than providing care for the person with that problem, or being the person with the problem.

Cultural *health* capital draws from this theoretical background, but is specifically focused on the forms of capital (economic, social, and cultural) necessary to successfully navigate medical systems. It is the "socially transmitted and differentially distributed skills and resources . . . critical to the ability to effectively engage and communicate" with health care providers (Shim, 2010, p. 1). These cultural health abilities include knowledge of medical vocabulary, understanding what information is relevant to health providers, skills to communicate in a medically intelligible and efficient manner, and an orientation toward the future that promotes adherence to medical treatment. People with high cultural health capital are easily engaged, knowledgeable, eager to address their health problems, and have the skills and resources to do so—in short, the kinds of patients most people enjoy working with. People with low cultural health capital may not "fit" in typical health care schedules, need more time and patience in order to transmit information and ensure that it has been understood, may not believe that behavior change is possible or desirable, and often lack the material, that is, financial resources, to implement a health treatment plan—they are the "difficult" patients in the health care system.

Cultural health capital is not usually consciously acquired, but arises from one's position in the social hierarchy and the general styles or habits of action that are tied to social position. Unlike financial capital, cultural health capital is not usually directly sought out by people outside the health care system, but is the product of social connections, educational background, and other experiences. The habits instilled by different forms of cultural health capital include "common sense" notions about what is good and valuable in terms of health behavior. Within medical systems, cultural health capital is dynamic—health care providers can contribute to their patients' acquisition of cultural health capital, given the time and inclination. The accumulation of skills associated with high cultural health capital are "intrinsically social and relational in their origin, [but] *are perceived to be* individual in their accumulation and expression" (emphasis in the original) (Shim, 2010, p. 5). In other words, the forces that create "easy" and "difficult" clients are products of the larger social structures that shape behavior, but many times individual patients are perceived as the source of problems.

Like obtaining any form of symbolic or material capital, the ability to acquire cultural health capital is embedded within systems of social inequality, favoring people with access to more wealth, better education, or other social resources. Patients within the health care safety net are more likely to have lower levels of cultural health capital, just as they are more likely to have lower levels of financial capital. A higher proportion of patients within these systems will need increased assistance to develop their ability to effectively negotiate their care with health providers, and to successfully implement agreed upon treatment interventions. Unfortunately, health care safety-net systems are among those that have the fewest resources (including staffing) to support patients and providers trying to create the conditions most likely to lead to successful patient outcomes (Shim, 2010).

Health literacy is a component of cultural health capital that specifically addresses the "degree to which individuals have the capacity to obtain, process, and understand basic health information and services needed to make appropriate health decisions" (Ratzan & Parker, 2000, p. vi). Almost half of the U.S. population is unable to perform reading or math tasks necessary to carry out health care treatment (Foust, 2007). People with lower functional health literacy have poorer health overall, less adherence to prescribed treatment plans, make more serious medication errors because of their inability to read prescription labels, and more often use the emergency department to receive primary care (Foust, 2007). Adherence is more challenging when a patient has low health literacy because these patients have difficulty with recall of unfamiliar information and are less able to ask questions within the language of the environment (Alexander, Sleath, Golin, & Kalinowski, 2006). People of color, immigrants, and those who are poor are more likely to have inadequate health literacy (Institute of Medicine, 2004); these same groups are disproportionately represented among the clientele of the health care safety-net system.

Provider Factors

Health care providers have considerable influence in helping patients to understand and respond to their health conditions and behaviors. Clinicians teach about illness self-management and health-promoting behaviors (Goldstein, DePue, & Kazura, 2009) and, as such, are valued guides to the landscape of the human body. Effective clinicians take responsibility for ensuring that patients understand what the provider has communicated, view adherence as a skill to be learned, and anticipate problems the patient might have with engaging in the treatment plan (Alexander et al., 2006; Levensky & O'Donohue, 2006). For instance, communication theory indicates that the most effective way to ensure that information has been transmitted between two people is to ask the person hearing the information to repeat their understanding in their own words (Foust, 2007), but studies of communication in medical interviews show that this technique is not frequently used (Schwartzberg, Cowett, VanGeest, & Wolf, 2007). In addition, clinicians spend relatively little time in clinical interviews assessing patient adherence strategies (Schwartzberg et al., 2007). Patients may adhere to the treatment plan while symptomatic, but may discontinue treatment once they feel better; they may go on regimen "holidays"; or never initiate the treatment in the first place (Reickert, 2006). By understanding the pattern of the patient's adherence choices, new opportunities for communication about the health condition, the treatment plan, and the patient's lifeworld context may be uncovered.

Unfortunately, providers regularly miss opportunities to address long-term health risk behaviors associated with chronic illness such as weight management or substance use in favor of approaches that focus on acute problems in the present moment. One factor in the reluctance of health care providers to promote health behavior change may be providers' tendency to measure their own success in getting patients to "final outcomes" such as abstinence, rather than realizing that behavior change happens over time and has many starts and stops (Goldstein et al., 2009). For example, people who successfully stop smoking have often tried to quit several times before they reach their goal (U.S. Department of Health and Human Services, 2010). Behavior change rarely happens on the first effort. The more awareness health providers have of typical behavior change processes, the more helpful they can be to patients who become demoralized as their initial efforts are not immediately successful.

Modern medicine has become more technologically sophisticated, but it has been increasingly critiqued for overlooking the importance of the healing relationship. In some environments, this has led researchers to suggest that modern health providers treat machines (i.e., the technology providing clinical information) rather than people (Almerud, 2008; Barnard & Sandelowski, 2001). Even in noncritical care situations, clinical interviews are overtly structured in ways that limit patients' opportunities to tell their stories and build relationships with their health care providers. For example, most clinical interviews are composed of a series of questions from health care providers, and frequent provider interruptions of patients if they stray from the interview agenda of presenting what the provider sees as clinically relevant information (Clark & Mishler, 1992). These actions on the part of providers prevent patients from sharing their stories in ways that reflect their own understanding of their illness, information that is critical to understanding patients' rationales for nonadherence. Eliciting more of the patient's experience and responding empathetically to these revelations may actually improve physiological control of disease (Rodriguez-Gomez & Salas-Serrano, 2006).

As people intrinsically interested in health and devoted to caring for our patients, health care providers may be at a loss to understand and respond to patients who do not follow through on treatment plans. The divide between "us" and "them" can seem wide, but this distance may be lessened if health care professionals consider the ways in which they too do not adhere to recommendations.

For example, a body of literature has arisen that focuses on provider adherence to clinical practice guidelines. Clinical practice guidelines are intended to improve the quality and consistency of care to patients and are developed based on research evidence and the consensus of experts in the field (Weinberger & Salz, 2006). As shown in Table 9.3, the reasons for provider nonadherence to clinical guidelines often mirror reasons that patients give for not following through on treatment plans. These reasons include knowledge, skill, resource deficits, and attitudinal barriers to change. By looking at parallels between the experiences of health care providers and patients, it is possible for the "professional" to gain insight into the experiences of the "patient." This self-reflective process can enhance the development of understanding on the part of the health care provider (Miller, 2004) and help practitioners to respond empathetically to patient confusion, frustration, and resource problems, as we share the problems our clients experience.

TABLE 9.3
Parallels Between Patient and Provider Experiences With Adherence

PROVIDER REASONS FOR NONADHERENCE TO CLINICAL TREATMENT GUIDELINES[a]	PATIENT REASONS FOR NONADHERENCE TO MEDICAL TREATMENTS
Knowledge Deficits	
Lack of awareness of guidelines	Lack of information about illness or condition and its treatment
Inconsistency across guidelines creates confusion	Differing opinions among valued referents (medical provider, family, faith community, etc.) create confusion
Attitudinal Barriers	
Viewing guidelines as "cookbooks," which are too rigid for use in real life	Viewing health treatment plan as a suggestion to be modified based on lifeworld experiences
Adhering to guidelines will not lead to desired outcome	Adhering to treatment plan does not improve the patient's condition or is not aligned with the patient's beliefs
Skills/Resource Deficits	
Provider cannot perform what is required by the clinical guideline	Patient cannot do what is required by the treatment plan
Provider does not have the resources to implement the clinical guideline	Patient does not have the resources to implement the treatment plan

[a] From Cabana et al. (1999) and Weinberger and Salz (2006).

EXEMPLARS OF SPECIAL ADHERENCE-RELATED NEEDS

As we have stated earlier, adherence is a transactional process between patients and their health care providers, which is further affected by the organizational issues of the safety-net health care system. Adherence issues are particularly prominent within the safety-net because this system serves a disproportionate number of people who have special adherence-related needs. Various research studies have documented differences in adherence based on age, homelessness, substance abuse, and poverty (Bosworth et al., 2006). For example, age affects adherence in the management of diabetes both in adolescence and in old age. Adolescents are more likely to be noncompliant with insulin administration than younger children (Cramer, 2004). Among adolescents, adherence is often related to emerging developmental tasks in the transitions between childhood, adolescence, and young adulthood, during which responsibility for diabetes management is transferred from a parent or guardian to the adolescent/young adult (Dovey-Pearce, Hurrell, May, Walker, & Doherty, 2005). In the case of an older adult, diabetes management is often accompanied by the challenge of managing the medication regimes for multiple chronic conditions (Williams, Manias, & Walker, 2008).

In this section, we provide a deeper exploration of three groups with special adherence-related needs that we use as exemplars of the complex ways in which social location and diagnosis affect the clinical encounter and adherence behaviors. All three of these groups are disproportionately overrepresented in safety-net settings and have adherence-related struggles because of a complex set of historical and socioeconomic factors. These groups provide examples of the kinds of issues faced by populations at risk for being in the safety-net health care system, examples that we hope readers will extrapolate from when working with other populations (such as the homeless, elderly, or others) who are also more likely to be served in safety-net settings and who might encounter adherence-related issues.

Racial and Ethnic Minorities

People of color experience a disproportionate burden of chronic disease because of the combination of structural forces such as racism and poverty, and certain health behaviors (Williams & Mohammed, 2009). As an example of the association between racism and health, Chae and Walters (2009) found that persons who report higher levels of racial discrimination reported more pain, impairment, and over-all poorer health. People of color may distrust health messages that come from outside their communities (Whitt-Glover, Beech, Jackson, Loftin-Bell, & Mount, 2009) because of the legacy of discriminatory behavior they have experienced. Many people are aware of the Tuskegee experiments in which almost 400 African American men were not treated for syphilis when they could have been. By the end of the 40-year experiment, almost half of the men had died of syphilis or related conditions and dozens of women and children were also infected with the disease after treatment with penicillin became standard in the 1950s (Reverby, 2009). Scholarship among American Indian/Alaska Native communities points to similar conflicts with biomedical providers such as forced sterilization of Native women by the Indian Health Service during the 1970s (Lawrence, 2000). In the contemporary health care system, African Americans and other minorities experience more misdiagnoses and inappropriate services that may lead these groups to perceive their care as ineffective (Rodriguez-Gomez & Salas-Serrano, 2006).

In addition to historical reasons for marginalization and distrust that affect their relationships with health care institutions, people of color also experience a disproportionate number of health behaviors associated with poor health. For example, African Americans, Latinos, and Native Americans are all at risk for poor nutrition as a result of poverty, but also from living in "food deserts," or geographical areas in which access to healthy, nutritious food is limited (Walker, Kean, & Burke, 2010). These same groups are also more likely to live in neighborhoods with increased rates of violence, making physical exercise more difficult. Poor nutrition and physical inactivity can lead to obesity, which is further linked to heart conditions, cancer, and diabetes (U.S. Department of Health and Human Services, 2001). Obesity is highest among African Americans and American Indians/Alaska Natives, particularly women (Whitt-Glover et al., 2009). Smoking is another health risk behavior deeply associated with poverty—about one-third of all people who smoke live below the poverty line (Husten & Jackson, 2004). American Indians/Alaska Natives have the highest rate of cigarette smoking among racial and ethnic groups (Whitt-Glover et al., 2009). These examples point to the fact that certain barriers to adherence are more prevalent among racial and ethnic minorities, largely because of poverty and the stress it induces. Adherence is affected by other obstacles that people of color are more likely to experience including a lack of access to high-quality, affordable health care; difficulty in securing health-promoting resources; multiple role obligations, particularly as caregivers both within and outside the home; and higher numbers of stressful life events such as death, imprisonment, and unemployment (Whitt-Glover et al., 2009). Taken together, this information suggests that adherence to health-promoting lifestyle change is more problematic for members of racial and ethnic minority communities.

Immigrants

Immigrants make up a significant and growing part of the population in the United States and often do not possess the characteristics that are associated with a higher likelihood of adherence to conventional approaches to treatment: English language literacy, health insurance, and a cultural understanding and affinity with Western medicine. According to the Census Bureau, there are 38.5 million immigrants in the United States; 20% of the U.S. population are either immigrants or the children of immigrants (U.S. Census Bureau, 2009). In contrast to the mid-1900s when most immigrants came from European countries, in the past 30 years, most immigrants now come from Latin American countries, including Mexico (Center for Immigration Studies, 2007). In some areas of the United States, people who speak a language other than English are the majority, or close to the majority (Kritz, 2010).

Many health care institutions do not have diverse clinical staffs, or easily accessible language interpreters and cultural brokers available during health care transactions. As was mentioned in Chapter 1, some urban locations have dozens of language communities. Safety-net health care providers are more likely to serve these communities, in part because immigrants are less likely to have health insurance than native-born persons and also are more likely to fall below the poverty line (U.S. Census Bureau, 2009).

People With Mental Illness

Safety-net health care systems provide a disproportionate share of the mental health treatment in the United States. Historically, state health insurance programs such as Medicaid have not always covered mental health care (Kaiser Family Foundation, n.d.), leaving people who are both poor and mentally ill to seek care through publicly funded systems. People with mental health emergencies, such as being at imminent risk of suicide, or being so disabled by their psychiatric illness as to be unable to function, are often treated first in the emergency department of a safety-net hospital. As noted in Chapter 1, three-quarters of safety-net hospitals have psychiatric emergency units, as compared to fewer than half of non-safety-net settings (Bazzoll, Kang, Hasnain-Wynia, & Lindrooth, 2005). Policy efforts aimed at achieving "mental health parity" (i.e., providing equivalent services for physical and mental health problems) have been incorporated into the Patient Protection and Affordable Care Act, so more resources may become available for mental health treatment in non-safety-net settings in the future.

As a symptom of their illness, people with mental illness often behave in ways that either interfere with their adherence to treatment or reduce a provider's willingness to work with the patient (Beitz & Hall, 2009). For example, conditions such as schizophrenia or bipolar disorder are characterized by patients' lack of insight into aspects of their illness when acutely ill—they may believe that delusions are true or that manic behaviors are normal (Mahadun & Marshall, 2008). With other mental disorders, people may be more emotionally volatile, have difficulty with relationships, or feel hopeless about change. People with mental illness generally experience a high degree of suffering, which is often disturbing to the people living or working with them. Social psychology research suggests that "When a clinician cares about a patient yet is unable to reduce a patient's suffering, clinicians have a tendency to blame the patient for that suffering" (Beitz & Hall, 2006, p. 402) instead of seeing the suffering the patient experiences as a result of the disorder for which they are seeking treatment. This fundamental cognitive error of blaming the patient and not the disorder (Linehan, 1993) can result in iatrogenic, or provider-caused, harm to the patient as clinicians become more distant and less willing to provide help.

Treatment for mental disorders usually includes a combination of both psychological counseling and psychotropic medication use. National epidemiological studies indicate that fewer than half of people with a serious mental illness received any treatment for that illness in the previous year (Kessler et al., 2001). Of patients prescribed medications, one-third to one-half did not take the psychotropic medication as prescribed (Akincigil et al., 2007; Calhoun & Butterfield, 2006; Gianfrancesco, Sajatovic, Rajagopalan, & Wang, 2008). The medications used to treat mental illnesses often have serious and sometimes irreversible side effects. For example, antipsychotic medications have adverse neurological effects known as extrapyramidal symptoms. These symptoms may include muscular tics, tremors, or involuntary movements of the face. Nonadherence to psychotropic medication is associated with increased hospitalization and mortality (Calhoun & Butterfield, 2006).

Serious mental illness is also associated with nonadherence to treatment for physical health disorders. Depression and anxiety are two of the most common mental illnesses, and each has been studied for its effects on adherence in a variety of illnesses. For example, depression has been associated with nonadherence in HIV/AIDS (Starace et al., 2002), cancer (Spiegel & Giese-Davis, 2003), diabetes (Gonzalez et al., 2007), and cardiac rehabilitation (McGrady, McGinnis, Bandehop, Bentle, & Rajput, 2009). In a meta-analysis of the effects of depression and anxiety on adherence, DiMatteo, Lepper, and Croghan (2000) found that depression substantially increased the likelihood of nonadherence to medication regimens across a variety of illnesses, whereas anxiety had only a minimal effect. Being able to recognize and treat mental illness is important for both mental and physical health outcomes.

Within American medical systems, people with serious mental illness remain one of the most highly stigmatized groups, as noted in our previous discussion of "gomers" (patients whom the provider wants to Get Out of My Emergency Room) and "difficult" patients. Often people with serious mental illness are stigmatized as "gomers" because their conditions may be chronic and difficult to treat effectively and their behaviors unusual or strange. Health care providers in the safety-net care system must develop advanced skills for working with clients with serious mental health problems, even if their specialization is not in psychiatric care.

APPROACHES THAT IMPROVE ADHERENCE

Since the 1950s, researchers have developed and tested theories to understand how individuals make health behavior changes. Some of the most widely used theories are summarized in Table 9.4 and are discussed more fully elsewhere (see, e.g., Martin et al., 2010). These theories provide general information on health behavior change and help practitioners to concentrate on skills development and communication interventions such as those that focus on underlying beliefs, norms, or motivations that are most likely to support behavior change.

A variety of experimental evaluations of treatment adherence strategies have been reported in the literature in response to various conditions. Table 9.5 summarizes some of the key intervention techniques and their use during the evolution of the treatment relationship.

TABLE 9.4
Behavioral Change Theories Relevant to Adherence to Treatment

THEORY	SUMMARY
Health Belief Model	The likelihood of engaging in a new behavior is a result of how a person perceives his or her susceptibility to illness, the severity of the potential illness, the benefits and barriers to change, self-efficacy, and environmental and demographic factors
Theory of Planned Behavior	Behavior is the result of an intention to change; this intention is influenced by a person's beliefs, norms of meaningful others, and self-efficacy
Transtheoretical Model of Change	Behavior change progresses in a series of stages ranging from precontemplation to contemplation, preparation, action, and maintenance of change
Information Motivation Strategy Model	Health behavior is a product of having information about what change is necessary, the desire to change, and the skills/resources to be able to implement the change

Adapted from Martin et al. (2010).

For example, early on and throughout the period of active treatment, the provider should evaluate how well communication is occurring between the provider and the patient by assessing the patient's knowledge of the condition and treatment plan. As the treatment plan and relationship progress, the provider can assess adherence behavior and, when barriers are anticipated or identified, work with the patient to develop greater knowledge or skills or to address attitudinal barriers. In addition to these general techniques, skills focused on eliciting the patient's cultural beliefs and motivation to treat the illness, along with approaches that focus on patient–provider communication and systems-level interventions may help improve patient adherence to identified treatment plans.

Culturally Relevant Information Gathering With Patients

A culture clash may exist between the worldview of biomedicine with its focus on mechanistic, individualistic, and materialistic explanations and many patients who are more oriented to spiritual accounts and family or community beliefs about their condition and the appropriate way to treat it. In this sense, health care practitioners treat disease, whereas patients experience illness (Frank, 1991; Kleinman, Eisenbert, &

TABLE 9.5
Evidence-Based Methods to Promote Patient Adherence

When Starting a Treatment Plan

Assess patient's readiness to begin the treatment plan

Assess patient's knowledge of the condition and treatment that is prescribed

Assess that the patient has the resources and skills to carry out the treatment plan

Provide both written and verbal information about the condition and treatment

As Treatment Plan Continues

Ask about adherence in a supportive, nonjudgmental way

Anchor requests for adherence information to short, recent time frames

Assess patterns of adherence

Engage in problem solving when barriers to adherence are identified

When Nonadherence Occurs

Assess degree of agreement between patient and provider in terms of understanding of the condition and the treatment plan

Focus on adherence skills (medication organizers, cues to engage in treatment behavior, etc.)

Increase access to material and psychosocial resources and support

Increase motivation to enact the treatment plan

Maintenance of Treatment Plan

Provide regular follow-up opportunities (email, in person, or over the phone)

Reassess emerging barriers to treatment

Focus on relapse prevention skills

Adapted from Levensky and O'Donohue (2006).

Good, 1978). Medical anthropologists have long taken up the question of how to bridge the communication divide between health care professionals and nonmedically trained patients and family. One of the leading figures in cross-cultural medicine is the psychiatrist and anthropologist Arthur Kleinman. Earlier, we recounted the story of Lia Lee, a Hmong immigrant girl. In reflecting on her situation, Kleinman made the following observations about the cultural differences between Lia and her health providers around the issue of nonadherence:

> First, get rid of the term "compliance." It's a lousy term. It implies moral hegemony. . . . Second, instead of looking at a model of coercion, look at a model of mediation. . . . Remember that a stance of mediation, like a divorce proceeding, requires

compromise on both sides. Decide what's critical and be willing to compromise on everything else. Third, you need to understand that as powerful an influence as [a person's culture] is, the culture of biomedicine is equally powerful. If you can't see that your own culture has its own set of interests, emotions, and biases, how can you expect to deal successfully with someone else's culture? (Fadiman, 1997, p. 261)

In this passage, Kleinman is reflecting on how medical terminology implies a certain worldview that is believed to be more legitimate and real than that of nonmedical actors, that is, a "moral hegemony." From a cross-cultural point of view, the important task is to come to some shared sense of what is most important to advance the health of the patient.

For over three decades, Kleinman has advocated for an approach to patients that takes into account their beliefs and ideas about their illness or condition. Table 9.6 presents a series of questions that Kleinman has suggested be asked of patients to explore their conceptualization of their condition. These questions allow the clinician to explore the patient's beliefs about illness and their concerns about treatment in a nonjudgmental, supportive fashion. Successful treatment depends upon a shared understanding of the problem at hand and what will be done about it. For this understanding to be shared, the clinician must become familiar with the patient's feelings, beliefs, and concerns about the condition; know what the patient's family thinks about the condition and treatment plan; and understand how the patient's community and social context will influence treatment decisions (Goldstein et al., 2009).

TABLE 9.6
Assessing Cultural Beliefs About Health Conditions and Treatment

1. What do you think has caused your problem?
2. Why do you think it started when it did?
3. What do you think your sickness does to you? How does it work?
4. How severe is your sickness? Will it have a short or long course?
5. What kind of treatment do you think you should receive?
6. What are the most important results you hope to receive from this treatment?
7. What are the chief problems your sickness has caused for you?
8. What do you fear most about your sickness?

Adapted from Kleinman et al. (1978).

Cross-cultural communication builds upon the abundant literature in other areas of health care that advocates a "patient-centered" style of communication. In contrast to medical communication models that focus on the expertise of the health care practitioner, patient-centered communication explores the disease and illness experience from the point of view of the patient, understands the illness in the context of the whole person, determines patients' goals and concerns, provides information in a way that the patient can understand, and facilitates patient and provider negotiation of a treatment regimen (Stewart et al., 2000). With this kind of deeper understanding, it becomes more possible to develop a collaborative treatment plan.

Understanding and Increasing Patient Motivation for Change

Change is developmental—a person acquires competence in new activities in a process that evolves over the course of an illness or condition (Goldstein et al., 2009). People are often able to make change initially, but have difficulty maintaining these changes over time. Sustaining change is not easy! Patients have to maintain behavior changes (such as stopping smoking) over long periods of time to have this change make a difference to overall health (Bowen & Boehmer, 2009).

Because change is developmental, it is important to match clinical interventions to the patient's current level of commitment and ability. Prochaska and colleagues (see Prochaska, Norcross, & DiClemente, 1994; Prochaska, Wright, & Velicer, 2008) have developed a stage-based theory of change known as the Transtheoretical Model that reflects various orientations to change (see Table 9.7). From this perspective, expecting a patient to be in "action" (i.e., ready to implement a treatment plan) when a health problem occurs may be unrealistic.

TABLE 9.7
Stages of Change

Precontemplation: Not thinking about change, may not believe the change is necessary, may not feel able to make the change
Contemplation: Weighing benefits and costs of behavior and the proposed change
Preparation: Experimenting with small changes
Action: Taking a definitive action to change
Maintenance of change: Maintaining new behavior over time

Adapted from Prochaska et al. (1994).

A clinician can be most effective in addressing issues of adherence to treatment plans by assessing the patient's readiness to change, and matching interventions to the patient's particular stage in the change process.

When requesting behavior changes, even those that may appear simple from the outside such as medication taking, it is important to assess with the patient his or her own motivation (or lack thereof) for making the change suggested by the clinician. Motivational interviewing (MI; Miller & Rollnick, 1991; Rollnick, Miller, & Butler, 2008) is an empirically based, patient-centered communication intervention designed to explore and increase a patient's commitment to changing behaviors. Originally developed to help engage people with addiction problems in treatment, MI is particularly helpful in work with people in the precontemplation or contemplation stages of change—that is, those who aren't sure about change such as people who may not adhere to a prescribed treatment plan.

The ultimate goal of MI is to help the patient to become more convinced of the importance of the change and of their ability to enact it. Instead of arguing with the patient or becoming frustrated when the patient does not follow a prescribed plan, MI relies on reflective listening, and the ability to hear discrepancies between the patient's goals and what the patient is doing. MI works to increase awareness of ambivalence about change within a context that supports the patient's ultimate right to choose his or her own path. Clinicians skilled in this communication intervention provide information about what the risks of change are as well as the value of change, and seek to explore the patient's own reasoning about what is the stronger priority—the risk or reward of behavior change. Practitioners also work to enhance a patient's sense of self-confidence or self-efficacy in his or her ability to change by reviewing past efforts where the patient was successful at change, encouraging small steps that can lead to success rather than a "final outcome" approach to change, and teach problem-solving skills when obstacles to change are encountered.

Provider Communication Strategies

Clinicians, when frustrated by nonadherent behaviors of a patient, may translate their negative emotions into erroneous negative assumptions about the client. Health care professionals may come to believe that individual patients don't care about their health, or that people from already stigmatized groups (such as the mentally ill) don't learn from experience. Attitudes and beliefs are powerful antecedents to anyone's behavior (Martin et al., 2010). In the case of health care providers, frustration and negative assumptions may lead to less empathetic communication and other behaviors that affect the quality of care.

Although patients ultimately make the choices they make, the way the provider offers information, frames behavior change, and addresses adherence issues can be critical to whether the patient adopts the recommended treatment plan. Research indicates that there is an association between clinician demonstration of empathy for the patient as indicated by the clinician responding to, supporting, and respecting the patient's feelings and whether the patient adheres to the treatment plan (Goldstein et al., 2009). Particularly in regard to chronic conditions, clinicians need core competencies to support patient self-management, including relationship building, information sharing, collaborative goal setting, action planning, skills building, and problem solving.

Health care practitioners are responsible for the transmission of knowledge about a health condition and a treatment plan to the patient. Certain techniques are more likely to improve patient retention and acceptance of information. For example, patients had the highest adherence to treatment when they were provided information about their health condition and a treatment plan in writing and verbally by the clinician (Oser, 2006), *and* when the practitioner assessed the patient's comprehension of the illness and treatment regimen (Alexander et al., 2006). Given the health literacy concerns of patients within the safety-net health care systems, written materials should use language at less than a fifth-grade level; this is equivalent to writing that does not include words longer than two syllables, sentences longer than seven words, and paragraphs longer than seven lines (Foust, 2007).

Mental health clinicians suggest that health care providers working with clients with adherence problems or difficult behaviors "acknowledge and describe the problematic behavior and [the provider's] responses to it, generate hypotheses about the cause of the behavior, and address it openly and directly with patients, all without judging the behavior as good or bad" (Beitz & Hall, 2009, p. 403). For example, a provider may have a belief such as "this client is noncompliant." Reframing this thought as a nonjudgmental description might result in a sentence like, "this patient misses appointments, does not take prescribed medications, and I feel frustrated about this behavior "(Beitz & Hall, 2009). Two possible hypotheses that explain this behavior might be that the patient does not understand the reason for the treatment plan or that the patient disagrees with the plan. Each of these hypotheses could be evaluated with the client, in addition to asking the patient to hypothesize about the reason for the behavior. To be most effective with clients with difficult behaviors, health care providers must conceptualize these behaviors as part of the reason the patient is there—they are part of the patient's underlying problem, and as such, represent significant targets for clinical intervention. Psychologist Marsha Linehan advises clinicians to "adopt the perspective that, at all times, *patients are doing the best they can* [and] . . . *they want to improve*" (Linehan, 1993, p. 102). This nonjudgmental approach can help clinicians to take an active role in supporting patients to develop skills in adherence.

Health System Structures

Up to this point, we have focused on techniques practitioners in safety-net settings can use within these settings to promote adherence to treatment plans among their patients. However, as we noted at the beginning of this chapter, adherence is a transactional process that is deeply influenced by the environmental system of care. Health care systems, even those that primarily serve a safety-net population, do not reflect the communities where care is provided. Although we have stated that all transactions between members of the medical establishment and those outside of it constitute cross-cultural interactions, communication is made more difficult when cultural groups are not reflected within the health care workforce. For example, among physicians, "in 2000, 1.6% of medical students and 5.5% of medical school faculty were from American Indian, Latino/a, and African American groups, although these traditionally underserved groups collectively represent greater than 25% of the population in the United States" (Whitt-Glover et al., 2009, p. 597). Until populations within the country are equally reflected within the workforce of health care institutions, health systems will have to make concerted efforts to provide culturally congruent care to their clientele that supports patient acceptance and adherence to treatment plans.

Table 9.8 describes a core set of techniques that promote and support culturally competent care within health care settings. These techniques have been compiled by researchers with the Agency for Healthcare Research and Quality and are reflected in the guidelines published by the Joint Commission on Accreditation of Healthcare Organizations (Joint Commission, 2010). By increasing the systemic resources to support work with people who are not members of the biomedical subculture,

TABLE 9.8
Cultural Competency Techniques at the Health Care System Level

1. Provide interpreter services
2. Recruit and retain a culturally diverse staff
3. Train all staff in cultural awareness, knowledge, and skills
4. Coordinate care with traditional healers when patients utilize them
5. Use community-based health workers to connect populations to health service systems
6. Provide information about culturally congruent health promotion practices
7. Include family and community members in health care decision making at the patient's request
8. Provide opportunities for immersion experiences in other cultures
9. Provide administrative and organizational accommodations to promote service delivery

Adapted from Brach and Fraserirector (2000).

these institutional practices reflect an ongoing commitment to working with diverse populations that will have differing approaches to adherence-related concerns.

CONCLUSION

Adherence to health care treatment plans is a complex, multifaceted process that operates at patient, provider, and system levels. Safety-net systems are chronically under-resourced, and therefore have fewer systemic tools available to help promote patient adherence to care. Patients who have multiple challenges to adherence are also more likely to be clients of safety-net health care systems. As other authors have noted, "if we want to change behavioral patterns that lead to a negative health outcome, we need to consider the larger forces at play in shaping and influencing our individual choices and, ultimately, our health" (Bowen & Boehmer, 2009, p. 789). These larger forces are at play not only in the lives of our patients, but also within the patient–provider relationship, and the settings in which health care professionals provide care.

Promoting adherence and dealing effectively with nonadherence entail the application of sophisticated diagnostic skills and a deliberative treatment strategy that incorporates the considerations identified in this chapter. With deeper engagement in the underlying issues that are at play at patient, provider, and system levels, practitioners can resist the temptation to view nonadherence as a frustrating "patient" issue. By framing nonadherence as a normative and intriguing problem to be addressed through the clinical encounter, practitioners can open dialogues with their patients that enhance the exchange of cultural information, advance understanding of the health condition, promote motivation for change, and provide support for the difficulties involved in changing behavior.

REFERENCES

Akincigil, A., Bowblis, J. R., Levin, C., Walkup, J. T., Jan, S., & Crystal, S. (2007). Adherence to antidepressant treatment among privately insured patients diagnosed with depression. *Medical Care, 45*, 363–369.

Alexander, S. C., Sleath, B., Golin, C. E., & Kalinowski, C. T. (2006). Provider-patient communication and treatment adherence. In H. B. Bosworth, E. Z. Oddone, & M. Weinberger (Eds.), *Patient treatment adherence concepts, interventions and measurement* (pp. 329–372). Mahway, NJ: Lawrence Erlbaum Associates.

Almerud, S. (2008). The meaning of technology in intensive care. *Connect: The World of Critical Care Nursing, 6,* 39–43.

Anstrom, K. J., Weinfurt, K. P., & Allen, A. S. (2006). Estimating causal effects in randomized studies with imperfect adherence: Conceptual and statistical foundations. In H. B. Bosworth, E. Z. Oddone, & M. Weinberger (Eds.), *Patient treatment adherence concepts, interventions and measurement* (pp. 453–474). Mahway, NJ: Lawrence Erlbaum Associates.

Barnard, A., & Sandelowski, M. (2001). Technology and humane nursing care: (Ir)reconcilable or invented difference? *Journal of Advanced Nursing, 34,* 367–375.

Bazzoll, G. J., Kang, R., Hasnain-Wynia, R., & Lindrooth, R. C. (2005). An update on safety-net hospitals: Coping with the late 1990s and early 2000s. *Health Affairs, 24*, 1047–1056.

Beitz, K., & Hall, M. L. R. (2009). Treatment adherence in difficult (personality disordered) patients. In S. A. Shumaker, J. K., Ockene, & K. A. Reickert (Eds.), *The handbook of health behavior change* (3rd ed., pp. 401–415). New York, NY: Springer Publishing.

Bosch-Capblanch, X., Abba, K., Prictor, M., & Garner, P. (2007). Contracts between patients and health care practitioners for improving patients' adherence to treatment, prevention and health promotion activities. *Cochrane Database of Systematic Reviews, 2.* doi: 10.1002/14651858.CDC004808.pub3

Boston Women's Health Collective. (2005). *Our Bodies, Our Selves.* New York, NY: Touchstone Publishing.

Bosworth, H. B., Weinberger, M., & Oddone, E. Z. (2006). Introduction. In H. B. Bosworth, E. Z. Oddone, & M. Weinberger (Eds.), *Patient treatment adherence concepts, interventions and measurement* (pp. 3–12). Mahway, NJ: Lawrence Erlbaum Associates.

Bourdieu, P. (1986). The forms of capital. In J. G. Richardson (Ed.), *Handbook for theory and research for the sociology of education* (pp. 241–258). Westport, CT: Greenwood Press.

Bourdieu, P., & Wacquant, L. J. D. (1992). *An invitation to reflexive sociology.* Chicago, IL: University of Chicago Press.

Bowen, D. J., & Boehmer, U. (2009). Lessons learned: What we know doesn't work and what we shouldn't repeat. In S. A. Shumaker, J. K. Ockene, & K. A. Reickert (Eds.), *The handbook of health behavior change* (3rd ed., pp. 785–793). New York, NY: Springer Publishing.

Brach, C., & Fraserirector, I. (2000). Can cultural competence reduce racial and ethnic health disparities? A review and conceptual model. *Medical Care & Research, 57,* 181–217.

Cabana, M. D., Rand, C. S., Powe, N. R., Wu, A. W., Wilson, M. H., Abboud, P. A. C., Rubin, H. R. (1999). Why don't physicians follow clinical practice guidelines? A framework for improvement. *Journal of the American Medical Association, 282,* 1458–1465.

Calhoun, P. S., & Butterfield, M. I. (2006). Treatment adherence among individuals with severe mental illness. In H. B. Bosworth, E. Z. Oddone, & M. Weinberger (Eds.), *Patient treatment adherence concepts, interventions and measurement* (pp. 307–328). Mahway, NJ: Lawrence Erlbaum Associates.

Center for Immigration Studies. (2007). Immigrants in the United States, 2007: A profile of America's foreign-born population. Retrieved from http://www.cis.org/articles/2007/back1007.html

Centers for Disease Control. (2010). *FastStats: Death and mortality.* Retrieved from http://www.cdc.gov/nchs/fastats/deaths.htm

Chae, D., & Walters, K. L. (2009). Racial discrimination and racial identity attitudes in relation to self-rated health and physical pain and impairment among Two-Spirit American Indians/Alaska Natives. *American Journal of Public Health, 99*(s1), s144–s151.

Clark, J. A., & Mishler, E. G. (1992). Attending to patients' stories: Reframing the clinical task. *Sociology of Health and Illness, 14,* 344–372.

Committee on Quality Health Care in America, Institute of Medicine. (2001). *Crossing the quality chasm: A new health system for the 21st century.* Washington, DC: National Academies Press.

Cramer, J. A. (2004). A systematic review of adherence with medications for diabetes. *Diabetes Care, 27*(5), 1218–1224.

Davies, P., Taylor, F., Beswick, A., Wise, F., Moxham, T., Rees, K., & Ebrahim, S. (2010). Promoting patient uptake and adherence in cardiac rehabilitation. *Cochrane Database of Systematic Reviews, 7.* doi: 10.1002/14651858.CD007131 .pub2

DiMatteo, M. R., Lepper, H. S., & Croghan, T. W. (2000). Depression is a risk factor for noncompliance with treatment: Meta-analysis of the effects of anxiety and depression on patient adherence. *Archives of Internal Medicine, 160,* 2101–2107.

Dovey-Pearce, G., Hurrell, R., May, C., Walker, C., & Doherty, Y. (2005). Young adults? (16–25 years) suggestions for providing developmentally appropriate diabetes services: A qualitative study. *Health & Social Care in the Community, 13*(5), 409–419.

Duncan, E., Best, C., & Hagen, S. (2010). Shared decision making interventions for people with mental health conditions. *Cochrane Database of Systematic Reviews, 1.* doi: 10.1002/14651858.CD007297.pub2

Fadiman, A. (1997). *The spirit catches you and you fall down: A Hmong child, her American doctors, and the collision of two cultures.* New York, NY: Farrar, Straus and Giroux.

Foust, R. F. (2007). *Engagement strategies in health and disease management: Best practices for boosting participation.* Marblehead, MA: HCPro, Inc.

Frank, A. (1991). *At the will of the body: Reflections on illness.* New York, NY: Houghton Mifflin.

Gianfrancesco, F. D., Sajatovic, M., Rajagopalan, K., & Wang, R. H. (2008). Antipsychotic treatment adherence and associated mental health care use among individuals with bipolar disorder. *Clinical Therapeutics, 30,* 1358–1374.

Gibbons, A. (1992). Exploring new strategies to fight drug-resistant microbes. *Science, 257,* 1036–1038.

Goldstein, M. G., DePue, J., & Kazura, A. N. (2009). Models of provider-patient interaction and shared decision making. In S. A. Shumaker, J. K. Ockene, & K. A. Reickert (Eds.), *The handbook of health behavior change* (3rd ed., pp. 107–125). New York, NY: Springer Publishing.

Gonzalez, J. S., Safren, S. A., Cagliero, E., Wexler, D. J., Delahanty, L., Wittenberg, E., . . . Grant, R. W. (2007). Depression, self-care and medication adherence in type 2 diabetes: Relationships across the full range of symptom severity. *Diabetes Care, 30,* 2222–2227.

Halpern, V., Grimes, D. A., Lopez, L. M., & Gallo, M. F. (2006). Strategies to improve adherence and acceptability of hormonal methods of contraception. *Cochrane Database of Systematic Reviews, 1.* doi: 10.1002/14651858.CD004317.pub3

Haynes, B., McDonald, H., Garg, A. X., & Montesqieu, P. (2002). Interventions for helping patients follow prescriptions for medications. (Cochrane Review). *The Cochrane Library, Cochrane Database of Systematic Reviews,* (2):CD000011.

Haynes, R. B., McKibbon, K. A., & Kanani, R. (1996). Systematic reviews of randomized trials of interventions to assist patients to follow prescriptions for medications. *Lancet, 348,* 383–386.

Husten, C., & Jackson, K. (2004). Cigarette smoking among adults—United States 2002. *Morbidity and Mortality Weekly, 53,* 427–431.

Infection Control Today. (2005). New research estimates MRSA infections cost U.S. hospitals $3.2 billion–$4.2 billion annually. *Infection Control Today.* Retrieved from http://www.infectioncontroltoday.com/news/2005/05/new-research-estimates-mrsa-infections-cost-u-s-h.aspx

Institute of Medicine. (2004). *Health literacy: A prescription to end confusion.* Washington, DC: National Academies Press.

Joint Commission. (2010). *Advancing effective communication, cultural competence and patient-and family-centered care: A roadmap for hospitals.* Oakbrook Terrace, IL: The Joint Commission.

Jordan, J. L., Holden, M. A., Mason, E. J., & Foster, N. E. (2010). Interventions to improve adherence to exercise for chronic musculoskeletal pain in adults. *Cochrane Database of Systematic Reviews, 1.* doi: 10.1002/14651858.CD005956.pub2

Kaiser Family Foundation. (n.d.). *Medicaid benefits: Online database.* Retrieved from http://medicaidbenefits.kff.org/

Kessler, R. C., Berglund, P. A., Bruce, M. L., Koch, J. R., Laska, E. M., Leaf, P. J., . . . Wang, P. S. (2001). Prevalence and correlates of untreated serious mental illness. *Health Services Research, 36,* 986–1007.

Kleinman, A., Eisenbert, L., & Good, B. (1978). Culture, illness and care: Clinical lessons from anthropologic and cross-cultural research. *Annals of Internal Medicine, 88,* 251–258.

Kritz, F. L. (2010, December 27). Medical interpreters are a patient's right. *Los Angeles Times.* Retrieved from http://articles.latimes.com/2010/dec/27/health/la-he-medical-interpreters-20101227

Laine, C., & Davidoff, F. (1996). Patient-centered medicine: A professional evolution. *Journal of the American Medical Association, 275,* 152–156.

Lawrence, J. (2000). The Indian Health Service and the sterilization of Native American women. *American Indian Quarterly, 24,* 400–419.

Levensky, E. R., & O'Donohue, W. T. (2006). Patient adherence and nonadherence to treatments. In W. T. O'Donahue & E. R. Levensky (Eds.), *Promoting treatment adherence: A practical handbook for health care providers* (pp. 3–14). Thousand Oaks, CA: Sage Publications.

Linehan, M. (1993). *Cognitive-behavioral treatment of borderline personality disorder.* New York, NY: Guilford Press.

Link, B. G., & Phelan, J. C. (1995). Social conditions as fundamental causes of disease. *Journal of Health and Social Behavior, 35*(extra issue), 80–94.

Mahadun, P. N., & Marshall, M. (2008). Insight and treatment attitude in schizophrenia: Comparison of patients on depot and atypical antipsychotics. *The Psychiatrist, 32,* 53–56.

Martin, L. R., Haskard-Zolnierek, K. B., & DiMatteo, M. R. (2010). Understanding behavior change: The theory behind informing, motivating and planning for health. In S. A. Shumaker, J. K. Ockene, & K. A. Reickert (Eds.), *Health behavior change and treatment adherence: Evidence-based guidelines for improving health care* (pp. 3–23). New York, NY: Oxford University Press.

McCloud, M. T. (2010). *Living Well . . . Despite Catchin' Hell*. New York, NY: New Life Publishing.

McGrady, A., McGinnis, R., Bandehop, D., Bentle, M., & Rajput, M. (2009). Effects of depression and anxiety on adherence to cardiac rehabilitation. *Journal of Cardiopulmonary Rehabilitation & Prevention, 29*, 358–364.

Merck. (2008). Hodgkin lymphoma. In *Merck Medical Manual, Online: Home Edition for Patients and Caregivers*. Retrieved from http://www.merckmanuals.com/home/sec14/ch177/ch177b.html

Miller, S. (2004). What's going on? Parallel process and reflective practice in teaching. *Reflective Practice, 5*, 383–393.

Miller, W. R., & Rollnick, S. (1991). *Motivational interviewing: Preparing people to change behaviors.* New York, NY: Guilford Press.

Northrup, C. (2010). *Women's Bodies, Women's Wisdom*. New York: Bantam Books.

Oser, M.L. (2006). *Patient education to promote adherence to treatments*. In W. T. O'Donohue & E.R. Levensky (Eds.), Promoting treatment adherence. (pp. 85–97). New York: Russell Sage Foundation.

Peleg, A. Y., & Paterson, D. L. (2006). Modifying antibiotic prescribing in primary care. *Clinical Infectious Diseases, 42*(9), 1231–1233.

Peterson, A. M., Takiya, L., & Finley, R. (2003). Meta-analysis of trials of interventions to improve medication adherence. *American Journal of Health System Pharmacy, 60*, 657–665.

Phelan, J. C., Link, B. G., &Tehranifar, P. (2010). Social conditions as fundamental causes of health inequalities: Theory, evidence and policy implications. *Journal of Health and Social Behavior, 51*(1 suppl), S28–S40.

Prochaska, J. O., Norcross, J. C., & DiClemente, C. C. (1994). *Changing for good*. New York, NY: Morrow.

Prochaska, J. O., Wright, J. A., & Velicer, W. F. (2008). Evaluating theories of health behavior change: A hierarchy of criteria applied to the Transtheoretical Model. *Applied Psychology: An International Review, 57*, 561–588.

Ratzan, S. C., & Parker, R. M. (2000). Introduction. In C. Selden, M. Zorn, S. Ratzan, & R. Parker (Eds.), *National Library of Medicine current bibliographies in medicine: Health literacy. NLM Publication #CBM 2000-1* (pp. v–vii). Bethesda, MD: National Institutes of Health.

Reickert, K. A. (2006). Integrating regimen adherence assistance into clinical practice. In W. T. O'Donahue & E. R. Levensky (Eds.), *Promoting treatment adherence: A practical handbook for health care providers* (pp. 17–34) Thousand Oaks, CA: Sage Publications.

Renders, C. M., Valk, G. D., Griffin, S. J., Wagner, E., van Eijk, J. T., & Assendelft, W. J. (2000). Interventions to improve the management of diabetes mellitus in primary care. *Cochrane Database of Systematic Reviews, 4.* doi: 10.1002/14651858.CD001481

Reverby, S. M. (2009). *Examining Tuskegee: The infamous syphilis study and its legacy.* Chapel Hill, NC: University of North Carolina Press.

Rodriguez-Gomez, J. R., & Salas-Serrano, C. C. (2006). Treatment adherence in ethnic minorities: Particularities and alternatives. In W. T. O'Donahue & E. R. Levensky (Eds.), *Promoting treatment adherence: A practical handbook for health care providers* (pp. 393–400). Thousand Oaks, CA: Sage Publications.

Rollnick, S., Miller, W. R., & Butler, C. C. (2008). *Motivational interviewing in health care: Helping patients change behavior.* New York, NY: Guilford Press.

Rueda, S., Park-Wyllie, L.Y., Bayoumi, A., Tynan, A. M. Antonious, T., Rourke, S., & Glazier, R. (2009). Patient support and education for promoting adherence to highly active antiretroviral therapy for HIV/AIDS. *Cochrane Database of Systematic Reviews, 3.* doi: 10.1002/14651858 .CD001442.pub2

Satcher, D., & Higginbotham, E. J. (2008). The public health approach to eliminating disparities in health. *American Journal of Public Health, 98,* 400–403.

Schedlbauer, A., Davies, P., & Fahey, T. (2010). Interventions to improve adherence to lipid lowering medication. *Cochrane Database of Systematic Reviews,* (3):CD004371.

Schroeder, K., Fahey, T., & Ebrahim, S. (2004). Interventions for improving adherence to treatment in patients with high blood pressure in ambulatory settings. *Cochrane Database of Systematic Reviews,* (2):CD004804.

Schwartzberg, J., Cowett, A., VanGeest, J., & Wolf, M. (2007). Communication techniques for patients with low health literacy: A survey of physicians, nurses, and pharmacists. *American Journal of Health Behavior, 31,* S96–S104.

Scott, E. M. D. (2010). The term "patient" may describe me . . . but it does not define me. *Journal of Participatory Medicine, 2,* e22.

Shim, J. K. (2010). Cultural health capital: A theoretical approach to understanding health care interactions and the dynamics of unequal treatment. *Journal of Health and Social Behavior, 51,* 1–15.

Shryock, T. R., & Richwine, A. (2010). The interface between veterinary and human antibiotic use. *Annals of the New York Academy of Sciences, 1213*(1), 92–105.

Sparks, L., & Villagran, M. (2010). *Patient and provider interaction.* Boston, MA: Polity Press.

Spiegel, D., & Giese-Davis, J. (2003). Depression and cancer: Mechanisms and disease progression. *Biological Psychiatry, 54,* 269–282.

Starace, F., Ammassari, A., Trotta, M. P., Murri, R., De Longis, P., Izzo, C., . . . Antinori, A. (2002). Depression is a risk factor for suboptimal adherence to highly active antiretroviral therapy. *Journal of Acquired Immune Deficiency Syndromes, 31,* S136–S139.

Stewart, M., Brown, J. B., Donner, A., McWhinney, I. R., Oates, J., Weston, W. W., Jordan, J. (2000). The impact of patient-centered care on outcomes. *Journal of Family Practice, 49,* 796–804.

U.S. Census Bureau. (2009). *Place of birth of the foreign-born population.* Retrieved from http://www.census.gov/prod/2010pubs/acsbr09-15.pdf

U.S. Department of Health and Human Services. (2001). *The Surgeon General's call to action to prevent and decrease overweight and obesity.* Washington, DC: U.S. General Printing Office.

U.S. Department of Health and Human Services. (2010). *How tobacco smoke causes disease: The biology and behavioral basis for smoking-attributable disease: A report of the Surgeon General.* Atlanta, GA: U.S. Department of Health and Human Services, Centers for Disease Control and Prevention, National Center for Chronic Disease Prevention and Health Promotion, Office on Smoking and Health.

Vermeire, E., Wens, J., Biot, Y., Hearnshaw, H., & Lindenmeyer, A. (2005). Interventions for improving adherence to treatment recommendations in people with Type 2 Diabetes Mellitus. *Cochrane Database of Systematic Reviews, 2.* doi: 10.1002/14651858.CD003638.pub2

Volmink, J., & Garner, P. (2007). Directly observed therapy for treating tuberculosis. *Cochrane Database of Systematic Reviews, 4.* doi: 10.1002/14651858 .CD003343.pub3

Walker, R., Kean, C., & Burke, J. (2010). Disparities and access to healthy food in the United States: A review of food deserts literature. *Health & Place, 16,* 876–884.

Weinberger, M., & Salz, T. (2006). Physician adherence to clinical-practice guidelines. In H. B. Bosworth, E. Z. Oddone, & M. Weinberger (Eds.), *Patient treatment adherence concepts, interventions and measurement* (pp. 373–390). Mahway, NJ: Lawrence Erlbaum Associates.

Whitt-Glover, M. C., Beech, B. M., Jackson, S. A., Loftin-Bell, K. A., & Mount, D. L. (2009). Health disparities and minority health. In S. A. Shumaker, J. K. Ockene, & K. A. Reickert (Eds.), *The handbook of health behavior change* (3rd ed., pp. 589–606). New York, NY: Springer Publishing.

Williams, A., Manias, E., & Walker, R. (2008). Interventions to improve medication adherence in people with multiple chronic conditions: A systematic review. *Journal of Advanced Nursing, 63*(2), 132–143.

Williams, D., & Mohammed, S. (2009). Discrimination and racial disparities in health: Evidence and needed research. *Journal of Behavioral Medicine, 32*, 20–47.

Wolfe, W. (2009, November 6). Daniel Hauser finishes his cancer treatment. *Minneapolis-St. Paul Star-Tribune.* Retrieved from http://www.startribune.com/projects/45440392.html

10

Thriving in Stressful Environments

INTRODUCTION

*I've learned that people will forget what you said, people will forget what
you did, but people will never forget how you made them feel.*
—Maya Angelou

Working in safety-net health care settings is not for the faint of heart.
As we have described throughout this book, these institutions are
characterized by resource scarcity while caring for patients with
complex problems who are also physically, psychologically, and
socially vulnerable to the consequences of poverty and stigma. To be
present day in and day out in the safety-net health system requires
a capacity to encounter what is most difficult in human relations—
hopelessness, victimization, abandonment, trauma, serious mental
illness, and death. People working in these settings are called on
to be conscious and compassionate witnesses to suffering that is
borne of the regularities of life, human perversity, and our societal
willingness to allow structural inequalities to continue unabated.
Each day in safety-net health care settings is a confrontation with
social inequality and our own responses to these disparities in our
society and world.

And yet many health care professionals survive and thrive in safety-net institutions, offering compassionate care and kindness to patients and colleagues alike. People who flourish in these settings have been "knocked around" by the realities of safety-net care, but have found ways to manage the stress of these environments without becoming "stressed out" themselves. Clinicians develop the capacity to keep engaging in the care of complex clients, even when easy solutions are not available. In fact, as we pointed out in our discussion of homelessness, many professionals in safety-net settings become leaders in community organizations and larger movements to address clinical problems that have systemic root causes. Health care providers who "make it" in these environments are flexible, humorous, creative, and able to endure. In this final chapter, we consider strategies for successful long-term work in health care safety-net settings. To do so, we remind ourselves about underlying motivations for the provision of humane health care, explore the conceptual landscape of occupational stress and its effects on care provision, and discuss core strategies that help us to cultivate wellness for ourselves in the midst of challenging circumstances.

THE "CARE" IN CLINICAL CARE

All of the health professions have deep roots in religious and philosophical systems that call on us to care for one another in times of pain and sorrow. The terms *patient* and *compassion* come from the same Latin word which means "to suffer," just as *hospital, hospice, and hospitality* all derive from an older term meaning "guest." These common expressions remind us of the fundamental nature of our work—to suffer with the guests who come through our doors.

Some of our best teachers of these concepts in the health care arena are people who are doctors, nurses, social workers, rehabilitation specialists, and others who end up on the "night-side of life,"[1] experiencing serious, potentially life-threatening illness. William Hurt, an award-winning actor, starred in a movie that stands as one of the great illustrations of the way in which

---

[1] Sontag (1988) wrote one of the more important cultural critiques of serious illness in the 20th century in her widely-quoted book *Illness as Metaphor*. She said, "Illness is the night-side of life, a more onerous citizenship. Everyone who is born holds dual citizenship, in the kingdom of the well and the kingdom of the sick. Although we all prefer to use only the good passport, sooner or later each of us is obliged, at least for a spell, to identify ourselves as citizens of that other place." This book questioned the ways in which cancer and tuberculosis have been associated with certain desirable (or undesirable) character traits. Later, she made a similar argument about AIDS.

experience as a patient can transform a professional's approach to people who are ill. In *The Doctor*, Hurt is surgeon Jack MacKee. MacKee has years of experience diagnosing and treating serious health problems as a highly skilled technician whose focus is on the problem more than the patient, until his world is suddenly turned upside down when he discovers he has throat cancer. MacKee becomes a patient being treated by the same people who are his medical colleagues in the hospital. He is shaken by how dehumanized he feels by the impersonal treatment from his colleagues during this period of intense fearfulness and physical pain. While sitting in a waiting room one day, he meets June, a young woman with brain cancer. She comments on his remote, unemotional manner and challenges him to live more fully. In a later unforgettable scene, the two are in a field in the sun, and she begins to dance her happiness in life at that moment. Slowly, MacKee begins to mirror her movements until he too is able to express his joy. MacKee recovers from his cancer and takes his newfound compassion for his fellow beings into his medical practice. In one of the final scenes of the movie, MacKee is training new medical residents by having them experience what their patients will face by laying on a gurney in a gown and being asked personal questions. MacKee's transformation mirrors the conclusion of a noted scholar of genocide and reconciliation, "A person's own suffering can become a source of especially pronounced awareness of human suffering, empathy with others in need, and feelings of responsibility for their welfare, resulting in a strong commitment to helping" (Staub & Vollhardt, 2008, p. 276). Professionals in health services choose this career path because of their desire to help others, many times in response to our own experiences of suffering.

Figure 10.1 gives some other common synonyms for the word "care." These terms compose an "emotion family" (Ekman, 1994, p. 19), or a group of highly related affective states that share a common feature. The commonality in these words is that action is directed to another, rather than focused on the self. Historically, pity and sympathy were

FIGURE 10.1 Common Synonyms for Care

also terms that expressed similar feelings of concern for another, but in contemporary times, both terms now have more pejorative meanings. In this section, we will consider three core ideas that are closely related in the literature on health care: altruism, compassion, and empathy.

Altruism

Safety-net justice can be understood as a socially formalized version of the basic motivation of altruism . . . The fact that altruism is natural does not make it inevitable. Altruistic motivation is easily overridden, is in keen competition with other goals, is extremely fragile, and has not of late been socially nurtured. Thus, in devoting ourselves to altruistic ideals . . . we are preserving and nurturing for our entire society a public manifestation of our natural altruistic motivational heritage that recent ideological currents have tended to sweep out of our sight.
— Wakefield, 1993, p. 454

Altruism is usually defined as unselfish concern that results in help for others; its opposite is egoism or devotion to one's own interests. We have commented in passing on the concept of altruism in previous chapters, mostly to note its discrediting as a source of explanation for caring behavior. A debate has raged for the past century as to whether altruism exists, or whether all altruistic acts are actually egoistic in nature, designed to serve one's own needs by minimizing self-distress caused by another's suffering or producing self-pleasure through doing good for others. The egoism argument builds on the deeply entrenched ideology of economic rationalism in American culture, which sees all persons as acting to maximize their own benefit and minimize their costs. Self-interest is a motivating virtue in capitalism that only reluctantly (if at all) recognizes the role of altruism in human societies. Authors who disagree with egoistic explanations of altruistic behavior contend that when altruism results in positive feelings, these are by-products, not the primary motivation for altruistic behavior (Staub & Vollhardt, 2008). The person's inner motivation to help another without expectation of self-benefit is the chief differentiation between an altruistic or egoistic act (Wakefield, 1993). The debate as to whether altruism is always a form of egoism is likely a matter of perspective, as the same evidence has been interpreted to support either position.[2]

---

[2] We refer readers to Wakefield (1993) for a detailed review of the historical debate and about altruism and its detractors, and how various theories of human behavior account for altruism.

To be a professional is to share an underlying ideology that focuses on the social (other oriented) benefit of the work performed, rather than solely on the money made by the practitioner (Relman, 2007). Yet a definition of altruism as action for the good of another without expectation of self-benefit raises a paradoxical question for professionals—"How can one at the same time be professional and altruistic? The two terms conjure up competing images, one of a job undertaken for personal remuneration and mediated by scientific calculation, the other of a spontaneous act of generosity" (Wakefield, 1993, p. 409). This question is a serious one on two different fronts. First, particularly for physicians, the escalating focus on issues of profit in medical practice in the past 50 years may come at a cost to care for patients. Medicine has shifted dramatically from its solo practice origins at the turn of the 20th century in which the physician was deeply integrated into the community in which he practiced.[3] Medicine now is a highly commodified industry and its trainees usually accrue significant financial debt in order to be credentialed in its practice. The issue of financial conflicts of interest in which medical practitioners and establishments favor themselves over their patients has become widespread, leading to calls for a return to "professional altruism and the moral commitment to patients" (Relman, 2007, p. 2669). Here, one physician is pleading with his profession to recenter the social, altruistic nature of the medical profession. Being able to practice with a sense of altruism may ultimately lead to a deeper sense of satisfaction and commitment to the profession of medicine (Young, Webb, Lackan, & Marchand, 2008).

In direct contradiction to the need for altruism among those who receive the greatest financial benefit in health care, the second issue is that altruistic behavior may actually be detrimental to already socially exploited groups such as women and people of color. One social welfare scholar notes, "The existence of 'helping' professions with low economic rewards, such as social work and nursing, in which the participants are predominantly women, requires either an assumption of a disproportionate inclination toward . . . 'altruism' among women, or an assumption of a persistent pattern of social and economic exploitation within a patriarchal system" (Austin, 1994, pp. 438–439). Some evidence exists that women *are* more altruistic, although the reason for this finding can be interpreted in several ways.[4]

---

[3] We use this pronoun intentionally, recognizing that women were excluded from medical school for most of the first half of the century.

[4] For instance, altruism among women may have strong biological underpinnings related to child care (which are evolutionarily advantageous for species survival); or women may be socialized into altruistic behavior as a consequence of gender role expectations for care work, as just two possible interpretations.

Among students in the professions of medicine, law, and business, women are more altruistic than men, and African Americans and Latinos are more altruistic than Whites (Coulter, Willkes, & Der-Martirosian, 2007). In fact, altruism may be more pronounced in socially disadvantaged groups precisely because they have had to cope with exploitation. In this case, altruism may support actions that help other members of one's group, without necessarily being of direct advantage to oneself. People from historically oppressed groups are also more likely to know others living in poverty, and to interpret poverty from a more structural than individualistic perspective, as we discussed in Chapter 2. This discussion indicates that altruism in gender- and race-segregated occupations may be a response to social inequality *and* a contributor to it.

Through our own reflections and observations, we have come to believe that altruism *as altruism* exists and can be drawn on as a support for practitioners in safety-net settings. Yet we also realize that altruism is deeply personal and context dependent. Wakefield's quote that opens this section points to the "fact that altruism is natural,"[5] and has a long historical trajectory. The safety-net health care system can be seen as an institutional reminder of the importance of altruism in human societies. We see altruism as being "driven by an inner core of compassion" (Coulter et al., 2007, p. 341) directed to the benefit of the other person, without expecting benefit for oneself, and oftentimes actually accruing "altruism" costs, as we will return to in our discussion of occupational stress. For people working in safety-net health care settings, consideration of altruism directs us to personal reflection on the existential question of why we have undertaken this work. We will return to this thought when talking about wellness.

Compassion

> *If compassion is to be acknowledged as an important aspect of the concept of care,*
> *compassion needs to be unconditionally available towards everyone who suffers.*
> — van der Cingel, 2009, p. 132

Compassion is one's own internal emotional response to another's suffering (Goetz, Keltner, & Simon-Thomas, 2010), which creates a desire to relieve the other's distress, even if at a cost to oneself (i.e., to behave

---

[5] Wakefield's use of this term derives from his analysis of the evolutionary advantage that altruism provides a social species such as humans. A similar argument on the evolutionary advantages associated with altruism has also been made by a leading scholar of animal behavior, De Waal (2008).

altruistically). Suffering, in this context, is understood as an ongoing distressing experience such as pain, trauma, or existential loneliness, rather than a transient event. Compassion makes suffering visible, but, "Suffering does not disappear because of compassion . . . suffering will exist more than ever when compassion has made it visible, but it also shows the other person is not left alone" (van der Cingel, 2009, p. 133). In this way, compassion requires active engagement between the care provider and the patient (or colleague, friend, or family member). Although central to health *care*, compassion receives little attention in most professional training programs. We are more likely to be taught "skills" that often require the opposite of compassion as our current treatment procedures rely on the detachment of the human being from the care being provided. One could argue that practices such as stripping away people's individuality by requiring patients to wear hospital gowns is, in part, an attempt to avoid viewing people as suffering individuals. Seemingly benign practices such as impersonal patient clothing designed for easy access to the body by clinical staff facilitate a view of the "patient" at a technical rather than human level. The preoccupation of the health care system with the depersonalized patient was demonstrated in *The Doctor* in MacKee's surgical competence and interpersonal incompetence.

Because what is distressing to one individual may not be to another, it can be difficult to recognize and acknowledge suffering, particularly if the other's suffering contradicts social or personal values. For example, people who are grieving a significant loss may experience intense sad and angry feelings for months or years, but they are often discouraged from sharing these emotions because of social pressures to "get on with life" (Worden, 2002). In this case, well-intentioned others avoid the suffering of the grieving person in favor of enforcing social norms of positive emotionality that are more comfortable for the unaffected person. Compassion in clinical care requires a health care provider to "de-self," or to temporarily set aside one's own values in order to understand the experience of the other person (van der Cingel, 2009). To be compassionate is to appreciate things that are important to the other person, but not necessarily to you.

Goetz et al. (2010) describe a series of appraisals, or assessments, that are necessary to transform awareness of suffering into compassion for the suffering other. For instance, if someone else's suffering actually satisfies a goal one has, such as the infliction of revenge, then suffering will not elicit compassion. Of particular interest to safety-net care providers are the final two appraisal components associated with compassion—deservingness and resource capacity. Compassion is elicited when the person who is suffering is judged to be deserving of help.[6] This dynamic is certainly at play when people with lung cancer are asked if they smoked. By smoking, a person who develops lung cancer may be seen as responsible for his or her own suffering, and hence, undeserving of compassion (or at least its fullest manifestation). In contrast, patients who develop lung cancer but who never smoked often receive more compassion because they are judged as not contributing to their illness. These patients often quickly inform new providers that they never smoked in order to avoid the possibility of being stigmatized as to blame for their illness. The social purpose of stigma (to shame people for nonadherence to socially expected, normative behaviors) directly contradicts the idea of compassion.

The cultural judgment of deservingness required for compassion to be conferred is at odds with professional ethics that requires practitioners to practice nonjudgmentally. Determining responsibility and deservingness is one of the most challenging inter- and intrapersonal issues faced in health care settings. Ethical decision-making exercises such as those that force the participant to choose who he or she would prioritize for services such as liver transplants, access to scarce flu vaccinations, or receiving HIV drugs make clear that issues of deservingness are matters of life and death every day in the health care arena. The challenge of compassion is to learn how to work with our judgments related to deservingness. As we discussed in the chapters on stigma and privilege, it is easier to feel compassion for people who are most like us. For health care practitioners who smoke, it is likely easier to find compassion for the difficulties involved in quitting smoking than for clinicians who don't use cigarettes or have successfully quit. Our own suffering may (but not always) make us more aware of the suffering underlying another's behavior. When a clinician unreflectively decides that a person is responsible for their own suffering, then the opportunity for compassion may be lost.

To move from the recognition of the suffering of another to compassion, the final appraisal that is made is whether one has sufficient internal resources available to experience compassion. These resources include things as basic as feeling well rested and fed, knowing that one is valued by others, and having a sense of one's

---

[6] Evaluations of deservingness are often affected by attribution bias—the tendency to see someone else's difficult circumstances as a consequence of their behavior, whereas we are more likely to attribute our own difficulties to bad luck or fate.

own efficacy in responding. Without internal resources such as these, the presentation of suffering that is deemed deserving of relief may actually result in anger, distress, or anxiety for the overtaxed practitioner instead of compassion. We will pursue the issue of resources at greater length when talking about stress paradigms in professional practice.

Patients rely on the compassion they experience from their care providers to help them cope with their conditions, and more importantly, to reaffirm their intrinsic value. How health care providers respond to suffering can have critical effects for clients, as is illustrated in the following example.

> Inordinately high suicide rates were reported among Scandinavian patients with advanced cancer, who were offered no further treatment or contact with the healthcare system. While the rationale for this may have been based on considerations of resource allocation or medical futility, the psychological and spiritual fallout is clear: people who are treated like they no longer matter will act and feel like they no longer matter. In other words, patients look at healthcare providers as they would a mirror, seeking a positive image of themselves and their continued sense of worth. In turn, healthcare providers need to be aware that their attitudes and assumptions will shape those all-important reflections. (Chochinov, 2007, p. 185)

This story demonstrates the profound effect that our recognition of suffering, or our lack thereof, can have for our patients. When patients felt that their health care providers no longer cared about them, no longer paid witness to the suffering they were experiencing, they killed themselves to end their own pain. Chochinov points to possible systemic explanations for the decision to withdraw care that was not preventing death. We could read these rationales as institutional manifestations of the lack of resources needed to move from recognition of suffering to compassion.

In summary, in order to experience compassion, a series of decisions are made, often at a depth that is below conscious awareness. In safety-net health care settings, the suffering created by illness is complicated by the presence of stigma that functions as a social tool for delegitimizing the claim of the individual to the care and concern of others. In the final section of this chapter, we will talk about approaches to increase compassion in professional work.

Empathy

Empathy may be uniquely well suited for bridging the gap between egoism
and altruism, since it has the property of transforming another person's
misfortune into one's own feeling of distress.
— Hoffman, 1981, p. 133

Empathy is the ability to relate to another's emotional state—some would say it is putting ourselves in the other's shoes. It is a fundamental attribute of compassion and altruism. People with severe deficits in empathy are often diagnosed with psychiatric disorders such as psychopathy (the inability to feel another person's suffering, which leads to destructive antisocial behavior) and autism (difficulty with social interaction, in part, because the person is unable to decipher emotional cues). Empathy is essential to moral development (Jolliffe & Farrington, 2006), healthy parenting (Strayer & Roberts, 2004), and marital happiness (Waldinger, Schulz, Hauser, Allen, & Crowell, 2004). A well-functioning organization, community, or society needs a healthy dose of empathy in order to enable social interactions, cooperation, and work toward shared group goals.

Empathy involves both unconscious affective responses and conscious cognitive and behavioral processes, all of which are deeply affected by the stability of emotional relationships and nurturing by caregivers early in life. Childhood deprivation deeply affects later empathetic capacities; children who have not had stable, loving relationships show less brain activity in areas associated with empathy (Gerdes, Segal, Jackson, & Mullins, 2011). Stress early in life can affect the development of empathy; stress during adulthood can also diminish a person's ability to display empathy, particularly job-related stress (Stebnicki, 2000).

Evolutionary psychologists have studied the development of empathy across species, and historically among humans. Current understanding of empathy suggests a "Russian doll" model, in which the doll's outer layer (which we would define as empathy) is contingent on underlying neurological and cognitive processes related to emotional contagion and perspective taking (De Waal, 2008). Emotional contagion is at the core of the "Russian doll," and it is one's physiological experience of another's personal distress. As the term "contagion" implies, distress is communicated to another, often involuntarily. In the past two decades, neuroscientists have been able to identify underlying neural pathways that are activated when people communicate emotions. When a person observes another, the same nerve cells that would be used if the person was to exhibit similar emotions are stimulated. Mirror neurons create an "echo" of another's experience, enabling humans to understand one another (Rizzolatti & Craighero, 2004). Emotional contagion operates at this physiological level. We can observe emotional contagion at movies when people will cover their eyes or avert their face when something horrible is about to happen to someone (De Waal, 2008), viscerally anticipating a distressed other's feelings. Emotional contagion can also transmit positive emotions, as when in *The Doctor*, June was able to transmit her joy in a moment of sunshine to MacKee.

At the next level of the "Russian doll," cognitive processes are used to understand the difference between self and other. In order to experience empathy for the other, a person has to learn which emotions are one's own and which are the feelings of the other. We have to know that the sadness we feel when a patient discusses a loss is sorrow for the patient, not for ourselves, in order to feel empathy; otherwise, we are still at the level of emotional contagion. Developing boundaries between the self and others is part of the emotion regulation process (Gerdes et al., 2011). By being able to separate self from other, it is then possible to engage in perspective taking that allows us to see the emotional experience from the other's point of view (Wakefield, 1993). By being able to take another's perspective, it is possible to then target helping behaviors at the particular needs of the other—in other words, to engage in empathetic behavior. Empathy, thus, is not just feeling someone else's feelings (emotional contagion), but the ability to differentiate self from other in such a way that we can act in a way that is helpful to the other to relieve distress. Interestingly, De Waal (2008) provides a number of examples of targeted helping in animals that imply the presence of empathy, indicating that these processes are not unique to human beings. In each of these examples, the animal recognizes distress, understands that it is the other who is hurting (not the self), and acts in a way specifically designed to alleviate the companion's suffering. Examples of targeted helping recorded among animals include

- Dolphins biting through harpoon lines or nets to save distressed companions.
- Whales putting themselves between a hunter's boat and an injured companion, or even trying to capsize the hunter's boat.
- Elephants supporting each other to stand and eat when weak or ill.
- Chimpanzees trying to save companions who have fallen in the water even though they cannot swim; some have died in these efforts.

The ability to show empathy to patients is "arguably the most important psychosocial characteristic" of a person engaged in any kind of human service or health care practice (Colliver, Conlee, Verhulst, & Dorsey, 2010, p. 588). Without empathy, compassion, and altruism, health care practitioners are more akin to mechanics than the healers most desire to be. In Table 10.1, we provide a beginning set of questions that can help us to reflect on our practice of empathy with our patients. These questions move us beyond technical proficiency to evaluate our interpersonal competencies. Although most of us strive to embody care ideals, the day-to-day sorrows and dilemmas in health care can challenge even the most committed individuals.

STRESS PARADIGMS IN PROFESSIONAL PRACTICE

We are more likely to be able to enact our ideals related to humane care when we have a deeper understanding of stress processes and their relationship to empathy (Table 10.2). Providing care to others is a stressful occupation (Yoder, 2010). Epidemiological research in the United Kingdom shows large variation in the proportion of people who report high levels of stress in their jobs—31.5% of nurses say they experienced high levels of stress compared to 14.2% of secretarial workers, 13.0% of scientists and engineers, and 41.5% of teachers (Smith, Brice, Collins, Matthews, & McNamara,

TABLE 10.1
Questions to Promote Self-Reflection on Empathy With Patients

How would I be feeling in this patient's situation?

What is leading me to draw these conclusions?

Have I checked out that my assumptions are accurate?

Am I aware of how my attitude toward my patient may be affecting him or her?

Does my attitude toward being a health care provider enable or diminish my ability to establish an open and empathic professional relationship with my patients?

What behaviors am I using to show compassion to my patient?

What new learning am I seeking to understand situations that are challenging for me?

Adapted from "Dignity and the essence of medicine: The A, B, C and D of dignity conserving care," by Chochinov, 2007, *British Medical Journal, 335,* 184–187.

TABLE 10.2
Symptoms Associated With Different Stress Paradigms

PARADIGM	SYMPTOMS
Occupational Stress	Depression, emotional depletion, callousness, tension, fatigue, health problems, headaches, stomach problems[a]
Burnout	Emotional exhaustion, erosion of idealism, diminished morale, reduced sense of accomplishment[b]
Compassion Fatigue	Anxiety, depression, stress, weariness, somatization, exhaustion[b]
Vicarious Trauma	Changes in meanings, beliefs, schemas,[c] nightmares, fearful thoughts, intrusive images, personal vulnerability, cynicism, pessimism[a]
Secondary Traumatic Stress Syndrome	Reexperiencing traumatic event, avoidance, numbing, persistent arousal, work conflict, missed work, insensitivity to clients, reduced social support[b]
Moral Distress	Violation of personal beliefs and values due to external constraints, anger, guilt[d]

[a] From "An institutional ethnography of nurses' stress," by McGibbon et al., 2010, *Qualitative Health Research, 20,* 1353–1378.

[b] From "Issues and controversies in the understanding and diagnosis of compassion fatigue, vicarious traumatization, and secondary traumatic stress disorder," by Thomas and Wilson, 2004, *International Journal of Emergency Mental Health, 6,* 81–92.

[c] From "Vicarious traumatization: Implications for the mental health of health workers?" by Sabin-Farrell and Turpin, 2003, *Clinical Psychology Review, 23,* 449–480.

[d] From "Moral distress: A growing problem in the health professions?" by Ulrich et al., 2010, *Hastings Center Report, 40*(1), 20–22.

2000).[7] Similar studies show that workers in the public sector report substantially higher rates of stress than private sector workers (Blaug, Kenyon, & Lekhi, 2007). Increased occupational stress is associated with more organizational turnover with high costs to individuals and institutions (Barak, Nissly, & Levin, 2001). This research suggests that health professionals in public safety-net health care settings may experience increased pressures both because they are in care-providing professions and because of the issues surrounding public institutions. Stress has personal, interpersonal, and organizational effects. While health professionals are taught about the effects of stress for our patients, it is equally important to understand how the stress response affects our own work.

---

[7] Other health professions were not identified in the report.

Understanding the Stress Response

Stress is both a physiological and psychological experience that, at its most extreme, evokes the "fight-flight-or-freeze" response to an identified threat. In the body, stress acts on the brain, heart, lungs, and the endocrine and immune systems. In particular, the hypothalamic–pituitary–adrenal system produces adrenaline and cortisol in response to threats perceived as serious (Farmer, 2008). Unlike acute situations that usually resolve fairly quickly, chronic stress occurs over long periods of time and can change the physiology of our bodies. Chronic stressors can include interpersonal conflicts or situations that are symbolic in nature such as threats to competence or self-esteem. These types of stress are common in modern societies. Neuroscientist Bruce McEwen explains how the body responds to the flood of hormones released when under stress to illustrate why chronic activation of the stress response can be so damaging:

> To fight or flee, an animal needs an increased flow of oxygen to its muscles, particularly the large muscles of the legs. So breathing accelerates to bring in more oxygen, and the heart rate speeds up to deliver that oxygen through the bloodstream to the major muscles. The blood vessels in the skin constrict so that there will be as little bleeding as possible in the event of injury; this constriction produces the sensation of the hair standing on end. To provide sufficient fuel for the exertion, our glands liquidate stored carbohydrates into blood sugar. Under acute stress, the immune response is enhanced. The infection-fighting white blood cells attach themselves to the blood vessel walls, ready to depart for whatever part of the body is injured. But if a stressful situation goes on too long, the immune response is dampened in favor of the primary systems—the heart and lungs—that need the energy most. Already, you can see the potential for trouble if this system gets stuck in the "on" position. (McEwen, 2002, p. 6)

Clearly, jobs are not the same as being attacked by a tiger, yet our bodies may react in similar ways to perceived threats in the workplace. In many health care settings, clinicians are confronted with situations in which stressful events such as unexpected death or other serious traumas can occur on a routine, repetitive basis, and for some, this will elicit an increase in stress hormones. Although the acute stress response can save a person's life, or the life of others, when stress pathways are chronically activated, this can have serious detrimental effects on health including cardiovascular disease, immune dysfunction, and mental illness (Thoits, 2010).

However, not all potentially threatening events are perceived as stressful. Psychosocial theorizing on the stress response notes that a physiological reaction is elicited through a cognitive appraisal process (Lazarus & Folkman, 1984). Before stress hormones are released, a person has to recognize that harm or loss could occur; without an awareness that material or symbolic threat exists, stress is not induced. People vary in terms of what kinds of situations are stressful to them. For example, a health care provider in a hospice setting is likely to have a very different reaction to death than a clinician in an ICU trying to prevent death. Once a threat is identified, a person focuses next on what can be done about the event, a process known as "secondary appraisal." People with the intrapersonal, interpersonal, or social resources to respond effectively to a potential threat may avoid a stress response by activating these capacities. An experienced critical care nurse who has participated in many resuscitation efforts will have training, skills, and a support system to cope with the stress of a code—things that may not be available for a less-seasoned care provider. Finally, situations that are neutral emotionally will not be stress invoking. It is the feeling of potential loss that activates physiological stress.

When stress hormones are chronically released, these can result in allostatic load or the long-term "wear and tear" on the human body caused by repeated or unremitting elicitation of the physiological stress response. This concept is important for safety-net care providers both in terms of understanding the experience of many of our patients and for recognizing when our own coping capacities have been exceeded. Different patterns of allostatic load exist, of which three are particularly relevant for clinicians in safety-net health care settings (McEwen & Seeman, 2009). First, a person can experience stress overload, as it occurs when multiple traumatic events occur (a "pile up" of stressors), or are unremitting in nature (such as poverty). In the second pattern, a person has difficulty in adapting to situations that are initially stressful, but would be expected to be less difficult over time. For example, some people experience high levels of stress every time they are confronted with a test, even when they have successfully navigated exams in the past. Third, when stress interrupts the body's normal cycles of eating and sleeping, allostatic load can occur. Allostatic load, or being "stressed out," can lead to increased risk for mortality and morbidity over time (Seeman, McEwen, Rowe, & Singer, 2001).

Occupational Stress Models

*Did you hear about the emergency ward nurse who died and went straight
to hell? It took her two weeks to realize that she wasn't at work anymore.*
                                                                    — Anonymous

Thus far we have focused on the individual experience of stress from
a physiological and psychological perspective; social models that
look at job stress in physical and mental health care occupations reveal dynamics that are unique to these systems. As the "joke" above
indicates, sometimes work in health care settings (and we would
argue, safety-net health settings in particular) can engender chronic
stress responses. We will focus on models that look at organizational
practices and stress; however, the point of demarcation between
stress that is considered work related and pressures that occur outside the workplace is not necessarily clear. Tensions from work
can increase conflict at home and vice versa. The pervasiveness of
stressful events in modern society makes it difficult to draw distinct
boundaries around locations that are stress generating; however, the
National Institute for Occupational Health and Safety (1999) notes
that 40% of all workers feel their job is "very or extremely" stressful.

Reasons for stress change depending on the institutional location
of the worker. A large body of research shows that "demand" and
"control" features of work affect experiences of stress. People with
the highest demands from their jobs and the lowest levels of control
over their work have the highest levels of stress. For instance, in a
study of employees of elder care facilities, those workers with high
demands in their job, particularly for emotional care, and low-job
control had higher rates of sickness and more reports of stress symptoms than people who had high control in their jobs (De Jonge, van
Vegchel, Shimazu, Schaufeli, & Dormann, 2010). Control over work is
highly gendered in medical settings, with nurses, in particular, consistently reporting issues related to hierarchy within medical institutions as a major source of stress (McGibbon, Peter, & Gallop, 2010).
Within nursing, nurse assistants are more likely to have high demand/
low-control positions, and consequently report more job strain than
nurses (Morgan, Semchuk, Stewart, & D'Arcy, 2002). Specialties within
medicine also differ in the amount of stress experienced. Research on
burnout and mental health symptoms among physicians suggests that
surgery (Shanafelt et al., 2011) and psychiatry (Miller & McGowen,

2000) may have higher levels of stress, burnout, and depression than other medical specialties.

Researchers have been concerned for many years with how care providers experience stress in health occupations; however, no comprehensive research model has yet been proposed that accounts for the varied responses to occupational stress in health care settings. Figure 10.2 illustrates six different conceptual models that have evolved over the last several decades to explain job-related stress, and Table 10.2 notes their associated symptoms. As can be seen from the table, many of these symptoms overlap between the different conceptual classifications. It may be that each of these models points to a similar experience that has been named differently, or different conceptualizations may indicate differing levels of intensity of symptoms, or there may be clear and nonoverlapping distinctions between different experiences captured by each model. We have organized these models into three rows—from more general on the bottom, to more specific at the top (Figure 10.2).

General Stress Models

On the bottom row of Figure 10.2 are models that are more general in their descriptions of factors related to job stress and that generally originated earlier in the literature. Emotional depletion, exhaustion, and weariness are all similar symptoms that are catalogued in the literatures on occupational stress, burnout, and compassion fatigue. Occupational (or job/work) stress is the oldest term and refers to physical, mental, and emotional effects of job-related strains. Burnout has been defined as a state of cynicism and exhaustion accompanied by a

FIGURE 10.2 Models for Understanding Stress Paradigms in Professional Practice

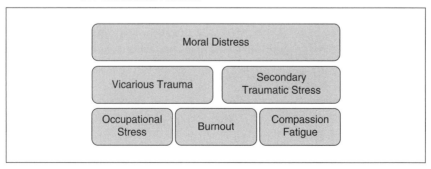

reduction in accomplishment and effectiveness (Brazeau, Schroeder, Rovi, & Boyd, 2010). Compassion fatigue, originally labeled "compassion stress" (Figley, 1993), focuses more directly on the symptoms of emotional withdrawal within professions such as health care that rely on emotional connection and empathy in order to perform job roles (Thomas & Wilson, 2004). Some authors distinguish burnout from compassion fatigue by describing the former as stress caused by a failure to accomplish goals, whereas compassion fatigue is seen as stress caused by a failure to save others from harm (Yoder, 2010).

Occupational stress tends to be viewed as an individual phenomenon more than an organizational one (McGibbon et al., 2010), although organizational factors such as caseload and working conditions are associated with job-related stress. As noted in Chapter 1, safety-net health care settings are providers of "last resort," so these institutions are more likely to care for people with serious and complex conditions such as burns, trauma, HIV/AIDS, and mental illness. Within safety-net health care settings, organizational issues may be more prominent as stressors because of resource constraints. For example, most safety-net settings have large caseloads and concomitant longer waiting times for care, a situation that is stressful for patients and for health professionals who have to cope with patient and family distress. Another resource, the physical environment of the institution, also affects working conditions in safety-net settings. As an example, prior to Hurricane Katrina, Charity Hospital in New Orleans, Louisiana's largest public hospital, had operated for almost 70 years in a building built in the late 1930s. Hospital care was provided in large wards with multiple beds that offered little privacy to patients or clinicians; likewise, clinic visits usually occurred in small cubicles separated by flimsy curtains. For practitioners who want to offer the highest quality of care, long-term work under conditions such as these can result in feelings of demoralization and stress.

Certain factors may be more likely to trigger work stress. For example, Yoder (2010) in her study of compassion fatigue found that nurses reported three main areas of stressful interactions: patient care issues (such as the patient's condition, providing care the nurse felt was futile, or challenging patient and family behavior), system issues (workload, conflicts with management), and personal issues (limits, experiences outside of work). McGibbon et al. (2010) also note that nurses face special stressors as a result of being constantly present, negotiating hierarchical power and engaging in bodily caring. Social workers also face profession-specific stressors resulting from the lack of financial reimbursement for their services in hospital-based settings and the concomitant downsizing and restructuring that have occurred to contain costs (Lloyd, King, & Chenoweth, 2002). Being in a safety-net health hospital is associated with higher levels of job-related stress for social workers in terms of interprofessional conflicts, work schedules, and critical decision making when compared to social workers in non-safety-net settings (Gellis, 2001).

In terms of looking at general models of occupational stress, research on coping suggests several possible methods for handling work-related distress. For example, some health care providers report individually focused strategies such as changing levels of personal engagement or involvement in stressful work situations, or focusing on personal self-care by developing a life outside work, engaging in spiritual activities, and introspection (Yoder, 2010). At the organizational level, having strong support from one's work team, peer debriefing, and access to supportive supervisors also help counteract stress symptoms (Lloyd et al., 2002).

Trauma Models

The middle row of Figure 10.2 differentiates general stress responses from trauma responses or situations where health care providers may exhibit symptoms associated with severe anxiety. Anxiety symptoms reported in both vicarious trauma and secondary traumatic stress disorder include fearful thoughts, intrusive images, and withdrawal as a response to traumatic experiences. Trauma models differ from general stress models in their focus on the anxiety symptoms that arise as a response by the clinician to empathic identification with a suffering other. For example, a health care professional who cares for a severely burned individual may experience anxiety as a result of the disfigurement, pain, and distress of the patient. Depending on the level of anxiety created by a situation, a care provider may experience nightmares, avoidance of the patient, or other troubling symptoms as a result of his or her exposure to another's trauma.

Vicarious trauma refers to having negative experiences as a result of hearing, seeing, or knowing about a traumatic event experienced by another person (Thomas & Wilson, 2004). Secondary traumatic stress disorder is similar in its focus on the personal effects of being a witness to another's trauma, but proponents of this model believe that the associated distress for the worker is severe enough to indicate that the person may have a disorder similar to posttraumatic stress disorder (PTSD; American Psychiatric Association, 2000). These models have been particularly developed to explain stress reactions experienced by some emergency workers or mental health care providers who treat individuals who have suffered intense abuse, victimization, or trauma (Thomas & Wilson, 2004). As Thomas and Wilson note, "There is a cost to caring. Professionals who listen to clients' stories of fear, pain and suffering may feel similar fear, pain and suffering because they care" (2004, p. 81). This empathetic connection is necessary for the provision of compassionate health care, but it can also become incapacitating in some circumstances.

Drawing on work that has been done to define PTSD, occupational trauma models describe symptoms such as intrusive memories of the event that were experienced as traumatizing by the health care provider (i.e., nightmares, flashbacks, or distressing recollections); avoidance of stimuli associated with the trauma or estrangement from others; and increased arousal such as difficulty sleeping or concentrating. Working with severely traumatized people may have a toxic, contaminating quality for health care professionals (McGibbon et al., 2010) and lead to changes in the clinician's identity and sense of goodness of the world (Thomas & Wilson, 2004). When confronted with horrifying events, some people may become cynical or despairing when their efforts to prevent harm or provide care are inadequate for the situation at hand.

It is unclear from this body of literature to what degree anxiety symptoms should be seen as an expected outcome of encounters where clinicians are exposed to severely distressing or appalling situations. If these are expected responses, labeling these experiences as "trauma disorders" may be unnecessarily pathologizing (McGibbon et al., 2010). However, research reports and personal anecdotes in the literature indicate that some health care providers develop anxiety symptoms that become disabling as a result of their exposure to certain traumatic situations at work. In these cases, help from formal sources such as counseling professionals, employee assistance programs, or psychiatrists may be warranted.

A Moral Distress Model

The top row of Figure 10.2 is a more recent model of job-related stress that focuses on moral distress, or the inability of a person to act in accord with his or her own personal values (Jameton, 1984). Morality is our personal and cultural sense of right and wrong. Here, a judgment is made as to what the just and desirable action *should* be in a particular circumstance. This approach differs from both general stress and trauma models because of its focus on an idealized set of actions or outcome. Practitioners who experience moral distress report emotional exhaustion, recurrent nightmares of clinical situations, or increased pessimism (Sheldon, 2010), symptoms similar to both general and trauma models of occupational stress.

All health care providers are faced with moral questions about whether it is right or wrong to offer a certain treatment or undertake a procedure (Ulrich, Hamric, & Grady, 2010). However, moral distress occurs when the morally correct thing to do is known, but institutional constraints prevent care providers from pursuing the right action (Sheldon, 2010). These situations can invoke feelings of helplessness and anger for clinicians. The following are examples of situations that might elicit moral distress for a health care practitioner:

- A patient needs a liver transplant, but can't afford it and subsequently dies.
- A woman works at a job that doesn't provide health insurance; she has HIV/AIDS and is put on a years-long waiting list to receive antiretroviral medication, even though she could benefit from the medicine immediately.
- An elderly man with diabetes needs a specialized pump to control his insulin dosage because of frequent bouts of hypoglycemia, but Medicare doesn't pay for this particular equipment. He has an acute hypoglycemic attack, lapses into a diabetic coma, and ends up in the emergency room.
- A family wants to continue pursuing aggressive treatment for a loved one with chronic organ failure who is being kept alive on a ventilator, even though the health care team sees no benefit in further treatment.

These examples represent relatively common events within health care settings; in fact, their ordinariness may mask the complexity of the moral calculus they reveal. Is it right that a person's health is worsened, or that he or she may die, as a result of available, but socially (meaning politically and financially) unobtainable resources? These examples highlight why one might expect practitioners in safety-net settings to have an increased risk for this type of stress, as many situations that are morally distressing may have an underlying link to poverty or stigma. Moral distress may also occur more frequently in high-intensity or high-conflict care settings such as intensive care units or emergency departments (Ulrich et al., 2010) that are more typically present in safety-net settings. Moral distress affects the individual, but it can also lead to conflict or difficulty within the larger health care team. Shared practice models where health care providers grapple together with the difficulties in patient care may offer some assistance to those experiencing high levels of moral distress (Ulrich et al., 2010).

General stress, trauma, and moral distress models all describe ways in which the work of being a health care provider may create internal difficulties that lead to feelings of exhaustion, anxiety, and larger existential concerns. The special issues of safety-net settings, particularly as these relate to resource limitations, heighten the possibility of stress responses among the health care professionals who work within these institutions. A common underlying component of these various forms of occupational stress reactions is their effect on the ability to experience compassion for others and to express that empathically to clients.

Effects of Stress on Empathy Behavior

In order to be effective health care practitioners, we must be able to recognize and respond to another's meta-emotional communication—to recognize and respond to the distress, suffering, and confusion that accompany serious illness. The experience of chronic stress is often most noticeable in its effects on a person's capacity to experience feelings of warmth and care for others, particularly others who may be socially stigmatized in some way. The following story illustrates some of the tensions between stigma, empathy, and compassion:

> One night, in the emergency room at a county hospital, an ambulance brought in a homeless person who had been found unconscious in an alley. The man was filthy, his breath reeked of alcohol, and he had lice crawling on his body. It took two nurses more than an hour just to clean the man up enough for admission. It was difficult work and the nurses' senses were overwhelmed with unpleasant sights and smells. One of the nurses read the intern's admission note on the way up the elevator. It said, "Patient carried into emergency room by army of body lice, who were chanting, 'Save our host. Save our host.'" The nurse laughed heartily at this amusing picture. Suddenly the struggles of the last hours were put into a humorous perspective, and she felt a lot less anger and a lot more compassion. (Wooten, 2009, pp. 243–244)

This story is interesting on many levels. First, the patient in this anecdote is one who would typically be cared for in a safety-net setting, given his homelessness, substance abuse, and hygiene issues associated with poverty. The term "county hospital" is sometimes a synonym for a public safety-net hospital. Second, the nurse felt angry instead of compassionate, which may indicate either her estimation that the patient was not deserving of compassion (that he was responsible for his condition), or that she did not have the internal resources at that moment to feel compassion for the patient. Feelings of anger and being overwhelmed are often symptoms of occupational stress and internal resource depletion, and this story illustrates how they can interfere with feelings of compassion for patients. Third, the intern used humor that, in this instance, was at the expense of the patient, a not uncommon event in stressful hospital settings as was discussed in the chapter on stigma. This kind of joking, sometimes referred to as "gallows humor," is a coping response to trying or tragic situations. Gallows humor is often used to define group boundaries—outsiders find it offensive, whereas those in on the joke find gallows humor comforting, as did this nurse.

Occupational stress, trauma, and moral distress can all result in a loss of compassion and empathy for patients. A body of literature has developed in medical education assessing the level of empathy among students during their training. Several studies have indicated that empathy decreases among medical students, although this finding has been contested (Colliver et al., 2010). As students experience higher levels of burnout (defined as emotional exhaustion, cynicism, and reduction in effectiveness), they also report lower levels of empathy (Brazeau et al., 2010). In a longitudinal analysis of empathy, Hojat et al. (2009) concluded that "the devil is in the third year," as students showed a marked decline in reported empathy at this stage in their training. Technology-oriented specialties (anesthesiology, pathology, radiology, and surgery) had lower empathy scores and were significantly different from the more "people-oriented" specialties such as family medicine, internal medicine, and obstetrics-gynecology.[8] The authors point to several factors that may account for declines in empathy including increased stress, an overreliance on technology for

---

[8] Decisions on specialization in medicine show distinct gender trends with women more heavily represented in "people-oriented" specialties. As women also report higher levels of empathy, empathy scores in these specialties may be more related to gender than to either the technological or person orientation.

diagnosis, and a concomitant lessening of the importance of empathetic interactions in human encounters. In addition, they also note that "changes in the market-driven health care system have a ripple effect on medical education, combined with the belief that a controlled clinical trial is the royal road to advances in medicine, can also lead to a false idea that empathy is outside the realm of evidence-based medicine, and thus, has no importance in . . . education" (Hojat et al., 2009, p. 1188).

Although trends in the erosion of empathy were similar (but of different magnitudes) for male and female medical students, one-quarter of students reported no decline in empathy. Students with higher levels of empathy noted the importance of the role modeling of superiors in encouraging empathy (Hojat et al., 2009), a finding further corroborated by Brazeau et al. (2010). This research points to the importance of the "hidden" or "implicit" curriculum in education—we learn from what we see modeled as much as what is presented through didactic methods. In one of the first studies to test whether intervention can preserve empathy, medical educators found that routine reflection on intrapersonal challenges in clinical practice was successful at helping students to maintain the same level of empathy as when they entered medical school (Rosenthal et al., 2011).

In summary, occupational stress can interfere with our personal ideals and professional intentions toward altruism, compassion, and empathy. Stress is a normative, albeit difficult human experience. Years of study about coping with stress show that there are actions we can take to strengthen our ability to respond to challenging circumstances. We turn now to ways that we can cultivate inner wellness to help us live joyfully and work effectively in safety-net settings.

CULTIVATING WELLNESS

Many persons have a wrong idea of what constitutes true happiness.
It is not attained through self-gratification but through fidelity to a
worthy purpose.
— Helen Keller

Wellness is a virtuous circle, whereas stress is a vicious cycle. What we mean by this is that processes that support self-care build on each other—caring for our bodies through exercise promotes better sleep; high-quality rest helps us to be mindful in our daily activities, which further promotes caring relationships that foster wellness. In contrast, increasing levels of stress are likely to lead to dysfunctional eating patterns, which affect our ability to care for the body through exercise and sleep. Being tired is more likely to lead to conflict in interpersonal relationships that increase stress. In behavioral terms, these are examples of positive feedback—more of A (exercise) leads to more of B (rest), which creates more of A (exercise).

Regrettably, although most health care professionals have intensive learning experiences in how to care for others, fewer are taught to focus on their own self-care—most academic training programs do not explicitly focus on self-care strategies. This omission is a missed opportunity, especially since younger and newer helping professionals are at higher risk for occupational stress and burnout (Shapiro, Brown, & Biegel, 2007). Burnout and poor self-care skills are often found in tandem. For instance, residents who reported high levels of burnout were also more likely to see self-care as "inconsequential" (Shanafelt, Bradley, Wipf, & Back, 2002). Burnout has a negative effect on patient care, collegial relationships, and personal feelings of self-efficacy and worth. New professionals are in need of more training and intervention to promote self-care skills.

In Figure 10.3, we show five "petals" of the wellness or self-care "flower" that we consider core self-care activities.[9] These behaviors have been consistently identified as supporting physical and psychological wellness across a body of studies in varied populations of people who have clinical health problems and those who are currently healthy. Although they do not represent all of the things we can do to care for ourselves, they do form a foundational set of behaviors that are most likely to reduce stress and promote wellness, especially if learned early in the process of professional practice.

High-Quality Nutrition

Our bodies are created out of and renewed from the food we eat. If we pause a moment to consider this simple but profound truth, the importance of high-quality nutrition becomes clear. For example, even small deficiencies in the iron levels in the blood can diminish the supply of oxygen to the brain, with a concomitant increase in feelings of irritability and fatigue (Benton & Donohoe, 1999). This example shows how poor nutrition itself can increase feelings of stress. But the opposite

---

[9] We propose this model to emphasize ongoing health-inducing activities, rather than focusing on the elimination of activities that are known to damage health (i.e., smoking, excessing alcohol use, drug use, etc.).

FIGURE 10.3 The Virtuous Circle in Wellness

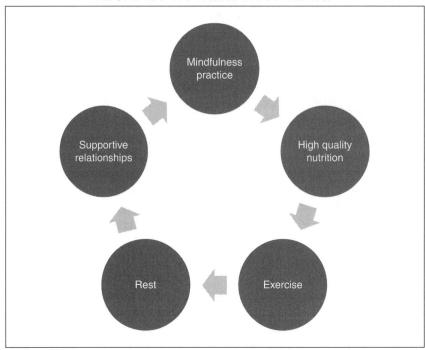

is also true—stress can cause nutritional difficulties. As a person feels increasing stress, more cortisol is released in the body driving down levels of the neurotransmitter serotonin; this drop induces strong cravings for carbohydrates (especially sweet or salty carbohydrates) that restore the body's serotonin levels, creating a feeling of calm (Somer, 1999). As we have discussed in this chapter, work in safety-net health settings can be stress inducing, so attention to nutrition is an important self-care strategy. Practitioners need to particularly concentrate on nutritional strategies that balance needed nutrients rather than reaching for easily available salty and sweet products.

Debates rage in nutrition sciences about various approaches to healthy eating. The American Diabetic Association and the American Heart Association have been in a decades-old argument as to whether low-fat or low-carbohydrate diets are the best for overall health. Rather than advocating for a particular nutritional approach, we rely on Michael Pollan's (2007) unpretentious recommendation: "Eat food. Not too much. Mainly plants." Whereas the last suggestion is self-evident, the others are less intuitive. The first statement refers to eating food that is as close to its natural state as possible, a "whole"

TABLE 10.3
Questions to Ask to Determine Whether Something Is a Whole Food[a]

1. Can I imagine it growing?
   "It is easy to picture a wheat field ... tough to picture a field of marshmallows."
2. How many ingredients does it have?
   "A whole food had only one ingredient—itself."
3. What has been done to the food since it was harvested?
   "Read the list of ingredients ... if you can't pronounce it or can't imagine it growing, don't eat it."
4. Is this product "part" of a food or the "whole" entity?
   "Juice is only a part of a fruit. Eat whole entities as much as possible."
5. How long has this food been known to nourish human beings?
   "Most whole foods have been on the dinner table for centuries."

[a] Adapted from "Feeding the whole family: Cooking with whole foods," by Lair, 2008, p. 3, Seattle, WA: Sasquatch Books.

food—that is, eat an orange rather than drinking an orange-flavored soda or even a bottle of orange juice. As Pollan notes, "food" is something your great-grandmother would recognize as opposed to what passes for nutrition in the highly processed and refined foods that are common to the Standard American Diet.[10] The second suggestion, to eat "not too much," is embodied in the revised nutritional standards issued by the U.S. Department of Agriculture (USDA) in 2011. Using a diagram of a plate, the USDA recommends that half of any meal be vegetables and fruits (with more vegetables than fruits), grains (preferably whole grains), and a small serving of protein and dairy.[11] In an era of highly processed foods, identifying a whole food might be difficult for some. Table 10.3 suggests a set of questions that help to determine whether a food is whole or not.[12]

Exercise

Moderate aerobic exercise is wellness enhancing through its actions on body chemistry, including the release of endorphins that promote feelings of well-being. Several studies in both clinical and nonclinical

---

[10] The Standard American Diet is often referred to by its acronym SAD and is characterized by high intake of meat, processed/refined foods, high-sugar drinks, and high-fat foods.

[11] More information on the revised USDA nutritional standards can be found at choosemyplate.gov

[12] Several websites and blogs exist that discuss whole food nutrition. One example is by Cynthia Lair, a nutritionist at Bastyr University, one of the first naturopathic universities in the United States. Cookus Interruptus provides videotapes on how to eat and cook whole foods "despite life's interruptions." The website is located at CookusInteruptus.com

samples suggest that exercise is associated with decreased levels of depression and anxiety, and may even be as effective as psychotherapy in the treatment of depression (Stathopoulou, Powers, Berry, Smits, & Otto, 2006). A dose–response relationship exists in which higher intensity or more frequent exercise showed larger decreases in symptoms of stress when compared to low-intensity/low-frequency exercise, with aerobic exercise five times a week showing the greatest effect (Dunn, Trivedi, Kampert, Clark, & Chambliss, 2005). Routine exercise has also shown benefit for decreasing anxiety, alcohol abuse, and eating disorders (Stathopoulou et al., 2006). Exercise may exert these positive effects by boosting serotonin, improving sleep (which we will discuss next), increasing a cognitive sense of self-mastery, and decreasing rumination, or repetitive, worrying thoughts (Stathopoulou et al., 2006).

Unfortunately, most Americans do not achieve the minimum suggested 30 minutes daily of moderate activity. The American economy has transitioned from labor- (and exercise-) intensive farming and manufacturing to service occupations (such as health care) that require less physical activity and are frequently associated with hours in front of computer monitors. Many activities associated with health care practice have a sedentary quality to them such as listening and talking with patients and colleagues, or reading and writing documentation. Within the medical field, half or fewer physicians engage in moderately intense physical activity three times a week (Feller & Hatch, 2004), whereas over half of nurses in one national study report being overweight (Miller, Alpert, & Cross, 2008). Integrating daily activities such as taking the stairs instead of the elevator, walking or biking rather than driving, and taking breaks to walk around are all ways to expand physical activity.

Rest

A significant number of Americans do not sleep the recommended 7 to 8 hours nightly. The less sleep a person obtains, the higher his or her risk of hypertensive disease (Gottlieb et al., 2006) and all-cause mortality (Kripke, Garfinkel, Wingard, Klauber, & Marler, 2002). In addition, sleeping less than 4 hours per night has been shown to impair glucose tolerance and increase cortisol levels (Alvarez & Ayas, 2004), thereby intensifying the physical stress response and leading to more impairment in sleep. Less sleep is associated with poorer overall health, increased risk of alcohol and drug use, and cognitive difficulties, especially in attention (Brown, Buboltz, & Soper, 2002).

For health care practitioners, getting adequate rest can be a particular issue as many physicians have long work days, and nurses and others work nightshifts to care for patients. Medical intern and resident shifts can be 24 hours long, several days in a row, with little time for sleeping. Longer shifts are associated with higher rates of errors, including medication and diagnostic errors; increased risk for motor vehicle accidents; and increased levels of depressive symptoms (Reed, Fletcher, & Arora, 2010). As a result of findings such as these and others documented by the national Institute of Medicine (2008), medical education accreditors have instituted new standards that limit shifts to 16 hours for interns and 24 hours for residents, with night coverage limited to six consecutive nights (Reed et al., 2010). Although napping is strongly encouraged during long shifts, previous studies of protected sleep time indicate that clinicians generally do not nap because of their focus on patient care (Reed et al., 2010). Clearly, work practices affect sleep behavior. Health care professionals will have to make concerted efforts to ensure that they receive enough rest on a routine basis.

The American Psychological Association has recommended several interventions as empirically validated in treating insomnia or sleep difficulties (Morin, Bootzin, Buysse, Edinger, Espie, & Lichstein, 2006). These treatments include stimulus control, relaxation training (which we discuss in the next section on mindfulness), sleep hygiene, and cognitive interventions. Stimulus control focuses on increasing behaviors that are associated with higher sleep quality, including getting up at the same time each morning, stopping napping, and getting up at night when unable to sleep. Increasing attention has been placed on educating people about "sleep hygiene," or habits that are associated with adequate rest. These practices include health-related factors (good nutrition, avoiding caffeine at least 6 hours before going to bed, exercising, and limiting use of substances such as alcohol that can interfere with sleep), and environmental routines such as ensuring quiet as much as possible, and decreasing light and temperature to promote sleep. The more people know about sleep hygiene, the more likely they are to have sleep habits that promote high quality rest (Brown et al., 2002). Cognitive interventions emphasize changes in maladaptive thoughts about sleeping, including worry associated with insomnia and its consequences (Morin et al., 2006). Changes in thinking are often paired with efforts to improve relaxation before sleep.

Supportive Relationships

Over 30 years ago, the first longitudinal study of mortality and social support found that people who were more isolated were more likely to die than their counterparts with higher numbers of social contacts (Berkman & Syme, 1979). Social support includes both the direct provision of help from caring others (instrumental support) as well as receiving reassurance (emotional support). Health is associated with social support through multiple pathways, including the effects of others on our own health behaviors, our psychological processes, and potentially on underlying biological processes. People who participate in relationships that have high levels of empathic engagement (i.e., social support) report better health over time (Little, 2004). Caring and supportive relationships have multiple health benefits—they reduce loneliness, increase motivation to care for oneself, offer numerous opportunities to gather information important to health, and decrease the production of stress hormones (Cohen, Gottlieb, & Underwood, 2000).

Increases in the stress hormone cortisol have been consistently linked to diminished levels of social support (Uchino, 2006). Increased stress and low levels of social support are important factors in the development and progression of cardiovascular disease and have also been implicated in cancer-related mortality among women (Astin, Shapiro, Eisenbert, & Forys, 2003). Decreased social support is associated with higher levels of plaque in arteries that can lead to heart attacks or other cardiovascular events (Uchino, 2006). The effects of social support on health are as significant as the "risks associated with cigarette smoking, high blood pressure, and obesity" (Cohen et al., 2000, p. 6). Whatever the mechanism, high-quality social support is clearly an important component of wellness and stress reduction.

One particularly important aspect of support for health care providers is the development of collegial relationships (ideally across disciplinary boundaries) that help us to reflect on our practice. This form of social support encompasses both instrumental and emotional support, but is specifically focused on professional development. These relationships may or may not be supervisory in nature, but, when consciously developed, they are safe spaces for discussing difficult encounters for the purpose of learning and stress relief. Reflective practice involves thinking from a "bird's-eye view" about one's own behavior, thoughts, and feelings in relation to challenging work situations; it is most effectively practiced in dialogue with others (Scaife, 2010). Schön (1990), a leading scholar on educational theory related to professional development has suggested that reflection on practice is needed both in the moment and as a process of looking back on critical events. Through active reflection with others, practitioners can consider, "what may have contributed to the unexpected event, whether the actions taken were appropriate, and how this situation may affect future practice" (Kaufman, 2003). These skills are best practiced within the context of supportive relationships that allow for risk taking in revealing vulnerabilities.

Mindfulness Practice

The final petal on our flower is the emerging awareness of the role of mindfulness in promoting well-being. Mindfulness is both a psychological and a spiritual state—it incorporates the use of the mind and those aspects of experience that are not confined to material reality. The term mindfulness is most clearly associated with Buddhist spiritual practices, but it has clear parallels in contemplative traditions within Christianity, Islam, and Judaism. The leading developer and researcher on mindfulness and stress reduction, Kabat-Zinn (1990), notes that mindfulness does not employ a particular religious view, so it can be utilized by anyone. As a physician at the University of Massachusetts, Kabat-Zinn developed an 8-week intervention known as Mindfulness-Based Stress Reduction (MBSR) for medical students and patients suffering from a number of health problems, including chronic pain, psoriasis, anxiety, and cancer treatment.[13] MBSR has been taught to several thousand students, health care practitioners, and patients, and training in the practice is offered across the country (Irving, Dobkin & Park, 2009).

Mindfulness describes a state of heightened attention, awareness, and intentionality toward peace; it is "a particular kind of attention characterized by a nonjudgmental awareness, openness, curiosity, and acceptance of internal and external present experiences, which

---

[13] For a listing of peer-reviewed evaluations of MBSR, see the University of Massachusetts Center for Mindfulness in Medicine, Health Care and Society bibliography at http://www.umassmed.edu/Content.aspx?id=41286. This website also provides information about the Center's MBSR training program. MBSR-trained practitioners provide courses throughout the United States.

allows practitioners to act more reflectively than impulsively" (Chiesa & Serretti, 2009, p. 593). It is the opposite of the stress response and of multitasking in current work environments. Mindfulness is associated with increased self-compassion, empathy, and compassion for others (Chiesa & Serretti, 2009; Shapiro et al., 2007), so it is a skill that is of great use to practitioners within health care settings. Given the particular stresses associated with safety-net health care settings, mindfulness practice would likely be a useful organizational as well as intrapersonal intervention.

We have talked earlier about the physiological manifestations of stress—heightened heart rate, muscular tension, increased respiration. It is possible to calm the body through conscious activation of the relaxation response, the down-regulation of the stress response. Eliciting relaxation requires four elements—muscular relaxation, quiet, disregard of everyday thought, and intentional mental focus (Jacobs, 2001). Most mindfulness programs integrate some form of meditation that focuses on "here and now" experiences. One particular technique used to develop this focus is the body scan, during which a person sits quietly and mentally connects with each part of the body, sensing any stress or relaxation in each region.[14]

Ongoing practice of the relaxation response is associated with reduced stress hormones and changes in brain wave patterns that are associated with subjective feelings of well-being (Jacobs, 2001). In Table 10.4, we give three brief examples of techniques for increasing mindfulness and eliciting relaxation. These methods can be utilized in a few minutes, but longer periods of engagement in mindfulness activities increase the benefit. These techniques have been associated with significant clinical benefit for severely ill patients as well as decreased stress symptoms among healthy people (Chiesa & Serretti, 2009). For instance, the combination of mindfulness practice with other lifestyle changes (low-fat diet and exercise) resulted in improvement in arterial stenosis in patients equivalent to that found with the use of medication (Ornish et al., 1990). Mindfulness promotes wellness for patients and practitioners alike—we hope this is one prescription you take every day for your own health.

---

[14] The University of Pittsburgh offers a 20-minute audio body scan meditation at: http://www .counseling.pitt.edu/ShortBodyScan.html. Guided body scan meditations are also available through several internet sites.

TABLE 10.4
Mindfulness Meditations

Breathing Meditation[a]

Breathing in, I calm my body.

Breathing out, I smile.

Dwelling in the present moment.

I know this is a wonderful moment.

Progressive Muscle Relaxation

Find a comfortable place to sit or lay and close your eyes.

Beginning at the bottom of your body with your toes, tense your toes to a count of 10, then relax them.

Notice the difference between tension and relaxation.

Next tense the muscles of the feet for 10 seconds, then relax them. Notice the difference.

Continue up the body, tensing muscles for 10 seconds, then relaxing and noticing the sensation.

End by tensing the muscles of your face for 10 seconds, then relaxing.

Breathe and notice the feeling of relaxation in your body.

Listening Meditation[b]

Find a quiet place where you won't be disturbed and invite your mind to become still and calm.

Close your eyes, and focus your attention on ambient sounds—the sounds that surround you.

Listen to each sound until it fades. Rest until another sound rises into awareness. Let it come, let it go.

Now extend the listening to more distant sounds—sounds outside your immediate area.

Let the listening become very large, very open.

Find the farthest, most distant sound. Listen to it until it completely fades away.

Open your eyes. Say to yourself: I am here in this moment. I am here.

[a] From "Being peace," by Hanh,1987, p. 15, Berkeley, CA: Parallax Press.

[b] From "Mind-body medicine." by Little (2004). In B. Kligler & R. Lee (Eds.), "Integrative medicine: Principles for practice (pp. 37–69)," New York, NY: McGraw Hill, p. 55.

CONCLUDING COMMENTS

This final chapter has focused on deepening our understanding and commitment to humane practice within the context of the stressful environments of safety-net health care settings. It is tempting to insulate ourselves from others' suffering in an effort to protect our own hearts from the enormity of the pain and sorrow we encounter in health care settings on a daily basis. Although working in safety-net settings has challenges not found in other settings, we are reminded that "Dealing with difficulty signifies mastery rather than weakness. Olympic dives are rated in terms of difficulty, as are mountain climbs, hiking trails, musical works, crossword puzzles and highly technical procedures" (Kroenke, 2009, p. 334). Many practitioners (ourselves included) know that working in these environments teaches skills and life perspectives that are in direct relation to our mastery of the difficulties inherent to work in the safety-net.

We hope this final discussion has suggested alternatives to the stance of cynicism and disengagement that some practitioners adopt to cope with the effects of this work. Our brief journey through perspectives on altruism, compassion, empathy, and wellness is intended to heighten your desire for more information and reflection on these topics, rather than being a definitive statement on them. Ultimately, remembering the ideals that led many of us to choose careers in health care can help carry us through the hard times in this work.

REFERENCES

Alvarez, G. G., & Ayas, N. T. (2004). The impact of sleep duration on health: A review of the literature. *Progress in Cardiovascular Nursing, 19,* 56–69.

American Psychiatric Association. (2000). *Diagnostic and statistical manual of mental disorders IV-TR.* Arlington, VA: American Psychiatric Publishing.

Astin, J. A., Shapiro, S. L., Eisenberg, D. M., & Forys, K. L. (2003). Mind-body medicine: State of the science, implications for practice. *Journal of the American Board of Family Practice, 16,* 131–147.

Austin, D. (1994). Altruism. *Social Service Review, 68,* 437–440.

Barak, M. E. M., Nissly, J. A., & Levin, A. (2001). Antecedents to retention and turnover among child welfare, social work and other human service employees: What can we learn from past research? A review and meta-synthesis. *Social Service Review, 75,* 625–661.

Benton, D., & Donohoe, R. T. (1999). The effects of nutrients on mood. *Public Health Nutrition, 2,* 403–409.

Berkman, L. F., & Syme, S. L. (1979). Social networks, host resistance and mortality: A nine-year follow-up study of Alameda county residents. *American Journal of Epidemiology, 109,* 186–204.

Blaug, R., Kenyon, A., & Lekhi, R. (2007). *Stress at work*. London: The Work Foundation.

Brazeau, C. M. L. R., Schroeder, R., Rovi, S., & Boyd, L. (2010). Relationships between medical student burnout, empathy, and professionalism climate. *Academic Medicine, 85*, S33–S36.

Brown, F. C., Buboltz, W. C., & Sofer, B. (2002). Relationship of sleep hygiene awareness, sleep hygiene practices and sleep quality in university students. *Behavioral Medicine, 28, 33–38.*

Chiesa, A., & Serretti, A. (2009). Mindfulness-based stress reduction for stress management in health people: A review and meta-analysis. *Journal of Alternative and Complementary Medicine, 15,* 593–600.

Chochinov, H. M. (2007). Dignity and the essence of medicine: The A, B, C and D of dignity conserving care. *British Medical Journal, 335,* 184–187.

Cohen, S., Gottlieb, B. H., & Underwood, L. G. (2000). Social relationships and health. In S. Cohen, L. G. Underwood, & B. H. Gottlieb (Eds.), *Social support measurement and intervention* (pp. 3–25). New York, NY: Oxford University Press.

Colliver, J. A., Conlee, M. J., Verhulst, S. J., & Dorsey, J. D. (2010). Reports of the decline of empathy during medical education are greatly exaggerated: A reexamination of the research. *Academic Medicine, 85,* 588–593.

Coulter, I. D., Wilkes, M., & Der-Martirosian, C. (2007). Altruism revisited: A comparison of medical, law and business students' altruistic attitudes. *Medical Education, 41,* 341–345.

De Jonge, J., van Vegchel, N., Shimazu, A., Schaufeli, W., & Dormann, C. (2010). A longitudinal test of the Demand–Control model using specific job demands and specific job control. *International Journal of Behavioral Medicine, 17*(2), 125–133.

De Waal, F. B. M. (2008). Putting the altruism back into altruism: The evolution of empathy. *Annual Review of Psychology, 59,* 279–300.

Dunn, A. L., Trivedi, M. H., Kampert, J. B., Clark, C. G., & Chambliss, H. O. (2005). Exercise treatment for depression: Efficacy and dose response. *American Journal of Preventive Medicine, 28,* 1–8.

Ekman, P. (1994). All emotions are basic. In P. Ekman & R. Davidson (Eds.), *The nature of emotions* (pp. 15–19). New York, NY: Oxford University Press.

Farmer, R. (2008). N*euroscience and social work practice: The missing link.* Thousand Oaks, CA: Sage Publications.

Feller, D. B., & Hatch, R. L. (2004). Do physicians take care of their health? *Psychiatric Annals, 34,* 763–768.

Figley, C. R. (1993). Compassion stress: Toward its measurement and management. *Family Therapy News (January),* 1–2.

Gellis, Z. D. (2001). Job stress among academic health center and community hospital social workers. *Administration in Social Work, 25*(3), 17–33.

Gerdes, K. E., Segal, E. A., Jackson, K. F., & Mullins, J. L. (2011). Teaching empathy: A framework rooted in social cognitive neuroscience and social justice. *Journal of Social Work Education, 47*, 109–131.

Goetz, J. L., Keltner, D., & Simon-Thomas, E. (2010). Compassion: An evolutionary analysis and empirical review. *Psychological Bulletin, 136*, 351–374.

Gottlieb, D. J., Redline, S., Nieto, F. J., Baldwin, C. M., Newman, A. B., Resnick, H. E., & Punjabi, N. M. (2006). Association of usual sleep with hypertension: The Sleep Heart Health Study. *Sleep, 29*, 1009–1014.

Hanh, T. N. (1987). *Being peace* (p. 15). Berkeley, CA: Parallax Press.

Hoffman, M. L. (1981). Is altruism part of human nature? *Journal of Personality and Social Psychology, 40*, 121–137.

Hojat, M., Vergare, M. J., Maxwell, K., Brainard, G., Herrine, S. K., Isenbert, G. A., . . . Gonnella, J. S. (2009). The devil is in the third year: A longitudinal study of erosion of empathy in medical school. *Academic Medicine, 84*, 1182–1191.

Institute of Medicine. (2008). *Resident duty hours: Enhancing sleep, supervision and safety.* Washington, DC: National Academies Press.

Irving, J. A., Dobkin, P. L., & Park, J. (2009). Cultivating mindfulness in health care professionals: A review of empirical studies of mindfulness-based stress reduction (MBSR). *Complementary Therapies in Clinical Practice, 15*, 61–66.

Jacobs, G. D. (2001). Clinical applications of the relaxation response and mindbody interventions. *Journal of Alternative and Complementary Medicine, 7*, S1, S93–S101.

Jameton, A. (1984). *Nursing practice: The ethical issues.* Englewood Cliffs, NJ: Prentice-Hall

Jolliffe, D., & Farrington, D. P. (2006). Development and validation of the Basic Empathy Scale. *Journal of Adolescence, 29*(4), 589–611.

Kabat-Zinn, J. (1990). *Full catastrophe living: Using the wisdom of your body and mind to face stress, pain and illness.* New York, NY: Dell Publishing.

Kaufman, D. M. (2003). Applying educational theory in practice. *British Medical Journal, 326*, 213–216.

Koekkoek, B., Hutschemaekers, G., van Meijel, B., & Schene, A. (2011). How do patients come to be seen as 'difficult'?: A mixed-methods study in community mental health care. *Social Science & Medicine, 72*, 504–512.

Kripke, D. F., Garfinkel, L., Wingard, D. L., Klauber, M. R., & Marler, M. R. (2002). Mortality associated with sleep duration and insomnia. *Archives of General Psychiatry, 50*, 131–136.

Kroenke, K., (2009). Unburdening the difficult clinical encounter. *Archives of Internal Medicine, 169,* 333–334.

Lair, C. (2008). *Feeding the whole family: Cooking with whole foods* (p. 3). Seattle, WA: Sasquatch Books.

Lazarus, R. S., & Folkman, S. (1984). *Stress, appraisal, and coping.* New York, NY: Springer Publishing.

Little, S. (2004). Mind-body medicine. In B. Kligler & R. Lee (Eds.), *Integrative medicine: Principles for practice* (pp. 37–69). New York, NY: McGraw Hill.

Lloyd, C., King, R., & Chenoweth, L. (2002). Social work, stress and burnout: A review. *Journal of Mental Health, 11,* 255–265.

McEwen, B. (2002). *The end of stress as we know it.* Washington, DC: Joseph Henry Press, National Academies Press.

McEwen, B., & Seeman, T. (2009). *Allostasis and allostatic load. Report to the Research Network on SES and Health.* Retrieved from http://www.macses .ucsf.edu/research/allostatic/allostatic.php

McGibbon, E., Peter, E., & Gallop, R. (2010). An institutional ethnography of nurses' stress. *Qualitative Health Research, 20,* 1353–1378.

Miller, S. K., Alpert, P. T., & Cross, C. L. (2008). Overweight and obesity in nurses, advanced practice nurses and nurse educators. *Journal of the American Academy of Nursing Practice, 20,* 259–265.

Miller, M. N., & McGowen, K. R. (2000). The painful truth: Physicians are not invincible. *Southern Journal of Medicine, 93,* 966–973.

Morin, C. M., Bootzin, R. R., Buysse, D. J., Edinger, J. D., Espie, C. A. & Lichstein, K. L. (2006). Psychological and behavioral treatment of insomnia: Update of the recent evidence (1998-2004). *Sleep, 29,* 1398–1414.

Morgan, D. G., Semchuk, K. M., Stewart, N. J., & D'Arcy, C. (2002). Job strain among staff of rural nursing homes: A comparison of nurses, aides and activity workers. *Journal of Nursing Administration, 32,* 152–161.

National Institute for Occupational Health and Safety. (1999). *Stress. . . . at work. Report No. 99–101.* Washington, DC: U.S. Department of Health and Human Services, Centers for Disease Control.

Ornish, D., Brown, S. E., Scherwitz, L. W., Billings, J. H., Armstrong, W. T., Ports, T. A., . . . Gould, K. L. (1990). Can lifestyle changes reverse coronary heart disease? The lifestyle heart trial. *The Lancet, 336,* 129–133.

Pollan, M. (2007). Unhappy meals. *New York Times.* Retrieved from http:// www.nytimes.com/2007/01/28/magazine/28nutritionism.t.html

Reed, D. A., Fletcher, K. E., & Arora, V. M. (2010). Systematic review: Association of shift length, protected sleep time, and night float with patient care, residents' health and education. *Annals of Internal Medicine, 153,* 829–842.

Relman, A. S. (2007). Medical professionalism in a commercialized health care market. *Journal of the American Medical Association, 298,* 2668–2670.

Rizzolatti, G., & Craighero, L. (2004). The mirror neuron system. *Annual Review of Neuroscience, 27,* 169–192.

Rosenthal, S., Howard, B., Schlussel, Y. R., Herriget, D., Smolarz, G., Gable, B., ... Kaufman, M. (2011). Humanism at heart: Preserving empathy in third-year medical students. *Academic Medicine, 86,* 1–9.

Sabin-Farrell, R., & Turpin, G. (2003). Vicarious traumatization: Implications for the mental health of health workers? *Clinical Psychology Review, 23,* 449–480.

Scaife, J. (2010). *Supervising the reflective practitioner: An essential guide to theory and practice.* New York, NY: Routledge.

Schön, D. (1990). *Educating the reflective practitioner: Toward a new design for teaching and learning in the professions.* San Fransisco, CA: Jossey-Bass.

Seeman, T. E., McEwen, B. S., Rowe, J. W., & Singer, B. (2001). Allostatic load as a marker of cumulative biological risk: McArthur studies of successful aging. *Proceedings of the National Academy of Science, 98,* 4770–4775.

Shanafelt, T. D., Balch, C. M., Dyrbe, L., Bechamps, G., Russell, T., Satele, D., ... Oreskovich, M. R. (2011). Suicidal ideation among American surgeons. *Archives of Surgery, 146,* 54–62.

Shanafelt, T. D., Bradley, K.A., Wipf, J. E. & Back, A. L. (2002). Burnout and self-reported patient care in an internal medicine residency program. *Annals of Internal Medicine, 136,* 358-367.

Shapiro, S. L., Brown, K. W., & Biegel, G. M. (2007). Teaching self-care to caregivers: Effects of mindfulness-based stress reduction on the mental health of therapists in training. *Training and Education in Professional Psychology, 1,* 105–115.

Sheldon, L. K. (2010). Moral distress: A consequence of caring. *Clinical Journal of Oncology Nursing, 14,* 25–27.

Smith, A., Brice, C., Collins, A., Matthews, V., & McNamara, R. (2000). *The scale of occupational stress: A further analysis of the demographic factors and type of job.* Cardiff, UK: Cardiff University.

Somer, E. (1999). *Food and Mood, 2nd Ed.* New York, NY: Henry Holt & Company.

Sontag, S. (1988). *Illness as Metaphor.* New York, NY: Farrar, Straus and Giroux.

Stathopoulou, G., Powers, M. B., Berry, A. C., Smits, J. A. J., & Otto, M. W. (2006). Exercise interventions for mental health: A quantitative and qualitative review. *Clinical Psychology: Science and Practice, 13,* 179–193.

Staub, E., & Vollhard, J. (2008). Altruism born of suffering: The roots of caring and helping after victimization and other trauma. *American Journal of Orthopsychiatry, 78,* 267–280.

Stebnicki, M. A. (2000). Stress and grief reactions among rehabilitation professionals: Dealing effectively with empathy fatigue. *Journal of Rehabilitation, 66,* 23–29.

Strayer, J., & Roberts, W. (2004). Children's anger, emotional expressiveness, and empathy: Relations with parents' empathy, emotional expressiveness, and parenting practices. *Social Development, 13,* 229–254.

Thoits, P. A. (2010). Stress and health: Major findings and policy implications. *Journal of Health and Social Behavior, 51*(S), S41–S53.

Thomas, R. B., & Wilson, J. P. (2004). Issues and controversies in the understanding and diagnosis of compassion fatigue, vicarious traumatization, and secondary traumatic stress disorder. *International Journal of Emergency Mental Health, 6,* 81–92.

Uchino, B. N. (2006). Social support and health: A review of physiological processes potentially underlying links to disease outcomes. *Journal of Behavioral Medicine, 29,* 377–387.

Ulrich, C. M., Hamric, A. B., & Grady, C. (2010). Moral distress: A growing problem in the health professions? *Hastings Center Report, 40*(1), 20–22.

Van der Cingel, M. (2009). Compassion and professional care: Exploring the domain. *Nursing Philosophy, 10,* 124–136.

Wakefield, J. C. (1993). Is altruism part of human nature? Toward a theoretical foundation for the helping professions. *Social Service Review, 67,* 406–458.

Waldinger, R. J., Schulz, M. S., Hauser, S., Allen, J. P., & Crowell, J. A. (2004). Reading others' emotions: The role of intuitive judgments in predicting marital satisfaction, quality, and stability. *Journal of Family Psychology, 18,* 58–71.

Wooten, P. (2009). Humor, laughter and play. In B. M. Dossey, L. Keegan, & The American Holistic Nurses' Association (Eds.), *Holistic nursing: A handbook for practice* (pp. 239–258). Sudbury, MA: Jones and Bartlett Publishers.

Worden, W. (2002). *Grief counseling and grief therapy* (3rd ed., pp. 51–81). New York, NY: Springer Publishing.

Yoder, E. A. (2010). Compassion fatigue in nurses. *Applied Nursing Research, 23,* 191–197.

Young, R., Webb, A., Lackan, N., & Marchand, L. (2008). Family medicine residency educational characteristics and career satisfaction in recent graduates. *Family Medicine, 40,* 484–491.

Index

Abuse. *See* Alcohol abuse disorder;
     Child abuse; Domestic
     Violence, Substance abuse
     and addiction
Access to Housing program, 190
Accidents, 79, 240, 241
ACE. *See* Adverse childhood
     experiences
Acute care models, 8–9
Acute stress response, 344–345
Adapting Your Practice: General
     Recommendations for the Care
     of Homeless Patients, 176
Addictions
  homeless persons with
     alcohol, 188
     chronically homeless, 188
     "Common Themes in Effective
        Substance Abuse Programs,"
        190–191
     drug, 197
     substance abuse, 187–188
     "successful" treatment, 189–190
     treatment problem, 189
Adherence to care. *See* Care,
     adherence
Adverse childhood experiences
     (ACE)
  health conditions and behaviors
     associated with, 258

and health
  adult psychiatric illness, 259
  childhood traumatic events, 257
  dose–response relationship, 258
  health outcomes, adulthood,
     256–257
  heart disease, 259–260
  psychosocial harm, 256
  race and gender differences,
     257–258
  smoking, 260
  potential influences throughout
     the lifespan of, 259
  screening for
     domestic violence, women, 262
     instruments, 261
     questions, 261–262
AFDC. *See* Aid to Families with
     Dependent Children
African Americans
  alcohol consumption of, 206
  homicide, 243–244
  illicit drug uses of, 201
  racial and ethnic composition,
     123, 124
"After-tax/in-kind transfer" income
     inequality, 59
Age groupings, leading causes of
     death for, 241
Age variation, in poverty, 48–49

371